JOYCE CARY

A BIOGRAPHY

JOYCE CARY

A BIOGRAPHY

MALCOLM FOSTER

LONDON
MICHAEL JOSEPH

First published in Great Britain by
MICHAEL JOSEPH LTD
26 Bloomsbury Street
London, W.C.1
1969

© 1968 by Malcolm Foster

Printed lithographically in Great Britain by
Hollen Street Press at Slough
and bound by James Burn at Esher

7181 0345 9

FOR CAROL

. . . the man was as memorable as his work. He made a picturesque and exhilarating first impression. His elegant, virile handsomeness, his racy, vivid, appreciative talk, and something at once heroic and debonair in his whole personality, suggested a gentleman rider in the race for life, risking his skin for sport rather than for a prize, and looking on every crisis of existence as a hurdle to be surmounted gaily and gallantly, however many bruises and spills might be incurred in the process. This was a true impression but a partial one. The gentleman rider was also a sage and a saint.

Lord David Cecil
The London *Times*

PREFACE

MALCOLM FOSTER

TWENTY YEARS AGO, Joyce Cary was on the brink of becoming a popular success, and, for the first time in his sixty years, was seeing his books begin to sell in quantities and his income soar. Today, his novels are enjoying a certain academic success — students write Ph.D. theses about them, academicians compose articles for the literary journals and books for the university presses about them. Yet both these successes, the popular and academic, distort the nature of Cary's novels, and, even more, the nature of Cary's aims as an author. For he was neither intent on becoming a best-selling novelist, nor did he wish to have his writings encrusted with footnotes and varnished with interpretations which might prevent the "common reader" from experiencing the works in their initial vividness.

My own discovery of Cary was quite accidental and came at a difficult time in my teaching career. Casting about in the library for something to read, I came upon *The Horse's Mouth*. Almost at once I was captivated by this story of an old, down-and-out painter who, fresh out of jail, comes home to find his paintings vandalized and his paints stolen by the neighborhood boys, yet manages through force of will to laugh off the damage and reequip himself once more for work. The impact of Gulley Jimson's tremendous vitality sent me back to the college library for its only other Cary novel, *Mister Johnson*.

Later, while teaching at the University of Cincinnati, I read the remaining Cary novels then in print and became more and more interested in their author. However, I found very little information available about Joyce Cary.

It was a friend and colleague, Mrs. Gilbert Bettman, who induced me to think of doing some serious research on Joyce Cary. She had written a thesis on his novels and had met him in Oxford. Her enthusiasm prompted me to ask her one day in October, 1962, why she had not undertaken his biography since one was so obviously needed. Her reply, which pleaded everpresent family obligations, served to launch me on the task myself.

And it has been a rewarding, fascinating adventure, if at times an arduous and frightening one — frightening because of the sense of responsibility I felt toward Joyce Cary, his family, his friends, and his admirers. In the course of research I learned how easy it would be to create a false impression of the man through the misuse of facts. But to write of Cary, happily, is simply to make use of the facts, for there was nothing in Cary's life that required glossing over. In the end, I can only hope that I have succeeded in making him live for others as he has lived for me.

Occasionally, I have altered Cary's punctuation in his letters, largely for the sake of clarity. For instance, the end of the line sometimes served him for a comma, so I have put the commas in. I have added apostrophes where clarity demanded, as Cary often left them out because he disliked them. Further, I have omitted the names of two or three persons in the text, because I felt it necessary to do so. But I have not tampered with Cary's misspellings, which were so much a part of his personal writing.

I wish now to thank all those who helped me with this work. First, I am grateful to Mrs. Bettman for having got me started. Next, I should like to thank all those members of the Cary family who have shown me kindness, cooperation, and forebearance: Miss Sheila Cary, Commander J. P. Cary, Sir Michael and Lady Cary, Mr. and Mrs. Peter Cary, Mr. and Mrs. Tristram Cary, Mr. and Mrs. Cary Clark, and Mr. and Mrs. J. Thompson. Then, I should like to thank Mr. T. F. Higham, who filled in the many gaps in my knowledge of Joyce Cary.

I should also like to thank Walter Allen, H. E. Bates, Prof.

and Mrs. James Boyd, J. B. Brown, Spencer Curtis Brown, Miss Joyce Carey, Lord David Cecil, Mr. and Mrs. Richard Cochrane, H. W. Cowper, Mr. and Mrs. Dan Davin, Thorold Dickinson, Percy Diggle, Rev. R. F. Diggle, Mr. and Mrs. Frank Doherty, John Fischer, Prof. M. G. Fisher, Miss Anne Freegood, George Graves, Mrs. Edith Haggard, Ernest W. Harvey, Frank Hauser, Sir Alan and Lady Herbert, R. M. Hone, Sir Donald Hurst, A. Y. Jackson, the Misses Kane, Miss Elizabeth Lawrence, Mrs. Laura Lightburne, Robert Lusty, Mr. and Mrs. Ruari McLean, Hugh MacLennan, Prof. John MacMurray, Patrick McSheffrey, S. J. McWatters, Prof. M. M. Mahood, Miss Iris Murdoch, Mrs. Mary Middleton Murry, A. L. P. Norrington, Sir Heneage Ogilvie, Lady Mary Ogilvie, Halvor Olsson, Dr. Gordon Ostlere, Sir John Patterson, Mrs. Helen Robertson, Norman Rosten, E. H. F. Smith, Gilbert Spencer, Prof. Enid Starkie, Prof. Lionel Stevenson, J. I. M. Stewart, Mr. and Mrs. Bruce Stovel, Frank Swinnerton, Adam Bruce Thomson, John Wain, Miss Mimi Wakeham, Prof. John Dover Wilson, Prof. Andrew Wright, and Prof. Austen Wright.

Thanks must go to the following institutions for the use of their facilities: the BBC Library and North American Service, the British Museum, the University of Cincinnati Library, Clifton College, The Dragon School, the Edinburgh Public Library, London University's Goldsmiths Library, Londonderry City Cemetery, Londonderry Library, the Londenderry *Sentinel*, Oxford Public Library, Oxford University's Bodleian Library, Oxford Civil Defence Service, the Royal Scottish Academy, and the Scottish National Academy, together with the James Osborne Trust, which made possible the Bodleian Library's Joyce Cary Collection.

My only regrets arise from the conditions under which the Cary Collection is kept in the Bodleian Library, for many documents are becoming illegible, are disintegrating, or are being misplaced and lost.

I wish to thank Joyce Cary's British publishers, Michael Joseph Limited, and his American publishers, Harper and Row, for allowing me to quote from his novels and short stories.

Finally, may I thank those whose support made this book possible: the British Council, the Canada Council, Houghton Mifflin Company, especially my editor, Daphne Ehrlich, and Jeffrey Smith, and Sir George Williams University.

MALCOLM FOSTER

Sir George Williams University
Montreal, P.Q.
Canada
1968

CONTENTS

PART III

A Rising Reputation

PART IV

Triumphs and Tragedies

Contents xv

ILLUSTRATIONS

Between pages 286 and 287

I

CHILDHOOD AND
A VARIED EDUCATION

1

INISHOWEN

In 1880 the members of Parliament for the Irish ridings elected Charles Stewart Parnell their leader and spokesman. Despite the fact that he came from the Protestant, Anglo-Irish, landholding aristocracy, Parnell devoted his great energies and talents to bringing about home rule for Ireland and ending the domination of the landholding class.

That same year the Irish Land League launched its effective campaign of boycotting the estates of oppressive absentee landlords, driving the worst and most vulnerable of them out of Ireland and into bankruptcy. It was a campaign that resulted inevitably in lawlessness, violence, and suffering, for it involved people who were without rights or land or legal redress; people who had been driven out of their homes and had seen those homes torn down behind them while they were forced to live in roofed-over ditches and worse; people who remembered the great famine and ensuing plague just over thirty years before that had wiped out more than half of Ireland's population, only a trickle of food and aid having been sent them from England.

The beginning of the boycotts and Parnell's elevation to leadership opened a decade that offered the majority of Irishmen their first real hope of justice in the whole of the nineteenth century. But if the 1880's were a decade of hope for most Irishmen, they were years of despair and ruin for others, the members of the landlord class, and the best of these were made to suffer with the worst.

For there was another sort of landlord besides the absentee, rack-renting, tenant-evicting sort who caused the class as a whole to be viewed as the great villain of Irish history. Some landlord families had lived in Ireland for nearly three hundred years and considered themselves far more Irish than English. They concerned themselves with their land and their tenants. For instance, when the famine had come in the 1840's, they had done all that they could to relieve the suffering and prevent the deaths that had come with it. They were a ruling class, but their rule was not harsh, for many let their tenants fall into arrears in their rents and carried these debts for years.

The Carys of Inishowen Peninsula were of this latter sort.[1] The family had come to Ireland during Queen Elizabeth's reign, fighting under Lord Mountjoy and Sir Arthur Chichester. In 1621 George Cary, who had fought under Chichester against the O'Doherty clan of Inishowen Peninsula, Donegal, was awarded a great chunk of that peninsula — almost a quarter of it — for his aid. He was rich in acreage, but the land wasn't worth much. A topographical survey of the land published in 1837 spoke of it as "in general of inferior quality . . . a large portion of the parish consists of rocky barren mountain. . . . The land is generally light, and everywhere encumbered by rocks, heath, and whins; the greater proportion of the rocks are clay-slate."[2] Clay, bog, gravel, and rocky hills hardly make the best sort of farmland and a farmer on such land is not apt to get rich. Nor is his landlord.

But in a quiet way the Carys prospered and the *Civil Survey* of 1634 speaks of the property as containing "two Castles, the one called Redd Castle and the other called White Castle both belonging to Major George Carey* as tenant of the Lord Chichester." Although they came as conquerors, the Carys had on the whole good relations with the Irish. When Henry Cary, who was made Lord Falkland for his services to the Crown, became Lord Lieutenant of Ireland in 1622, he began the restoration of the Roman Catholic abbeys, allowed masses to be celebrated in the churches, and even issued writs calling for an Irish

* The family name was variously spelled Cary, Carey, and Carew.

Parliament. Some elections, in fact, did take place under his rule, but the question was vetoed by King Charles I. So under a Cary, Irish Roman Catholics briefly enjoyed toleration and hope.

The Carys remained one of the most important families in Londonderry and Donegal for the next 250 years. A George Cary ("George" was a very common name in the family, so confusingly so that George Carys had to be identified by their homes, e.g., "George Cary of Whitecastle") was one of Londonderry's first aldermen and its first recorder when the city was given its charter by King James I in 1613. And when the city was besieged by the Catholic forces of James II in 1688–1689, Edward Carey was among the leading citizens who signed the "Declaration of Union" which bound them to the Protestant cause of William and Mary.

After the successful defense of Londonderry and its relief by ships which sailed into Lough Foyle to disperse the army of King James, thus leading to James's final defeat at the Boyne River, Donegal settled into nearly two centuries of peaceful vegetation. Like an enchanted princess, she slept on while decades passed, a kind of backcountry Byzantium, with a nearly feudal social structure that scarcely changed even with the coming of the railways and the steam packet boats that crossed the Irish Sea from Liverpool to Belfast, Moville, and Londonderry, making Donegal only a day's journey from London.

The Carys lived as seventeenth- and eighteenth-century country gentlemen until well past 1850. They married into the other Anglo-Irish families of the province of Ulster: the Wrays, Beresfords, Lunelles, Gilfoyles, Hamiltons, Graysons, Kennedys, and a dozen others. They were easy landlords, letting their tenants fall deep into debt to them while they themselves were obligated to merchants, banks, and their less prodigal neighbors, so much so that in 1822 one of their three grand houses, Redcastle, was put up for sale by the Court of Chancery and was bought by the Doherty family, descendants of the O'Doherty clan from whom the Carys had won the land two centuries before. While the poorer members of the clan had become tenants of their new

English landlords, the clan leaders had gone into exile in France in "the flight of the earls" of 1607, and now in 1822 their descendants returned to take back a part of their former holdings.

The Redcastle Carys had been dogged by disaster, though. George Cary died six weeks after his marriage. His posthumous son, also George Cary, died while a boy. The elder George Cary's brother, Francis Lucius, then inherited the estate and passed it on to his son, Lucius. But the sole son of Lucius was burned to death while an infant, and Lucius himself, the last Cary of the Redcastle branch of his family, went mad and died in a Glasgow asylum. It was at that point the Dohertys bought the property.

The luck of the Carys of Whitecastle and Castle Cary held out a while longer. But when the great famine of the 1840's came to Ireland and Donegal, they suffered along with their tenants. The Reverend Anthony Cary of Castle Cary, who cared for his parishioners and tenants all during the famine, died in 1848 of the "plague fever" that followed the famine. He left his wife Charlotte with seven children, five of them under twenty-one. Two of the five sons became clergymen, one, Tristram, studied medicine, and the remaining two ran the estate.

One of these last, Arthur Lunelle Cary, intended to stem the ebbing tide of his family's fortunes. He was a strong-willed man, full of life, ready to take on anything, including huge debts. After a bout of gold prospecting in Australia, he returned to Ireland, took over Castle Cary, and began to make it prosper. In time he rebuilt the house into a great Georgian-style home, a fit setting for the Victorian-size family he and his wife Jane produced: four sons and five daughters.

Arthur and his brother Tristram, who, after studying medicine abroad, had married and returned to Ireland in 1852 to farm an estate of his own, were great sportsmen. They favored shooting, greyhound racing, and horse racing. Racing tandem carts, though, was Arthur's favorite. After petty sessions court in Moville, where he was a magistrate (magistrates came from the ranks of the landlords), he and a colleague would race their tandems along the Moville-Londonderry road the two miles to Cas-

tle Cary. The road was unpaved, narrow, and abounding in
hills and turns as it wound around the shore of Lough Foyle,
and it was bounded by stone walls so that any miscalculation
was almost certain to end in a fatal smashup, which made the
race all the more exciting.

Once, after an operation for gallstones, Arthur Cary, racing
against his friend, and accompanied by his small son Arthur, felt
the stitches pull loose and cried out to his son, "Hold me together, Arthur — I'm bleeding!" and, with the boy thrusting his
hands up under his father's shirt to hold the gaping flesh together, the race went on.[3]

Only a few days later when a young horse was being broken at
Castle Cary, Arthur watched as the men failed time after time.
Finally he waved them away and jumped up on the horse himself, fresh wound and all, and sat the animal through all its attempts to throw him until it stopped its nonsense and quieted.[4]

But while Inishowen, remote and conservative, remained a
place where country squires raced greyhounds, the ferment of
revolt was alive elsewhere in Ireland, reaching its peak in the
1880's. In 1882 while they passed through Dublin's Phoenix
Park, the chief secretary for Ireland, Lord Frederick Cavendish,
and the permanent under-secretary for Ireland, Thomas Henry
Burke, were assassinated, a crime in which Parnell was impli-
cated in 1886 by what proved to be forged documents. Soon
after the Phoenix Park Murders a James Carey, a Dublin
builder and contractor, was arrested and informed on his associates in the murders. He was shot by Michael O'Donnell while
fleeing to South Africa, but his name haunted the young Carys
years afterward when they were taunted as betrayers (in fact,
James Carey was no relative of theirs).

But the Phoenix Park Murders was not an isolated phenomenon. The newspapers of the 1870's and 1880's abound with
stories of beatings, bombings, stonings, shootings, incendiarism,
and murder and imprisonments, as the Land League's policy of
boycotts took increasing effect, and tenants who had endured
generations of evictions, poverty, and starvation, as well as the
Great Famine of the 1840's, began to feel their power. Bailiffs

were murdered, policemen and troops were stoned or fired on and in turn fired on mobs who confronted them, and livestock were stolen, slaughtered, or poisoned.

One of the most fantastic acts took place in the Connemara country of western Ireland and was followed closely by the Londonderry *Sentinel* and other Irish papers during the summer of 1883. A woman on her way home one evening came upon three men who were getting rid of the bodies of two murdered bailiffs. She slipped away home unseen and for days after kept the horrifying news to herself. But finally she was unable to keep it bottled up and so she told her husband one night. For all her secrecy, her children overheard. Then one day when the youngest child, a boy, was being bullied at school by the sons of two of the men the woman had seen, he burst out at them, "I suppose you'll murder me like your fathers murdered the bailiffs." That night the three murderers came to the family's house and slaughtered them, the grandmother, the mother and father, and the two sons, all but the seventeen-year-old daughter, whom they stabbed and left for dead. Soon after, and before the daughter had recovered, the three murderers were informed on by two other men. All three were arrested, tried, and hanged. The grotesque footnote to the whole story is that two of the three murderers were named Joyce, the family they attempted to wipe out was named Joyce, and one of the two informers was named Joyce. And as footnote to footnote, Connemara is known as "Joyce country."

But the sort of violence that Connemara, Dublin, and much of the rest of Ireland knew was felt very little in Inishowen. Yet there was unrest all the same; it was a peninsula, not an island, and could not remain untouched. Once, for instance, there was a Land League meeting held at the gates of Castle Cary. Arthur Cary, hearing the crowd gather, armed himself with a horsewhip and strode down the long drive to break up the meeting. But when he arrived at the gates he found a young woman in charge. Hiding both the whip and his embarrassment, he invited the young lady, who introduced herself to him as Miss Parnell, the sister of the "uncrowned king of Ireland," up to the house for tea.[5]

This was as close as trouble ever came to the Cary lands, for the Carys were not hated. From the time of the religiously tolerant and politically liberal Henry Cary down to the time of Tristram and Arthur Cary, whose father had died in the service of his people during the Great Famine, the family had been good resident landlords, who increasingly identified their interests with Ireland rather than England.

The relationship between Tristram Cary and Barney Magonegal reveals the feelings of responsibility and duty that existed on both sides. One day Tristram invited a number of country gentlemen to a shoot on his land. Several boys, the children of tenants, hung about, ready to fetch the dead birds. In return for their retrieving, they expected to be rewarded with a few pennies apiece, or even a sixpence if the shoot went well. One of them, Barney Magonegal, crouched behind a stone wall with the others, popped up to see what was happening. It was a bad moment. One of the men fired his gun at the same instant and Barney was blinded in one eye by bird shot. Tristram Cary, a medical doctor, did all he could for the boy, but nothing could save the eye. So Tristram promised the boy that there would always be a place for him with the family. Barney entered Tristram Cary's household as soon as he was well enough and kept his position for life. When the Carys lost their lands in Ireland, Barney went with Tristram Cary to his English exile to work as butler, coachman, dogman, and even medical consultant when Tristram had again to earn his living as a doctor.

For in the 1880's both Tristram and Arthur Cary were ruined. When William Gladstone's Liberal Government passed the Irish Land Act in 1882, the arrears of the Irish tenantry were wiped out. Despite the attempts of Sir Henry Stafford Northcote and others to tack a rider onto the Arrears Bill to relieve the landlords as well, those in debt were ignored. So, caught between their own obligations and the Land Act, the Carys, along with many of the other benevolent landlords (the gouging landlords, of course, were owed no back rents — if a tenant could not pay, he was promptly evicted — so they suffered far less than the rest of their class), were ruined.

Tristram Cary was better able to make the adjustment to the

new circumstances than Arthur Cary. Tristram's wife, whom he had married in Belgium, was French-speaking, belying her maiden name of Oakes (her father, who had fought against Napoleon at Waterloo, had then settled in Belgium), and as a consequence he knew England and the continent well. He settled first in Kent, where he attempted to continue his life as a gentleman farmer, but it was a time of desperate agricultural depression in England and he was forced to sell his newly acquired lands. Then he moved to Gunnersbury, at that time a suburb of London, and began to practice medicine. His moderate success might be considered surprising in view of the fact that he had been trained in the 1850's and was thus more than thirty years behind the times in his medical knowledge.

As for Arthur Cary, he was Irish, loved Ireland, and could not accept what had happened to him. It broke him to lose his lands. He died in March, 1885, at the age of fifty-one. His widow, Jane, was left with nine children, seven of them minors. With five of the children she settled into the dilapidated Falmore House about six miles from Castle Cary. The other four of her children, Tristram (known as "Big Golliloh," because of his height, his huge hands, and great blond head), Arthur (called "Young Arthur" to distinguish him from his father), George, and Olive, had left home by then. Tristram had gone to the United States and enlisted in the 8th Cavalry, where he rose to the rank of Post Sergeant Major; he later fought as a U.S. Marine in the Spanish-American War campaign in Puerto Rico. (A somewhat maudlin letter he wrote before the battle for San Juan Hill became a family classic as "Tristram's before the battle, Mother, letter.") George also went to America, joined the then Northwest Mounted Police in Canada, and took part in putting down the Second Riel Rebellion in Manitoba. (He was just seventeen and lied about his age in order to enlist.) After he left the Mounties he prospected in Nevada and Arizona. He was the crack shot in a family that did a lot of shooting, and one of his stories was of an encounter with a train robber in the American West. The robber was nervous enough to start with, but when George Cary quietly told him, "Put down that gun or

I'll put a bullet between your eyes," the would-be Jesse James threw away his gun and jumped off the train.[6]

Olive Cary, the eldest of the children, took a job as a governess in England.

As for Arthur Pitt Chambers Cary, he too went to England, to study engineering, rather than follow his brothers on their romantic quests for adventure and gold. His father had avoided facing the world as it was and had been ruined and killed by it and its harsh realities. Now his two brothers in their turn were avoiding the real world, and Young Arthur Cary had no intention of doing thus. He had a strong sense of responsibility toward himself and his family, so much so, in fact, that he took it on himself to restore the family name from failure to strength. His brothers Tristram and George, however much he loved them, had defaulted, and his other brother, Lionel ("Leo"), was only thirteen at the time of Old Arthur Cary's death, suffered from bad eyesight, and had the weakest constitution of the four brothers. As for his five sisters, all with their own strengths, they would marry someday, of course. So if anyone was to redeem the family name, it would have to be he. His relatives were helping him to gain his education, so he could repay them in this way, and he worked hard at his apprenticeship to the engineering firm of Randall, Palmer, and Tritton.[7]

Not that Arthur Cary was a narrowly ambitious man, out for money and respectability at all costs. What he meant to do was to be done for the family as much as for himself. And as for being meanly ambitious, he was not this either. In fact, he was a gay man, who loved life, shooting, fishing, dancing, and fun of all sorts. He was only bantam-size, especially when compared with his brother Tristram, but his strong, handsome face and electric blue eyes were very attractive to women. Although his family had lost their money and their home, Arthur Cary was considered a prize catch for the girl who got him. He was going somewhere and it would be exhilarating to be the one who accompanied him.[8]

He did not wait very long to make his choice, either. On August 15, 1887, when he was twenty-three, he married Charlotte

Louisa Joyce, the quiet, pretty daughter of one of Londonderry's most prominent men, James Joyce, manager of the Belfast
Bank. It was a triumph of a marriage, connecting, as Mayor
Thomas Lecky said, "one of the oldest county families in the
North of Ireland" with one of the new, rich, and vigorous families there. The wedding was almost a civic celebration in Londonderry. On the Saturday preceding it, the Mayor and the
Corporation of Londonderry presented Mr. Joyce with a casket
of money for the couple, contributed by one hundred and
twenty-nine subscribers, and over one hundred wedding presents poured in on Charlotte Joyce Cary and her new husband,
everything from a piano down to several brass gongs, pincush-
ions, and a satin coverlet from a Miss Agar. The marriage took
place at Christ Church and was conducted by the Reverend Joseph Potter, who had confirmed Charlotte Joyce.[9]

Just over a year later Arthur and Charlotte Cary had their
first child, a son, Arthur Joyce Lunel Cary, born December 7,
1888, at the Joyce family home over the Belfast Bank, just within
the Shipquay Gate of the old city of Londonderry, thereby making the boy Joyce an "Apprentice Boy" of Londonderry.[10] (Exactly two hundred years before Joyce's birth other apprentice
boys had shut Londonderry's gates in the face of the troops of
James II and thereby began the siege of 1688–89.)

The 1880's ended with expectations of national triumph in
Ireland. In 1886 Thomas Stewart Parnell had been cleared of
charges that he was involved in the Phoenix Park Murders and
was winning a more respected place for himself, for the Irish
members of Parliament, and for the cause of home rule for
Ireland. In 1889 he was given the freedom of the City of Edinburgh and as "the uncrowned king of Ireland," was respected,
admired, even worshipped. But in 1890 he was named as corespondent in Captain O'Shea's divorce of his wife Kitty, and in
less than a year he was repudiated, abandoned, dead. The cause
of home rule was fragmented and rendered impotent.

Old Arthur Cary was dead too, and his family dispersed. But
young Arthur Cary was determined to pick up the pieces, and his
marriage and the birth of his son Joyce and a second son, John
Pitt Cary, meant, he hoped, a new beginning for the family.

2

CROMWELL HOUSE

Although Joyce Cary was born in Londonderry (often called simply Derry), Arthur Cary soon moved to London, and the city increasingly became the hub of the family. Arthur's uncle, Dr. Tristram Cary, was there, and his sisters Olive, Hessie, Agnes, and Antoinette (Netta), as well as his brother Leo, gravitated to the metropolis while Dora, their youngest sister, stayed in Ireland with their mother. Agnes, like her older sister Olive, worked as a governess and sometimes as a lady's companion. Hessie studied painting and then earned her way as a magazine illustrator and as a painter of animals and, occasionally, portraits. Leo, although color-blind, worked in a carpet factory. Netta, the second youngest and a strikingly handsome young woman, followed her brother Arthur's lead in fitting herself for the modern world: she learned to type and became one of the first young women employed as a secretary-typist in the London business world.[1]

The Cary girls and their brother Leo set themselves up in a home they named "Poker Flat." The name referred, of course, to their sense of exile from Donegal, an exile they could face but did not have to like.[2]

The real heart of the family was neither at Poker Flat nor at Arthur Cary's home in Kitto Road, but at Cromwell House, the home of their childless Uncle Tristram and Aunt Doll. The house had been named by a previous owner; the Carys were monarchists and most of them Conservatives, since Gladstone had stripped them of their lands.

As for Dr. Cary, he had studied medicine in the 1850's but had abandoned the field to run his Inishowen estate. When he lost his land, however, a few years before his brother did the same, he had moved to England and relaunched his medical career. But in the 1880's and 1890's he still practiced the sort of medicine — or as much of it as he remembered — that he had learned thirty and forty years earlier. The family claimed that he had two standard remedies for everything: his red mixture and his blue mixture, supposedly stocked in barrels in a back room. Barney Magonegal, the boy wounded years before at Dr. Cary's bird shoot, and now butler, coachman, dogman, and general factotum at Cromwell House, served as Dr. Cary's medical assistant. Dressed in his black suit, black stock, and black shoes, his black moustache drooping in apparent disapproval of the goings-on, Barney watched Dr. Cary's cursory examination of patients and went to fetch a bottle of whichever mixture the doctor prescribed. Sometimes, too, he reminded Dr. Cary that a particular patient had been given the blue mixture on his last visit, so it was time now for the red.[3]

Dr. Cary's wife, Dorothy, a tiny little woman known as Aunt Doll, exuded enough vitality to compensate for her husband's rather melancholy air and even Barney's aura of disapproval. She wore an apron with more than a dozen pockets, a walking set of pigeonholes, with thread, handkerchief, money, and chocolate for whatever children were about, each item in its proper place.[4]

Cromwell House was big enough to shelter all the London Carys when they needed it and warm enough to make them forget their exile. It was a good place to come for a "loan," or even better, so as to leave no residual guilt at the loan's not being paid back, to win money from Uncle Tristram at cards. For Dr. Cary had as bad luck at cards as he had had as a landed gentleman.[5]

Croquet was his game. But it was a serious game when he played. When the doctor took up his favorite mallet, it was for blood and money. Bets were made, and a pile of silver and even gold coins was set on the final stake on the croquet lawn. The player whose ball slammed into that stake and sent the coins flying came away with a pocket full of cash. Young Arthur's son Joyce, and in time Joyce's younger brother Jack, would leap at the coins to collect them for the winner, pretty sure of at least a penny or two or even a sixpence for gathering up the cash.[6]

It was Joyce and Jack who almost ruined Dr. Cary's croquet game, though, when they decided one day on a game of polo. Using his croquet lawn and mallets and their bicycles, they played until the lawn was full of divots and their great-uncle's favorite mallet was shattered. Then, realizing the fix they had gotten into, the boys went in shame to Barney. Barney replaced the divots and tamped them down while Aunt Doll hid the broken mallet. The boys kept out of the doctor's way. When he was not able to find his favorite mallet, Dr. Cary chose another, and only when he had gotten thoroughly used to it was he told what had happened to the old one. It was the only time Joyce remembered Barney's not telling anyone the whole truth and he was more ashamed of being the cause of the man's lapse than of being the vandal of the croquet lawn.[7]

Cromwell House saw a lot of Joyce and Jack Cary, because their father often was away from London as a consulting engineer. (Among other tasks he helped in the laying out of the Indian Railway.) One of the special fascinations of the house for Joyce, besides the back room where Dr. Cary kept his barrels of red and blue mixtures and his other medical supplies, was the room occupied from time to time by Aunt Doll's brother, Hildebrand Oakes. Hildebrand, a world traveler and hunter, had stocked it with every sort of trophy, from tiger skins to his father's sword worn at the Battle of Waterloo. The room, whether Hildebrand was at home or away, always remained locked. Joyce, a rather sickly boy who had had several attacks of pleurisy, was a great reader and addicted to stories of adventure and fantasy. So the room drew him as a cave of treasures.

One day when the maids were cleaning the bedrooms, Joyce managed to sneak into Uncle Hildebrand's room and hide there until they had finished their work and gone downstairs. Then he pulled a chair to the wall and climbed on it to gaze at the famous Waterloo sword that hung above him. His hands could

B

not stay away from it, and he reached to pull it from the scabbard. He was just drawing out the sword when the door swung open. It was Uncle Hildebrand. Joyce, startled and horror-stricken, clutched at the sword. It pulled from its nail and clattered across the floor. Joyce found himself lifted from his chair by his tall, erect, awesome great-uncle.

"Ha," said Hildebrand, "I thought so! Don't you know you're not allowed in my room?"

Joyce, petrified, could not speak.

"Of course you know. You've been told often enough. It's no place for children. You've no sense — you just break things. Don't do it again, you understand. Or I shall have to go away and live somewhere else."

Joyce was then led by his ear to the door and shown out. He never entered the room again. It was not being caught that kept him from it, nor was it fear of physical punishment; it was Hildebrand's threat of moving away that shook him. As with the episode of Barney and the croquet mallet, Joyce was overwhelmed by the knowledge of his own power. His actions had forced Barney to lie; now what he did might drive Uncle Hildebrand from his home. It was a responsibility and a guilt that he could not bear.[8]

He loved the life at Cromwell House with his uncles and aunts, its talk and fun, cards and croquet, and its hundred boyish pleasures. Besides his great-uncle Tristram's storeroom, which was not nearly so sacrosanct as Hildebrand's bedroom, there were the kitchen and the servants' quarters and the dining room, where, long after he was supposed to be in bed, he could sidle in, sit in a corner or lounge under the table to hear the grown-ups talking of old times and recent fun. The conversations grew so animated that sometimes Uncle Tristram could only attract Aunt Doll's attention by pelting her plate with nuts or pellets of bread, and a boy could easily go unnoticed.[9]

When he was old enough he was allowed to go out in the fields with Barney to train Uncle Tristram's greyhounds. Joyce held the dogs on their patent leashes while Barney, with a stopwatch, paced off the course, then gave the boy the signal to re-

lease the catch on the dogs' leashes, whereupon they raced to the
waiting Barney.

It was a place of warmth and shelter for all the family, and
even Aunt Doll's shows of wrath and disgust at her nieces for
their cigarette smoking and her complaints of what young
women were coming to were part of this sense of concern and
home.[10] So when Uncle Hildebrand threatened to jar this pattern by moving away, Joyce was badly shaken.

When he was in his sixties, Joyce looked back on Cromwell
House and made these comments:

> To us from earliest childhood, in England or Ireland, the fun-
> damental injustice and instability of things, the cruelty of blind
> fate, was as natural as the air we breathed, and, I think now,
> probably as important to our health. Cromwell House and the
> Irish households of my various relations had a sense of life, both
> older and more modern than that of our English cousins. We
> lived more intensely, and we set a far higher value on what we
> had of secure happiness. We were more eager in our attachments.
> We knew, more consciously than other children, what family affec-
> tion meant, as the one trustworthy thing among so many treach-
> eries.[11]

3

CLARE COTTAGE AND RAVENSCLIFFE

THE KNOWLEDGE of just how unstable the world was and how
cruel "blind fate" could be was pressed home when the boys'
mother, Charlotte Joyce, died of pneumonia on October 1,
1898. Jack was just six and Joyce nine when their mother was
taken back to Ireland to be buried in Londonderry, where she
had been a bride only eleven years before.[1]

Charlotte Joyce Cary remains a figure very much in the background. Her sons were too young, Jack in particular, to remember her clearly. What Joyce remembered was more of a feeling,
a sense of love and warmth, that remained long after he had
forgotten the sound of her voice and the look of her face. He
remembered learning his prayers from her, cuddled in her lap,
prayers that grew longer and longer as he added more names to
those he hoped God would bless. The list

> included Dan Kane, my grandmother's gardener, Mrs. Tobin her
> cook, and Bridget Tobin her maid, and Barney Magonagle my
> great uncle's dog man, to whom I was devoted; and it ended with
> "all whom I love and all who love me." In fact I well remember
> at about this time, when I was eight or nine and the list was
> always having new additions, I had a feeling that it was not only
> wrong, but dangerous, to leave out anyone at all whom I knew.[2]

He was conscious of this ritual, perhaps due to his mother, and
remembered, "Often too — especially on a cold night — I
would gabble them so fast that I probably had very little

thought of what I was saying, yet I would have felt guilty if I had not said them, and if I had not said them too in a proper manner, on my knees outside the bed." [3]

Bedtime had always been a ritual. When he was two or three, his mother had tucked him in with a wooden horse he loved, and the toy became a vital part of that procedure until "This horse, having lost its legs and its head, became at last a battered cylinder of wood, spotted here and there with patches of paint. But it was still a god. . . . When I was punished for some mischief I found comfort in my horse." [4] And when, one night, the horse disappeared, Joyce would neither sleep nor be consoled until it had been found and tucked beneath the bedclothes beside him.[5]

Like all children, Joyce wanted stability and order. Perhaps this need was accentuated by the sense of disruption that pervaded the family — the outcasts of "Poker Flat" — the tragic look that Uncle Tristram always wore, his own father's constant journeys in his engineering work, and his grandmother, Jane Cary, now resettled in Clare Cottage just across the Derry-Moville Road from Castle Cary, which had been meant to house the family for centuries to come. The death of his mother must have been a shattering experience, driving the boy, already shy and withdrawn, even further into himself.

When Arthur Cary's sister Netta came into the household at Kitto Road to care for the two boys, Jack took to her at once, but Joyce did not.[6] Jack seemed better able to roll with the punches; he was an outgoing, healthy, and happy boy, good at games, and he loved the out-of-doors. Joyce, though, wasn't terribly strong and was nearly blind in his right eye, a fact that simply was not noticed until after he had learned to read and so often was seen curled up with a book held so close to his face that his nose sometimes rubbed on the pages.[7] Besides this there was the pleurisy, a tendency to rheumatism, and sometimes fainting spells. He was a bookworm from the time he could read, apt to stay indoors reading or dreaming when he was in London unless he and Jack were visiting at Cromwell House. It took him a month or more before he warmed to his young Aunt

Netta, an attractive woman with the piercing Cary eyes.

She was a regular Shavian "New Woman" in many ways: she had worked as a typist in an office when that occupation was considered exclusively men's work, she smoked cigarettes in public when that sort of behavior was associated with the Scarlet Woman (smoked so much, in fact, according to her son, that when her hair had grown white it was streaked blond in front from the smoke and nicotine), and she was apt to speak her mind without any of the traditional feminine decorum. But with her looks, she could get away with it all; if she couldn't silence a critic with her beauty, she could glare him down with her Cary blue eyes.

Once Joyce had gotten over his first diffidence with Netta Cary, however, he came to love her very much with a love that remained strong and vital until the end of her life more than forty years later. She had little influence on him in one area, though: she gave him piano lessons, but Joyce had a tin ear and they made no lasting impression.[8]

Not all of Joyce's London time was spent mooning about. Once, for instance, when Jack was having a rough time at a game of king of the castle, Joyce dashed up, grabbed a toy rifle on the ground, and cracked one of the roughest boys over the head with it, breaking the gun in two. Jack raged, though, because it was his rifle that Joyce had used.[9] But Jack got his own back, despite the more than three-year difference in their ages.

Once Arthur Cary came home to be met by Netta, who told him that Jack had broken a window that day. "But don't punish him, Arthur," she said. "He's punished himself more than you could, fretting about it all day." Arthur Cary went up to see his son and when Jack fearfully told him, "Dad, I broke a window," Arthur Cary replied, "Oh, that's all right, old man. How did it happen?"

Jack, collapsing back on his pillow with relief, said carelessly, "Oh, I only threw a knife at Joyce." [10]

Aunt Netta had a special way of dealing with the difference in size and age between Jack and Joyce. Whenever the two boys were having a friendly fight that seemed to be getting out of hand, with Jack getting the worse of it, she would step in and say, "All right, now let Jack do whirlwind," which meant that Joyce had to stand still, his hands at his sides, and let Jack come in at him, fists flying, until their referee called a halt.[11]

There was a period when Netta Cary became disturbed over a developing trait in Joyce; she told her brother Arthur that Joyce seemed to be growing quite miserly. Jack would spend his penny-a-day allowance as soon as it was in his hand, but Joyce spent nothing at all. She was worried, she told Arthur. But the problem resolved itself when, a few weeks later, Joyce gave Jack a toy train the younger boy had been eyeing and pining for since he had first glimpsed it in a shopwindow. Joyce had saved every scrap of money to buy the gift.[12]

The times when Joyce really came alive, though, were those he spent in Ireland, in Inishowen, at the home of his Grandmother Cary, Clare Cottage, or with his Joyce grandparents at Ravenscliffe. It was the Cary home that drew him more strongly, and he wrote twenty years later:

> We had a most splendid sunset this evening and as I sat out in a cool breeze with the smell of wet grass, the hills and the big clouds, I remembered Ireland. How I loved Clare, the clouds, the wind, the rain even, and the mountains, with the lovely Lough Foyle below. Clare is the only place that ever tasted of home to me, not that I was ever long there or even there very often, but because Ireland is my country, and Clare was then the place that was Cary.[13]

Both Ravenscliffe and Clare Cottage offered bathing in Lough Foyle or at one of the gorgeous beaches at the top of the peninsula. Joyce could explore the heathery hills, go boating, or play at any number of games with his brother Jack and the cluster of cousins usually present, most often the Beasleys, the children of Charlotte Cary's sister. Joyce, as the eldest boy and probably the most imaginative, was the crew's ringleader.

There were plenty of places to lead them, too. One of the great places for exploring was Greencastle, just three miles along the Lough Foyle coast from Moville, a spot that com-

manded the entrance to the lough. Because of its strategic position, the area had been fortified for centuries so the ruins of
both a Knights Templar castle and a later castle built by the
O'Dohertys, in addition to a Martello tower built against the
threatened invasion of Napoleon, were still there. For playing
at war games, ghosts, or almost anything else, there could be
no finer place.

There was the shore, too, with its treasures: ironwork from
long-sunken ships, shells of all kinds, interesting bits of wood,
and other prizes cast adrift from ships at sea. Close to Clare Cottage was the old Cary family chapel, now derelict, and its burial
grounds with a unique family tomb, a grave vaulted over with
stone to form a sort of grotto. The grave was that of an eighteenth-century Cary wife. At the time of her death, the story
goes, the various branches of the family were feuding, so when
she was buried, one of her husband's antagonists used to make a
point of driving his rig over her grave every time he went to
chapel. The widower had built the grotto over his wife's grave
to put a stop to this desecration.[14] If the graveyard and its ruined
chapel were frightening, on a dark night the grotto, reputed to
be haunted, was a place of utter horror. In his autobiographical
novel *A House of Children,* Joyce described a nighttime foray
on the grotto as one of the epiphanies in the narrator's life, and
it seems likely that the grotto held a fatal fascination for them
all, Carys and Beasleys, on stays at Clare Cottage.

On rainy days there were plays to be planned, great epic dra-
mas in which each of the children made up his own lines as he
went along. None of the parts related to the others, for the plays
were an excuse for declaiming half-remembered scraps from
books, ranting, or sometimes just horseplay. But there were
wonderful old clothes to dress up in and swords and spyglasses to
wave in the air to make a grand show of drama. But, as Joyce
related in *A House of Children,* the children's first glimpse of a
real play destroyed their own urge for the stage, at least for a
time.

All the same, for a boy of Joyce's imaginative and dreamy
temperament, no place could be better than Inishowen, and he

loved it. It brought him to life as London never did. He was a different boy, leading the crew into adventures and into mischief, breaking and stealing not to make trouble or for gain but simply as a means of exploring the world and its possibilities. When a constable nabbed them or some adult chased them, they were as surprised as any innocent bystander — or pretended to be.

Ravenscliffe was a little less rowdy than Clare Cottage. There were even lessons, or at least a pretense of them, with a governess sitting the children down in the schoolroom to keep them quiet for an hour or two. One young woman who was more conscientious or more naïve than the others actually tried to give them proper instruction. After their initial astonishment wore off and unbearable boredom set in, the children, under Joyce's lead, abandoned ship. When their governess turned her back for a moment to write on the blackboard, they tiptoed to the back of the room, climbed over the low window sill, and dropped one by one to the lawn a yard below. When the governess turned to face the room again, she found it completely empty.[15]

There were more interesting things to do than study. Once Joyce built a hut of driftwood and scrapwood on the shore at Clare Cottage, and there were the evening *caelidhs,* with their storytelling, music, and dancing in the cottage of some farm family or even the kitchen of Ravenscliffe. The best *caelidhs* of all occurred when a tinker came by, because the people could pump him for news and gossip. Tinkers were the best tellers of ghost stories, tales of banshees, and other strange goings-on,[16] too. There are plenty of people in Donegal who still believe in such tales; to this day, the gatepost tops are made round to keep the fairies from dancing on them.

It was in Ireland that Joyce first fell in love, when he was ten. The girl was his cousin, Helen Beasley, nearly Joyce's age, a pretty girl with blond hair down to her waist. For a summer they were inseparable and were certain that someday they would marry.

Once, in that summer of 1899, coming home from a Londonderry shopping trip with Helen, Joyce had his first direct experience with the bitterness of Irish politics. Parnell, of course, had been brought down because of his affair with Kitty O'Shea, destroyed as leader of the Irish forces, and sent to his grave. The unity of the home rule movement had thus been demolished in a turmoil of bitterness. The Belfast Bank, where Mr. Joyce was manager and where the Joyce family had their home, too, was just inside the Shipquay Gate of the old walled part of the city. The tunnel formed by the gateway was filled with fighting men when Joyce and Helen arrived. "There was a terrific noise of yelling and cursing," Joyce wrote of it. "But after a moment one of the men recognized us and began to yell, 'Hi — stop — stop — it's Miss Helen and Master Joyce, they want to go through.' And the men did stop and we walked through — they only started again when we had passed safely." [17]

There were other reminders of the bitterness that the Irish troubles had caused. Aunt Netta, for instance, insisted that the initials "G.O.M." used to refer to Prime Minister Gladstone did not mean "Grand Old Man" but actually meant "Gordon's Old Murderer." And further, that Gladstone, in not sending a relief force promptly enough to General Gordon in the Sudan, had caused the general's death — and by extension had caused the death of the Anglo-Irish by not allowing them a release from their debts although his Irish Land Act had freed the Irish tenants from their burden of back rents. [18]

And there were other signs, too. There was Joyce's uncle, Jim Joyce, his mother's brother, who had meant to be a writer, a tall and terribly thin young man, who drank instead of wrote, perhaps because of some inner flaw or perhaps because he did not have the strength to break with Ireland although he was surrounded with evidence that he had not much claim any longer to being an Irishman. Joyce's first clue to Jim Joyce's state was his uncle's giving an absolutely perfect imitation of a dog for him one day, scampering about on all fours, barking, howling, and rolling over on his back. Then abruptly Uncle Jim left the room, hurried up the stairs, and locked himself in his bedroom. Next, Joyce was confronted by his grandmother and his aunt, who asked if he had seen his uncle drinking anything.

"It might be like a medicine bottle," his aunt said.

"With water in it," his grandmother suggested. For the local poteen was uncolored like gin.

Jim Joyce stayed in his room all day, making no sound and not answering anyone who came to the door to ask after him or call him for meals. By bedtime, Joyce, upset by the strained mood of the household, was in tears, and his aunt took him on her knee and told him not to worry about his uncle, who would, she said, never be ill in this way again. She gave "a little sermon on drink," he wrote, "said it was the ruin of Ireland and advised me never to drink whiskey, except perhaps a little now and then, on special occasions." He wondered how much was a little and just what made a special occasion but never dared to ask.

The next day, though, his uncle, dressed in a sailing jersey, was down to breakfast as if nothing had happened and ready to take Joyce boating on the lough. Moville was readying itself for its annual regatta and an Englishman who had come to Inishowen to shoot grouse had entered the sailing race. He fascinated Jim Joyce, since the man had planned on paper just what he should do for every contingency. The Englishman failed miserably in the race, but Jim Joyce still marveled at the "paper studies" of the English.

To Joyce, who would be going to school that fall, Uncle Jim repeated the same advice: to plan everything and not go off halfcocked like the Irish. "It's the only way. Make sure of your ground before you trust your foot on it, for I tell you, me boy, there's no taking your foot back again. Now in the matter of boats, MacGill there will build you the prettiest wee boat you could dream of — to make you think when you were in her you were sitting on a dolphin's back. But in England they've got it all down on paper and they've got it all drawn out into figures so that a fella that never saw the sea or felt the kick of a tiller could build you a boat would sail three rings round MacGill's best while you were sneezing."

Jim Joyce stayed sober for six months in one last desperate attempt to reform his life and worked steadily at his writing. Then one day he went off to the hotel in Moville and got

drunk; from then on the fight was lost. He drifted out of the
family and life itself into the dim world of his defeat.[19]

But by then Joyce, who had been in Ireland partly for a holiday and partly because his father had married a second time and
was away with his bride, Dora Stevenson, a cousin, on their honeymoon in France, was off to school in England.

Joyce summed up the summer in a letter to his father dated
September 2, 1900:

DEAR DADS

I am enjoying myself. Jack has found an elephant's tooth
set in gold Jack can swim but not dive. I have learnt overhand
stroke from Bryne. Bryne won a dressing case at Portknish yesterday. Harold Bryne, in Siam, shot a tiger last Monday all by
himself and the skin is being cured in London. Did you get my
last letter about Navel engineering. Helen's thought me knitting
and has thought me to play the piano by notes in stead of ear. A
week ago Cecile Bryne and me (I hope they teach grammer at
Tunbridge) were walking to Cockhill for yellow daisys when a
boy who was standing near a headge said don't come hare ye'l git
stunkted its a wopse nes, we laughed. My love to Dora and the
Bulivants and a jolly holiday to you all.

Goodbye for the present

JOYCE

And he finished the letter off with the picture of a fierce Chinese
and a flag.

Going off to school was the end of an idyll, one that, unfortunately, had not been entirely untroubled. His mother's death
had been the worst happening of all, and there had been illness
and uncertainty as well. Now the sense of home which Ireland
had given him was finished. It might be glimpsed on short holidays, but that was all.

4

HURSTLEIGH AND CLIFTON

JACK AND JOYCE arrived that autumn at Hurstleigh School, Tunbridge Wells, with Irish accents that at first made them outsiders and the butt of jokes, a pair of Paddys.[1] Jokes were more apt to slide off Jack than Joyce, because Jack was pretty much game for anything and much more easygoing. His sturdy build made him one of the school's stars at games, so much so that a few years after this he wrote to Joyce in his blasé manner,

> I had my usual luck I won the 100 yds and the Quarter mile (440 yds) and I came second in the hurdles and the broad jump, and I had my pick of four prizes a cricket ball, a bat, a racquet, and a pewter mug, I picked the pewter mug, the ball, and the racket, because I have got 2 last year's bats. . . .[2]

If Jack could run and jump well, he, like Joyce, could not sing for anything. Both brothers sang in the school choir at chapel along with the rest of the boys until Jack's unique way with a tune made itself felt on more tender ears and he was weeded out. Instead he was forced to sit through chapel with the headmaster, Mr. Buston, and the Buston family, including a young daughter who made a habit of dropping her hymn book so as to make Jack get down on his hands and knees to find it. Joyce, older and wiser, found he could stay in the choir by making a decent show of things: he mimed the words without letting out a sound.[3]

The young Miss Buston evidently had inherited her knack for

making Jack Cary's life miserable from her father. Mr. Buston
had a foul temper and a strong arm. When he got into a rage
the boys' only resort was to make him even angrier, because
when he was driven past a certain point, Buston so entirely lost
control of himself that he could not do a thing but shake and
writhe with impotent rage. Unfortunately, this was not true of
one of the other masters, a huge Welshman who used to box the
boys on the head and literally knock them down to the ground.[4]

Joyce was not a terribly good student, perhaps because of
coming rather late into the system of regular schooling. He read
and wrote and drew a great deal, as he'd done before coming to
Hurstleigh, and these talents helped him to get by. If he shone
in anything at school it was in writing and drawing and,
surprisingly enough, considering the scrapes he was always
getting into in Ireland, manners. During Joyce's time at Hurstleigh, Mr. Buston was replaced by a much pleasanter man, Mr.
Honeywin (the names could have been made up by Dickens),
who urged Mr. Cary to let his older son stay on an extra year
because he was such a good example to the younger boys.[5]

While Joyce and Jack were at Hurstleigh, the school underwent a religious revival. A rather formidable missionary came
to lecture to the boys, an enthusiastic, masculine type of person,
and the wave broke. A bible-reading society was formed, and
tuck money was saved to send to the missions, rather than spent
on candy. The pariah of the school, at least for the moment, was
a day boy who expressed doubts "about the existence of God and
His power to do miracles," Joyce remembered. "But he had no
effect on our belief. We detested him for the very force of his
arguments, and I daresay we should have knocked him about if
he had not been large and tough. We were highly intolerant of
disbelief, and we had no more critical sense than savages. We
were ready to accept everything we were told by our masters and
pastors." [6]

During this time Joyce was visited by the man who had married his parents and buried Joyce's mother, Canon Potter. "I
remember him," Joyce wrote, "as a giant with an immense red
beard — but perhaps he was not so big." [7] Canon Potter went

out of his way to call on the two Cary boys to talk with them of their mother, to whom he had taught the catechism and who had sung in his church's choir, and to urge them to always remember her in their prayers. The visit further strengthened Joyce's religiosity.

But his religion and a good deal more suffered some bad shakes when he went to Clifton College on the outskirts of Bristol in the autumn of 1903.

Clifton in those years was a solidly middle-class school, with a reputation mainly for preparing boys for Sandhurst and the Army. Field Marshall Lord Douglas Haig, Commander in Chief of the British Expeditionary Force in France and Flanders from 1915 to 1919, was only one of several important military leaders who had been educated at Clifton. The school was army- and empire-oriented (many of the boys were sons of fathers in the Indian Civil Service or Army), and one of the great events of the school year was the army maneuvers in the spring. Sports were big at Clifton, too, especially so at Tait's House, the dormitory in which Joyce lived.[8] He was as temperamentally suited to the place as a duck is to a desert.

Not only was Joyce bad at games because of his poor sight, but he had not grown much. At fourteen he had yet to reach puberty,[9] and his growth in height had not come either. In each picture of the boys of Tait's House, the forlorn boy who looks as if he had just stepped in something clammy and rank and is trying to hide the fact is Joyce.

He settled not very happily into Tait's House and found that his one talent was a godsend. He could tell good stories. He could reel off episode after episode of serial stories in the dormitory after lights-out and gain an audience.[10] If he was not terribly good at any sport but swimming (with the grand beaches of Inishowen, together with instruction on his father's part, Joyce had developed into quite a decent swimmer of the trudgen stroke), he made a small niche for himself this way. And his writing and his drawing helped keep his grades up considerably.

But in the spring a real blow fell. His stepmother, Dora Stevenson Cary, whom he had come to love very much, had caught a cold that lingered on. She had borne Arthur Cary two children, Sheila and Anthony. Anthony was just a baby, so Mrs. Cary had continued to care for him and look after the house until one Sunday the cold grew markedly worse, and by early evening Arthur Cary decided a doctor was needed. He went to the nearest surgery, but of course it was Sunday evening, and the doctor was not in. So he tried another doctor and then another. All Sunday evening he looked for doctors, and when he finally found one and hurried home with him, the cold had gone into pneumonia. Soon after Dora Cary was dead.[11]

Joyce was informed at once of his stepmother's death. It was a great shock, coming at a time when he was so forlorn anyway. Out of his misery and out of a pathetic, boyish desire to comfort his father, he hurried away from Clifton to Bristol, caught a train, and went to London. But his trip was aborted at Paddington Station and he was brought back to Clifton without ever seeing Arthur Cary. His running away was entirely hushed up at school, of course, considering the circumstances. He was treated with sympathy rather than severity.[12]

His father, immediately on learning from Joyce what had happened, wrote the following letter:

> MY DEAR OLD BOY —
> I am sure you are bitterly sorry but you must not make me a greater burden to bear than I already have —
> Your letter was another blow to me for you know old boy that there are times in this life when we must not give way no matter how we feel so my dear old boy you must be brave now and do your very very best for my sake and the sake of dear Dora — We are going to take her to Rusthall Church tomorrow her Mother & Father are there —
> Goodbye for the present. I know you will try to be brave for my sake. Work and play with all your might.
> > Your loving father,
> > Arthur Cary.

The letter which Joyce wrote and to which his father refers must have expressed his profound misery and his longing to come home because of his unhappiness at Clifton and perhaps because his gesture of sympathy failed.

At first glance Arthur Cary's letter seems somewhat harsh. But he was a strong man, not a harsh one. He too had suffered: the loss of his home, of his future in Ireland, and of his own father had all come to him as a very young man. And he had lost two wives, both of whom he loved. But he believed in courage and duty and sticking things out rather than being defeated by them. Arthur Cary's father and his brother-in-law, Jim Joyce, were instances of what happened to a man when he buckled. Rather than a rebuke, the letter is simply a statement, as tenderly put as Joyce's father could make it, of what he truly believed a young man, even a boy, must sometimes do in life if he were determined to survive.

Joyce must have known his father well enough to take the letter to heart, because from then on he changed his life at Clifton. He built a whole new life for himself there, and the cornerstone of it all was his ability with stories. Some of the new friends he made through his tales took him in hand and set out to make at least a passable athlete of him. Perhaps they felt some pity for him because of the death of his stepmother. But boys can be terribly savage and if one of them gives way too much to self-pity, the others often will turn on him in mockery or affronted dignity and destroy him. So Joyce, after getting over his initial grief, must have presented a brave enough front so that he earned his schoolmates' sympathy rather than their derision.

At any rate, they set out to teach him football, practicing with him in the mornings and evenings in the dormitory, kicking around a hairbrush case for a ball, and encouraging him all they could.[13]

On his own he worked at his swimming to make what was already passable a good deal better.[14]

More important, and a real sign of either bravery or foolhardiness, he went out for boxing, despite his height, weight, and sight. He never became very good at it, but he said later that "the great thing was to have lots of blood and I was a great

bleeder." [15] There is not much that will impress boys more than
the capacity both to dish it out and to take it, to get a bloody
nose and swollen eye and still throw punches. Joyce both bled
and got his nose broken, a break that troubled him for years
afterward, but it paid off. He belonged. He had proven himself
to both the boys of Tait's House and himself. Nobody could
ignore him. Even more, nobody could sneer at him. It was the
sort of triumph every ignored or picked-on schoolboy dreams of,
even if in Joyce's case it didn't come in one burst of glory but
had to be won bit by bit. It taught him a crucial lesson.

That summer Joyce went to France with his Aunt Winnie
Chambers (a cousin, actually) on a sketching trip. Winnie
Chambers, like Arthur Cary's sister Hessie, was an accomplished
painter, who used her talent professionally. And since Joyce was
very interested in art and needed a diversion after the death of
his stepmother, the two of them set off with sketching pads and
paint boxes.

Painting and writing were talents highly acceptable in the
Cary family, perhaps because in Inishowen the family had lived
such an old-fashioned and isolated life. The family magazine
was a home product that circulated from household to household when Arthur Cary was a boy and young man. Each member of the family was expected to contribute something, a story,
poem, or picture and then circulate the magazine on to the next
Cary household where new creations would be added and criticisms made of previous contributors' work. This practice provided good training and enabled the amateurs in the family,
who, out of economic necessity, sometimes had to turn professional, to accept criticism.

The trip to France, coming after the beginnings of Joyce's
victory at Clifton, was a heady experience. In France he came
up against the new art, the revolutions that were going on one
right after another and which didn't hit England until Clive
Bell and Roger Fry organized London's Post-Impressionist Ex-
hibition in December, 1910. It was impressionism, however,
that won Joyce's favor. He became an ardent convert, and it was
as a fifteen-year-old impressionist that he met an old academic

painter whose art had gone out of style with the new age. The old man, finding Joyce was interested in art, took him to his house and his garden to show Joyce his most recent works, all of which had been submitted to the Academy, rejected, and returned to him. Nothing he painted now was accepted. Nothing was sold. Nowhere could his paintings be hung. But, the man insisted to the boy, weren't they just as good as those he had done twenty and thirty years before when everything had been sold almost as fast as the paint dried? What was wrong? he demanded. Where was the justice in that? He had lost none of his talent, yet nothing sold now. And he had a wife and family to support.

He brought out his paintings into the garden for Joyce to see and admire. There was one of a girl in a swing, smiling, golden, surrounded by flowers. Joyce knew it was trash and wondered how the old man could be such a fool as to think this sort of work was art. Didn't he know anything about painting? But however cocksure Joyce was, he said nothing.

The old painter, once respected and well-to-do, poured out his grievances to the fifteen-year-old student, complaining that the only thing the public wanted nowadays was this modern trash, these daubs, these monstrosities. There was no justice, no taste.

The boy went away wondering how the old man could be so blind and how he could fail to see that impressionism was the only real art, the only worthwhile approach to painting.[16]

The episode left a permanent impression, one he recalled time after time. He used it in several articles, and the old man became Gully Jimson's father in Joyce's novel *The Horse's Mouth*. He was to have appeared again, transformed somewhat, in another novel Joyce planned but never wrote. The old painter, betrayed by a change of time and mood, bearing his terrible sense of grievance, became a part of Joyce's concept of life, fitting into experiences closer to home: the apparent injustice of his family's fall in Ireland, his mother's and stepmother's untimely deaths, and his own physical disabilities. He had, eventually, to understand *why* these happened, whether they were caused by chance or by some more meaningful force. He could not fit them into the conceptions that orthodox religion gave him.

For that matter, other experiences he had would not fit into that pattern either. Back at Clifton that autumn, he was being prepared for confirmation by Mr. Rintoul, his housemaster at Tait's House. Mr. Rintoul was his science master and he, along with Joyce's other teachers, had encouraged the boys in the classroom to question everything, to prove everything, and to doubt that which could not be proved. Joyce "found geology incompatable with Genesis" [17] but expected that this and other incompatibilities and problems that disturbed him would be explained by Mr. Rintoul.

But when he asked about "the Trinity, the Incarnation, the problem of evil, miracles, and so on," Joyce was given "simply a set of dogmatic statements without any explanation."

The effect was not immediate. As Joyce later wrote,

> I was duly confirmed, with great emotional effect. But soon afterwards my faith began to wither like a plant whose root has been cut. . . .[18]

Over the next few years he lost all his religious faith and came to think of himself as an agnostic, unable to come to any terms with the church and thinking it quite irrelevant. The inconsistency of his ideas didn't bother him. "I accepted," he said, "the world as science described it, a complex kind of machine; I also admired poets, painters, as great creative minds, and deeply respected goodness, courage, whenever I saw it." [19] The idea of a mechanistic universe's being incompatible with human emotions and ethical values did not trouble him. He simply ignored the question.[20]

In the classroom, he blossomed as a student, just as on the playing field and in the swimming pool he had made a respectable mark as an athlete. His studies and athletics went together, both of them coming from a new desire to succeed in spite of the problems he encountered and he was bolstered by the new contentment he felt at being able to prove himself ready to take it. He won prizes with his drawings and some of his verse. His ability to reel off stories in the dormitory was matched by a talent for writing page after page of verse in the classroom, all of it very conventional and bad. Nevertheless, it was far better than most of the other boys were capable of. In fact, his ability to pour it out was a cause of amazement to at least one of them, a boy named Fisher, one of those who had coached Joyce in dormitory football.[21]

The poems were about what could be expected of a boy who has a flair for writing but is by no means an embryonic genius, as the following example, written in January, 1905, proves:

to my pen.

To what base uses has this pen been put,
The humblest cousin of some mighty quill,
Which has in some strong hand been made fulfill
A nation's degradation, at the foot

Of ruthless conqueror. What inspirations
Have defiled thy nib, worthy a better end.
What strange and crooked writings hast thou penned,
And called them English in thy high ambitions.

How oft, twixt thumb and finger, posing thee,
In pensive meditation have I conned
The ceiling, in an anxious hope, too fond,

Of finding there a tardy inspiration,
When my dull memory is failing me,
And I am lost in tangles of translation.

It isn't much of a sonnet, but at least it *is* a sonnet, and for all its archaic language it moves along at a good, flowing speed, rather than being all sharp and ghastly angles. And it and its kind made him the star of the English class. Obviously his masters hadn't heard of or else weren't in tune with the newer poetry.

The painting trip in 1904 and the prizes he won at Clifton for his drawings had a much more immediate effect on Joyce than his success with writing. He decided he wanted to become a painter.

In December, 1904, he came into a small income left him by his mother and, with that security, he made the choice definite.[22] It was only a matter of persuading his father.

Meanwhile he continued to be happier at Clifton, making friends and enjoying the life there rather than fleeing from it. One friend, who admired Joyce for his stories and who in turn was honored by Joyce, was Heneage Ogilvie, born in Chile, the son of a Scottish merchant in the import-export trade. Heneage Ogilvie was tall and handsome, an athletic boy who managed to be a dreamer as well. He was on the football fifteen, won the House Cup in 1905, and came second in the Long Penpull that year (the Long Penpull was a ten-mile race — participants took a train from Bristol to Pilning Station, then ran back to Clifton; the Short Penpull was only seven miles). In 1906 he was sergeant of cadets, but in addition to proving his leadership, he demonstrated his dreaminess, for he absentmindedly rested his blank-filled rifle on his foot and pulled the trigger, giving himself a nasty wound from the burn and not doing his foot much good either.[23]

By the end of his time at Clifton, Joyce had hit it off well with Ogilvie, Fisher, Graeme Paterson, and several other boys, some of whom, like Ogilvie and Fisher, were "bloods" but didn't make a profession of it, for they had other interests besides athletics and army life.

One of the last experiences Joyce had at Clifton was the spring maneuvers in 1906, when the boys went out on the downs with knapsacks full of apples, chocolate, meat pies, and such; one army was then put in charge of defending a position which the other army was to try to take. Joyce, on the defending side under Heneage Ogilvie, was delighted with his army's success.[24]

This was the proper ending to his three years at Clifton. He had fought a battle, largely with himself, and had won, had secured his position in the school, and could come away with a far better idea of exactly where he stood.

Now he brought off another victory. He convinced his father that art was the field for him and that Paris, as the artistic capital of the world and its experimental laboratory as well, was just the place for him to study. That being the case, there was no sense staying any longer at Clifton preparing for either a university or an army career.

So, at seventeen, he set out for Paris.

PARIS AND EDINBURGH

To be a seventeen-year-old art student in the Paris of 1906, with the certain knowledge that he would not starve, that there was always plenty of money to bail him out, and that there was a home he could go to in London if ever he needed it must have seemed the best of all possible worlds. Yet Joyce felt a bit of envy for his brother Jack, who had just gone into the Navy as a cadet. Joyce had once hoped to enter the Navy himself until it became obvious even to him that with his eyesight it would be impossible.[1] Paris, though, was a great place to console himself.

The dealers' galleries were full of the newest works, those of the newly discovered Rousseau and many of the audacious young painters — Braque, Picasso, and others; the theater was exploding with new works meant to shock, where the playwright's greatest triumph was a riot that needed the police to break it up. The cafés, though, were best of all; there a young man could meet the world.

And he could do it for practically no money at all. As a young Canadian art student found the next year, 1907,

> One of the attractions that brought thousands of students to Paris to study was the low cost of living. Looking over an account book recently, I found such items as meals at twenty-five cents — and good meals too — and a seat at the cinema for ten cents. The two rooms I shared with the [two] New Zealanders cost us each two dollars a month. . . .[2]

That was one of the great benefits of Bohemia: it was cheap as well as interesting.

Joyce, with some facility at drawing and painting, and always ready to talk or to listen, easily made friends, endless friends: Frenchmen, Americans, Serbians, Russians, painters, anarchists, prostitutes, journalists, frauds. Having a bit of money with which to buy drinks was a help. Joyce went Bohemian and at the same time put on his best Irish accent — an Irishman was more immediately accepted than an Englishman — and spent hours and days and weeks in conversation and argument on everything from painting to Irish home rule.

Not far from the Luxembourg Gardens was Joyce's favorite café, the Closerie des Lilas, a gathering place for Satie, Picasso, and other leaders of the new movements in the arts. Here they met regularly each week for a symposium. Ezra Pound, a few years later, also frequented the Lilas. If Joyce met any of the great men, though, he never mentioned them to anyone, either then or later.

Besides Paris, there was Étaples, ten or so miles south of Boulogne on the coast,

which at that time was an art centre for Britons and Americans who were attracted by studios, models and hotels, all at moderate prices, a fishing fleet, sand dunes, and a bathing beach at Paris Plage.[3]

Joyce traveled up there with his friends, for Étaples gave him a chance to laze and to show off his excellent swimming. He blossomed in this atmosphere of art and talk, becoming increasingly animated and gay. With his Irish-accented French, his curly brown hair, and his youth, he evidently attracted several girls, if the number who wrote him letters is any indication. Among them was a Scottish girl, Dorothy (Dot), who was a pupil of Augustus John, the great English painter.

In fact, happy as he was, Joyce might have frittered away the rest of his life in Montmartre and Étaples (provided his father didn't cut off his money), if it hadn't been for a Scottish painter he met who thought the adolescent Irish café-habitué had a talent that was worth training.

Charles Mackie had already begun to establish himself when he met Joyce in Paris. He had been chairman of the Society of Scottish Artists in 1900 and 1901, and in 1902 he was made an Associate of the Royal Scottish Academy. Mackie, a painter of landscapes and portraits, was as sympathetic as Joyce to the new trends in art, perhaps more so. But he saw that if Joyce were to use his talent and zest, rather than dissipate them in cafés, he must get proper training, and he told him so.

Edinburgh was the place Mackie suggested. Paris could ruin a young man, even an ambitious one, if he hadn't self-discipline and were allowed to talk away — or drink away — his talent. With some proper training behind him, a sound beginning, Joyce would be better able to take Paris in his stride.

Evidently Mackie's interest and persuasiveness overwhelmed Joyce because in 1907 he followed his friend's advice. He packed up, left Paris, and entered classes at the school which Mackie suggested in Edinburgh, the Board of Manufacturers School of Art. Despite its name, it was a good school offering sound instruction, and a few years later it became the Edinburgh College of Art. Edinburgh in those days was no Paris, but a young man could live an inexpensive and reasonably Bohemian life if he liked and yet not go so far astray as he might in Paris.

The School of Art held its classes upstairs in the Royal Institute Building (now the Royal Scottish Academy) on The Mound, the road running from Princes Street up to the top of the hill on which Edinburgh Castle stands. The Mound is right in the middle of Princes Street Gardens, probably the handsomest setting in all Edinburgh, a perfect place from which to watch Edinburgh go by.[4] Not only is there the panoramic view from the Castle, stretching out to the Firth of Forth and beyond on a clear day, but there was the constant parade of people to watch. The Mound and Princes Street are the center of the city. If the cafés were the place from which to see Paris, The Mound was the place to be in Edinburgh.

In 1942, when he was about to make a trip to Scotland, Joyce wrote to a friend,

> It is years since I have been in Edinburgh. I look forward very much to seeing it again, even tho I can no longer sit on the steps of the Mound, in a dirty painters blouse, and contemplate the passers, from that Bohemian other world which seemed to me then so much better furnished, for entertainment, than the Heavenly Mansions.[5]

In those days Edinburgh was a much older, slower city than now, with more sharp angles and dark corners and less gloss. It did not have hairdressing shops with yards of windows over-looking Princes Street, for instance, with rows of women under driers like a showcase full of dolls. Nor were there shiny windows full of pseudo-Scottish souvenirs to entice the tourists — Tartan was what people wore to demonstrate their clans, not a backdrop for trinkets made in Hong Kong.

The back streets and alleys, the closes and slums, were often filthy places full of disease, and along the Royal Mile the slops, or at least the wash water, could still come down in a torrent from windows four and five stories above. There was dirt, but to a young artist, at least, it was a vital place, where one could see "scenes in the old Carengate which would rival Steen or Goya," Joyce said later. "It is a pity that as the world gets cleaner and less brutal, it loses its bravura." [6]

While there was a great deal of pleasure to be had outside the Art School, Joyce had plenty of hard work as well. There were sketching and drawing classes with still life and modeling, end-less drawing from plaster busts, painting classes when the students were quite advanced, and even more classes in the evening, organized informally by the students themselves. And there were evenings spent at Charles Mackie's studio in Murry-field, where the students — all of them young men — discussed the new art and argued fauvism versus impressionism and agreed to despise the set pieces of Victorian art, the paintings of tippling monks and jolly tavern scenes that continued to domi-nate provincial galleries in Britain until the 1920's and 1930's.[7]

Joyce must have talked about the Paris scene he had so recently inhabited, because he always liked talking and was good at stories and because his fellow students surely would have been interested in learning everything they could about the city, even second hand, since all young painters considered it Mecca.

Joyce's passion remained impressionism, but he was caught up by the Celtic aura of Edinburgh, an aura half real and half bogus. The Scottish "Celtic Twilight" was dimmer than that of Ireland, producing nobody to match the people it spawned in Ireland — no Synge or Yeats, for instance — but there was enough of it to infect Joyce. Impressed with Celtic crosses, runic writings, wandering bards (or at least an old man who played the Celtic harp and sang the old songs in pubs for pennies[8]), and the dramatic sight of the ancient castle itself and Holyrood Palace, Joyce began to use a monogram of Celtic design to sign his drawings; he designed a costume for himself, that of a Celtic demon with horned helmet and fur cloak, to wear to a student masquerade ball, and he wrote some abominable poetry, half cavalier and half rotten Rosetti.

By the end of the first year his instructor, Mr. Blacklock, let him begin with oils, and he painted by day and drew at the evening sessions of the sketching club, mastering the basics and learning them so well that more than forty years afterwards he claimed he could still draw a cross section of the human body at any point his listener cared to suggest.[9]

That first year, despite his progress, was not entirely satisfactory for Joyce. In his second Edinburgh year he turned more and more to poetry (for he had never abandoned it entirely). It was poetry not much advanced in craft from that of his Clifton years and, adulterated by its Celtic sludge, poetry totally out of harmony with the type of painting he was doing and equally out of harmony with the new literary movements in France, England, and America.

He was beginning to realize, as he approached his twentieth birthday, that he simply wasn't good enough as a painter and never would be — at least not good enough to measure up to his own ambitions. At best he would be third-rate. Although he had a greater technical skill at painting, writing seemed to him to be the field in which he could achieve what he wanted.

Besides, there was his sight. With one eye almost blind, he had a handicap for which technique could never compensate. He decided he'd gone about as far as he could in painting, even though he had won a few prizes for his work, including one for a sketch of his brother. He therefore reached the conclusion that writing must be his vocation and painting just a hobby.

First he had to be sure of his ground before approaching his father. His initial move was to publish some of his work. Instead of submitting to magazines or publishing houses, he had a volume of his poetry privately printed by an Edinburgh stationer. The slim, paper-covered book, *"Verses* by Arthur Cary," was handsomely printed: the title and author's name with scarlet initial letters and a runic symbol also done in scarlet were impressed on a cream cover. Although since he was born he had been called "Joyce," so as to avoid confusion with his father (if his father was "Young Arthur," what could they call *him?*), he chose to use his first name on the book's cover, which suggests he was making a diplomatic gesture toward his father. This impression is confirmed by the dedication which read, "To Arthur Cary my father."

The poems show a variety of influences: Celtic romanticism, the Cavalier poets, and William Blake (who became an increasingly important influence and is at the core of *The Horse's Mouth*), as in this one:

SONNET

He built his house with squarely hewed stones
Upon a shaggy-headed cliff, set high
That every roof and tower did cut the sky
Enduringly in old Chaos' bones.
And sometimes rolled an Organ's soaring tones,
Setting the air a-tremble; sometimes high
Upon the terrace, while the winds ran by,
He meditated old temptations;
Yet in a while, as't seemed, Earth's blood ran slow

> And slower in its walls, and it was cold.
> But he was strong and said, "This house doth grow
> Into a prison;" and he took nor gold
> Nor carven jewel, but straightly forth did go
> In's tattered coat, as he had come of old.

But for the most part, the poems are on the level of "Song":

> Out of bed, o yawn o' Morn,
> For Father's blown his hunting horn,
> And Mother's sewn my frock that's torn,
> And Lanky John has gone away
> To see the Indies and Cathay
> And won't be back for many a day;
> And here I'm waiting all forlorn
> For you, get up now, Yawn-o' Morn,
> Dear Yawn-o' Morn.

T. S. Eliot, born in the same year as Joyce, wrote "The Love Song of J. Alfred Prufrock" two years after this volume was published, which shows just how far behind the times Joyce was as a poet. He sent copies of *Verses* to his father and his friends, who were impressed by it all the same.

Joyce's next move was to write some of his former teachers at Clifton, sending them manuscripts of his work. Did they see any real talent in it, he asked, and if so, did they think he had a chance of succeeding as a writer? He also traveled to Clifton on the excuse that he wanted to see some friends there. But he had been away from Clifton for two years and since boys were not allowed to have more than a scant association with those not in the same class, it seems unlikely that he went so far a distance to visit boys he hardly knew. The reason for the trip must have been to consult with the teachers to whom he had sent his work about a literary career.

He needed all the advice he could get, not so much to reassure himself that his new choice of career was the right one, but to convince his father. After all, Arthur Cary had seen what improvidence and lack of direction could do. These tendencies had reduced his family from the rank of country gentlemen to that of outcasts and exiles. Improvidence had ruined the Carys of Inishowen, and he had been forced to work desperately hard to educate himself and build a career, to start a family on a more prosperous road, and to educate his children at the best schools he could afford.

He had allowed himself to be persuaded that Joyce should leave Clifton since his son had been certain then that painting was the only possible life for him. He had supported Joyce's term in Paris and his education in Edinburgh. Now Arthur Cary's eldest son and his namesake, having abandoned the conventional life for the world of painting, wanted to abandon *that* world as well for literature. Joyce knew it would be a shock to his father and apparently expected a fight over it.

So he wooed Arthur Cary with the dedication in *Verses* and armed himself with the endorsements of his teachers. Finally, when there was nothing else left to do, he declared himself.

The plan Joyce proposed was that he should go to Oxford to take a degree in law. In this way he'd be prepared for both a literary career and a more conventional one, possibly in the Civil Service, should it happen that he hadn't the talent or the luck to succeed as a writer. The idea of an Oxford degree and the preparation it would give, the doors it would open to a solid profession and a place in the social establishment, were exactly what would appeal to Arthur Cary.

All the same, Joyce's father could not help expressing in his letter of agreement some of the misgivings he had about Joyce's fickleness. He reminded the boy of what had happened to the family in the past and of what he had suffered in order to become a man of substance. He agreed to Joyce's plan, but with reluctance and misgivings.

His son was quick to reply in the following undated letter that he fully understood the situation:

16. St. Bernards Crescent
Edinburgh

MY DEAR DAD,

I am very sorry that I have made you anxious about me. Truly I realize the importance of this choice — and that is my only excuse for delay. I meant in my last letter to tell you I leant towards

the varsity, and indeed, I have been expecting your advice on that
project. So many people — of critical knowledge and some literary standing — advise me to write & since I find I spend most of
my time thinking about that kind of work, whatever is going on,
and since I seem to be able to labour at it without tiring — as I
have done these weeks — I am encouraged to decide for it. Will
you then tell me what you think? My best love to you all,

Your affectionate son
Joyce

Arthur Cary conceded. Joyce could go to Oxford, then give
writing a determined try, and, if that failed, go into the Civil
Service or teaching, at any rate into something that was sound
and respectable, something that would give him a decent living.

His father's concession was particularly generous because he
had been saddled with other troubles in the past two years. In
1907 Arthur's mother, Jane Cary, had died, as had his uncle, Dr.
Tristram Cary, and he had been devoted to them both. His sister Mab and her husband, Henry Stevenson (the brother of Arthur's second wife, Dora), now moved to Canada. So the final
break had come with Donegal; the last of the Carys had gone
from it.

A further tragedy of 1907 was Arthur Cary's third marriage.
He was only forty-three and as vigorous and handsome as ever
(whenever he swam underwater the family always feared he'd
drown, he stayed under so long; and once at a country fair he
had taken two troublesome hulking ruffians twice his size and
had thrown them out of the place, as much by his forceful manner as his strength), so he could have had his pick of new brides.
But his family cautioned him, "Don't marry a gel, Arthur.
Don't start another family. Marry a settled older woman." Unfortunately he took their advice and proposed to the Miss Agar
who had sent the gift of a satin coverlet to his first bride. At first
she seemed a perfect choice, for besides being in love with Arthur, she had some money of her own and professed an overwhelming affection for the two children of his second marriage,
Sheila and Tony, who were her "darling little pets." And she
wanted to be "pals" with Jack and Joyce.

After the marriage, the new Mrs. Cary got on well enough with the two older boys, perhaps because they were so seldom at home and needed no attention (Jack, after training as a naval cadet, was at sea most of the time). It was Tony and Sheila who suffered from the marriage; apparently their stepmother had meant to pack Sheila off to a boarding school and felt that Tony, since he was extremely delicate, might well die, leaving her to share Arthur Cary with nobody. As she increasingly revealed her dislike of the children, the marriage began to crumble until finally she walked out on her new husband and family. Her stepdaughter felt "This was the happiest day of my life," a feeling the rest of the Carys shared.[10]

But in the spring of 1909, when Joyce told his father of his new plans, Arthur Cary was in the midst of this unhappiness at home. His ability to display tolerance and magnanimity toward his son's waverings at a time when he was suffering such strains speaks well of him. He agreed to support Joyce in his new venture to Oxford.

6

OXFORD

ALTHOUGH JOYCE had made up his mind about Oxford and Arthur Cary had accepted the idea, there was a third party, the university itself, to be reckoned with. Having dropped out of Clifton early, Joyce had a good deal of work to make up before he had any hope of passing the entrance exams for Trinity, the college he had chosen. His Greek was impossible and his mathematics both slim and rusty. While these subjects were the worst, the others needed work, too. So in the early spring of 1909 he signed up with an Edinburgh "crammer" school for tutorials as he was in a hurry to get started for the first examinations in May.

His decision to stay in Edinburgh, rather than go home to London, seems odd. After all, London offered a far greater choice of tutors, was close to Oxford, and allowed him to live at far less expense, since he would not have room and board to pay. Joyce explained to his father that he felt a responsibility to his landlady, a Miss Yule, who was having an impossible time making a go of her boardinghouse. But since Miss Yule was managing to lose money with a full house because the boarders were costing her more than she was charging them, he would have done her a bigger favor by moving out.[1]

Joyce had been on his own for nearly three years, and while his concern for Miss Yule was probably real enough, it was also a good excuse for maintaining his independence. That way he could move from Edinburgh to Oxford with no more than a brief visit or two at home with his father and stepmother. A visit would be far more comfortable for him in his present scapegrace state than actually living there. So he went to Arrowsmith's for his tutoring and received encouragement and advice from Mr. Tait, his former housemaster at Clifton, now retired and living in Edinburgh.

"My Mathematics are practically safe now," he wrote to his father in April. "I can get 75% on former college papers. Latin Prose is getting very much better (and ought to improve my English style later) and History goes on evenly. Greek of course is the doubtful subject, but if I do well in English, so Blakiston the President says, Trinity will excuse a failure in Greek. All the same, it is wonderful how fast they teach you." He added as an obvious piece of soft soap, "As you say, I find this return to hard and fast routine does me a great deal of good."

Through the spring he sweated it out with his books, breaking the routine with a stay at the country home of a friend, Arch Sturrock, a fellow art student. "Arrowsmith, the Crammer, especially advised me to go away if I could," Joyce explained, "so that the invitation came at a fortunate time." [2] In May he sat for the first entrance exams, managed to pass them, and squeezed his way through the rest of the entrance requirements that would enable him to enter Trinity that October.

His transformation was remarkable. He completely abandoned one world and way of life for a new one. From the sophisticated and Bohemian student of painting, he became the ingenuous freshman. Although he was two years older than most of the new students, a significant difference at that age, he entered into this new life with as much enthusiasm as the rest, and perhaps even more; apparently he lived by the lesson he had learned at Clifton, that the only way to survive and triumph was to throw himself into everything and squeeze out of life all that it had to offer.

Life at Oxford before World War I was much less serious than nowadays and often more riotous. There was the Freshman Wine Party, held in Trinity's hall, to repay those senior men who had invited freshmen to their rooms for breakfast shortly

after the beginning of term. The Wine Party took up where a
Bacchanalia left off. It was dedicated to wine and fire, in that
order. After the students had enough wine, they got started on
the fires. College linen hampers were one of the first targets:
their wicker burned so well. So did the chairs and tables, once
the fires were started. When the evening was well along, there
might be a dozen bonfires burning in the college quad, with the
dean of the college, whose charge was discipline, running from
blaze to blaze, attempting to salvage what was not yet burning
and writing down the names of as many fire stokers as he could
so that the proper people could be billed for damages later.

Finally, with the wine gone, the fires flickering out, the dean's
notebook filled, and both the freshmen and the seniors exhausted, the party broke up and people went off to their beds —
if these had not been thrown into somebody's fire, too.[3]

Joyce also went out for the tamer sport of rowing and was
stroke for his college four. They raced through November and
just missed winning the contest with Brasenose College, after
breaking an oar in one heat and having their number two man
go sulky on them in the final moments, thus giving the crew
only half the effort that he could have. The enthusiasm Joyce
showed in his letters to his father that autumn may have been
given special emphasis in order to prove to Arthur Cary that
Oxford *was* the right choice. But Joyce always had a capacity for
enthusiasm, at least since that hard plunge into Clifton life after
the runaway episode. If he was going to be there and was going
to have to take part in certain events, he would enjoy them. He
would absorb every bit of pleasure that he could out of every
minute. So if he had to row, he did his damnedest at it and
expected the rest of the crew to do the same.

Impatience, in fact, was his worst fault; impatience with other
people's moods or sheer laziness. It was a failing that took a
great deal of time, effort, and experience to conquer.

But the group with whom Joyce fell in had more than sufficient enthusiasm for him. The men were different from the
usual Oxford students of the time. They were not the horsey,
country squire sort, nor were they the grinds, the overly serious

scholars. And they certainly were not the type who had come to loaf and get a veneer of culture before they went into the family business. They were more men of the world — in the best sense as well as one or two of the worst ones — than anything else. The critic John Middleton Murry, who as a student came into much contact with them, described them this way:

> They were a little older than the average undergraduate. Some of them had come from Scottish universities, while Joyce had put in a year at an art school. Something had intervened for them between the public school and the university, which made the difference. They were neither overgrown sixth-form boys, like me, nor pass-men up for a good time. There was nothing precocious about them, yet their intellectual interests were various and widespread; and they judged for themselves.[4]

Duncan MacGregor, a classical exhibitioner at Oxford, was the man from a Scottish university whom Murry mentions. Of the others, two were South Africans on Rhodes scholarships, Gerhardus Maritz and Lennox Ross Broster. They and another South African, Percy Horsefall, were known in the group as "the native troops." Philip Mitchell was the liveliest of the group, always ready for high jinks, and finally was sent down (expelled) from the University for one of his pranks, no easy accomplishment back then. Thomas Higham and Joyce made up the rest of the group's core.

They were bright, lively, witty, and worldly, and they knew how to drink; all of this impressed Murry, a boy from a rather strict, lower middle-class family, up at Brasenose College on a scholarship. Jack Murry, young and impressionable, was just then discovering the world of art, a world Joyce had had three years' experience in, so the two were drawn together by their mutual interest. Joyce, in a sour mood years later, said that in introducing Murry to the Bohemian life, he had ruined a good civil servant. But Murry had caught the art fever before coming to Oxford; Joyce encouraged the infection. In any case, they met, got on well, and Murry, for the moment, adopted Joyce as big brother, which probably flattered the chosen one. Joyce talked — bragged, perhaps — about his painting days in Paris, and the artists, exiles, anarchists, and others with whom he had consorted. Perhaps he talked about the girls, too, and, of course, he was a grand storyteller, always able to embroider a bit. Jack Murry was filled with the desire to go to Paris.

In their second year they took rooms together in the Broad Street, and the plans for Paris developed into a concrete proposal to spend their Christmas holiday there. When the end of term came, Joyce went down to London for a brief visit at home, but Murry, eager to plunge into Bohemia, bypassed his own home in London and went straight to Paris, armed with introductions from Joyce to various old friends in Paris — painters, mostly, and a few writers and other persons of the sort he wanted to show off to Murry.

Jack Murry was delighted with Paris. He was drunk with the place from the day of his arrival and amazed at how fast he made friends with the habitués of the Closerie des Lilas. Why, he wrote to friends, they even let him pay for their drinks! And they considered him so much a kindred soul, a friend even, that they allowed him *to lend them money!* He never realized he was a lamb among the wolves and was quite broke before Joyce ever arrived. Murry had to write to Joyce to ask for some money so he could live until his friend finally arrived to shepherd him about the place.

Joyce, who had come of age during his first year at Oxford, December, 1909, had inherited from his mother an annual income of nearly £300, a very handsome sum of money in those days, and he was free with it, too free perhaps, especially with Murry, who had his scholarship and not much more. Murry, unsophisticated in so many ways, seems to have caught on to the matter of money and the ways of borrowing it fairly early in his student career. So Joyce bailed him out and found Murry quite happy when they met again in Paris.

In the meantime, Murry had met a girl, Marguerite, a young prostitute, and was convinced that he had fallen in love with her. Joyce walked in on Murry and Marguerite's light housekeeping, but the three got along well under the circumstances. Murry was very upset at the idea of Marguerite's staying on the streets and wanted her to stop, so this made Joyce's presence a financial necessity.

As for Joyce, he spent his vacation with bad digestion — stomach cramps — and dreams of Marguerite. It wasn't easy to relax or read in the sitting room when the bedroom next door was occupied.[5]

However, he renewed a number of old friendships and flirtations, particularly with Dot, the Scottish girl of 1907, who had written several times to him in Edinburgh and may even have visited him there. She seems to have been more interested in Joyce than he was in her, for she went into jealous sulks when he talked to the prostitutes at the Lilas and the d'Harcourt. One night, as Murry and Joyce were walking her home to her studio after dinner and drinks, she suddenly hit Joyce in the face. Joyce swore at her and walked off in a sulk of his own, only to be chased after by Dot and Jack, and it was Murry, desperately turning somersaults in the middle of the street, who calmed the star-crossed couple down.

Dot caused Murry some trouble, too, because Marguerite glimpsed her with Murry one night and was furious. Marguerite was very jealous. As Joyce noted: "Marguerite has always said she would put a knife in him if he left her, & I believe she would." Murry was in a terrible state when he learned of Marguerite's rage, not because he was afraid she would knife him but because he was afraid he would lose her. So he rushed off to her with flowers, only to find her coldly putting on her street-walking powder and rouge. He gave her the flowers, but she would say nothing. Finally he gave up in despair and walked home. Then, at six that evening, Marguerite burst into Joyce and Murry's rooms, proclaimed her love for Murry, and everyone forgave everyone else.

After the high-pitched tone of the vacation, Joyce and Murry must have been glad to get back to Oxford again, although their return left Marguerite in a terrible state, for she was desperately afraid that Murry, like other English students who had taken up with French girls (one of the girls at the d'Harcourt had just been deserted), would leave, forget her, and never come back again. Whether or not she loved him — and both Joyce and

Murry were convinced that she did — he was her salvation from
streetwalking, and it must have been very hard for her to see
him go. And Murry, too, even if he may have found college a
bit more relaxing, was not happy over their good-byes.

In fact, he found it impossible to settle down to studies again
after his love affair and his first taste of Bohemian life. He wrote
letter after passionate letter to Marguerite throughout the term
and despaired that Easter would ever come when he would see
her again. The fact that Murry went back to Paris alone at
Easter while Joyce went home suggests that Joyce was ready for
a little peace and quiet for a change.

Actually, although he and Murry continued to room together
for a time, their friendship was ending. Joyce saw more and
more of Tommy Higham, Duncan MacGregor, and the others,
although by now Philip Mitchell had been sent down, leaving a
gap in the original group.

Not that Joyce and Murry failed to keep in touch during the
vacation. For on April 1, Murry, sitting in the Lilas, set his wallet on the table in the middle of a conversation, then, getting up
to go, forgot all about it. He walked a dozen yards or more
down the street, then suddenly remembered his loss and raced
back to the café. But the wallet was gone. No one had seen it;
they were sure of that. And Murry was left as stony broke as he
had been at Christmas, and this on the first day of his visit. It
was a perfect All Fools' Day. What made it worse was that the
French friend with whom he had meant to stay was out of Paris,
and his flat was locked up.[6]

The "friends" to whom Murry had loaned money last time
evidently were neither able nor ready to repay the loans even in
part. But Murry finally found someone who would give him a
small sum and rushed off to a post office to send a flock of tele-
grams to his Oxford friends, begging for help. This one to Joyce
is an example of Murry's distress:

> Joyce, for God's sake send me 2 or 3£. The very fiends of hell
> have dogged me since I've been here. Delacroix with whom I was
> to stay has cleared out of Paris. And now at the Lilas last night I
> lost every damned penny in my purse, by leaving it on the table.

195 francs — at the present time I have 2 fr. 30. It's enough to make a man turn god knows what. I'll pay that to you in time for your [?] as my school comes in then. The beauty of it all is that I haven't paid for my room and have lost my return ticket. Marguerite has chucked the d'Harcourt; turned typist and lives en pension.

I'd write more only I'm too anxious.   Yours Jack.[7]

The letters worked so well that Murry was able to spend his vacation quite comfortably with Marguerite, even perhaps buying more drinks for his café friends, and still return to Oxford for the spring term with more money than he'd had when he first arrived in France.[8] If he paid off any of these debts or other loans for that matter, he did not pay Joyce, who would get irritated by the fact years after when he remembered it.

Again Murry returned to Oxford and to the rooms on the Broad Street he shared with Joyce, and he thought and talked of Marguerite. Only now, Murry began to think more and more along the same lines as Joyce: he wanted to be a writer. With Joyce lying on the floor of the sitting room scrawling Cavalier lyrics, with all their talk of art and literature and the glimpses they had had of Bohemian life in Paris, and with other friends having already made the big decision, Murry was carried away by the idea.

The product of his ambitions was *Rhythm*, a magazine devoted to the new literature fathered by Dostoevsky, Chekhov, and the other great Russians, and mothered by Constance Garnett, who translated so many of them. The Russian Ballet of Diaghilev came to London in June, 1911, creating a great sensation. Samovars and batik dresses were the rage, and short stories revolving around the pathetic and fruitless, stories of mood, not plot, synthetic Chekhov, were being written in little rooms near the British Museum. In fact the new literature, especially the short story, was Russian; the new poetry was French; and the new art, promoted by Roger Fry and Clive Bell, whose Post-Impressionist Exhibit created a sensation in London in December, 1910, was French too. The magazine, promoted and edited by Murry, on borrowed money, was devoted to these new elements and to the destruction of Victorianism.

With a new career opening for him, Murry was in a quandary. He could chuck it all and marry Marguerite. Or he could get rid of Marguerite. Life with her would be full of pitfalls. It seemed unlikely that she would be happy in England among the literati. And it would be a great deal harder to edit a magazine — one in English — from Paris than from London, at least so that it would pay. London was where the audience was and the backers, too. Murry had endured enough of pinchpenny living at home. He did not feel he could face a lifetime of it. The break with Marguerite looked inevitable. So he stopped writing to her. He decided he could not keep his promise to spend the summer of 1911 with her in Paris. Instead he would devote himself to art and, in order to drown his sorrows, to debauchery.

But debauching himself in Oxford presented problems. Just where could one go to accomplish it?

Joyce had been the only person at Oxford to know of the Marguerite affair. He had advised Murry against it from the start. One could go off to marry prostitutes in novels or operas, but to do it in real life, Joyce had suggested, meant tragedy. Now it was Joyce to whom Jack turned to talk about his future and to whom he announced his decision to break things off with Marguerite.

In his autobiography, *Between Two Worlds,* Murry tells of his attempt to smother his sorrows in sensuality. A friend, he said, the only friend in fact who knew of the affair in Paris, came to his rescue.* The friend obliged Murry by taking him biking out into the country to a quaint little bordello. While the friend chatted happily with the girls, Murry, terribly embarrassed, sulked silently until he was led off upstairs. Soon, even more dejected, he came down again to his friend. Off they went to Oxford, the debauchery completed.

Not long afterward Murry, feeling distinctly unwell, went to see a doctor, who told him he had a clear case of gonorrhea. Fortunately, the doctor told him, the disease could be remedied quickly since it was in an early stage. Murry was well soon

---

* Since it seems that only Joyce knew of the Murry-Marguerite affair, he must have been the anonymous friend described in Murry's story.

enough, cured of both the disease and desire for a life of debauchery. In fact, when he moved in with Katherine Mansfield, his future wife, shortly after this, for months they led a totally celibate life, partly because Murry for the time being had no appetite for further sexual experience.[9]

Murry, when he moved off to the greener literary fields of London, drifted out of Joyce's life. They did not meet again for over forty years.

7

THE OGILVIES

JOYCE HAD HIS OWN UPS AND DOWNS in romance. Early in his Oxford days he was infatuated with a niece of his new step-mother. She in turn seemed friendly enough. So, when she asked him for a loan of several pounds, he was glad to oblige, then crushed when she disappeared and he found she had wanted the money to finance her elopement with another man.

Although there were other girls with whom he had better luck, there was one in particular who gave him a persistently difficult time. She was the sister of two friends, Heneage and Frederick Ogilvie, both of whom he had known from Clifton. Heneage, the dreamy sergeant of a few years before, was in his final year at Oxford, preparing to study medicine, when Joyce was a freshman. Freddy, a few years younger, didn't come up to Oxford until 1910.

The two Ogilvies had three sisters, Florence, Elsie, and Ger-trude, and Heneage several times had one or another of them come up to Oxford from their home on London's outskirts for a dance or Eights Week, the week of boat races and college balls, a kind of Mardi Gras before the Lent of exam time. The girls would arrive in the company of Gwen Quilter, a girl of whom Heneage was rather fond. Joyce, who was invited to the Ogilvie home in Harrow Weald, a lovely big place with sweeping lawns, had flirted with all three of the girls, but it was Gerty, the youngest and shyest of the three, who caught his fancy.

Heneage and Joyce saw a good deal of each other. Each possessed traits the other admired and perhaps envied. Joyce, to Heneage, seemed very free and Bohemian; he himself came from an extremely strict Calvinist home, where soundness and piety were the important values, although his parents loved music a great deal. Heneage's tall, straight figure, his good looks, and his sense of direction were characteristics Joyce admired. Joyce was several inches the shorter and described himself as "sallow." What both men had in common, however, was their idealism.[1]

Now that he had come into more contact with contemporary poetry, Joyce had become much shyer of showing people his writing, particularly after what he now regarded as the fiasco of his publication of *Verses*. The fact that he showed Heneage one of his most recent poems — Murry was about the only other person at Oxford who even knew Joyce was writing — shows how close they were. However, the poem, one about the Virgin Mary, shocked Heneage, although it was not irreverent, and this made Joyce all the more reluctant to show anyone his creative work.[2]

He did write for a public, but in the form of essays for various societies to which he belonged at Oxford. He was a great joiner of Oxford clubs — the Milton Society, where he had met Murry; the Gryphon Club, a very serious literary group that was founded by Sir Arthur Quiller-Couch; the Elizabethan Club, which was founded by Joyce and his friends; the Petronius Club, where Petronius's *Cena Trimalchionis* was read and discussed. There were others, some of them short-lived affairs, or ones in which Joyce did not participate so much as he did in those mentioned above. The meetings were informal, held in someone's rooms, with whiskey and soda, wine, or coffee for refreshment. One or two members would read a paper which the others would attempt to tear to pieces. Sometimes this effort caused such a wrangle that the club broke up, as the Elizabethan did one time. At this particular meeting, Tommy Higham made off with the club's total assets, a dozen or more oranges, so, when the members got together again, he got himself elected president.[3]

Murry said years later that, even though he had lived with Joyce, he never saw him do a spot of work at Oxford, except for scrawling poems on the floor of their sitting room.[4] But while that may have been true of strictly academic work, Joyce did go at his essays for his various clubs with great diligence. He learned early that he had to, because an Oxford undergraduate group can be one of the most critical audiences in the world.

Besides, very soon after coming to Oxford he was invited to the home of H. A. Prichard, a philosophy don at Trinity who had gone to Clifton. Joyce was a bit contemptuous of the fusty pictures he saw on Prichard's walls, and they got into a discussion of painters and art in general. Joyce complained that good painters so often starved while bad Royal Academy painters made money. The Royal Academy, he maintained, was opposed to really original work. Prichard led him on, gradually closing a trap on this freshman who was so full of his own opinions, and forced him by the end of the visit to admit that all his absolutes were relatives, that in fact in art absolute values did not exist. Joyce went away very upset and feeling he'd been had. When he complained that night to his friends, he found that rather than sympathizing with him, "they were greatly amused. I discovered, in short, that, like Prichard, they regarded me as an innocent. . . ."[5]

He found that all of the principles he had taken for granted in Paris and Edinburgh were treated with argument, amusement, or disdain. When he tried to explain a point, even his terminology, the jargon of the painter which his fellow students in Edinburgh had accepted totally and understood, was called into question. This highly critical reception, Joyce remembered, "surprised me very much. I had been talking art for years with other art students, and I had not found any difficulty in the use of terms."[6]

It was his first real introduction to dialectics, to sophisticated debate, and after the first shock, he did his best to cope with it. This was a difficult proposition, since so many of his friends were philosophy students, and had been trained in methods of analysis and in the use of terminology. Although they disputed his artist's jargon, they accepted their own philosopher's vocabulary, and they were in the majority.

So when he was getting a paper ready for one of the clubs, he worked to make it as airtight as possible, whether it was on painting or literature or politics, his favorite subjects. This concise type of writing was a vital experience, and out of it he got most of the education he took away from Oxford in 1912.

He took away a few other things, too. One of them was a photograph of Gerty Ogilvie, which he stole from Freddy Ogilvie's rooms.[7] The girl fascinated and confused him at the same time. Her shyness often expressed itself as rudeness toward Joyce, which utterly frustrated him. He tried to penetrate her defenses, to get to know her, but she would have none of him. It is difficult to explain her behavior, just as it is difficult to fathom why he continued to be fascinated by her.

She had been brought up under extremely strict and sheltered conditions, despite coming into the world in the middle of a Latin American revolution. For in August, 1891, Chile, where the family had then been living, was in ferment. The Chilean Congress and Army revolted against President Balmaceda, and a pitched battle was fought at Placilla, a few miles from the Ogilvie home in Valparaiso, on August 26. As her father later wrote,

> While this battle was going on, Gertie was born to the sound of guns. When the fighting began, English blue-jackets were landed from a cruiser in the bay, to protect the English colony. The password was "The Queen" and we often used to hear this called out in the night on the road in front of our house.
>
> I had also six men from the works, armed with iron bars, to protect the house in case it should be attacked during the interregnum, when the defeated troops came pouring into the town and the victorious opposition had not yet taken charge. All the policemen had cleared out.
>
> The night after Gerty's birth, the town, at least the lower part of it, was given over to fire and pillage. From our house on the hill I counted as many as fifteen incendiary fires at one time.[8]

It is tempting to ascribe her volatile nature to these pre- and post-natal influences.

More likely, however, her parents' characters and the atmosphere of her home were what made Joyce attractive to her at the same time she was repelled by him, fascinated yet fearful, and consequently rude. For Mrs. Ogilvie was the strictest of Calvinists with an overlay of Victorian gentility, while Mr. Ogilvie's Calvinism was tempered with a romantic streak and an undercurrent of adventurousness. He went along with his more rigid wife, but not always. Gerty was educated at home in a circumspect way, and taught to be a lady but not necessarily a woman. She studied music, painting, and the other arts, but only in the limited way that a gentlewoman should. And her reading was carefully censored.

Yet, like her brothers and sisters and her parents, she had a stubborn streak, a certain willfulness, that would make her do what *she* wanted, if she wanted it strongly enough. But first she had to make up her mind after brooding over matters. What appeared sometimes to be rudeness or perversity, and sometimes sheer cussedness, was the result of this sort of internal battle between what she wanted and what she knew she *should* want as a lady and an Ogilvie.

Joyce was a prime case in point. He was totally alien to the Ogilvie world view. He had wallowed in the fleshpots of Paris, leading an artist's life — and everyone knew what artists were like. He had drawn and painted from the nude; he had sat up half the night in Montmartre cafés, talking and drinking and carousing with prostitutes. At Oxford he went with a pretty fast crowd, so fast that one of them had been sent down for some wild escapade, and they all drank. He was Irish, too, or nearly so, and everyone knew what the Pope-ridden Irish were, just a bunch of drunken layabouts. To top it all, he wanted to be a *writer!* He definitely was not husband material, and a really nice girl would have nothing to do with him.

At the same time, he was a window on a whole new world for Gerty, a world of color, gaiety, and art. His slim, dapper (at least dapper when he wanted it to be) figure, his curly brown hair and blue eyes, his cocky grin, and his obvious infatuation with her all attracted her. To allow herself to fall in love with him, and even worse to marry him, would be an act of willfulness that might cut her off from her parents forever. It very well might be the primrose path to Hell itself.

As for Joyce, his emotions are easier to grasp. Gerty Ogilvie was a good-looking girl and a challenge. She was tall, a fraction of an inch shorter than he was (or so he insisted to her), handsome, almost imperial, and her contralto voice, both when she spoke and when she sang, was like rich velvet, soothing and compelling. It was a voice he could listen to the rest of his life.

And like most young men with any self-respect, Joyce could not resist an enigma. Evidently, he felt he had to penetrate Gerty's austere defenses. He had to get to *know* her. She was a Gioconda, eternally fascinating.

Whatever their feelings toward Joyce as a possible match for one or another of their daughters, Mr. and Mrs. Ogilvie did not treat him as a pariah personally. They were quite hospitable when either Heneage or Freddy invited him up from Oxford, and in fact Mr. Ogilvie developed a certain fondness for Joyce, who perhaps appealed to his own sense of adventure. Joyce's visits at their home in Harrow Weald, "The Glade," were pleasant ones, except for Gerty's behavior. For she would virtually run from whatever room he entered, as if he were Satan himself.

However he tried to disarm her and ingratiate himself, she fled from him. He couldn't get a pleasant word out of her. The entire effort was frustrating and apparently hopeless. She seemed determined to hold him at sword's point forever.[9]

Thwarted in that direction and realizing that his studies were in bad shape, as the Schools examinations that would sum up three years' work were only six months away, it is little wonder that Joyce envied Jack Murry when he dropped out of Oxford and into London's literary world. He asked himself if he shouldn't do the same — just throw up Oxford and devote himself to his writing. The truth was that aside from his essays for the various clubs and his poems, he had done very little writing at Oxford, although he had arrived there with high hopes. He had even hired a typist in the fall of his freshman year, a fact he had confided to his brother Jack in September, 1909:

> I have got a secretary now, my boy, to run my shew. So that I can be as secret as I like. She is a Miss Foot (about 55, and not handsome, so don't grin) and lives in a flat in Hammersmith. I have a private name too — I am Thomas Joyce, only don't tell a living soul, you are the only person, except miss Foot that knows it. I am going to write under it and play any fools' games I like under it, and have Cary for the drawing-room.
>
> I shall advertise it too. "Read the Counter-Jumper's Magazine. So-and-So by Thomas Joyce" in all the Railway Stations.

But Miss Foot got very little work to do, and, with all the costs of being a university student, Joyce could not manage to keep her in hire. His father, who footed the bills for most of Joyce's clothes, would have been a little shocked if he had seen how his son dressed at Oxford, because at the time the fashion was to be as shabby as possible, and Joyce managed to live up — or rather down — to this style. One time, while out on the river with some friends, he saw an older man, quite distinguished, who had fallen out of his boat and was in difficulties in the water. Joyce and the others went to the rescue and pulled the old fellow out, and the man, seeing their clothes, gave them each a shilling, thinking they obviously could use the money. Joyce was rather proud of this shilling and spoke of it to a cousin years later as the first money he had ever earned.[10]

Now in the autumn of 1911 he wanted to try earning some money from his writing. So, after he had gotten up enough nerve, he broached the idea to his father. Arthur Cary showed Joyce his usual consideration in his reply but attempted to get his son to see reason:

> I should be very sorry if you left Oxford without taking a degree — the effect would not be felt so much now as later — & I am quite sure if you do leave you will regret it very much in after years — of course if you do not have any aptitude for Law — or so little that you could only pass with a struggle you could not

go on with it — but none the less a mans Varsity Degree is an asset which is very much worth while making even a sacrifice to obtain if you can make money by your pen *now* why not do so — I mean in a minor way — it would help and — I am sure you could get a tutorship in the Long Vac. — I hope you will not argue the matter over all by yourself — but ask the opinion of some men or man whose judgment is sound & unbiased. . . .[11]

Perhaps Joyce's desire to leave without a degree was the product of one of those moods that beset many undergraduates somewhere along the way, the feeling that the university is just too cloistered, that the real life is all going on elsewhere. Whether this was behind Joyce's idea or whether there were more serious roots, Joyce accepted his father's advice and stayed on at Trinity.

The highlights of the year, Eights Week, and Trinity's Commem Ball, saw Joyce's best attempt to ingratiate himself with Gerty Ogilvie. But everything he did went wrong. At the Ball, in his anxiety, he held her too tightly when they danced and half squeezed the life out of her.[12] One of his dancing partners from those days calls him "a personal dancer," rather good in his odd way,[13] but at the Commem Ball he was too distracted to dance well, and the impression he made was all wrong.

The next day he had a date with her to go punting on the Cherwell, a chance to get her alone, or at least as alone as possible on a Sunday afternoon when everything that could float was apt to be on the river. This outing would give him a chance to talk to her, he hoped, as well as an opportunity to show off a bit, because he was an excellent punter. Punting is one of those English sports that looks terribly easy until one tries it and then discovers what a vast amount of technique it requires. A novice punter is apt to find his punt, that long, lean, unmanageable boat, lunging into the river bank every five feet. He is bound to get his shirt and trousers sopping from water dripping from the pole, and, if he is not careful, may get the pole firmly stuck in the bed of the river at one of its muddier spots. When the pole does get stuck, he may in despair continue to cling to it as the punt moves out from under him, then he and the pole slowly bow down until he is up to his neck in the slow-flowing Cher-

well. Joyce, though, was the sort of punter who not only did not
have to come dressed in a swimming suit but could actually keep
his shirt cuffs buttoned and dry as he sent his boat smoothly and
straight up the river, while he either gave the other punters a
bored look or chatted to his passengers. So Sunday afternoon
was to be the highlight of the weekend, the final chance to break
the ice with Gerty.

He arrived promptly at the appointed meeting place. But
there was no Gerty. Worried that she might have misunderstood and was waiting elsewhere, growing impatient with him,
and also afraid that perhaps she'd simply been delayed and
would be there in another few moments, he made forays in
different directions for her, coming back to his original spot
each time in case she had arrived. His searching became more
frantic and desperate, and the idea that she was not coming at all
took hold of him. Finally he found her with a companion, another girl, and, relieved, he invited her to join him in his punt.
She went along — as did the other girl.

So Joyce had his afternoon on the river, but Gerty spent all of
it talking with her friend, while Joyce played mute gondolier.[14]
That night, after they had seen Gerty off on her train to London, Joyce went back with Freddy Ogilvie to Freddy's rooms
and, frustrated, gave way and wept on the shoulder of his
startled and embarrassed friend.[15]

His examinations soon after were just as disastrous, as he was
almost totally unprepared for them. So, with two fiascos behind
him, he raced off to London as soon as he was able. Oxford and
Gerty were behind him, for now writing was all that counted.
He went off to Soho and took a room for himself where he
could write.

8

STORE STREET AND ANTIVARI

AT 10 STORE STREET off the Tottenham Court Road, Joyce settled down in Bohemian squalor to begin a novel. It was to be
about the Paris he had known in 1906 and 1907 and then had
seen again in January, 1911, during his hectic vacation with
Murry.[1] He may even have had the novel in mind during that
vacation, because he had kept a diary then, a rather unprece-
dented activity for him. The diary is full of notes on the cafés,
the artists and émigrés, and especially the prostitutes: Maria,
nicknamed the Pirate, who, Joyce noted, "does catch rather well;
she has a buccaneering way that is not to be escaped"; Eugenie,
who, in 1911 was in despair, because "The little boy she was so
fond of, has gone back to his people. He threw up his career to
live with her, & has no money to stay longer"; Philippe, who
"found out that she was with child, & her man has run away";
Jeanette, "a pale dark red-lipped, sunken cheeked girl" just
lately let out of "a hospital for hysterical people." [2] This was
the material he wanted to put into the novel.

As for the Soho address, Joyce moved there to be in the Bohemian atmosphere he enjoyed so much, a suitable enough environment considering the book he was working on. But it was
not just for that reason. He was broke.[3]

His own expenses at Oxford, where he hadn't stinted himself,
had been heavy enough. He had bought a lot of clothes and rare
books (an edition of Blake, for example, that he kept the rest of
his life) and had gone off to France or Ireland for vacations

as well. In addition, he had been free with his money to Murry
and others and was not the sort to dun people for what he had
loaned them, nor even to remember how much it had been and
to whom it was loaned. So when he went down from Oxford he
was rather badly in debt and had to live as frugally as possible —
all the more so after he received a telegram in July:

Class 4 words fail us Thomas Spider Teddy

A Fourth was a disastrous degree, the lowest given. Several of
his friends had taken Firsts or Double Firsts; others at the very
least took decent Seconds. Even Murry, who had quit the University, or even Philip Mitchell, who had been sent down, had
more honor than he had. Any hope of entering the Civil Service
or of teaching, except at the worst of provincial schools, was
gone with that telegram from his three friends.
   It would be impossible to go to his father and ask him to pay
off the Oxford debts when he had let him down so badly. Besides, even under more favorable circumstances, Arthur Cary
must have had a horror of debt after his family's experiences.
All Joyce could do was sit down in his grubby room, in his self-
imposed poverty, and get on with the job.
   It must have been a miserable summer, because not only was
there the matter of the degree and the debt, but Joyce again
tried to kindle some sort of affection for himself in Gerty Ogilvie. "Gerty's the only girl I want," he wrote to her friend, Gwen
Quilter. "You may think I race about, but I'm entirely faithful
to her and I hope I get her." [4] He certainly tried hard enough.
   The Ogilvies spent a month or more each summer in Scotland, and Joyce was invited to join them that July. They went
that year to Balmacara, in Inverness, just across Loch Alsh from
the Isle of Skye, a very remote part of the British Isles in those
days and remote enough now. But again everything went wrong
for Joyce. When Gerty, Joyce, and the other young people went
across to Skye on a painting trip one day, Joyce hovered as close
as he could to her and once dared to criticize the perspective in
the sketch she was doing. While he was pointing that out with

one hand, he rested the other on her shoulder. She literally fled
from him to Freddy, and the two of them sat and scowled at
Joyce until he went back forlornly to his own canvas.[5]

One day he finally got her alone in the schoolroom of the
Ogilvies' house and, perhaps despairing of ever getting her all to
himself again, blurted out a proposal of marriage. Gerty evidently mistook the proposal for a proposition and again she fled
from him, horrified.[6]

The upshot was that when she later found him fiddling about
with his pipe in the schoolroom and scolded him for making
such a mess on the mantelpiece with his tobacco, he had had
enough. He roared that she was just a beast for the way she
treated him, and Gerty was stunned into silence.[7] He stalked
out of the room and encountered Mrs. Ogilvie just outside.

To her Joyce blurted out everything, and she was as shocked
as Gerty had been just a few moments before. When Joyce said
how much he loved Gerty and how miserable he was, Mrs. Ogilvie told him she had no notion "it was as bad as that." [8] Earlier
she had spoken to him of her feeling that he was treating Gerty
rather badly, and Freddy, too, had taken Joyce aside to urge him
sternly to stop tormenting the poor girl.[9] Now to find that he
was in love with Gerty put a different slant on Mrs. Ogilvie's
outlook.

Joyce, though, felt he could not stay, and soon after this he
left Balmacara, but not before Mr. Ogilvie had given him his
first real sympathy and encouragement. He told Joyce not to
give up hope. Gerty had a temper and was headstrong, he said,
but she was a girl worth fighting for, and he wanted Joyce to
persist.[10]

Soon after this, when Joyce was visiting Heneage at Guy's
Hospital in London, where Gerty's older brother was doing his
medical training, Joyce met Gerty again. When they talked of
Joyce's writing, she was scornful of his novel and asked him with
great sarcasm why didn't he write something to make money,
why didn't he write "a play or something." [11]

Under these circumstances, it's a wonder he was able to write
anything at all. And it's no surprise that he took the first real

opportunity that presented itself to clear out of London, and out of England in fact.

War had broken out in the Balkans between Turkey and the small states of Montenegro, Bulgaria, Serbia, and Greece. Turkey in 1912 still possessed the area of Macedonia straight to the Adriatic Sea. Her misrule of this area had prompted a good deal of resistance by the Macedonians, and now the four small countries bordering Macedonia declared war on Turkey in order to aid their brothers — and perhaps to add to their own territory.

Joyce decided he would somehow go to the aid of Montenegro. As much as offering a change of scene, the war provided two other opportunities: it was a chance to express the strong idealistic feelings which had been fostered by Graeme Paterson at Oxford;[12] it was a chance, too, for a unique experience, a view of war. If he was to be a writer this was an opportunity he could not miss, one of the great experiences of life.[13] It might be his last chance, too, he thought, since it was extremely unlikely that there would be any more wars, at least in Europe, an idea he certainly was not alone in believing.

Like many other would-be writers hungry for first-hand experience, he forgot that Tolstoi had not seen the Napoleonic War nor had Stephen Crane seen the Civil War, although *War and Peace* and *The Red Badge of Courage* became classics. The irony would be that this was the only time he ever underwent a series of events simply to write about them someday, yet he never incorporated any of this material into a novel. The one piece he did write about the Balkan War, *Memoirs of the Bobotes,** was not published until several years after his death.[14]

Early in October he set out, traveling straight through by train to Trieste, then by an Austrian Lloyd Line ship to Kotor (Cattaro then), and on to Cetinje by post carriage. He was accompanied on this leg of the journey by a correspondent for the *London Daily Mirror* named Hey. Mountain roads and a gay, drunken driver made it an exciting trip. Joyce had with him a letter of introduction to an English lady-in-waiting to the Princess Royal of Montenegro, but rather than rushing off to the

---

* The title comes from the name of the people of the region.

palace and presenting himself, he and Hey collapsed into the
Grand Hotel — the town's only hotel — to find food and lodging. They found the food, but were put up in a private house
opposite the hotel.

Joyce spent four days in Cetinje attempting to enlist in the
Montenegrin Red Cross and introduced himself to the British
Minister and to Miss Olive Daubeny, the lady-in-waiting at the
palace. Then he decided to go on to Antivari (nowadays Old
Bar) to try to join a British Red Cross unit there.

Off he set in another carriage, with a driver more drunk than
the previous one and "a very ragged old gentleman," picked up
along the way. They were joined soon by an old woman and the
son she was taking off to the war front. Among themselves the
Montenegrins discussed Joyce and decided he must be a Russian. Since Russia was the patron of the Balkan peoples at the
time, this supposition was very much to Joyce's advantage.

At an inn where they stopped in Rjeka another passenger was
added to Joyce's hired carriage, a Lieutenant Popovic, formerly
of the Serbian Army, who had fled Serbia because he chose the
wrong side in its dynastic disputes; now he was anxious to join
the Montenegrin Army in order to fight the Turks. The two of
them, Joyce and Popovic, could talk to each other only in
French, "and neither of us spoke it well, so we did not converse
very much." The old people left them at Rjeka, and now the
carriage stopped to pick up two soldiers heading for the Scutari
(Skodra) region. At Virzipar they boarded a train on Montenegro's only railroad, with rolling stock that looked as if it had
been loaned from railway museums.

Finally they arrived at Antivari on a Saturday night, in the
midst of a gale that "was tearing tiles off the roofs and making a
cannonade of all the windows and doors in the place." [15] Antivari, already crowded, had just received the King of Montenegro and his military entourage, jamming the town even more.
Joyce and his Serbian friend asked the landlord of the only
hotel if they might sleep on his balcony despite the gale, but a
colonel who overheard them sent one of his soldiers to scour the
town for a proper place for the two strangers. Joyce, as he con-

tinued to be, was amazed and delighted at this display of Montenegrin kindness and politeness and noted,

> These men had never seen us before, and we were not very
> clean looking — we did not tell them we wished to help their
> country, because we were neither of us sure of what we would next
> be at — we were merely strangers, and men doubtful of a bed.

The private returned to report he'd had no luck. All the officers
in the place conferred; a lieutenant decided to go and look himself, despite Joyce's protests. He returned to say he had found
"at least a roof," and the private was told to lead Popovic and
Joyce there.

It was a blue wooden hut on the shore of the bay, with neither
lights nor lamps and full of holes for the wind to rush through.
Joyce was to share a bed with a longshoreman, but the three
women of the house gave each of their two guests a glass of raki
and showered them with so many questions and such interest
that Joyce felt both pleased at his welcome and glad to get into
the bed so the questions would cease.

In the morning he went off to find General Burke, commander of the British Red Cross unit in town. But when Burke
said he could do nothing for him, Popovic suggested that Joyce
come along with him and they would both enlist in the Montenegrin Army. A lot of the troops were men who had emigrated
to the United States and who now had returned to fight for their
homeland, so Joyce could pose as one of these and completely
forget the Hague Convention. "Very well," said Joyce, and off
they went to the governor's house. Since the governor was away
Joyce could not be properly enlisted, but the matter seemed a
mere formality now — Joyce would be issued a uniform the
next day, he was told.

To while away the time until they were proper soldiers, Joyce
and Popovic went to see the town, particularly the old quarter,
whose principal feature was a citadel built during the heyday of
the Venetian city-state. They headed first for the citadel, "about
an hour's walk along a road bordered with sombre olive trees"
that rose "steeply and narrowly towards the fortress, now noth-

ing but an ivied ruin, though the mosque and the bath have survived the dead centuries." [16] They went up the steps to the only gate, but were stopped by the guards, who, sitting smoking around a brazier, asked the two if they had a pass. As soon as Joyce identified himself as an Englishman, they were allowed to enter the citadel.

Among the ruins was a new, domed building of concrete, not at all scenic, so they ignored it. Instead, they admired

> the beauty of the ruins and the remnants of Venetian carving over the porticoes. They had a glimpse of soldiers sawing wood, of a packing of shells into cases, of work with hammer and nail on the ammunition boxes that are strapped to the sides of the mules who walk to the front.[17]
>
> Then they sat down on a mound quite close to the arsenal. . . .

And they soon found out the function of the new concrete building, for almost immediately after they sat down,

> There was a hellish roar of incredible immensity . . . heard three miles away in Antivari. The ground heaved beneath him as though an earthquake had overtaken the place, and . . . "the air rained bricks and stones and lumps of iron." There were three other quick bangs. The roof of concrete lifted in the air and came down with a mad confusion of sound.[18]

By some miracle neither Popovic nor Joyce was injured. Then after a stunned moment, Popovic cried, "Let's run back! If the sentry finds us here we shall be arrested!" Joyce, though, wanted to stay to watch. All this in the midst of a terrible din in which, he reported,

> Shells exploded every second. Then there would be a quick rattle of minor sounds — the boxes of cartridges had caught fire and were going off like Chinese crackers.

Finally Joyce agreed that it was not a good place in which to be found, so they decided to hurry off and then come strolling back as if they had not been on the scene. But a sentry came running up just then and took Joyce by the arm. Between the furious noise, the agitation of both of them, and the language barrier, Joyce was unable to make the soldier understand what he and Popovic were doing there.

The soldier, his teeth chattering from shock and excitement, was no man to argue with, for even in Scutari, three miles distant, soldiers were popping off with their rifles, perhaps believing the Turks had arrived. Thus, Joyce and Popovic were very much in danger of being shot. They allowed themselves to be led off to the gate, where they were questioned briefly by an army captain, while chunks of stone still rained down around them.

Apparently it began to dawn on Joyce that he was in real danger. The interrogation might easily turn into a drumhead court-martial, and in the confusion and noise it would be difficult to explain what he, an unaccounted-for foreigner in civilian clothes, was doing in the area at exactly the time the arsenal was blown up. With the state the Montenegrin soldiers were in, the situation could turn even nastier, and Joyce and Popovic might find themselves stood before a wall and summarily shot.

Instead the captain, after a few questions, put them in charge of an old, gray-haired soldier whose nose was bleeding into his moustache and whose uniform was torn apparently by stone splinters from the explosion. Joyce attempted to tend the old soldier's cuts — after all, that was what he'd come to Montenegro to do, to care for the wounded under the British Red Cross. Evidently it was a lucky move, for, although the old man refused to be tended to, he offered Joyce some of his tobacco, and the atmosphere seems to have lightened thereafter.

Where they stood with their guard was an exciting vantage point, because in one direction they could see shells still bursting from the burning arsenal, and in the other a pack of Turkish soldiers (Albanians serving in the Turkish Army) wedged between bayonet-wielding Montenegrin troops and a screaming crowd. The Albanians had been imprisoned at the citadel and apparently had attempted to escape. But a group of women had seen them and had set up such a howl that they brought both more women and children, who joined in the screaming, and half a dozen soldiers with bayonet-mounted rifles. The Albanians were in far more danger now than if they had simply stayed in their prison.[19]

After about half an hour, six or seven various officials arrived at the gateway and questioned Popovic, who, as he repeated his story time after time, became more and more angry. Joyce, in French, simply told everyone he didn't know anything about anything. Some British Red Cross personnel arrived and treated some of the wounded but then left the immediate danger area, as nothing more could be done until the fire and the ammunition had burned themselves out. Two of the men returned before that time, however, and when Joyce asked them, "What is it?" one of them replied, "There's somebody inside. They've heard shouts."

Joyce told the men to wait a minute while he got a guide and then he would go along with them to the remains of the arsenal to see what could be done. Joyce spoke in French to a captain, the one who had questioned him earlier, and the captain, after hesitating a moment, then asked for a guide, in Montenegrin. A soldier volunteered and proved to be one of the two seventeen-year-olds whom Joyce had picked up on the road to town the day before. He, Joyce, and the two Red Cross men raced from the gateway toward the arsenal, ducking down behind ruined walls and pieces of rubble as the explosions continued. They were followed at a distance by some of the soldiers from the gatehouse.

One of the Red Cross men cried out, "Look at that, Joe!" The others looked and "noticed something like a piece of withered branch with the bark on," Joyce related. "I picked it up and saw that it was a man's arm, the fingers blown away at the palm." [20] Joyce handed the arm to the guide, who tucked it in his belt. Further along they found the dust-covered body of the man from whom the arm had come. He was still breathing, so they dragged him to shelter. Apparently he was the one who had set off the first explosion. They turned him over to the troops, who carried him down to the gatehouse, where a dressing station had been set up by others from the British Red Cross group.

Joyce, the guide, and the two Britons with them, Williams and Baverstock, then scoured the ruins for more injured, but found only one man, whom they turned over to the Montenegrin stretcher-bearers.

Then Joyce returned to the gate, asked the captain there if he were still under arrest, and was at once told "no." Popovic, after the captain questioned him a bit more, also was released, and he and Joyce, finding themselves desperately hungry, went across to the new quarter of town to the inn.

The tavern was alive with English correspondents when Joyce walked in, asked, "Is my soup ready?" and then sat down to tell them his story:

I've been having a nutty time. Got arrested because I was sitting there when the beastly thing blew up. Then they let me go when I offered to help the Red Cross. Helped pull 'em out.[21]

At the inn Joyce met Dr. Bradford of the Red Cross, who asked Joyce if he still wanted to join the group. Joyce said that he did, and, after a lunch of sour cheese and wine, he was put to work clearing away boxes and bales at the cigarette factory the unit had been given as a hospital, a bit anticlimactic after all the blood, fire, and fury he had seen when he had not even been in the unit earlier that day, but a better preparation in most ways for the pattern of real war: tedium.[22]

9

MONTENEGRO

JOYCE WAS GIVEN the job of cook when the Red Cross group moved forward to the front near Scutari, the Turkish strong-point that was preventing the Montenegrin advance. The Montenegrins had had great successes in the first days of the war and, in concert with their allies, might have destroyed the Turkish Army completely, but they had been ordered to halt and hold their positions, lest they get too far ahead of their supply lines. This delay had given the Turks time to fortify Scutari with a network of trenches and barbed wire so that it was nearly invulnerable. The fortress city, at the foot of Lake Scutari, commanded the valleys of three rivers, the Drin, the Drinessa, and the Bojana. These provided the only routes the Montenegrins could take against the Turks. To attempt to move an army and its supplies across the mountains would have taken months longer and would have risked disaster. Scutari had to be taken.

At the Scutari front, then, Joyce saw plenty of action.

Meanwhile, he had become a seven-day hero in the London and Londonderry newspapers. On November 5, the *Times* carried a story of the explosion. The day before, both the *Daily Mirror* and the *Daily Telegraph* had stories, and the *Telegraph* carried a second account on November 7. It was the *Daily Express,* however, that really presented the best write-up. There was a report of the explosion on the 4th, and on the 8th a story exclusively about Joyce, "The Man Who Was Blown Up," ran a full column. The account told of the "clean-shaven, curly-

headed young man" from "Oxford and Carey Castle, Donegal"
(only the *Telegraph* managed to spell "Cary" correctly). "The
Irish love of adventure guides his life," the correspondent, Alphonse Courlander, wrote, and the tone of the story varied from
patronization to virtual hero-worship.

The news created a sensation at home, and Mr. Cary sent a
copy of the *Express* story to Jack at sea, who wrote Joyce, "I saw
a wonderful account of your being blown up, in a paper Dad
sent me, all about a curly headed Irishman with a love of adventure, they never mentioned all that harlene you used to keep the
curly hair going."

Joyce could be sure that Gerty Ogilvie saw the story, too, because if nobody else pointed it out to her, her brother Heneage
surely would, since he was in Montenegro as well. He had left
Guy's Hospital to join one of the Red Cross units, bluffing his
way in as an M.D., although he had not yet qualified.[1] But he,
like Joyce, felt that the opportunity to experience war and to do
good was priceless. And what better training could he get in
surgery than to tend the wounded? Although they were not in
the same unit, he and Joyce crossed paths fairly often during the
war.

As winter approached the campaign slowed, partly because of
the bad weather and partly due to the need for better artillery,
for guns had to be brought up and put in position before any
real attack could be made on the Turkish fortifications. Finally
on December 3 the countries agreed to an armistice which lasted
until February 3, and it seems likely that Joyce went home to
London for part of it, for he kept several invitations to parties
he received at this time. But he returned to Montenegro when
the fighting began again and in April wrote to his father:

> Up to last week the fighting went on here just as it was going
> when last I wrote. desultory skirmishing with maxims bombard-
> ment at night, and a small trickle of wounded.
> But on Monday last we had a pitched battle.
> It was the finest piece of work I have yet seen on the part of
> the troops. We were near enough to see the heads of the Turkish

sharpshooters through Capt. Leakes glasses as they sniped at us, — with small effect, — George Lazaravitch the interpreter was hit in the cap, and the rest sprinkled with splinters of rock.

The advance was carried out in regular parade order, and as the stormers crawled under the wire (only smashed at the bottom) the Montenegrin guns covered them with a very well directed fire.

This infantry advance began only after 5 hours of bombardment, at 2.15, and the first redoubt was taken at 2.30. By three we could see the wounded beginning to come down, and so waited for a salvo to make the Turks duck into their pits, before going across the open to the last village.

We arrived in the village at four, and found 60 wounded there already.

All three of us dressed the first batch, and then I went off to clean a room out and get wood & water before the fire got too hot.

We worked all that night and next day — there were from 400 to 500 came in, and the Turks (only 700 yards away) fired so steadily at the house that none of them could get out. One old man was shot dead at his second step from Cap. Leake's hands as he finished bandaging him — several were wounded again before they could find room to lie down under the wall of the garden.

On Tuesday there was a continuous shrapnel fire.

We became very anxious for the wounded. They could not get away and there was no food for them where they were. The place was an extraordinary sight. The house was entirely ruined except the roof, and one room on the second story which I had bagged for stores and a fire. Every time I went down my ladder I stepped over a dying man — the wounded were lying on top of one another in every imaginable attitude — we were all steeped in blood — as water was too precious to use for washing.

About four the fire slackened and the wounded ceased coming in.

We had only four hours sleep each and could hardly face another night, in [illegible], now that we were no longer needed.

We got away under the dusk without much trouble, leaving our stores in charge of a soldier, and slept in Bobote again.

Since then there has been a lull but new guns are coming and I expect to see some more good work.

D

The style of this letter is typical of the ones he sent home and of those he sent to other people when he had time to write: cool, factual, objective, simple, even more so than the book he wrote shortly after the war, *Memoirs of the Bobotes.* Cary's approach stands in great contrast to those of the various journalists who were sending off reports on the war, for their prose was far more purple. His writing is like a black ink line drawing compared to their garishly colored battle tableaus.

As to his expectation that he would "see some more good work," he was right. He stayed to the end of the campaign, suffering whatever the troops did: the bad food (plenty of tough goat meat that even the longest stewing could do little for), the danger of being frequently under fire from the Turkish artillery and sharpshooters, the discomforts of sleeping on floors, wearing threadbare and disintegrating uniforms whatever the weather, and having shoes that went to pieces when he carried supplies over stony trails through the mountains.[2] Worse in many ways were the small irritations such as first having to scrounge carefully for bits of wood for the cooking fire, only to find when he returned from getting water that the others had thrown his whole supply of wood into the fire. Often, he would come back to a blaze that was useless for cooking purposes and have to search for more fuel, while the others laughed at "Cookie's stinginess with the wood" and complained when the food was not ready on time.

The war went this way most of the time. Of course Joyce brought back stories of his exploits. For instance, there was the story he told of commandeering a train. The men at the front were desperately short of medical supplies, so, according to Joyce's story, he and a friend went off on a foraging trip and located a trainload of equipment. Looking as correct as possible, they marched up to the locomotive, saluting all and sundry, got up into the cab, and simply drove the train away.[3]

Another story was that King Nicholas of Montenegro had offered Joyce one of his daughters in marriage. When Joyce had protested that he was pledged to marry an English girl, the king had asked him why not have two wives. Joyce finally managed to convince the king that in England one was allowed only the one wife.[4]

But these were tales he told his young cousin years afterward. In reality the war consisted of a great deal of drudgery, interrupted from time to time by skirmishing, until the big offensive of April, 1913, the beginnings of which were described in Joyce's letter to his father quoted previously. Scutari surrendered later that month, and the members of the British Red Cross units were decorated by King Nicholas for their great aid to his army. Then they went home, without a single princess stowed in their luggage.

So sometime in May, 1913, Joyce was back in England. He had jumped the gun by a year and more. It would not be until the end of the next summer that so many other young men would go off to Europe to encounter death or disillusionment. Joyce, in facing war earlier, and a more meaningful war at that, was not let down in the collapse of belief experienced by such writers as Wilfred Owen, Siegfried Sassoon, Aldous Huxley, and Ernest Hemingway during World War I. In contrast, his philosophy, which he was only beginning to formulate, was based not on a single cataclysmic turn of history, but on a series of episodes and events of which the Montenegrin episode was only one.

Back in England he did not try his Bohemian life again. He lived at home, at loose ends, looking for a cause, anxious to give himself up to something as worthwhile as his Red Cross work had been. He considered various occupations, including the African services,[5] and meanwhile went down to Oxford to receive his degrees.[6] Then in July he found the cause.

Sir Horace Plunkett, member of another old Anglo-Irish family, had spent much of his life studying and putting into practice various agricultural and economic reforms. He had been a friend of the American President Theodore Roosevelt and had worked in the United States in the cooperative movement. Now he was doing the same sort of work in Ireland in the more backward agricultural areas. Joyce wrote to Plunkett when he heard of the project to see if he couldn't be found a place.

This desire was perhaps a bit self-consciously altruistic, for he would be going to Ireland to help the very class of people, the poor farmers and small-farm tenants, who had been the force that had brought about the Irish Land Act of 1881 that pushed the Cary family out of Ireland.

Plunkett accepted Joyce's offer, for he was anxious to enlist young men, fairly recently graduated from a university, who, like Joyce, had enthusiasm and dedication. He preferred them to agricultural experts, who might be less capable of adapting themselves to the circumstances of training uneducated and suspicious people. Plunkett theorized that the young men's enthusiasm would make up for their lack of specialized training, and it might be infectious. Joyce's familiarity with back-country Ireland based on his frequent visits in Donegal was considered a distinct asset.

So Plunkett and Joyce corresponded,[7] and it was decided that Joyce should come over to Ireland in August. Joyce, delighted, sailed to Ireland. But in less than a month he was back in England, defeated.

For some time there had been antagonism toward Plunkett's plans among the leaders of the movement. It was just his enthusiasm for eager young men and his objection to trained agricultural people that was the bone of contention. The battle was going on at the very time Joyce was preparing to go to Ireland, and in the next few weeks the side opposing Plunkett won.

Joyce arrived in Ireland to find himself unwanted. There was nothing to do but go home once more.[8]

He toyed for a while with the idea of taking a secretarial job in the administration of Cyprus.[9] Whatever the reason, whether he changed his mind or did not meet the qualifications for the position, he dropped the plan fairly soon. Instead he decided definitely on the Nigerian Service as the place for himself. He applied, wrote his examinations, and was admitted. He had no profession, no proper university degree — not with a fourth — yet he was almost ideally suited for the job.

In Montenegro he had learned the rudiments of medicine

after treating several hundred wounded soldiers and from his art-student days he had retained a fair idea of the human anatomy. The prepping he had done for Ireland gave him some knowledge of agriculture and administration. An ability to draw would be a great help in learning to prepare maps. And his recent war experiences had certainly proved him capable of roughing it. An assistant district officer in the Nigerian Service *had* to be a jack-of-all-trades; Joyce may not have been much else, but he was that.

He applied for Northern Nigeria. In 1913 the country was divided into two administrative areas, north and south, each with its own lieutenant governor, while the whole was ruled by Lord Lugard, Governor of Nigeria, at the time one of the most advanced thinkers in colonial government. Northern Nigeria was a tougher area than the South. It was a more sparsely populated territory and much more primitive, with few roads, scarcely any railway, vestigial telegraph and postal services, and several unruly tribes who less than ten years earlier were still making — or resisting — slave raids. The sort of young men entering Lord Lugard's Nigerian Service can be seen from the fact that, in Joyce's year, 1913, of the seventy men admitted to the Service, sixty-four asked for postings in the North. They were idealistic and adventurous, the sort Plunkett had wanted and the sort Lugard wanted now. Of the sixty-four volunteers for the North, only six were chosen, and Joyce was one of them.[10]

The young men entering this service could have been given one of two sorts of training: a thorough background of several years of lectures and practical work to prepare them for a country still very little known, or scarcely any training at all, with the men being thrown into the country while their enthusiasm was at its highest, to sink or swim. The Colonial Service, more for economic reasons than anything else, chose the latter training method — that is — no substantial training at all.

At the Imperial Institute there were a few lectures on medicine, some talks on Nigerian law, an introduction to surveying, and scarcely anything else. The young men, toting their huge

volumes of *The Laws of Nigeria,* were like recruits just out of
basic training who are put in charge of whole regiments or divisions and shipped off to fronts where scarcely anything is known
of the terrain or the enemy.[11] Joyce, when he sailed for Lagos,
probably was better equipped than any of the rest.

Which isn't saying much.

10

A STEADY JOB

JOYCE WENT TO NIGERIA prepared to give the Service his best. His zeal wasn't simply out of idealism, although that played a large part. He also needed to find a steady job. When he returned from his Irish fiasco, he was nearly twenty-five, more than a year out of the university, and still with no profession, not even a livelihood. People who had treated his wanderings with indulgence a few years before — and had even envied him, some of them — were growing convinced that he was incapable of settling down and holding a job.

Certainly, his father felt this was true, and the Ogilvies were even more convinced of it. In July, 1913, he had been invited to The Glade after taking his degree. He was made as welcome as ever, particularly by Heneage, who had grown closer to him because of their shared experiences in Montenegro. Heneage had been back at Guy's Hospital since the start of the year, having left Montenegro during the December–February armistice.[1] Joyce had proved himself to the Ogilvies, in a way, because of his service to the wounded. But now that it became increasingly obvious that he was in love with Gerty, his humanitarianism was offset by his insolvency. Mrs. Ogilvie, still dubious of Joyce, was decidedly against his marrying her daughter, at least with his present prospects and instability.

So it was put to Joyce that he would not be considered a serious candidate for their daughter's hand unless and until he took a steady job, stuck at it, and proved he could earn a proper living.[2]

As for Gerty, she still wasn't having any of Joyce. He had another try at proposing during his visit, but although he was understood this time, he certainly was not accepted. In fact, her rejection was so decisive that Joyce packed up and left at once, only to telephone the next day because, as he told her, he wanted to hear her voice.[3]

She had a voice worth hearing, too. Like the other Ogilvies, Gerty had musical training in the cello, the piano, and voice. She and Heneage often gave family entertainments, with Freddy accompanying their singing. Joyce's ear had not improved since Hurstleigh, but her soft contralto voice, singing "The Sally Garden," or "The Ash Grove," was a music that even he could appreciate. And perhaps he could imagine that the songs she sang and the words in them might be addressed to him someday — they were certainly more pleasant than the ones he got from her whenever he proposed.

So now when he went out to Nigeria, he felt he had a chance to prove what he could do. If he carried it off, perhaps he would have the elder Ogilvies on his side, and if he had that, then perhaps he could make some dent on Gerty. He hadn't forgotten Mr. Ogilvie's encouragement in 1912 either. And he was used to campaigning hard for what he wanted — although Gerty was as hard to capture as Antivari.

Today, after more than fifty years of tremendous change, the Nigeria of 1914 is difficult to imagine, and it is even more difficult to comprehend the attitude both of her administrators and of the western world generally toward the issue of colonialism. Having lived through the twilight of the great empires, people today find it hard to understand the imperial urge as anything other than the product of avarice, racialism, and rapaciousness.

But Britain had not wanted Nigeria as a colony, at least not at first. In the nineteenth century Britain was interested in West Africa only because she wanted to end the slave trade. The "do-gooders" of the Clapham Sect in the latter years of the eighteenth century and the early years of the nineteenth worked hard and long both inside and outside Parliament to bring about various reforms, and one of their greatest aims was to end the slave trade and slavery itself. After much hard work, perseverance, and the spending of their monies, the Sect finally won. Slavery was abolished in the British Isles. Next it was wiped out in the British West Indies by the extremely pragmatic act of paying the slave owners a fair price for their slaves and then setting them free.

Once the Clapham Sect and its disciples had accomplished abolition in the British Isles and British West Indies, the next step was to end the trade itself. Since the west coast of Africa was the great embarkation point for slaves, the coast from which the squalid, jammed slave ships sailed to the Americas, the British Navy was sent to patrol the area and to intercept the slavers at sea. Because the Royal Navy lacked landing stations where fresh foods and water could be obtained readily, some of the offshore islands were taken over for this purpose.

Britain persuaded Portugal to take her ships — officially, at least — out of the trade by paying the Portuguese Government a huge sum of money. But this did not prevent private ships, whether they had British, Portuguese, or other owners, from continuing to engage in the very profitable business. And when these ships were hailed by Royal Navy patrols, the practice was to dump the heavily-manacled slaves over the side, where they sank to the bottom, thus eliminating all evidence that there was any trading in human lives. So Britain's task was to create a wall between the inland slave traders and the slave ships at sea.

Step by step, then, the British became involved with the territories of the African west coast, particularly Nigeria, always at great expense to herself and for humanitarian motives.

The Niger River Company, chartered for exclusive trade in the Niger River area, was founded for slightly less humanitarian reasons perhaps, but again it must be remembered that trade in itself was regarded as an almost pure good in the nineteenth century, for it was believed to be a force that fostered education, general prosperity, and the strength of the state. Only when commercial effort reached the proportions of the bloody rapacity that King Leopold practiced in his private colony and ivory preserve, the Congo, was trade considered less than a blessing.

For Leopold, as a matter of policy, had people slaughtered to keep the population down. In addition, his private army troops were issued ammunition only if they turned in a number of human ears equivalent to the number of bullets they were requesting. But Nigeria, of course, was not treated by Britain as Leopold treated the Congo.

In fact, Lord Lugard, Nigeria's great governor, thought in terms of the eventual self-government of a unified Nigerian state. His policy was that of "indirect rule," although perhaps divided rule might be a better term. Local institutions, rulers, religions, and customs of every sort were to be maintained, bolstered where they seemed good, and changed gradually where they seemed bad. The value of these essentials was to be determined by the extent of their benefits to the local people, their welfare, and their ultimate contribution to the establishment of a viable, peaceful, and progressive Nigeria.

Even to glimpse in some distant future a Nigeria ruled as a modern state by Nigerians was an extremely utopian vision. To hold a policy of moving toward such a future was unthinkable in 1914. But it was Lugard's policy. He was an idealistic, paternalistic ruler, who controlled his administration closely. This policy would prove to have both advantages and disadvantages.

It was into this atmosphere of idealism and paternalism that Joyce was sent in the early spring of 1914, sailing from Liverpool in a ship of the Elder Dempster Line. His companions were miners and old colonial administration hands gloomily returning from leave, and young, raw recruits like himself, attempting, like youthful husbands on a honeymoon, to hide their anticipation, pleasure, and apprehension behind a mask of indifference. They tried not to gawk when the ship landed at Freetown and Accra and the other stops along the way to Lagos, and pretended indifference to the sight of the native traders coming on board or the laundry women who were hoisted up in cargo nets to do a rush job on dirty socks, shirts, and underwear for the perspiring passengers. When the laundry was hung on lines across the decks, the ship looked like a pleasure craft on a gala night.

Then, Lagos and the railway north to Zaria. This trip was different even from his travels in Montenegro. The trains, in which he baked at temperatures over 100 degrees by day, didn't run at night for fear of hitting something on the track and being derailed. So at six each night or sometime before, they pulled into a station and parked.

Joyce would unload his numerous boxes of clothing, food, tobacco, books, necessities and other luxuries, make camp on the station platform or somewhere close by, and perhaps have a bath in his own tub, while his cook made a fire and prepared dinner. He had to rise early, because the equipment had to be packed and reloaded on the train before its departure time at six in the morning.

At Zaria he detrained and waited for a special train that would take him to Naraguta. Joyce told the story of this leg of the trip in one of a series of short stories he wrote about his early days in Nigeria, several of them later to be collected in *Spring Song*.* In the stories he appropriately renames himself Evelyn Corner, a reference on the one hand to his often misleading first name (his readers and government officials in future years often sent letters to "Miss Joyce Cary") and on the other to the English translation of the Paris pronunciation of his surname as "Carré." In addition to appearing in the short stories, the name Corner was used by Joyce in his novel *Castle Corner*, loosely based on the life at Castle Cary, and in his autobiographical novel, *A House of Children*.

Although Joyce traveled with two other men new to the service,[4] in his story "Railway Camp" Evelyn Corner travels alone except for his servants. The special train to Naraguta does not arrive; in fact, "noone knew when it would arrive, except that it would not be to-day." So Corner sets up a semipermanent camp on the station platform, with his cook and his boy, Jamesu. It is a great place to see Nigeria passing in review:

---

* These stories are "Bush River," "Buying a Horse," "Gudu," "The Raft," "Railway Camp," "The Spell," "Too Good To Be True," and "Umaru." Another apparently autobiographical story (although its subaltern hero is not named Corner) is "Adamu."

Naked pagans, with their tickets in their wool, would knock over Corner's chair, and trample over him in their fear of missing a train, or their anxiety to salute the station master. Young clerks, going to their first official post, used his rug to wipe their patent leather shoes. The passengers of a local train coming in unexpectedly, while the young man was having his bath in a little ring of loads, would come to the windows to stare at him, and discuss his colour and shape and shout jokes at each other. But he was no more embarrassed than any animal at the zoo.

After Montenegro, Joyce was used to the total absence of privacy, but Nigeria provided new and more extreme experiences of this kind. Like Corner in the story above, Joyce found that when he took one of his public baths, especially those on railway platforms, he became the center of attraction — not because of his nakedness but because he showed the Nigerians something more than his tanned face, arms, and legs. They could get a good view of his torso in all its exotic Anglo-Irish whiteness.

In the story, after three days of camping out this way, Corner/ Cary is shaken awake before five in the morning:

the train has arrived and must leave within ten minutes, as the boat train is coming through at 5:15 and the track has to be cleared for it.

Corner threw himself into a new uniform, for the important day of his beginning duty. The boys, obviously enjoying the crisis, shewed the speed and dexterity of acrobats. The table was dismantled as he put down his razor; the chair folded up as he rose from it; like magic equipment.

In fifteen minutes, shaved and dressed, he sat in the flat truck, shivering in a British warm.*

Eventually the train reached the end of the rails and Corner's boys unloaded his luggage.

Suddenly about a hundred natives, some in turbans, some naked, some carrying spears, some swords, sprang up from a hollow and rushed at him. He was too stupified to feel alarm. He simply did not know how to think.

* A short army overcoat.

The horde races up to them and, when it is just two yards off, flings itself down on the ground, while Corner stands flabbergasted. "Dey salute you, sah," the cook says impatiently. "Dey say you king of de world." Then he sets about the unloading with the other servants.[5] This reception parallels the one Joyce and his two companions actually received.

They trekked into Naraguta, to be met there by District Officer H. S. W. Edwardes, Joyce's first superior in Nigeria. Edwardes, who had come to the country in 1905, was a bit of a swashbuckling eccentric and wore the enormous boots of a buccaneer. He was a great admirer of Edward Gibbon, whom he used to read aloud, and he knew his stuff.[6] It was Edwardes who wrote the manual on road building "by a District Officer" that was used throughout Nigeria and many other areas of British Africa. And, like many old Nigeria hands, he had a great love and sense of responsibility for the natives in his care: to him they were "*my* people" in every sense.[7]

Edwardes was an excellent man to start under. The only danger was that since he was so strong and so sure, a new recruit might be so utterly molded by him that he would be incapable of adapting himself to another superior. For instance, Edwardes had a passion for road building, which meant he carried on a sort of guerilla war with the Public Works Department, since the construction of roads was supposed to be their concern and district officers were meant to keep hands off. The title of Edwardes's pamphlet, *The Improvement of Native Paths,* suggests his ingenuity in dealing with rules and regulations which he regarded as too rigid. But even more revealing of the contempt Edwardes (and a good many other men in the field, for that matter) felt for the "desk jockeys" of the administration is this excerpt from a letter which he sent to Joyce in September, 1915:

I am going to get some roads made this dry weather if it lands me in Stellenbosch. There is humour in the fact that the opposition to and distrust of any beneficent measures always comes from above. One has to fight the Government all the time. The man who is discouraged by rebuffs and snubs never gets anything done. I enjoy the battle and in the end they usually let me do it to shut me up.

Bauchi Division, where Joyce was to work under Edwardes, was
a revelation (Joyce, who was sent out to the field at once, was an
exception to the rule for new recruits, who usually put in their
first two or three months at provincial headquarters), "a place
where, within two years, slave raiders had been defeated in battle; a division with a real Mohameden emir, harems, eunuchs, a
headsman & practically fresh blood spilled in its market
place." [8] It was an area still rebellious in parts, with few roads
or bridges and little in the way of medical help, a raw chunk of
country where local government, if it existed, was often ineffi-
cient or dissatisfied at having lost its free hand, a free hand that
often had been badly bloodstained.

Then, almost immediately on his arrival, Joyce was left entirely on his own for a month. As he wrote to his father, it
meant

(with a district bigger than Wales) that I shall be very busy. The
D.O. here is going off with some soldiers to tackle some rebellious
villages in the South. I had ten days in the saddle on the way
here for I did not come straight. I had to look over a new stretch
of country on the way, and enquire about boundary troubles.
They gave me authority to change the boundary if I liked, and
since it appeared to be the best thing, I did change it over a ten
mile line. More than a hundred farms are affected, and I don't
know whether my report will be well received — but I am pro-
tected from revision by my authority which I took care to get in
writing and as explicit as possible. This is a very bad station
among river swamps, and full of mosquitoes which bite morning
& noon as well as night. My house is leaky and literally an ant-
heap. I hung a strap on the wall the day I came and it was eaten
through the next morning. They eat all my chop-boxes, and would
eat my boots if I did not keep a close watch on them. They have
eaten also nearly all the supports of the house and a big tornado
might bring it down, but the tornado months are over and a tornado is now rare. There is no money here allowed for buildings
because they have spent so much on the house at the central station at Naraguta, that the vote for the Province is already exhausted. I shall probably have to do some roofing out of my own
pocket for at present I sleep in my oil skins and my kit is ruined

between the rain and the ants, and the rivers it has been dragged through on my travels. The natives are a bad lot, incompetent and surly — very different from the intelligent old aristocrats of the Bauchi Emirate. However I am settling down for a long time here — I shall clean the station and fill up as many pools as I can as soon as the convicts are available. . . .

(3 Aug. 1914)

After only a couple of months in the country, Joyce sounds like an old hand. However, the assurance that his letter conveys is that of a young man who wants to impress the home folks. For of course the letter would be seen not only by his father but by his stepsister and stepbrother, Sheila and Tony, along with other relatives and friends. It was a great chance to show off.

II

THE AFRICAN YEARS

1 1

CAMEROONS CAMPAIGN

JOYCE WAS NOT AWARE when he wrote this letter to his father, that during the week Europe had moved to the brink of chaos. On July 28, a month after the assassination of Archduke Ferdinand, Austria-Hungary had declared war on Serbia; Germany then declared war on Russia on August 1 after the Czar ordered mobilization along her borders and then on France on August 3, the date of Joyce's letter. At midnight, August 4, Britain declared war on Germany because of the German violation of Belgian territory. In eight days a rift in the Balkans had mushroomed into the First World War.

The war affected Africa, too, since Germany in 1914 owned the colonies of Tanganyika, South West Africa, and the Cameroons. With the Cameroons on her border, Nigeria was involved in the conflict as soon as word reached Lagos. Nafada, where Joyce was stationed, was just over one hundred miles from the border of the German colony.

The war in western Africa was pure surrealism. There were a few hundred troops on either side strung out along a border of seven to eight hundred miles. And this front abounded with elephant grass six or eight feet high, where in flat land a patrol could not travel more than a dozen yards without a compass, where there was no visibility and no landmarks, where sounds were so smothered that enemy patrols could pass twenty feet from each other and never know of the other's existence.

Joyce, however, was not yet involved in this nightmare. He was left at Nafada, gathering taxes and grain and other necessities of war and enlisting native troops, supplying the columns that moved through Nafada on their way to the border and the fighting around Gurin, Yola, and Garua. And while he watched the troops go through, he hoped that each mail coming by runner from Naraguta and Bauchi would contain his own orders of transfer to the military so that he could join the columns.[1]

The staff of Political Officers to which Joyce had been appointed was given military status as part of the WAFF (West African Frontier Force), and Joyce was given the rank of subaltern or second lieutenant. With his Montenegrin battle experience, a background that the vast majority of those passing through Nafada on their way to the front did not have, it rankled that he of all people should be left behind.

Meantime he was learning more about Nigeria than the somewhat superficial information he had flaunted in his early letters. Everything was not the "harems, eunuchs, a headsman & practically fresh blood spilled in the market place" which he had reported to his father. In late July, 1914, on his way to Nafada, he had passed through famine areas and was horrified to see people sitting in front of their huts, waiting stoically to die. Their faces expressed no hope, not even anger at the sight of their swollen-bellied, dying children, since starvation was a fact of life in these parts and had been for as long as anyone could remember. This picture impressed him so strongly that he could see and describe it thirty years and more later.

Then in early 1915 a smallpox epidemic hit the area, again impressing Joyce with the harsh realities of African life, for all that he could do, lacking money and medicine, was to attempt to isolate the infected people in a camp

> where whole families sat all day, with their enormously swollen faces, waiting upon fate with a submission so complete that I had to have some of them spoon-fed. They had lost all confidence in remedy and even in food. I daresay they felt that the familiar corn might poison them. They were some of those millions who have died every year, in peacetime, for countless thousands of

years, in misery which no war could exaggerate, and they accepted their fortune in such patience that they did not even resent it. They did not dream of blaming anyone for it. They were perfectly good-natured and ready to be cheerful. They laughed at a joke, especially if they thought they were meant to be amused.[2]

If Joyce had had any Rousseauian ideas of noble savages living an idyllic life in a state of nature (and his novel, *An American Visitor,* suggests he did) before he came to Nigeria, sights such as these surely destroyed them. Africa, he found, was desperately poor; the soil was worn out, and the people lived in every state of disease. The native who was without traces of syphilis, smallpox, hernias, or some other illness or disability was an exception. As for tribal life, it was so utterly stultifying for the individual that Joyce was hard put to see the good in it.

The cynicism of his immediate superior, J. F. J. Fitzpatrick, a strong critic of Lugard's policy of indirect rule, affected Joyce, but not so deeply as Edwardes's more buoyant attitudes. Fitzpatrick had little faith in the native regimes or peoples with whom he was supposed to work hand in hand, and, after years of attempting to cope with ruinous situations on the one hand and official rules and parsimony on the other, he had turned to venting his frustrations by writing a series of sketches which violently criticized colonial administration. These were published in *Blackwood's Magazine* and did him no good in Nigerian official circles. But he was not alone in his sense of defeat. Many of the officers who had been around a while felt the same way, but their frustrations did not necessarily manifest themselves in cynicism; drinking was a more common way of escape.[3] Edwardes's passion for road building was another form, perhaps, and in the end a far more constructive one.

Joyce had his frustrations in Nafada early in the war. Three routes of march to the front funneled through Nafada, which meant that plenty of men — "horse soldiers and foot soldiers, signallers, and doctors, machine guns and carriers, black soldiers, white officers, and small parties of Europeans — miners, traders, officials — volunteers for the Cameroons Expeditionary Force"[4] — needed to be supplied with food, as did their horses.

And Joyce had to feed them by imposing a grain levy on the local population. The famine conditions that existed made the problem even more acute. To extract grain from starving people was desperately difficult, and the troops on the march did not improve their relations with the local population when they stole or requisitioned without payment. Edwardes was outraged at this abuse of his people; Joyce fired off an apology to him and went to investigate and to make compensation to the natives who had suffered from this pillaging while at the same time he attempted to persuade the troops to pass through his territory in a more orderly fashion.[5] It was a rigorous form of training for a man only three months in the country.

Fitzpatrick was relieved by T. F. Carlyle in September, 1914, and Joyce at once took to his new chief, whose enthusiasm for his work matched that of Edwardes. On the leave from which he had just returned, Carlyle had spent his time writing a history of the Gombe district for which Nafada was headquarters. He was devoted to his corner of Nigeria and had won acceptance and respect from the extremely suspicious mountain tribes of pagans in his division as well as from the Moslems of the plains.[6]

This new superior was a bracing change after the disillusioned Fitzpatrick, and Joyce responded to him enthusiastically. Carlyle was one of the people who lived most vitally in Joyce's memory years afterward.

Yet Joyce remained anxious to get to where the fighting was and waited through the autumn and winter, more and more fretfully, for orders that did not come. Besides watching the columns of troops move on to the front, he was made impatient by letters from Duncan MacGregor and others in France who had seen action or would see it soon, and his own brother Jack was at sea with the Royal Navy.

Jack Cary's war was nearly over, however, before Joyce's began. In early 1915 Jack was in Australia, where he ran across a young Australian Navy officer who was anxious to get home on leave to see his wife. The Australian, an officer on the submarine *AE2*, was about to sail for European waters, which meant he might not see his wife for another year or more. Jack was eager to get home himself, so the two of them agreed to swap places and got official approval for the exchange. But instead of any pleasure cruise, the *AE2* was marked out for a special job.[7]

At the time the Royal Navy was trying to penetrate the Dardanelles with submarines which were to surface off Constantinople and lob a few shells at the city. It was hoped that this gesture would have a strong effect on Turkish morale and policy and in addition give a boost to the morale of the Russians, who needed it badly after their bloody defeat at Tannenberg in 1914. The *AE2* was assigned to the Allied squadron in the eastern Mediterranean for this task.

The operation, like the whole Dardanelles Campaign, was a disaster, and the *AE2* had nearly the worst luck of all. Not only did she fail to penetrate the Narrows, but she was caught on the surface by shore batteries and sunk. Her crew was rescued and imprisoned in an improvised camp in what had been an Armenian village before the murderous deportation of the Armenians, whom the Turks considered a potential fifth column.

The prisoners of war were treated better than the Armenians had been, but not much. The Turks had a rather unique way of running their camps, for they were concessions, to be bought and sold or awarded to favored officers, who then set out to make money from them. The prisoners were housed but not fed. Instead, the Turkish guards opened up several of the old shops and sold the prisoners food and other supplies. Since the shops did not have to worry about competitors, the prices charged were whatever the traffic would bear, with a bonanza of profits for the camp commander.

The prisoner who happened to enter camp without any money, dressed in oil-spattered navy dungarees, was out of luck. If he had a winning personality or was able to arouse enough pity among his more affluent comrades, he would survive. Otherwise, he might be kept on a bare subsistence diet by the Turks, and, since the camp's facilities deteriorated as the months passed, the consequent dirt and disease took a high toll among the half-starved prisoners.[8]

Jack Cary took much longer getting home than he had meant to; he was in the camp from early 1915 to November, 1918. three and a half years.

Then in April, 1915, Joyce was called into service, too, and sent off to the northern frontier east of Nafada. The war there was at a standstill. The Germans and their native troops were holed up in a mud fort on Mount Mora. The fort, like a huge clay ant heap, held up any major British advance. The Germans, although outnumbered, could not be routed from their position. Mass assaults up the jagged hill to the fort meant slaughter for the attackers.

The situation was almost exactly parallel to the one Joyce had seen at Scutari in the Balkan War, and consequently he was called on for his advice. The entrenchments that the Montenegrins had built around Scutari had been effective, so similar ones were dug around the German position. But it had taken guns to make the Turks surrender at Scutari. To attempt to ring Mount Mora with artillery was impossible.

Still, it was argued, if one gun could be brought up, the effect might be as good as a battery of fieldpieces. A few shells pumped into the German fortifications might create a sufficient gap for an assault force to enter. Even more important, the explosions might have a great psychological force on the German's native troops, the bulk of their force. They had never seen a fieldpiece, much less heard one or had shells bursting around them. The shock might demoralize them long enough to make the fort impotent against a sudden attack. In fact, in their panic they might surrender.

But there was a problem in bringing up such a gun. It could be carried partway from Lagos by rail, but at least half of the way it would have to travel overland.

Joyce was sent out with a party of native troops to clear a rough road for the gun's passage. This task involved devising means to carry the weapon over unbridged rivers, probably the hardest part of the preparations. The job would be all the more hazardous because the Germans might be patrolling some of the territory through which Joyce and his Nigerian soldiers had to pass. Joyce had been told to avoid all main trails because of this, and of course silence would be vital.

Joyce gave a portrait of himself at this time in his story "Bush River":

A young officer with an eyeglass in his right eye walked slowly round pony and groom. Now and then he glanced severely upon both. Everything about him, his clipped hair which left him almost bald, his clipped moustache, even his eyeglass increased this air of severity, of an austere and critical aloofness.[9]

At the head of his men, his monocle steamed up, leading his native pony Satan (astride, he would have been a fine target for snipers), Joyce must have been an impressive — and somewhat ludicrous — sight.

Another autobiographical story, "The Raft," deals with the sort of problems that faced Joyce and his men on their road-making expedition. In the story there is a river that must be crossed, so Corner marks some trees for his men to fell in order to make a raft. He is disconcerted by the giggling and laughter which accompany their work and tells his corporal to keep the men quiet.

The corporal began to reprove them, but burst into a neigh of laughter right in the face of the young officer. Corner was disconcerted, but he thought, "After all, it's a good thing they're not worried." He therefore smiled upon them as if to say, "Be happy, my children."

At this the men became almost hysterical. One young recruit made sounds like whooping cough and bent down till his woolly green cap fell right off.

Luckily Corner's breakfast was ready. He was able to withdraw with dignity. With dignity, good nature returned to him, and after breakfast he thought, "Really, they're nice chaps — it's not their war — and here they are laughing away." [10]

The young officer suffers through the hewing of the trees, with the cannon-like crashes they make when they fall, but the laughter is what unnerves him most. Only after the trees are felled, stripped, tied into a raft, and launched does he understand the laughter: the trees are ironwood. The raft sinks beneath the water and into the muddy riverbed the minute it is launched. The entire day had been one long practical joke, just the sort of humor the men delighted in.

Despite problems of this sort and a hundred natural obstacles along the way, the route was finished, Joyce and his men returned to H Company, and the heavy field gun, a French 95 mm., was brought to the assault on Mount Mora. The bombardment began on September 1 and the attack was ordered for the night of the 2nd, with two diversionary attacks to confuse the German defenders. But because of the impossibly rugged terrain, this attack failed.

The German fort was excellently located for defense. To reach it, the British force had to climb down a rocky ravine, then claw their way up the other side onto the mountain height, open to enemy fire at almost all times and unable to get off a shot themselves because the climbing was too treacherous for them to unsling their rifles.

Nevertheless a second attempt was made on the next night, and it also failed. A third attack, delayed because of filthy weather, finally began on the 7th, after a week of ineffective bombardment by machine guns and the French fieldpiece. Moving through darkness and mist, the assault force gained a foothold on the heights by dawn; then the bombardment burst forth to pave the way. At 7:30 the attackers moved forward for the final dash. They reached within sixty yards of the German breastworks before being turned back, their captain killed and many of their troopers dead or wounded.

Now they were in a hopeless position, unable to advance or to retreat, pinned down among the rocks. As the sun burned away the mist they were left with neither water nor food, helplessly waiting for nightfall, while bullets whined and ricocheted around them, dusting them with splinters of rock. All day they crouched and went without water. With nightfall their commander, Brigadier General Frederick H. Cunliffe, attempted to send more troops forward to consolidate the position, but he was not successful. Even supplies of food and water could not be brought forward. So at dawn of the 9th the remnants of H Company's assault force were even more desperately off than before.

General Cunliffe finally ordered them to retreat and the men, carrying their wounded, constantly under fire, and parched and tired, edged back from rock to rock.[11] Joyce, retreating with the rest, felt an explosion in his head; he had taken a bullet. In his last brief moment of consciousness, he knew he was dying ("It felt as if my brains were blown to pieces"[12]) and he thought, "Well, this is it, and it is easy."[13] He "had no unhappy thoughts or pain or fear — only a sort of surprise that such a terrible thing as death should happen so easily and suddenly."[14] Then he collapsed.

12

LEAVE, 1916

THE BULLET, which, in that brief moment, Joyce thought had killed him, had hit the mastoid process immediately behind the ear and had glanced off this bone. Coming from the rear, the bullet had then cut through Joyce's ear, leaving him unconscious and bloody but not too seriously wounded.

In fact, after treatment at the base hospital in Yola, he rejoined H Company on the 450-mile march south to the central plateau of the Cameroons, where French troops from French Equatorial Africa were to link with the British to clear the enemy out of the central areas of the colony.

The march took five weeks — ninety miles a week on foot or on horse. It was a unique experience in Joyce's life. The monotony of the landscape and his own activity turned him into an almost purely physical being by day:

I did not think, or reflect. I felt well, brisk in the morning, tired at night. I slept as soon as I closed my eyes, and waked at the rustle of a leaf. I can't remember that I ever laughed or smiled, and I walked through blood on the road (the blood of some fellow shot in the advance station) without interest of any kind, or any emotion that I can remember.[1]

It was life in a vacuum, life more as an automaton or an animal than as a man. Only on the days when the march was short did Joyce come alive and "recover enough activity to wonder where we were marching to, or where we would have more par-

cels of eatables; to enjoy conversation, and feel compassion for
others, the men and the beasts, my own poor pony; sometimes
even to enjoy a joke." [2]

His letter writing was almost nonexistent, his relations with
home minimal, his ambitions nil, and love had vanished from
his life; he wrote Gerty Ogilvie sometime after:

> . . . I did not think of you every day or even every other day.
> Just now and then I had a recollection of you which generally
> caused me to say "D***n girls." I fancy I had rather a reputation
> as a misogynist in those days. I know I used to scorn a fellow
> Joseland who was on the column with me, and who was engaged.
> While he sat with his nose buried in letters, I drank my drink and
> smoked my pipe like a free man, and thoroughly despised women. [3]

This 450-mile trek, like the wound that preceded it, had a
strong effect on Joyce. He saw that this kind of life was merely
an existence, barren and stultifying, like so much of the tribal
life of Africa wherein man had no chance to exploit his capacities, particularly his imagination and creativity. These two human values became increasingly central to Joyce's view of life.
Like his other beliefs, they were born out of experience rather
than achieved on a purely abstract basis.

Another experience at this time left a scar on him. It grew
out of the public indifference to and ignorance of the Cameroons Campaign, which, Joyce said, the men felt deeply:

> We knew well no one cared a damp what happened to us, neither
> for praise or blame. I remember a friend of mine, Charles Mar-
> wood, saying as much, when someone had remarked it didn't
> much matter where one fought, it was just the same if one was
> killed. Marwood said half and more of his Regiment were dead
> in France, and he would have wished to be with them, but he
> didn't want to be killed in the Cameroons, it was too lonely. And
> poor Marwood was killed — shot at ten yards out of the forest —
> he died in two hours — and is buried in a desolate waste of scrub
> and stone — a thousand miles from anywhere under a pile of
> stones to keep the hyenas from him — a lonelier place could not

be found. That was his long chair I had . . . and Marwood's head made that pillow black. I can understand what poor Charles Marwood felt when he said he did not want to be killed in Africa, but would not mind so much in France — and so I am anxious for the Mesopotamia troops. Africa, Mesopotamia, these are places men can live for a while and not be unhappy while they have work to do, but they are bad places to die in. Of course it is easy to die quickly anywhere. I thought I was killed when I was shot, and in the few seconds consciousness I had, I had no unhappy thoughts or pain or fear — only a sort of surprise that such a terrible thing as death should happen so easily and suddenly — but poor Marwood did not die quickly and I know from the man in whose arms he died (who wore his ring afterwards for safe keeping till he could give it to the girl Marwood was engaged to) that he was like a child afraid of the loneliness and the dark. Yet he was a very brave man and had done many things in those eighteen months to prove it.

Joyce brings the story to a close with these words: "Men and women are not born to be alone, they need one another, and others of their kind, and as they should live in friendship and love, so it is hard for them to die alone."[4] He would return to this episode several times in his letters, and the idea of how vital love was to sustain a man, an idea already impressed on him from Cromwell House days, never left him.

The column of troops moved on south to the German fortress at Banyo, which was very similar to that at Mount Mora: on a rise, surrounded by craggy rocks that meant slow progress for an attacking force, and thick-walled. Banyo, however, was even better defended and provisioned. Again the attackers had to struggle through impossibly rocky terrain up the heights to the fort, which stood on a piece of ground that rose a thousand feet above the plain around it. It took the troops, including H Company, two days to make their way over the approaches to the fort. But this time there was no fight; the garrison had evacuated during the Franco-British advance under cover of a storm. The entry into Banyo was an anticlimax.[5]

Joyce was attached to a force commanded by Brigadier General Cunliffe, which moved southwest to Foumban, then east across the M'Bam River to Ngambe, losing touch with the German troops retreating ahead of them. It was the southern force rather than that of Cunliffe in the north that brought matters to an end with the capture of the capital of the Cameroons, Yaoundé, in January, 1916.

Joyce had gone back to Yola on leave at Christmas. He was in very bad shape after the campaigning he had done and his wound, which hadn't entirely healed, was troubling him. Sometime during his adolescence he had developed asthma (his childhood illness diagnosed as pleurisy may have foreshadowed this); now the asthma was severe, and the act of breathing exhausted him during his day's work and prevented him from sleeping properly at night. The combination of the wound, asthma, and consequent insomnia wore away his physical stamina and left his nerves utterly raw.

The extent of this nervous deterioration was made apparent by an event in February, 1916. Joyce got into an argument with some men, apparently native carriers, and suddenly went berserk. He hit and kicked out at them viciously, so furious that afterward he could not remember what had happened. He had a complete blackout. One man, a fellow officer, told him afterward that he had killed one of the men during his seizure.

It was a lie, a bad joke. However much damage Joyce had done, he had not killed anyone or even caused serious injury. But he was terribly shaken by the experience.[6] He knew he had a temper and had been quite ready to believe what he had been told. It haunted him for a long time afterward, and later he used the experience in his writing. More immediately, it frightened him terribly and made him resolve that he must never let such a thing happen again. The occurrence, along with his general physical decline, also seems to have made an impression on his superiors, for he was sent home on leave very soon afterward, a leave he had been due for a few months earlier but had not gotten because of the campaign and the general disruption of normal policy in Nigeria. The wartime shortage of personnel made leaves scarce. Normally, a political officer

spent eighteen months on a tour of duty, then went on nine
months home leave to shake off the malaria and whatever ill-
nesses' he took home with him. The climate, the work load, and
the abundance of disease made such leaves absolutely essential.
Joyce should have received his in late 1915. Now in March,
1916, he was so visibly shattered that the physical examination
required for a wartime leave must have been a pure formality.

London in 1916 was a strange sight to him. He had left in
peacetime and returned in the middle of the war; there were
uniforms everywhere, women working in factories and on buses,
shortages and displacements, and his father was on Zeppelin patrol, an early version of the ARP (Air Raid Precautions),
watching for German aircraft coming over on bombing raids
(there were five Zeppelin bombing raids on London in 1915
and five more attacks on English targets in January–April, 1916,
with one raid killing 59 people in Shrewsbury. In May, 1916,
the Germans launched the first airplane bombing raids on England).

Any sight-seeing had to wait, however, since Joyce was a physical wreck: emaciated, wheezing, and still not sleeping properly.
But he was delighted to see his friends again, and when Freddy
Ogilvie invited him to spend a few days at The Glade, he accepted gladly. Freddy's friendship, the chance of perhaps seeing
Heneage, and the restfulness of the big house and quiet grounds
made up for his hesitancy at seeing Gerty Ogilvie again after his
last round with her in 1913.

As for Mr. and Mrs. Ogilvie, they had always accepted Joyce,
and in Mr. Ogilvie's case, liked him. Now that he was back from
the war front, wounded and ill, his welcome was a good deal
warmer than in 1913 — particularly because one of their sons-in-
law, a clergyman, the one in fact whom Mrs. Ogilvie must always have contrasted favorably with the (to her) more profli-
gate Joyce, had become increasingly rude to Mrs. Ogilvie
because of her German origin.[7] Of course in England during
World War I the mania against anyone and anything German
was almost universal, but to experience it so close to home must
have been extremely upsetting. Again she could contrast her
son-in-law with Joyce but this time to Joyce's advantage.

If Mrs. Ogilvie was happier this time to see Joyce, Gerty was
not. On coming to dinner that first evening, she caught sight of
Joyce and almost jumped with shock, then went to stand behind
her mother as if Joyce might attack her. She did sit down but
would not speak to him.[8] However, she was curious about him;
she had heard he had had his ear shot off in Africa and wanted to
see what he looked like in his new lopsided state.[9] But the damage to his ear, perhaps to her disappointment, was barely per-
ceptible, and as for the young man, in his present worn state, he
wasn't nearly so fierce as she remembered him. In fact, poor
fellow, he seemed nothing but skin and bones. So she finished
her dinner more calmly than she had begun it.

This was early in April. A month later she and Joyce were
engaged. And in early June they were married. Joyce had
vowed he would get her at last, and he did.

In April, no one would have believed this possible. If Gerty
was more interested in Joyce than she had been two or three
years earlier, she was too shy and stubborn to show it. Joyce had
given her up. So far as he was concerned, the closest he ever
expected to get to her came one evening when she was in the
sitting room singing old English songs, while he and Freddy sat
outside in the hall, smoking and listening quietly.[10]

Freddy and Joyce felt an extra kinship for each other during
this leave. Freddy was an officer in the 4th Bedfordshire Regiment, and early in 1915 he had been wounded. In April, at Hill
60, his left arm had been hit and the hand was amputated. His
parents visited him at the hospital where he was convalescing, at
Le Tréport, near Dieppe. Heneage, who was serving at a hospital at Bar-le-Duc, also visited Freddy, who needed all the morale
boosting he could get.[11] He had been a fine pianist before the
war, and it seemed obvious that he would not be able to play
again. So both Freddy and Joyce, in April, 1916, had suffered
and felt closer than ever before.

When Freddy was preparing to return from his leave, Joyce
consequently felt it was time for him to go, too. With Freddy
going, Heneage over in France, and their sister Elsie also in
France, where she was working as a volunteer nurse, there were
only Mr. and Mrs. Ogilvie, Gerty, and another houseguest at

E

The Glade. But Freddy persuaded Joyce to stay on a few more days after he himself had gone.

Perhaps Freddy had pleaded Joyce's cause to Gerty before he left because one night soon after, as Joyce sat talking to his fellow guest at the house, Gerty came flying into the room in a white dress, sat down next to Joyce, and, without saying a word, put her hand on his. This was the first sign she had ever given that she was fond of him. Joyce, although he was overwhelmed, did not lose a second. The moment they were alone, he proposed. To his delight, she accepted at once. He tried to kiss her mouth and, in his confused state, kissed her on the ear instead.[12] However much a man of the world he was, however much a jaded Bohemian and veteran of the wars, Joyce could still lose his bearings when it came to Gerty.

Freddy had pushed them together, and now, when Joyce shilly-shallied and argued that it was unfair to Gerty to marry her at once when he would be shipping out to Nigeria soon again, he overrode Joyce's protests and urged that they marry before Joyce's leave was up in August.[13] If they married in June they could have two months together, and that was a lot more of a marriage than many couples were allowed in those wartime days. There was Gerty's friend Gwen Quilter, for instance, who had married Alan Herbert on New Year's Eve, 1914, with a far shorter time before he was to leave for the war. Who could say when Joyce and Gerty would be together again? The system of granting leaves from Nigeria was so confused, it might be two, three, or even four years. And Joyce had waited four years already from the time he'd first proposed, hadn't he, so why should he wait longer?

It was ironic that Freddy, in so many ways more staid than Joyce, and the one who had urged Joyce to stop bothering Gerty in 1913, should now be pressing Joyce into an immediate marriage. But Joyce was grateful to him for doing so. It was the right moment, too, for approaching Mr. and Mrs. Ogilvie, when all Mrs. Ogilvie's feelings about Joyce's instability and irreligiosity were undermined by the war and by Joyce's state, so much like her own son's.

So Joyce was won over to the idea, as was Gerty. And Mr. and Mrs. Ogilvie were delighted. In fact, Mr. Ogilvie, always sympathetic to Joyce's cause, made a point of trying to explain Gerty to Joyce so as to make the first days of the marriage easier on the young man. As Joyce told Gerty about the talk later,

> He seemed to think you were decidedly a difficult proposition, while at the same time he assured me it was worth tackling. The picture left in my mind was rather of a golden-hearted porcupine, or a hedgehog with good intentions but a naughty temper.[14]

The couple began the formality of drawing up a marriage settlement, when Gerty objected partway through the proceedings that there was no need in the settlement for a provision in case of her being widowed: Joyce, she said firmly, would outlive her.[15] She was given an income of nearly three hundred pounds by her father, and Joyce's income from his mother varied between two and three hundred a year.[16] This, together with his pay and various allowances he received for service in Nigeria, would total about £900 a year, a very handy income for a young couple then, equivalent to more than $10,000 today.[17] Since Gerty, now 25, meant to live with her parents after Joyce's return to Africa (with Freddy, Heneage, and Elsie in France and Flo, the third Ogilvie daughter, married, Mr. and Mrs. Ogilvie would be very lonely otherwise; besides, with the wartime lack of servants, an extra pair of hands would be very useful in such a large house), they could save a good amount toward the time of Joyce's return when they would have a home of their own.

They were married in the first week of June, then went for a three-week honeymoon in Cornwall. Arthur Cary was very pleased at his son's marriage, for it was a sign that Joyce was settling down, for one thing, and this meant a great deal to Mr. Cary. And he was pleased that his eldest son, having come home in such wretched shape, should have this happiness. He was in the best of spirits, and at Joyce's bachelor party the evening before the wedding, Arthur, who had a fine wit and boisterousness when the time suited, hinted in his speech at some of the pleasures of marriage — to Joyce's embarrassment.[18] Joyce, who ordinarily could be as Rabelaisian as his father (neither liked smutty jokes of the sniggering sort though), was suffering badly from asthma at the time, perhaps brought on by the excitement and anxiety of the step he was taking, and so he was not himself — he looked particularly wretched the next day, his wedding day, and could only gasp out his responses at the marriage ceremony.[19]

The honeymoon, spent at Trebetherick on Padstow Bay in northern Cornwall, where Joyce and Gerty spent lazy days on the seashore in deck chairs or went walking in the hilly country behind Trebetherick, did wonders for Joyce's health, easing the asthma, putting some flesh on him, and bringing some color up through the tan on his face.

It also saw the first of the ruptures that continued through the marriage, the "massamoras" as they called them that both made life interesting and cleared the air when feelings built up, always ending in tears and kisses and *mea culpa*'s all round. This one was particularly wild and woolly, since Gerty and Joyce had so little experience with each other. Each was keyed up and Gerty's temper was matched by Joyce's, because the state of his health still made him sulky and moody. They shouted at each other, broke dishes, stormed and raged, and ended in each other's arms, while Gerty told Joyce, "I couldn't love you more." [20] Joyce, for his part, even let himself be persuaded to go to services each Sunday at the little white church nearby, something he hadn't done since Clifton.[21]

They returned to spend the last month and a half at The Glade, meeting friends, seeing plays, going to concerts, their marriage marred only by the arrangements in the bedchamber given to them by Mrs. Ogilvie, in which she had put two single beds, on opposite sides of the room.[22]

Despite Mrs. Ogilvie's discretion, in mid-July Gerty told Joyce she believed she was pregnant. Joyce was delighted. The news put the cap on the whole glorious leave: the proposal, the acceptance, the marriage, the honeymoon, and now the knowledge he was to be a father. Even the fact that he would have to be in Nigeria when the baby was born and might not see his child until it was one or two years old, that he might not be able to see its first steps and hear its first words, could not daunt him, at least for the moment. Joyce had a great talent for blanking out both past and future when he needed to, which made the last days of his leave far easier than they might have been.

Joyce left The Glade on the morning of August 9, hurrying away with his boxes and gear by himself. He hated making his good-byes in public on railway station platforms. Everything was too strained, too public, and too frantic. To leave Gerty at The Glade, seeing her for the last time in her proper setting, was a much better way.

The previous day had been spent quietly at the Ogilvie home, walking together, sitting by the pond, trying to be brave, although Gerty broke down for a few minutes in the afternoon at the prospect of their long separation, longer than that of couples where the husband was going off to France and might be home on leave again in a few months. That night Joyce watched her sit and brush her hair at her dressing table in her blue dressing gown. He tried to impress the picture as firmly as possible on his memory, because it was a scene he had loved since he'd first watched it on their honeymoon. It was the picture he most wanted to remember when he returned to Nigeria.[23]

13

THE NAFADA POLO CLUB

JOYCE SAILED FROM PORTSMOUTH on the 9th, aboard the *Abasso*. He was in far better shape than when he had arrived in England in March: his health was nearly restored, his asthma virtually was dormant, and he was having little trouble now with his nerves. Each morning and night he did setting-up and breathing exercises and planned to keep up this new regimen for his whole tour to prevent another collapse.

He hoped to return to military duty and, since the Cameroons campaign was settled, he hoped he would be sent on to Tanganyika, where the war still went on. The German commander in Tanganyika, General Paul von Lettow-Vorbeck, was fighting a brilliant campaign. Von Lettow, who had fought against the British in the Boer War, was using all his knowledge of British tactics and of the Boers' guerilla methods, together with his own dynamism and ingenuity, to avoid being surrounded and defeated. Cut off from supplies and communications with Germany, and with just a handful of German and native troops, he campaigned up and down Tanganyika for nearly four and a half years, dragging the Governor of German East Africa along with him to give a semblance of an unconquered Tanganyikan Government. His men made ammunition and other supplies on the march and finally surrendered only after the British got word to him that the war in Europe was over and the Armistice signed.

The British Army, which outnumbered von Lettow's troops by far, and had access to plenty of supplies and some excellent

commanders (one of whom was General von Lettow's former
Boer ally, Jan Christiaan Smuts), was, nevertheless, unable to
catch and corner him. The difficulties, at first an acute embarrassment, finally amused the British troops and their commanders, as they played hare and hounds through German East Africa, and their respect for von Lettow became so great that they
passed him word of his promotions and his newly-awarded medals (lacking communications with Germany, he'd never have
known of them otherwise) and in return received his thanks for
the messages.

Joyce hoped to be included in this campaign or, even better,
to be sent to the Middle East or one of the European fronts
where he would stand a greater chance of getting more frequent
home leave.

So he thought it was a fine piece of luck that he should find
himself not only on the same ship, but seated at the same table,
as General Cunliffe, formerly commander of the northern
Franco-British Army in the Cameroons, and now returning
from leave to prepare an army of 3,000 Nigerians for service in
Tanganyika. The two of them were among the half-dozen
guests at the captain's table.

Between the time Joyce said good-bye to Gerty at The Glade
and the time he boarded the *Abasso,* he began a series of daily
letters to her that ended only when he was on his way home
again on his next leave. In one of the first of these he sketched
the others at the table, particularly General Cunliffe:

> The other people at my table are the General (Cunliffe),
> Major Uniacke, Bovill, a D.O., Blackwood, a soldier, Captain
> Ford, a police commissioner, and myself. The General is the best
> sort of old soldier you could meet anywhere, very straight, very
> honest in his opinions, quite sure of what he ought to do, and
> doing it whenever he can. He tells a story in the most innocent
> and delightful sort of way, much better to listen to than much
> wittier talk. . . . He doesn't pretend to be wise, or pompous,
> and so always manages to be worth hearing & dignified. Ford is a
> comical card, very tall & chic. He served before the mast at one
> time, and laughs very loud at very small jokes of mine which flat-

ters me & makes me like him. Blackwood looks about him & tries
to find out what other people are at without committing himself
— Bovill is a solid official — painstaking, anxious to be fair, &
looking forward to a pension, the Major is at a loose end — ought
to have been a soldier but has drifted into the political & doesn't
like it — he expects his pension in four years — and will then
settle in a little flat in town & be an old clubman and something
of a vieux marcheur.

(13 August 1916)

The trip that began so pleasantly, however, went a little sour
when Joyce and his cabin mate caught colds. The two men,
cooped up in a small room with its windows sealed and painted
over because of the threat of submarines, in an increasingly
tropical climate, both of them coughing, sneezing, and having a
hard time getting proper sleep, could hardly stay on good terms.
The result, at least on Joyce's part, was an overwhelming desire
to be back home in England with his new wife. After only two
weeks away from her, with many months of duty ahead of him,
he missed her unbearably.

It was General Cunliffe who helped most to keep up Joyce's
spirits, with his talk of army life in the days before the war, of
India where he had served, and of all sorts of previous experiences.
One of Cunliffe's comments that most amused Joyce was
how disgraceful it was that so many young people, especially
young soldiers, should be marrying during the war. He was un-
aware that Joyce was married and, as Joyce wrote to Gerty,

said that in his old regiment the Seaforths, the only married officer was the colonel & any one who got engaged was at once sent
off to the Sudan for five years to get over it. A married man had
to pay £100 to the mess, and was transferred as soon as possible
to another regiment. . . . The old man didn't know I was married or I would have come in for it — the major did not give me
away.

(22 August 1916)

Two nights later, when at dinner the general did find out that
Joyce was married, he was full of apologies and explained, ac-

cording to Joyce, "but of course he only meant young chumps oughtn't to get married as its so hard on the women, but everybody else, exclusive of young chumps, ought to be married."

When Joyce and the general separated at Lagos, Cunliffe, to whom Joyce had indicated his desire to serve in Tanganyika, assured him that he wouldn't be forgotten when members of the WAFF were to be sent on to the army chasing General von Lettow-Vorbeck's elusive force. Joyce was elated. But the general, with an army to get ready and then to transport to East Africa, evidently forgot his dinner table companion. Or perhaps, remembering his feelings about married young officers and the sufferings of their wives, he decided not to have a young widow on his conscience.

Joyce headed north by train, then boarded a paddle wheel riverboat, *The Black Swan* (known to Nigerian hands as *The Black Swine* due partly to her habit of rooting in the mud of the riverbanks), for the trip along the Niger to Lokoja. The boat regularly ran aground during the thunderstorms that plagued the trip and made the banks unrecognizable. From Lokoja Joyce headed overland to Nafada, the post he had held in 1914. It was a twenty-eight-day march, more than 400 miles through bush, but surprisingly Joyce felt fitter at the end of the trek than when he had left the ship at Lagos.

Nafada had changed a great deal from its primitive state in 1914. The Cameroons Campaign had helped to see to that. Being used as a way station and training depot for the troops of the WAFF had left Nafada much improved. There were new houses, and more land had been cleared; in fact the administrative station had developed until it was almost a village in itself. But at the time of Joyce's arrival, it had gone slack, with the best of the native troops having gone off to the Cameroons to fight, then south to the coast for rest and reequipping. The remaining troops were rather motley.

Joyce, still an officer in the WAFF rather than a civilian administrator, was required to recruit additional troops for the Tanganyikan Campaign, and then to train them before they went south. He was an excellent training officer, perhaps because he wanted to make himself known to the higher-ups so as to be sent off with the men he instructed. Perhaps it was just because he did such a good job of training the troops that he was left back at Nafada instead.

His spirits were up again after their low aboard ship; they were raised by the work he was doing (work always perked him up), by the improved conditions at Nafada and the company there, and especially by his new pastime, polo.

This sport was another addition to Nafada in his absence. A polo ground had been cleared and ragtag games were played regularly. Joyce, who rode well, was anxious to learn the game, and was initiated into it by the others at the station. The personnel in Nafada when Joyce arrived there in October, 1916, included a Dr. Rolleston; three Assistant District Officers (A.D.O.'s), de Putram, Falconer, and Heathcote (de Putram, ill, was due for leave); Phillips, Joyce's subaltern; and the man who ran the Niger Company's store there, Hall, "an ex-sailor, small, wizened, with a big voice who tells me very long & pointless stories. . . ." They were a very mixed bag. Falconer was a university lecturer who was a war volunteer. Dr. Rolleston, the "Likita" (Hausa for doctor), was a very unassuming and generous man — he had ridden fifty miles through the bush in six hours to come to the aid of de Putram, who was ill and alone. Joyce came to like all of the men in time, but his first impressions of most of them (like most of his first impressions, which also tended to be wrong) were fair to bad.

Joyce settled into a regular and fairly vigorous routine at once. "You want to know how I spend the day," he wrote to Gerty on October 26, soon after he got her first letters (the first came on October 9, three months after he had said good-bye), and went on to give his schedule:

. . . 5.30 get up. I sleep in a mosquito house, that is a square wooden framework covered in with wire netting, in my verandah. The orderly wakes me at 5:30. then I do ¼ hour exercises in pyjamas and have my bath, ten minutes more exercising in nothing, put on a vest, and shave. While I shave I drink a cup of cocoa and

eat a couple of biscuits. At 6.25 I go on Parade — and parade till
7.45. Then to the office till 8.30. The office is a little mud house
in the Fort. at 8.30 I go to breakfast and about 9.30 back to office, without a belt, and smoking my pipe. Then I answer wires,
hear complaints, see defaulters and so on till 12 or so. At 1 I
lunch, at two I smoke, 2–4 I work. 4.30 change into boots and
breeches and have tea, unless I have an N.C.Os instruction from
4–5, when I tea at 4, and change at 5, about 5 to go off to the Polo
ground, back to bath at six (sundown) and about 6.30 go out to
wherever drinks are in a sweater and Mother's [Mrs. Ogilvie's]
scarf. There I sit and talk over the camp-fire, and smoke, till 8
or later. The orderly Sergeant reports to me and takes to-morrows
orders and about 8.30, I go to dinner with the boy carrying a lan-
tern and my chair. After dinner I smoke and write to you as I'm
doing now and perhaps you are doing to me.

Everything on the whole was tranquil. Polo tended to be a
little rough, however, as the ground was dotted with anthills,
hard clay abutments like small anti-tank dragon's teeth that
could trip up the horses or send a ball caroming off in a very
different direction from the one in which it was hit. And the
native ponies were half wild and even under ordinary
circumstances loved to bite, so they went into an absolute frenzy
during a fast game and were another hazard to the players.
Joyce was better off than the rest because his pony, Satan, was
the best biter. One day after the animal had bitten Dr. Rolleston in the backside, the players voted to ban Satan from the
game until Joyce argued that with only one pony he would be
unable to play.

But payday was the worst hazard of all, at least for Joyce's
nerves and temper. He told Gerty of a typical episode of paying
off the wives of the men who were either on the coast or off in
Tanganyika:

What is your name? A simper, are you the wife of no. 5689 Abdu
Bagasmi — a faint smile and some coquettish wriggles (Oh! Damn,
from Phillips — haven't you got any tongue from the Sergeant
Major) — finally a faint yes, and more wriggles — Yes what — are
you Abdu Bagasmi's wife — no — (Oh! Hell from Phillips and

ejaculations from the Sergt. Major in two or three languages —
then who are you — I'm Fatima — Abdu Bagasmi has put Fatima
down in the book as his wife, what Fatima are you — She's his
wife all right, from three other ladies outside in shrill voices, the
orderly Sergeant dashes out to restore order — I'm Abdu's wife
says the lady with more simpers (Blast the woman! says Phillips).
— whats his other name, I ask, where does he come from — from
Bagasmi (Phillips' face takes on a shade more gloomy despair
and the Sergt.-Major makes a short speech — I pay the lady ten
shillings — she goes off with more coquettish smiles and wriggles
— and the next is called) one person kept us for twenty minutes
— I came away with a headache and a very bad temper. Women
are the deuce — I wonder why God didn't arrange to do without
'em — how much less complicated the world would be. There's
not a row in barracks, but a woman's in it. . . .

   And their clothes — you never saw such robes — turbans —
beads — falling off all over the office, and away goes the money
(mostly 3d bits & pennies — I paid out £135 in these denomina-
tions so you can see what counting means) and its 2d short — o
dear! what a dreadful thing — where's my 2d — meanwhile sixty
or seventy of 'em talking as loud as they can in a crowd in the
fort just outside my door — squatting in bands and letting very
choice bits of gossip fly about like fireworks.

   The recruiting went famously, though. Old soldiers strolled
in from the bush at an increasing rate to apply for the WAFF.
The money was good, after all, and they were used to fighting.
It was just a few years before 1914, the year Joyce had arrived,
that the area had been pacified and the wars between tribes
stopped. Many of the recruits had fought then, while others
were old Niger Company soldiers. Still others, according to
their prison records, had been brawlers simply for the fun of a
fight. Joyce liked them. "Its quite delightful to see the
thoughtful villainy of their war worn countenances on Parade,"
Joyce wrote to his wife, "and they know their work too — anything from six to eighteen years Service."

   Joyce liked the occasional comic side of recruiting. One particular episode was a real practical joke, only this time Joyce was
the one to laugh. He wrote Gerty,

A mallam* tried to join yesterday — like a parson with you — I nearly collapsed with surprise and the Sergt. Major was convulsed with secret joy. We put him on parade and I heard the lance corporal teaching him the difference between his right and left hands at great length, and the Mallam feebly protesting he knew already, and the L/C still insisting it didn't matter if he did, he'd got to learn it on the first morning. The doctor threw the poor old thing out however for a most unromantic disease, and the Mallam has given up his hopes of glory and left us dull again.

The mallam's "unromantic disease," whether syphilis or gonorrhea, was commonplace, as Joyce had already found. He encountered not only venereal diseases but goiter, hernia, black water fever (on his first tour he had nursed a fellow officer through this deadly disease and had earned praise for his job), malaria, intestinal worms, the insidious and crippling guinea worm, and a host of other parasites, diseases and cripplings among the natives, as well as the recurrent famines.

Arthur Cary had learned to cope with change and live in a world of flux. Joyce had learned the lesson, too. Now in Nigeria he was beginning to recognize yet another truth: that man could not endure without change; he needed its stimulus in order to exist. Rather than a glib, "You can't fight progress," Joyce's belief became positive, pragmatic as well as idealistic. It was not the easy optimism of the Victorian and Edwardian belief that *all* progress was a natural force which men did not need to control or even initiate, that it just came of itself. Joyce's view was that man *must* initiate change and give it direction, preserving what deserved preservation and abandoning what was not worth saving.

He believed that change was good when old institutions had proved themselves empty or impotent. So long as they were vital, they possessed capacity for good. When they lost their vitality they became stultifying shells, keeping out light and air and life. Then they crippled people. Yet, inevitably, some people would have vested interests in them, and even more, many would still believe in them not necessarily because of vested in-

* A mallam was a native official whose duties were both religious and clerical; in fact his functions correspond roughly to those of medieval clerk.

terests but simply because they were used to these dying institutions; they had been raised among them and their familiarity was reassuring. Joyce was made to think of a toy he'd had as a small child, the wooden horse he had been used to sleeping with. The horse lost its head, tail, legs, and paint until it was just a battered lump of wood, shiny with dirt and handling. But young Joyce had continued to love it and take comfort in its presence, so much so that when the horse was lost, he would not sleep or be soothed until this talisman and symbol of security was found and given to him.

The battered and dying institutions of society, he felt, were like that horse, for they provided comfort and a sense of security for people, but at the same time they prevented growth and vitality.

This view scarcely made him a revolutionary, because Joyce loved the past as much as he believed in the future. He was very conscious of his family's history and took pride in it, even in its follies. He liked much about the past — family heirlooms, good manners, General Cunliffe's talk of the old British Army. Change was a matter of weighing alternatives in individual cases. And however much he enjoyed the panorama and pomp of the courts of the Nigerian emirs, he gradually came to see that they inhibited necessary progress in their country. Although the natives might find solace and identity in the tribe's life, Joyce saw that tribal ways helped perpetuate the recurrent famine that wiped out men, women, and children by maintaining agricultural techniques that eroded the land and sapped its vitality. And the famine that killed them physically had its equivalents in spiritual famines that killed their creativity and thought.

These ideas led Joyce away from Lord Lugard's gradualism and his theory of indirect rule. With Edwardes and Carlyle to spur his thoughts and actions, Joyce in time became one of the most advanced thinkers on Africa, and his ideas were based on practical experience.

But in the autumn of 1916 he had only begun to think along these lines. He was still just another well-meaning but rather rigid and conventional young man trying to do a decent job in a strange place, sometimes idealistic and sometimes cynical, but not yet sure just what he believed. It was not until he was put on his own a few months later that he really began to experiment with change. And then he was not even conscious that he *was* experimenting, he simply saw what had to be done and did it.

14

WRITING, 1916

JOYCE, now that he was leading a relatively settled life, married, and about to become a father early in 1917, was anxious to get some writing done. He didn't wait until he was settled at his post at Nafada to begin; instead, he started during the trip itself, while he was traveling through Nigeria. He was going on twenty-eight, and his slim book of poems was the only publication he had to show (not that he showed it — or even mentioned it nowadays — to anyone) for his ambitions to be a writer. Even that small volume had appeared eight years ago, when he was nineteen.

John Middleton Murry was established as a literary light in London now. He had had several books published; he was living with Katherine Mansfield and was the closest friend of D. H. Lawrence. Yet Murry in a way had been Joyce's protégé at Oxford seven years ago. Joyce was filled with regrets when he thought of how much time he himself had wasted at activities other than writing, as he said to Gerty in a letter of August 30:

> I wish I had had the courage years ago to defy all conventional notions of respectable living & write, write, write, for whatever I could make by it even nothing. This tour I had promised to try my hand & see if I could make MONEY the magic stuff that I must get for wife & family or stay in this exile for 12 years of my life and yours, the best of both of us — but nothing is possible now & I doubt if I will be able to do anything at all. The day is cut up in small jobs — there is no privacy (I share a bungalow

with another fellow) & you know how necessary that is to me to
work.

He allowed himself to show Gerty all the conflict and anxiety
he felt, and told her,

> You've married a queer fellow you know my darling. At any rate
> I shall make use of myself before I leave this job you may be
> sure of that — if only for my own sake, for if I failed you & found
> you suffering by my selfishly going my own way to happiness, I
> should not be happy either — but I know well in the bottom of
> my heart what is the way to happiness — my *work,* with you al-
> ways by me. To make sure may mean three or four years, perhaps
> I shall fail — of course I shall at first, but perhaps always I shall
> fail. Then I shall settle down here in the cellar to work out my
> freedom and at least we shall be old together. But think of the
> lovely years wasted apart. What is all this business of separation
> except for the war, a sort of superstition about what is proper
> work & what isn't, a superstition murdering two lover's two thou-
> sand miles apart. But perhaps you don't agree — you are not like
> me in some things — I don't know you as well as I love you
> yet. . . .

For all his talk of lack of privacy and consequent inability to
write, he did get to work and three days later, September 2,
wrote to Gerty,

> 10:30. Just going to bed — I've done a little work — not very sat-
> isfactory — but glad to have done something. If I go East [to Tan-
> ganyika] I think I had better send it all home to you — not to
> read though, until its finished, unless you want to awfully badly.
> And all this is not very good as its a first draft.

All the same, it was difficult to go off by himself to sit in some
quiet corner and write. To do so might be taken as a sign of
antisociality by the others when they clustered together around
a fire in their deck chairs to talk and smoke over a drink or two.
His behavior might be viewed as an eccentricity for them to
joke about. Or, worst of all, they might take an interest in what

he was doing and ask to see his work or even come and peer over his shoulder at what he was writing. Joyce was very shy of his work now, far readier to have a stranger, some editor of a magazine, look at what he had done than to have a friend read it.

Since publishing his *Verses* in 1908, he had hardly let anyone see his work or even know he attempted writing. He had shown his father an essay and had felt he was not much interested and looked on writing as a passing fancy. Then there was the Virgin Mary poem he had shown to Heneage at Oxford, which had shocked his friend. Jack Murry had seen some of his writing — mostly poems — at Oxford when they roomed together. These were the only people who had seen his work since Edinburgh.

Even Gerty, his own wife, had never read a word of his fiction, although apparently he had done some writing on their honeymoon and more when they had returned to The Glade. It was several years, in fact, before he got up courage to let her read any of it. So to have his companions in Lokoja and then Nafada read what he was doing was absolutely out of the question no matter how interested and considerate they might have been. This meant he had to keep his work a secret as long as possible.

There was another reason for secrecy. He knew he wasn't any good yet. In 1908 the feeling that just about everything he wrote was quite fine had prompted him to publish *Verses;* now he had learned enough and set himself such high standards that nothing he did seemed much good.

Yet writing was his only means of escape from Nigeria, as he told Gerty. It would be twelve years before he could retire from the Nigerian Service on a small pension, which, together with their family incomes, might give them enough to live on comfortably. Meanwhile, even under the best of peacetime conditions, he would have only his leaves after each 18-month tour, while Gerty and he and their children grew older. And a leave every couple of years, although it might be bearable for a bachelor, was not enough for a married man. So he must write and he must sell what he wrote. There was no getting around it.

He would have to endure his apprenticeship. He must learn how a short story or a novel gets written. His approach was as workmanlike as he could make it — probably too much so, as the following description to his wife, written on September 24, shows (the fact that he had finished the first draft of a novel in well under two months indicates how hard he was working):

> . . . the first draft is finished and I am beginning the first revision. That is I read the whole thing through this morning & considered it from every point of view — what parts were too short, what too unfunny and needing more explanation, where I had missed chances and where I had too many incidents crowded together — then I made notes and have started to add. First of all I add roughly, whole pages at a time — bringing in a character that does not appear often enough, in other places, or explaining the plot. For instance if a person only appears once or twice at either the very beginning or end, the character is almost wasted and also gives an appearance of only being dragged in to carry on the plan. When I write a first draft I don't worry about this but bring in a character only when wanted. Now I must weave them into the whole texture of the work. This is not at all difficult in the early stages as now. The first draft runs to about 40,000 words, and the book will have to be 100,000 or more so there's lots of room for expansion. Also the first draft reads too quickly of course and I must put in quiet places — little descriptions of people or places, or pieces of consideration of things in general. I write in the first person. It is an experiment, and does not prove easy — the chief person, I, that is, is a man of 45, and must not talk out of his age or character — and that I of the book is not at all the I of me, as you can understand. It is a fascinating amusement, and I believe makes the most absorbing hobby in the world — my hours fly away, I don't get into mischief, and I am happy all the time.

Those "little descriptions of people or places, or pieces of consideration of things in general" to keep the novel from reading too quickly show what stage Joyce had reached in his literary education. His writing technique was consciously mechanical, for he was learning about structure and pace, rather than attempting to indulge himself. He was not a precious young man who meant to write for himself alone. He intended to be published and allowed himself no room to be arty. If his writing was mechanical, with all the bones showing, at least he knew that good writing needs bones if it is going to hold up.

Now that he was settled, he became increasingly productive, despite the fact that his writing had to be confined to a very small corner of his day, after duties, polo, dinner with one or more of his companions, "small chop" around someone's fire, and issuing orders for the coming day. "I was in good vein and wrote some 3000 words," he told Gerty one night, and on another, "I have written 4000 words of moderate good sense, and feel very well, though a trifle over smoked" (Gerty thought he was too fond of his pipe and so he tried to cut down on his smoking).

Two, three, and four thousand words a day, especially under the circumstances, represent an extremely high rate. The amount of writing done shows how fertile his mind was, prompted perhaps by those years of storytelling at Hurstleigh and Clifton.

As yet, though, he had very little to say in his writing. He was working on plots rather than themes. The result was a series of works that pleased and amused him at the time he was writing them but which were frustrating to reread. Sometimes, in fact, his disappointment with their shallowness came before he was halfway through them. He was an author in search of a message without realizing it.

The subject of several of his stories was the one he had used in Store Street: the Bohemian life he had seen and experienced nine and ten years before in Paris. Nigeria did not appear in his writing perhaps because after only two years in the country he had not had time to assimilate its possibilities. Or perhaps he believed the Paris material would have more chance of selling — Bohemia and its artists and models were good standard stuff, whereas only the more bizarre aspects of Africa seemed to attract much attention.

Joyce had always been a reader and now, as he attempted to progress with his writing, he looked at novels with a different interest and insight. Among the books he read in the early part of this second tour were Balzac's *Père Goriot,* a collection of Tolstoi's stories and Thackeray's *The Great Hoggarty Diamond.* His interest in the newer novelists was small. Tolstoi, Conrad, Hardy, and Thackeray were among his favorites. And, of course, since he was so completely cut off from literary trends in England and elsewhere (his subscription to the *Times Literary Supplement* hardly kept him in touch with the *avant-garde*), he ran the risk of being entirely out of step with what was being written and read back home — but he was also freed from the risk of becoming a mere follower of trends.

His worst problem, because he was a beginner and not in touch with any other writers, was a lack of objectivity about his work. In his isolation it was even more difficult for him than for most writers to criticize his writing. Consequently his moods toward it varied more than they might have in England, with higher highs and lower lows. He channeled these moods of elation and depression into his letters to Gerty — this one of October 17, for instance:

> I've just read through the first 20,000 words, of the second draft, and don't know what to make of it. Its certainly very individual, and I don't know if its on account of its goodness or badness. It goes too fast, for one thing, and there's too much conversation in it and too little description. I think I've chosen a difficult form, too, writing in the first person. You see, I can't then explain what anyone is doing except in so far as the man who is speaking (writing that is) comes into contact with them. It has the advantage of giving a sort of unity, and that was why I chose it, but I think I should have been wiser to take an easier form. Also it is extraordinarily hard to critise one's own work.

And then, November 19, after carrying through the second draft of his novel nearly to the end, he broke off and wrote to Gerty,

> I've been suffering from a violent depression about my work. The truth is it is very hard to work in ungenial surroundings — just as if you tried to play and sing among a nation that knew

nothing but barrel-organs. That is one reason why painters, poets, novelists always tend to congregate together, while butchers, grocers and bankers are able to carry on by themselves. I put half my depression down to this — I have no standard of criticism and begin to tell myself my stuff's rotten, and ask myself what's the good of it, and so on. But I am going to make a determined effort to get on again next week.

He slogged on with the draft, as he promised, but now that the pleasure had gone out of the work and his faith in its quality was entirely gone, he dropped it. So, on his twenty-eighth birthday, December 7, he started a new novel. But for all the symbolic significance of the date, his enthusiasm for the new book ebbed quickly and two days before Christmas Joyce wrote,

> I'm a little melancholy, darling, and would like very much to have a massamora with you, to make it up again. My work is hopelessly stuck. I think of those old dirty glorious days in Store Street when I could work. The truth is that here only the worst part of my day is available for writing and the worst part of my mind. Most men here are tired by lunch time — they sleep or lounge all afternoon, and only wake up about half past four when it gets cooler, to take exercise and pay visits. This however is my time for work, and I find the work suffers, I scrapped that first thing, and looking at it again, I know I was right — I started another and am stuck already. How shall I face you if I come home empty-handed and what will you think of me. I am trying to find the courage to start again.

Writing at midday, as he now did, Joyce had to contend with not only the problems of any beginning author working in isolation but the additional ones peculiar to Nigeria. In the hot season he baked and broiled; sweat dripped off his nose and chin and made puddles of diluted ink on the pages even though he had tied a handkerchief around his forehead. Midges would twirl in front of his face and sometimes light on his pen so thick that he had to brush them off after every few words. In the rainy season the paper he wrote on was so sodden that it was like writing on blotting paper, with the words fuzzing, and his monocle steamed over so he had to wipe it off frequently or else work one-eyed. That he could concentrate at all and get some work done under these conditions seems a marvel.

On December 31, New Year's Eve, after working without success for nearly four months, he wrote to Gerty,

> I tried to write this afternoon & made a mess of it again — I'm quite in despair of doing anything, and I think thats why I'm low spirited. . . .
>
> I have made a dozen schemes for a book, but don't get at any of them. I know this country breeds infirmity of purpose in everyone and makes one lazy and unenterprising, as it does for its own people, and perhaps it is significant that I did so much on the voyage and in my first two months here, and so little since. I can only say I will try for I would be ashamed to come back to you empty-handed. But this writing is not like other work. . . . At the first hitch, it is easy to think another course would be better, and the choice is infinite. I suppose that is why people who must write or starve, often do better work than others with apparently much more leisure to perfect and polish what they do, because they can't stop to think and criticize themselves.
>
> Also there is this contest in me — whether to try and write for money, or to write merely what I think good — to try and catch the public eye with a few murders and adulteries, or to amuse myself with my own characters. I suppose I should do both if I can. Meanwhile I foresee a famine in foolscap. Please ask the A & N to send me some the same as I had. . . .

For all his despair, he had plenty to console him, as he told Gerty further on in the same letter:

> This is the end of the wonderful year that has seen me engaged, and married and very nearly a papa — and it leads to 1917 which promises to be a very lean year of separation — 1917 is no more than a space between 1916 and my leave, and I could not count it, if I was not going to grow a year older in it, a year balder, a year more wrinkled.

But he determined to make that next year, 1917, count for something with his writing. Since Gerty was going to bear their child, he should be able to give birth to something himself. And if he did not have to "write or starve," he still had to write if he meant to live the life he wanted at home with Gerty. So he would have to put aside his moodiness and depression ("What ups and downs I have —" he wrote December 7 "— I suppose its the Irish blood") and write his way home.

15

THE HAUSA FAREWELL

CARRYING ON A MARRIAGE by letter, as a lot of other people were finding out during the war, was very unsatisfactory. But when the mails took six or eight weeks each way as they did at Nafada, so that Joyce must wait three to four months to get a reply to a question or a response to a mood, and with the next leave a year and more away, problems did arise. With these conditions and such individual temperaments as Joyce and Gerty had, complications were inevitable.

For instance, Gerty, perhaps even more anxious than Joyce that he should come home to stay, was unable to understand why her husband should write that he was giving up a novel when only a few letters back he had been enthusiastic about it. In his birthday letter of December, 1916, Joyce replied to her temperately enough, but as the letter progresses there is an increasing testiness:

> I don't regret any of it but I have had 10 years now when I might have done something that would make me able to be with you always and leave this cursed mantrap of a country for good and all — and I've done nothing. Not only that but I haven't even stored up wisdom & knowledge towards the future for my memory, always bad and now worsened by quinine makes me always an ignoramus however much I have read or seen or thought. You said you supposed my second draft was a finale — it was darling for I've scrapped the whole thing and am struggling with a new theme. I have been for 3 weeks now but hadn't the courage to tell

you for fear you should say, he'll never do anything that boy. I
remember how you asked me in Heneage's room at Guy's Hospital with the most open scorn why I didn't write "a play or something." But mind you, that book was done — the first draft of it
was a complete short novel — I've thrown it away because it
wasn't good enough.

The letter is a compound of discontent, guilt, self-justification,
and a raking up of past unhappiness. Joyce's pointing to Gerty's
treatment of him in the past is an obvious plea for consolation
from her in his present misery and increasing anxiety over both
his writing and the birth that was coming.

Careening around the anthills on the half-tamed ponies during polo games, small talk with the others at the station, and
Gerty's letters, once they began to come regularly, were all con-
solations and diversions. Discussions between Joyce and Dr.
Rolleston about their mutual problem of developing baldness
were frequent, and Carlyle, Joyce's old friend from Nafada, arrived in late 1916 to make the days a little brighter. Gerty's
letters were barely readable, and Joyce often got more of a general idea of what she was talking about than a detailed picture
— ironically, his own penmanship left much to be desired.

Besides these activities, one of the Maxim gunners found a
baby antelope wandering alone and brought it back to the station, where Joyce took a particular interest in it. The animal
became a real pet, following him around on his walks and bedding down in his house. "The little berewa is sitting under the
China table looking at me all the time as if I was a great surprise
to him, he wonders what I'm glowing about and smiling over,"
Joyce told Gerty one evening in November, but a few days later,
the 17th, he wrote,

> The poor little berewa died this morning. I saw it fall down
> suddenly when it got up from sleep — and struggled. When I
> stroked it it lay still, but struggled again when I stopped. So I
> took it up and petted it and it died quite suddenly. It made no
> sound, of course, which seemed to make its poor quiet pains the
> worse to see. I'm afraid it ate some poisoned weed — it had no
> mother to teach it what was bad and good to eat.

There was a local snake charmer who performed at the station and also cleaned some snakes out of the local drinking well, thus providing the men with a diversion. There were people passing through, too: foresters, some French officers either coming to or going home from their own stations. And there was the polo which Joyce loved for the drama and excitement and kept at in order to stay in good health, besides doing his setting-up and breathing exercises.

On Boxing Day (December 26, when visits and gifts are exchanged in England) Joyce got himself a special Christmas present and wrote to Gerty in exultation,

> I SHOT A GOAL WHAT WHAT. I hit a ball back handed in front of goal for Heathcote to get, but his pony stood up suddenly and there was a wild scrimmage, and I galloped into it too, all dust and cusses and whirling sticks, and suddenly I saw the ball, so I said now then keep cool, and I kept cool and hit the goal. . . .

If the others at the station sometimes kept him from his writing, they also lifted him out of the black moods he was apt to slip into, the melancholy and depression that he ascribed to his "Irish blood." These moods could be a real hazard in Nigeria, as he knew. He had heard of, and on occasion had known, men who were drinking themselves to death from loneliness, frustration, or boredom, although a few years back they had been as young and idealistic as Joyce had been in 1914. There were men who committed suicide, some by blowing their brains out, while others took the less dramatic way of just letting themselves go, succumbing to one of the various diseases that could kill a man when he was not much interested in living.

Now in Nafada, Joyce was living on an English island in the middle of a Nigerian sea. He was dependent on the artificial culture of other whites for amusement, stimulation, and companionship. He had almost always relied on other Britons for his society, except, of course, when he was traveling through the bush with native troops on such treks as the one he took to pave the way for the French fieldpiece needed at Mount Mora. But even then the natives he traveled with were hybrids, British-trained and uniformed soldiers who followed ways similar to those of soldiers anywhere. In Nafada, he was studying Hausa, the *lingua franca* of much of Northern Nigeria, so as to be able to communicate with the natives other than in pidgin English or through interpreters, but it was with Dr. Rolleston, an Englishman and fellow student, that he practiced his Hausa conversation.

On January 3, 1917, Joyce returned to his civilian rank of assistant district officer. He expected to remain in Nafada to run the division, since Carlyle and Heathcote were due for leave. It would be a big job, with an annual tax collection of about £15,000, mostly in pennies and sixpences, a staggering amount of loose change that would have to be counted until Joyce dreamed at night of pennies. Then the money would be packed in old ammunition boxes and be carried to Lokoja by caravans of porters.

Five days later, however, he was ordered back into the WAFF to await further instructions. This state of affairs, of being issued orders and then having them countermanded, became so usual that Joyce now wrote to Gerty,

> Its a comical country, and the truth of all the shilly shallying is that the governor [Lord Lugard] is past his day, a shilly shallier, and very penny wise and pound foolish in all his shortsighted policies. . . .

Not that he minded being a soldier again, because he still hoped for transfer to Tanganyika, where the troops he had trained at Nafada were making a good name for themselves. He would get an extra allowance of pay for service at the front, which would be handy, and he was not worried about being shot, however much the possibility might worry Gerty. He explained his attitude toward battle in a letter to her:

> There is no doubt it has a sort of horrible fascination, even being shot at, as I have felt myself. Before a fight one feels the same as before a football match or more still a rowing race, not at all a pleasant feeling, but after it has begun, it is not as bad as it sounds.

In March Joyce received orders to move not to Tanganyika but to Naraguta and then even further east to Kontagora. This news meant both that he would have to be on the road at the time when he expected news of the baby and that he would be settled for the first time entirely on his own in a native area. The absence of news about Gerty and the birth of the baby was the more immediate concern.

They had written often about the baby, of course. One of the problems was the choice of a name. Since they were certain it would be a boy, Joyce wanted to use the Cary family names (his father suggested Arthur Lucius); Joyce himself, after thinking of Tristram, decided on Anthony. When Gerty suggested Mervyn, he nearly exploded, then carefully explained to Gerty his feelings that names should reflect nationalities and family traditions; since Mervyn was Welsh he wanted only Welshmen to suffer under the name.

He worried over her doctor and his treatment of her and was much relieved when she changed physicians, since he feared that she was being given too much medication (he had a phobia against pills and nostrums except for old and simple ones). He worried that she might hang some frightful name on the poor baby. But most of all he worried that she might have a difficult birth and that he, in Nigeria, could give her no comfort at all.

So his leave-taking of Nafada was hard. After the first day's trek, March 24, 1917, he wrote:

Barno. Here I am in the first rest house on my road, and I am very unhappy, darling. I always used to have my ups and downs, high ups and low downs, just like you, and this is a down. I feel very small and forgotten and lonely, and am very homesick too — not for home, for I haven't one yet, but for you and love. I've never had a home, you know, for I have never been happy at Gunnersbury or at any other place we lived in — my loneliest dreariest most friendless times were spent there, in spite of Dad. But Dad of course was always away, and I had no friends about the place, no men I knew, and Jack was always at sea — no amusements but reading and writing by myself for myself — how I loved Edinburgh, Paris, Ireland, Oxford by comparison. My dearest memories are of Ireland, my grandmother at Clare — that

place was like home and I loved it. This has struck me, because
I have just left Nafada, and was very much troubled by the kindness of everyone to-day — Silver especially [the captain who arrived two weeks before to take over Joyce's army duties] and the
Likita [Dr. Rolleston] — the guard turned out and the buglers
played the Hausa Farewell as I came away down the road. Gordon [his recentmost subaltern] walked out with me a mile or so
till it began to get dark, and then I got on my horse and rode on,
& he went back. . . .

The trek was bad, for Joyce's caravan consisted of fifty loads
borne by undependable porters. After a week of irritation, he
wrote from Domarguya, "I am having a rotten trek — four men
short this morning and no sleep again last night, my fourth
night running."

On April 1, when he reached Bauchi, where he hoped to receive news of Gerty, he was disappointed further. There was
nothing. And of the two men at the station, one was very ill and
the other was nearly dropping from the fatigue of doing two
work loads and nursing his companion. Joyce settled down to
take on the nursing of the sick man, G. W. Izard, until Dr.
Rolleston, who had been summoned by telegraph, could arrive
from Nafada. Izard, with a fever of 103, was in a bad state, so
Joyce was relieved when Rolleston arrived, as well as pleased at
seeing his old friend again. Then the three of them, with Izard
in a hammock, set out for Naraguta, six days away.

On reaching Naraguta he received a cable from Mr. Ogilvie:
Gerty *and* Arthur Lucius Michael Cary were well. "Darling,"
he wrote, "I had the Great News this morning, and am as
pleased as if I had had a bottle of champagne ever since." He
rushed about the station telling people his news and enjoying
their congratulations. He begged Gerty to send him photographs as soon as there were any, and two days later, still in a
euphoric state, wrote,

> My darling, I do hope you are looking after that there Kid
> properly. You must be careful not to drop him, for although it
> mightn't do him any harm, on the other hand, it might. I hope
> you are providing him with his Rations regularly. . . .

But on April 13 he had to be on his way again, catching a train at six in the morning, one that followed the usual schedule of starting at dawn and stopping at dusk, while Joyce and his fellow passengers camped out each night in order to escape temporarily the crowding and heat of the train. It was a wretched trip and his euphoria gave way to grouching:

14.4.17. Another wretched day — this Nigerian railway is the finest invention in the world for making one totally miserable — from six to six I was joggled about in a temperature of about 110 and from six to eight I walked about over railway lines in the dark, trying to find somewhere to put up my bed. But it has not turned out so badly — I found a rest house & am living in the Ladies Only, while there were a most interesting crowd at the Station — we have been bukking [gabbing] away at a great rate and drinking beer and smoking cigars, and I am feeling much better.

At Zungeru he left the train and started the trek for Kontagora. The first day there was a furious thunderstorm that soaked all his gear, and he camped that night with wet clothes, a wet bed, and soggy food. Besides this sodden state of affairs, he had another plague: a cloud of flying ants. "I have to stop sometimes," he told Gerty, "as they fly across the paper or sit down on my eye-glass. But I am very well my dear and very contented & happy too."

On April 29 he arrived in the province of Kontagora, having taken a month to travel nearly three quarters of the way across Nigeria. Kontagora was also the name of the capital of his new province, in which he would have the division of Borgu to care for. Both his division and the province generally were staggering: "the most backward and desert province in Nigeria," he moaned to Gerty, "with an average population of 4 to the square mile." Such a sparsely populated and poor province meant that only a few men would be spread over a huge area and that there would be scarcely any money to spend on improvements. As for his division, Borgu, it was even worse off than the rest of the province, since only a year before there had

been a rebellion against the native administration, and the emir
and two of the chiefs, together with over a hundred of their followers, had been slaughtered. "The people are not against the
white man, so don't be afraid for me, darling," he reassured his
wife, "they were against the bad officials of their own chiefs, who
were not properly looked after by an incompetent D.O."

Joyce revised his opinion of the "incompetent D.O." once he
had met him and had come to appreciate his capabilities (and
found that, on his own with no means of communication except
runners, he had more than enough problems to cope with in
Borgu).

But the recent rebellion meant that he had to start out among
a people in a state of unrest and with totally new officials whose
lack of experience meant he would have little help in settling
in. He was an old enough hand now to be rather apprehensive
about being the

> Lord of some 10,000 square miles, mostly deserted bush, with a
> large population of liones, snakes, crocodiles & mosquitoes — the
> administration is in confusion and the people backward. Hun-
> dreds of miles are swamp. However I am fit — and my tour is go-
> ing forward. Another 7 months should see the end of it.

He had immediate evidence of the state of things: the area
was too full of tsetse flies for him to take his horse, and of the
seven police given to him to run his 10,000-square-mile fief,
three were barely able to hobble around because they were con-
taminated by guinea worm, a parasite that infects the feet and
ankles, laying eggs in the tissue, thus creating great pain and
itching and making walking impossible at times.

If Joyce did not think much of his divison of Borgu, he immediately took to his new superior, the Provincial Resident,
Major Hamilton-Brown. Hamilton-Brown was a jovial older
man, and, since he was terribly understaffed, he was delighted to
see Joyce and made him most welcome. So did Mrs. Hamilton-
Brown, with intimidating fervor. She talked. She talked loudly,
endlessly, harrowingly. She talked to Joyce of her daughters, she
talked of her operations, she talked of her pregnancies and de-

liveries, of her one daughter's flat feet, of anything that came to mind. More than being bored, Joyce was shocked that a woman could talk to a complete stranger about things so intimate. In time he found she was famous for her garrulity, which was a great joke in the northwest.

From a distance it is easy to sympathize with Mrs. Hamilton-Brown. She was one of the very few British women in Northern Nigeria, the only one in a huge province. She had been faced with a dilemma years before: should she stay in England with her growing daughters or in Nigeria with her husband? Since she could not have both and since the daughters were becoming adults, she chose to live in Kontagora with her husband. But the consequence must have been immense loneliness. Her husband and the other men scattered through the province had their work to fill their days. But she had next to nothing. Day after day of emptiness and boredom made any face, especially a new one, a godsend. So she talked.

By the time he left Kontagora for his own divisional headquarters, Joyce could not stand the sight or sound of her.

But when he began the walk into his own vast corner of the province, he was too appalled at what he found to think much more of Mrs. Hamilton-Brown.

16

"OH TO BE IN BORGU, NOW THAT APRIL'S HERE!"

JOYCE MADE PART OF THE TRIP to Borgu with another A.D.O., H.
W. Cowper, whose own divisional headquarters was Yelwa, on
the east bank of the Niger River (Joyce's headquarters, Bussa,
was on the west bank, about fifty miles downstream); Joyce
stayed there for a week in order to get supplies and the records
for Borgu. Since Borgu had been abandoned after the uprising,
he had to make an almost completely fresh start and carry in
everything he imagined he would need for the next few months,
because there would be nothing in Bussa except what he
brought with him.

On the way to Yelwa, Joyce formed a different opinion of
Major Hamilton-Brown, his new Resident, not only from what
Cowper said but from what he saw himself. His original
enthusiasm ebbed rapidly. "In fact," he wrote to Gerty, "they
say he is merely marking time till he gets his pension and doesn't
care a hang for anything but his garden." This revised judgment, which was less than fair, did nothing for Joyce's morale as
he left Yelwa for Bussa.

Joyce's right-hand man in running the division was Musa, officially the Political Agent. He was a sort of liaison between
Joyce and the two local courts, those of the emirs of Bussa and
Kaiama, whose territories were roughly the northern and southern halves of Borgu. A fellow A.D.O. called Musa "A plausible
likeable old rogue, whom one couldn't trust but at the same
time couldn't help liking him." [1] Musa was a chunky, rather

pompous man, full of his own importance, and he confirmed Joyce's opinion that the situation in Borgu was bad. Joyce told Gerty:

> Musa the Political agent says I am going to have plenty to do down here. Noone has been down for a year, and there has been plenty of little kidnappings, affrays, robberies, abductions, and so on in the interval.

Added to the crime problem was the fact that Borgu bordered the French colony of Dahomey, "and Dahomey is not so well administered as Nigeria," Joyce reported; "they seem to be always having trouble, which makes our people restless. Our criminals all run over to Dahomey, and theirs come to us, it is not an advantage to be on a foreign border."

Joyce's most immediate task on arriving in Bussa was to get the paper work done, "answering, numbering, filing, cross-filing letters," and then to begin a census. The latter was essential, because without information on the division, he would have had an impossible time administering it. He had to know how many people he was ruling, what their industries and occupations were, how much livestock they possessed, how much tax he would have to collect; in fact, he would have to know everything possible about Borgu if he were to do a decent job of running the area.

After beginning the census, Joyce next had to clear away the backlog of legal cases that were pending, some of which had been awaiting decision for months. One of his duties in Borgu was to judge all cases that did not belong in one or another of the two emirs' courts, both of which were Class Four and as such could hear only the pettiest of cases. The reason for the limitation was that most of the native administration was new. Joyce dealt with the more important crimes: kidnapping, witchcraft, and murder, as well as instances of political corruption. Witchcraft still was rife in Borgu, which was very backward and, except for the Moslem ruling class, pagan.

Dealing with pagans who believed in witchcraft or juju presented a variety of special problems. An A.D.O. was apt to be

faced with situations that demanded every bit of his ingenuity.
For instance, one A.D.O., who alternated with Joyce in administering Borgu, had to cope with the case of a girl who was believed to be a witch and was therefore tied up and dumped in a
small thatch hut that was then set on fire. When the A.D.O.
found her, she was burned over every inch of her body. As there
were no doctors anywhere near and scarcely any medical supplies, all the A.D.O. could do was douse her with disinfectant
and bandage her up like a mummy. With constant changes of
dressings and liberal slatherings of antiseptic, the girl survived.
In fact, the only damage that remained was that the skin on two
of her fingers had grown together. So the A.D.O. told his orderly
to get a good hold on the girl, picked up a razor blade, and slit
the skin joining the fingers. The girl was completely healthy
again. The real problem was to convince her people that she
was not a witch.[2]

But since nearly everyone in Borgu believed in witchcraft
Joyce had to go slowly in attempting to modify the situation.
The would-be murderers who burned the girl might be punished with a year in prison while a successful murderer might
get a life sentence that would be commuted to five or fewer
years. However modest this judgment might sound to a west-
erner, it was extremely severe for a native of Borgu's backcountry, especially if served in a prison away from the convicted
man's native region. For these people were so attached to their
home country and tribe, and so afraid of foreign places, that
they might die of loneliness if left among "foreigners" twenty or
thirty miles from their village. To be a proper judge in Borgu,
Joyce had to be an educator, too, severing the people from their
ties with juju and superstition.

In order to become a teacher, though, he first had to be a
student, learning the native values, fears, and beliefs. Without
some real understanding of their feelings, he might commit
worse crimes in the name of justice than those he was trying to
correct.

Joyce had done some experimenting with changes of system in
Nafada, where the army wives presented a serious problem, not

just at pay days but all the time. Most of them were not flowers of Nigerian womanhood; rather, they were apt to be prostitutes or petty thieves, since those who were considered good girls usually, under Nigerian patterns, were so strongly attached to their parental homes that they would not move more than a short distance away. Soldiers, who were apt to be transferred anywhere, had to marry girls who would follow them, and such women very often were the ones who had been thrown out of their villages.

So, when the troops marched off to Tanganyika, leaving their wayward wives at Nafada or elsewhere, there was all sorts of trouble and mischief. In desperation, Joyce created a small police force, composed of some of the wives, to cope with the problems, as he told Gerty:

Last week I appointed a Serikin Mata, or queen of the women to look after them. Yesterday after the ordinary orderly room was over, and defaulters marched off — in came the Ser. Mata — a tall stately lady in a blue robe followed by a fierce little woman carrying a large stick scowling furiously — then two prisoners looking highly pleased with themselves — and then another policewoman with a stick and a scowl. The case was conducted with great solemnity — and the police were exceedingly officious about the etiquette of the court — wanting to knock the prisoners down whenever they opened their mouths. One lady was convicted of fighting, the other of loose behaviour in town, and they were both admonished — and warned that they will sit in the stocks at the next offence. The Serikin Mata has really shewn herself most capable — chose her own police — states a case clearly, and is keeping a very unruly crowd of exceedingly unscrupulous women in excellent order. The police take themselves very seriously — they are both rather pretty young ladies but their scowls are terrible to witness when they guard the prisoner and their tones awfully fierce when they admonish her not to shout or pull her clothes off. One lady this morning calmly undressed herself during the case — I suppose to shew her indifference to the proceedings — she was up for a violent assault and battery — and then put on her robes again with the most affected care — to the scandal of the whole court — I didn't laugh till they were out-

side again — one must look solemn on these occasions, — then I
laughed so much I dropped my eye-glass. You must tell Elsie of
these experiments — proving the capacity of women for positions
of authority.

(16 February 1917)

The Elsie to whom Joyce refers here was Gerty's sister, who was
a suffragette and a political activist generally. In 1912, when she
was working on *The Political Quarterly,* her mother found a
Communist pamphlet in her daughter's room at The Glade, literature Elsie was reading simply to keep abreast of the various
political movements. In a terrible fit of indignation, Mrs. Ogilvie ordered her out of the house.[3] Early in the war Elsie had
joined the V.A.D. (hospital volunteers) and had been sent to a
military hospital at Wimereux just north of Boulogne, where
she met and, in July, 1917, married Dr. H. G. Carlisle.

Although Joyce was pleased at the success of his experiment
with Nafada's women, his attitude was patronizing in the extreme, as the letter of February 16 shows. He felt no real sense
of unity with the people or the place, even though in February
he had written and passed his first Hausa examination. But this
proved his proficiency merely in the written, not the oral language. To a great extent he still had to use English with the
native population. And of course the Nigerian who spoke English usually was at a great disadvantage. He spoke it badly and
sounded like a child or a fool, and the listener, without thinking, regarded him as just that. But speaking in his own language, either that of his tribe or the more generally used Hausa,
he might be a very articulate, even poetic, person. Joyce had
not realized this and wrote of his amusement or anger with these
quaint, childlike people. For instance, he described his boy Ojo
going to look for his master's handkerchief:

"I find him, I find him, but I no look him" said Ojo. "Look
again" I said, and Ojo rummaged. "Well," I asked. "I find him,
I see him, but I no look him" said Ojo. This is the best Gold
Coast English, and means that Ojo has searched & searched but
can't set eyes on the handkerchief. To find means to search to see

means to use the eyes in searching, and to look means to see. "You look um proper" is what I say when I want Ojo to watch the house while I'm away. I tell Ojo he must learn Hausa, as coast English is too difficult. . . .

While Joyce could be patronizing to the natives he could also be vitriolic as illustrated by the following outburst of September 24, 1917:

But no black man on Gods Earth is reliable. Let those blasted "my brother the poor black" put that in his pipe. No black man is morally, or mentally, or even physically reliable. Not one can you trust. They're charming fellows plenty of them (not my foul cook, who has the face of a devil, and is morally and mentally a debased scoundrel) but you can not trust 'em. I don't know about Indians, and Aryans generally. They arn't black correctly speaking, I suppose, and I don't know 'em. But your black, your Negroid, and his near relations is a broken reed . . . I hate to lose my temper, I never know what I'm going to do, and it makes me feel a wreck afterwards. . . . If a fellow can't manage these people without violence and cruelty he ought to do something else.

This tirade came more than three years after Joyce first arrived in Nigeria and sounds as if he had learned nothing. But the letter was written when he was once more totally worn out physically and mentally, ready to attack and condemn anything that touched him. It is one of the last expressions of racism that can be found in his writings, private or public.

For that matter, Joyce's sentiments were no more racist than those of most Europeans at the time, and this group included some of the best scientists and medical men, as well as the general population. Today's insanity was 1917's gospel. That Joyce should express such ideas in 1917, whatever his experience, is not surprising; what really is astonishing is the speed and completeness with which he abandoned these thoughts.

17

"ANOTHER TORNADO LAST NIGHT"

THE SUMMER OF 1917 was miserable. It started off with tornadoes in June, and Joyce's house scarcely was ready for a rain shower, let alone a tornado or two. On June 7 he wrote home,

> Dearest, this is really a trying country. Just as I sat down to my soup, to-night, a tornado began. Imagine sitting in a house without walls, but just a roof on posts, with a forty mile wind blowing. I had to dash round to rescue my property, papers, books, clothes, all blowing wildly about. Musa managed to struggle across from the kitchen with the meat at last — but naturally there was more dirt than meat. I have eaten more than my allotted peck of dirt already in this country. I've rigged up an old tent now over my bed so that I hope to have a dry bed now in spite of rain. I am ashamed of the grubby state my letters get into, but the dust and damp is into everything, and can't be kept out.

Two days later he wrote:

> Another tornado last night, which kept me awake till 2 in the morning — all the net blown away, and the rain blowing straight across. I lay under the mat and kept wonderfully dry, but did not have a very good nights rest, as you can guess.

Besides the tornadoes almost every night in early June, he got a terrible scare on the 9th, when he got lost in the bush, where "You might walk 100 miles and never meet a soul." Fortunately, he instinctively followed the right direction, came across a trail, and made his way back to Bussa. He seemed to have been guided by the same sort of luck that had kept him from being blown up or shot at Antivari and had preserved his life at Mount Mora. Because, as he told Gerty,

> The last man I heard of who was bushed, was found eaten by ants — but of course he was badly bushed and noone knew he had gone out. These people always know when I am out, and I daresay they would take the trouble to find me, especially the Emir, as if anything happened to me, the rebels would shoot him. They were apparently doing so just before I came. . . .

The climate of Bussa didn't do him much good. The region was next to the Niger on low, swampy land, and the heavy humidity not only meant that everything, especially clothes, rotted away, but it provided a trigger for Joyce's asthma. The asthma caused sleeplessness, the sleeplessness caused asthma, and the climate caused them both. Joyce gradually sank into the state of bad health and nerves he suffered when he went home in 1916 and which he had determined not to experience again.

The result was a temper that was always on edge, ready to explode. And Joyce did lose control time after time. But now he had an outlet for it in his letters to Gerty and could keep his fury from manifesting itself in violence. On July 26, when he was about to go on a tour of parts of his division to begin a combination survey and census, he wrote:

> This is one of those days one would like to cross out. It is the day before I go and as usual everything has gone wrong — work has suddenly poured in, and I haven't had an instant scarcely to eat. On top of this the corporal of Police turns up mad drunk at 7 oclock and it took me two hours to unpack papers, files, etc and arrange for sending him in to the Resident, who will probably pardon him, as he also is getting superannuated. The state of this Province is rotten all through, police, native administrations and all, and it won't wake up till we change the Resident, who is simply marking time till he gets his pension. . . . Its a bad province anyhow, with a wretched small population of pagans little removed from monkeys, and so of course it is neglected, understaffed. 4 white men in a country as big as Wales. I believe I have

a filthy trek to-morrow with three rivers to cross, and no canoes, which means getting soaked to the neck, and the Emir insists on coming with me so I will have a lot of fools prancing round me on half broke horses all the way, and the drums and trumpets going for five hours. . . .

His criticisms were directed at far more than the province, though; they covered all Nigeria, her governor, Lord Lugard, and the British Colonial Office:

I really believe that there is no government in the world so mean as the British — so mean, so time serving, so short-sighted, so hypocritical. Do you know for instance what is the basis of government in Southern Nigeria, what pays the tax, what is the basis of trade, its gin, gin by the millions pounds worth. That very liberal party that was so mealy mouthed about temperance at home, and the treatment of subject races, stopped discussion on this very matter in Parliament, when it looked like danger to their profits — gin was sacred. And Southern Nigeria is enormously rich — one of the richest palm oil countries in the world — but 75 per cent of the oil nuts rot every year for lack of picking. The Government prefer to carry on on gin, rather than develope it. Northern Nigeria is honestly governed, but very meanly. A few hundred thousand on roads and bridges would be worth millions in a few years, but they won't do it. Instead of that the whole notion is to scrape a penny saving here or there and make the place pay, as Thingumbob made his bed do for him, by cutting off his legs. The latest notion is to make twopence half penny a year out of the A.D.Os (this is the sting you see that led me to all this fine indignation. Up to this, an A.D.O. doing a D.O.s work, that is, running a district of a quarter of a million or so, and taking responsibility for it, has drawn a D.O.s Duty pay. The Government did not suffer as only so many Duty pays are allotted to each province, and unless one were vacant, the A.D.O. didn't get it. Now no A.D.O. is to get Duty pay unless there is no D.O. in the province that could do his work, supposing he was free. This will save the Government possibly sixty pounds or so a year at the expense of the poorest and most over worked officials in the country. There is no redress, no Trades Union, noone to ask questions in Parliament. Any official who ever objected would be a marked man. Two men were hounded out of the country by the Government only a year or two ago, for trying to get better conditions for junior officials. It is easy enough to do. They send him to an unhealthy place, and kill him with overwork, refuse his increments, and pass him over for promotion. Lugard is a mean man, and a spiteful man. He will take a great deal of trouble to put an enemy or a critic out of the way.

(28 February 1917)

In August, Joyce found fault with the War Office, as well as the government, in criticizing the campaign in Mesopotamia to take and hold Turkey's principal oil fields:

That Mesopotamia is exactly what one expected knowing how Colonial Government is carried on. We also had our disaster for reasons still obscure, in the Cameroons, but luckily retrieved it by our own efforts, no thanks to any damn Cuthberts, and so pulled the chestnuts out of the fire for the high and mighty. This country out here is run as far as officials are concerned on purely Russian lines — with an iron censorship. If this letter was seen by any of the bigwigs, my promotion would probably be stopped, and I should find myself in some death trap of a station. Its Hush Hush when things go wrong, & blunders are made and some wretched A.D.O. gets chewed up, Mesopotamia on a small scale all over the Coast, and all through India too. The only way a Governor can commend himself to a Secretary of State is by economies (see the initial trouble in India) and the only people he can fleece are the Services, so he does. He does it all the time. All the time out here they make little sneaking amendments to the regulations knocking off a few shillings of allowance there, and a pound here — its very easy — noone can complain — if he does, he's fired out at an age when he can't make a new start, when he's rotten with the climate, and unfit for anything else. Look at the polite things said in Mesopotters to subordinates Carter and Cowper who ventured to suggest that things might be improved — they were both told flatly they would be turned out of their posts at once — what for — in this case for doing their duty. . . . Government is a trickster and a liar. They never keep their agreements — as I say they're always changing 'em now, and always for

the officials harm. I'm always wondering, like most of us, and
many poor devils worse off than me, who would have to take any
terms lying down, what they'll do next.

(22 August 1917)

This frequent lashing out at everything and everyone, particularly at authority, was a sign of Joyce's declining health and
was immeasurably compounded by the sheer loneliness of life in
Bussa, where, even had he wanted to chat with the natives, he
could not do so properly because of the language barrier. However he did not want to talk to them, because he wasn't interested in them, except from the administrative point of view.
Beset with a terrific amount of work, much of it a backlog, and
plagued by miserable living conditions and faltering health, he
drew into himself as sick people often do and became increasingly cranky, a cynic, a man with a grievance, who feels he has
not been dealt with honestly and justly.

Just how lonely he was is indicated in a passage from his letter
to Gerty of July 13:

> I was reduced to making faces at myself in my lamp-shade to-
> night, which acts as a distorting mirror, for a little human com-
> panionship and amusement. Really one gets a trifle weary of ones
> own company after a time — its impossible to play any games for
> instance, or get anyone else's opinion on anything.

Although he hated card games, he would even have played at
one for the company. Instead, each evening he took his one solitary drink and, dressed in pajamas and mosquito boots (high
boots of soft leather), smoked a lonely pipe in his ratty deck
chair in front of his shabby house.

Joyce lacked stimulus for the one available pursuit — writing.
He had commented in his diary in Paris during the Christmas
vacation he spent there in 1910–1911 with John Middleton
Murry:

> Talk and friends after all are more necessary than three meals
> a day. Indeed in Bohemia, than any meals, for with no talk, no

ideas, and with no ideas, no work, and with no work, neither happiness nor meals.

Now he had neither talk nor friends and certainly not much
happiness. But he tried hard to work all the same. He was irritated by a handsome review of a new novel by Murry in the
Times Literary Supplement and wrote,

> He was a scamp that fellow. The novel sounds just the sort of
> thing I would have expected from him — confused sex relations,
> neurotic love affairs — and a great anxiety for originality at all
> costs. But if he writes novels — why shouldn't I?? What darling.
> Except that he was a much cleverer fellow & gives all his time to it
> I see no reason at all.

Murry's success rankled. Several times Joyce wrote to Gerty that
he wished he had stayed in Store Street and done nothing else
but write — or not even gone to Oxford but just sat down and
worked at becoming a novelist. This idea must have made unpleasant reading for her, for had he not gone to Oxford, they
might not have met and married.

He started several novels, writing to ask Gerty to give him
information he needed: titles of Scarlatti's works, copies of the
Times, bits from *Burke's Peerage* and *Who's Who*. And he
begged for books, which she sent him in great quantities.

On July 4 he had bad news. He received new orders that his
leave, if and when he got it, would be for only three months,
rather than the nine he would be owed. He was ordered to send
in a medical certificate *at once* to indicate his fitness for active
service. Since the nearest doctor was 200 miles away, a journey
of about two weeks each way, he had to examine himself, judge
the results, and declare whether or not he was fit for active service — but where, though? Did the order mean he was going to
Tanganyika? Or perhaps France or Mesopotamia?

As there were only four men to run all of Kontagora Province, including the Resident, Major Hamilton-Brown, who was
getting closer and closer to retirement and had a bad heart as
well, and as there were no reliefs and not one new man coming

into the service at the time, Joyce scarcely believed he would be shipped out of the country. With Borgu's recent history of re- bellion and murder, and with the Iseyin Revolt of 1916, fo- mented by the Germans to drain off as many British troops as possible, the idea of further stripping the country of staff would be absurd.

But of course he hadn't much faith then in the sense of the government; it could do the absurd quite easily, he thought, and he would have been delighted to go. The order and the medical certificate, however, were just one more instance of red tape and nonsense.

Of course Gerty, receiving his letters that oozed misery, wanted him to come home even more than ever. She wrote to urge him to leave the Service. The idea of a separation lasting another dozen years and of their mutual misery and loneliness made her state her case as strongly as possible, too strongly, and on August 10 Joyce replied,

> My dearest I was made awfully unhappy by some things in your letter, where you say I have decided irrevocably to stay in Nigeria, and that I am wasting both our lives. My darling I have decided nothing. Michael and any other children I may have, decided that I must make money. I would give anything to be with you always, surely my dearest you know how miserable I am to leave you. . . . Do you not suppose life is dear to me? Do you not think I feel this exile from all I hold most dear, and the only things I like in ma- terial life, letters, and books and pictures? I dare not look forward to all the years, or think that this climate may shorten my life, and I don't, or I would never be happy for a moment. . . . I have made great efforts this tour already and written as much as would make three novels, but never finished anything. You may call me all the bad names you like, I deserve them. Here is my only chance, and I haven't the application to carry it through.

Once he had been able to blot out both the future and the past if they looked unpleasant. Now, however, he had a wife who shared his future, and he had to think of it. So he made a new attempt at writing. A plan, born out of his unhappiness and frustration and prompted by Gerty's letter, came to him the day after his August 10 reply to her. He announced with great pride,

> I've thought of a dabara (which is Hausa for a cunning plan, or gadget) to defeat myself over the writing. I shall vow to do 1000 words a day (this is not a very heavy task) till I have finished the novel I am working at, and I shall report to you every Saturday how much I have done during the week of the *same novel,* and certify to you that I have done also 1000 words a day. You must *keep me at it* sweetheart and damn me if I don't go on, and tell me again that it is important for both of us I should go on. This is Saturday. The novel is called provisionally "the Episode."
>
> (11 August 1917)

18

"A FAMOUS ACCORDION SOLOIST"

Now THAT JOYCE was again launched on a novel with a system he hoped would keep him writing until completion, he felt a new surge of self-confidence. "Darling I can write," he crowed to Gerty on August 12. "I am not at all a kind critic of myself, and reading old stuff to-day, I see that I can do quite as well as the average and better than some."

Besides forcing himself to continue writing a novel once he had begun, Joyce now was consciously working at a style, attempting to pare down his prose. "I seem sometimes to be too florid," he said, "sometimes too narrow, sometimes I have too large and full a canvas with too many figures, sometimes too bare and small with too few."

He kept his promise of a weekly report to Gerty for almost a month and a half, although midway through those six weeks he changed novels once again, scrapped the second one, and began a third under the scheme. The present novel must have been the sixth or seventh since New Year's Day, 1917, and, according to Joyce, "at least the 20th this tour, which, of course, began in August, 1916, and none finished." If this statement shows a lack of persistence, it also proves his inventiveness. He spilled over with plots, a position that many beginners would have envied. But the problem was still in finding ideas that continued to have meaning for him, and he had no real notion of where he was going yet or of what concepts he wanted to incorporate in his work or, in fact, what he wanted to use as a basis for his novels.

Since his writing was going somewhat better in August and September, Joyce's mood improved, and he rooted out his old concertina to give himself a few bush concerts and to do some singing, too (however bad his singing was, it was better than making faces at himself in his lampshade). He played every piece he could remember, sitting on the decaying verandah of his sleazy house in the evening and presenting an absurd sight to any traveler who might appear in the middle of the bush. The songs, he told Gerty, were

> Drink to me only with thine eyes, Cherry Ripe, Poor old Joe, the Swanee River, The Tarpaulin Jacket, My Bonny is over the ocean, what can the matter be, O where o where is my little dog gone, He that drinketh brown ale, So early in the morning, Daisy, Daisy, give me your answer do, The wearing of the green, Home Sweet Home, There is a happy land, King Alfred had three sons, Campdown Races, Tom Bowling, Green Grow the Rushes O and the Vicar of Bray.
>
> (Mosé, 16 July 1917)

"Refreshments were served during the evening," he announced, "and smoking was allowed. It is hoped to repeat this successful innovation, for the benefit of the Tobacco Fund for the Officials of Borgu Division."

What made him look even more like the village idiot at this concert "given by a famous accordion soloist" was his clothing. The myth that even in the heart of the jungle the Englishman always dressed for dinner was utterly exploded at Bussa. During the day Joyce wore a pair of one-legged riding breeches (the right leg had simply disintegrated, so if he wanted to make a formal appearance he had to stand sideways to his company), shirt, mosquito boots, and helmet and rode around on a native pony. In the evening he usually wore pajamas and mosquito boots. Everything he had was shabby, ragged, and rotten. The tremendous humidity of the rainy season saw to that, and the ants did their bit. Even though he dressed and undressed as carefully as possible, peeling off his clothes "like the skin of a banana," they ripped. They mildewed and rotted or simply disintegrated when they were laundered, and his boots lost their

soles. Since he had nobody to act as barber, he either cut his
own hair, using a distorted mirror, or else did not cut it at all,
thus adding to his scarecrow look. But there was no one to look
and laugh at him. The natives of Borgu had no standards by
which to judge him.

However unsuccessful he was in finishing his novels, Joyce
had made a good start at administering Borgu. His July survey-
census trek to Kaiama went quite successfully, and he was
pleased with himself:

> Last year the cow tax brought in £200. and as the place has now
> been administered 15 years, it might be supposed the cows were
> well counted. With any luck though I shall double this tax. I've
> put the fear of God in the mallams somehow, I don't know how,
> for I'm very polite, and already 2000 cows have been miraculously
> discovered that weren't last year. I have suggested to them that
> perhaps the cows in this part all have triplets, and then I laugh
> like mad, and they look at me as if I was a Dodo, or devil — I
> skirt round this subject till they're all so nervous they fairly
> jibber, and then I say how well they're doing the work and send
> them off. I've raised their pay too, and altogether I think they
> understand that bygones are bygones and if they do their work,
> I'll treat them properly. I am beginning to know how to manage
> the black man (dare I boast — not really) or think I do — the
> first thing is politeness, never be rude or violent, the second is
> patience, let 'em go slow if they want to as long as they are trying,
> the third is rigid justice, where a man wilfully does wrong and
> you're sure its wilful, jump with both feet, the fourth is, explain
> to them carefully and exactly their work, and *why* it is important,
> *why* you want it done this way, then all you've got to do is watch,
> watch, watch, distrust everything you don't see yourself, check
> everything yourself. Half of this small success here is due to the
> fact that they know I'm watching, and of course imagine I can see
> a hundred times more than I really can — conscience is all on my
> side.
>
> (Ibesha, 25 July 1917)

What Joyce does not mention in this letter is his monocle,
which earned him the nicknames "three eyes" and "glass-eyes,"

only two of the many he was given, most of which he never heard because they were not very complimentary. In a superstitious area, where an eyeglass had never been seen, Joyce must have inspired some fear in the natives of extra powers.

What he does mention in the letter is his prescription for dealing with the mallams of Borgu and even the general population — politeness, patience, justice, careful explanation of methods and reasons for them, and close supervision — a formula for good teaching anywhere and with anyone. He said "I am beginning to know how to manage the black man," as if the natives were a unique order of beings — and to Joyce they still were. At the same time, he shows he had learned some respect for their intelligence. These people of Borgu were ignorant, but they were not stupid. The same approach might be applied to them as to anyone. And when they learned not only how to perform a task, but why it was significant and how they might benefit from it (which was by far the most important aspect), then they could work well. The biggest problem was not stupidity but provinciality and tribal custom which caused all new ideas to be viewed as a threat. This feeling was especially true in the courts of the emirs, who saw innovations as threats to their own stability and power.

Joyce put into effect the lesson he had learned in Nafada when he created his Serikin Mata and her police force to keep the army wives in check. He began a small education project for the mallams in one area, as he explained to Gerty:

. . . a most exasperating afternoon with a dunder headed mallam who had all his cow lists in such a mess he himself couldn't make head or tail of 'em — the poor old boy sitting on the floor among a pile of dirty papers, wagging his old grey beard and wildly searching for some piece of very simple information, still makes me laugh and cuss at once to remember. He was an honest old man though, I think, and I fancy he is not quite so bribable as some of 'em. He is taking a lesson in arrangement of statistics from Audu dan Sakaba to-night. Audu is aged 16, and has come from School, where he has learnt to write English characters (not to speak or write English, but Hausa in English letters) and arith-

metic. He is a chief's son, and acts as assistant Treasurer to
Bussa Emirate. He is a blessing because he can really add up,
writes well, and has sense. Otherwise he is just an ordinary
Schoolboy, very bored at a long session, very fidgety, and inclined
to screw himself into a corner behind me somewhere, where he
curls up and dozes. I make him teach all the mallams. These
revered old gentlemen are very comical at their lessons. They are
very dignified, and at the same time very eager to learn. A learned
man out here is always anxious for new learning, contrary to the
European plan.

(Okuta, 27 July 1917)

The last comment marks quite a change of attitude.

And the evidence that Audu, a native of Borgu, could do an
excellent job once he had had a decent brush with education was
an important lesson for Joyce. His comment that Audu was
"just an ordinary Schoolboy" shows a penetration of the superficial barrier of color and a lessening of Joyce's feeling that these
Borgu people were a separate order of beings.

The problem of coping with witchcraft and superstition
remained, however, even if the mallams were learning something about statistics. In Bure on August 1 Joyce had to judge a
case of alleged murder and became thoroughly exasperated:

I spent the whole afternoon in a perfectly maddening contest
with superstition and stupidity. An old man accuses his brother
of killing all his children by witch craft, and nothing would shift
him. He went to some witch in the South who told him it was his
brother. I of course cannot tell them their religion is worse than
nonsense (those witches are the most awful swindlers), besides it
would do no good. I found out at last the children died of smallpox!! Even then he won't believe his brother didn't do it. I made
the brother say, if I killed the children, may the Safi (or religion)
kill me, which he did quite willingly, and this did a little appease
the other. You wonder why I take all this trouble. It is quite a
serious matter. Dozens of people came up to hear the case, and
feeling might easily run to bloodshed. I also told him to destroy
his old house, isolate his patient and so on. But small pox is well
known here, and fairly well understood. In spite of this, this old

man is sure his brother is killing his children with it, and makes no effort to use even native science. I am thankfull Mahomedanism is spreading. It does a great deal to stop all the witchcraft, at least the malignant kind.

(Bure, 1 August 1917)

Sometimes witchcraft could come in handy for an A.D.O. For instance, when Percy Diggle was sure that three witnesses were perjuring themselves, he took them to a juju priest and had them swear to the truth of their testimony in front of the holy man (who charged threepence apiece). Inside of a month all three were dead from "causes unknown." [1] Joyce, who detested the juju business thoroughly, would not use this technique; his monocle seems to have done almost as good a job of intimidating perjurers.

The survey-census Joyce began in July of 1917 was probably the greatest factor in his acclimatization. "I have 7 districts to report on," he told Gerty, "and each town in each district, Forestry, Agriculture, Geology, History, Flora and Fauna, Geneologies and titles of chiefs as well as population, local industries, and crops and average income."

This duty was a tremendous change from his initial job in Borgu of policeman, judge, and tax collector. As policeman and judge, he saw the worst side of Borgu. He was constantly exposed to robbers, murderers, swindlers, and liars. As tax collector, too, he had to cope with evasion and lying. Of course his picture of the area and its people was conditioned by these jobs and by the people he encountered in his ramshackle office-courtroom.

The survey, though, took him out of the office and away from a situation where he had to be constantly suspicious. It thrust him into the villages and the homes of more ordinary people, into conversations about the problems of the area and the ways its people tried to deal with them. It gave him a truer and better picture of Borgu. He grew more interested, more open, and more sympathetic.

And of course the people of the area felt increasingly at ease with him, sometimes too much so. For instance, one old woman came to see him while he was sitting in his little galvanized bath tub and poured out her troubles to him at great length while he sponged and soaped away. Musa, the Political Agent, was scandalized. But, as Joyce commented, there was nothing to be scandalized about, since "she had very little more on herself than me."

As an absentee father who saw his son Michael only in photographs and through Gerty's comments in her letters, Joyce was especially receptive to the children of the country and took great pleasure in watching them. He was particularly pleased when one day three policemen's children came to pay their respects to him, wearing respectively a necklace, an earring, and a bangle and nothing else. "The smallest girl who was not more than 3," he reported to Gerty, "lost her nerve when it came to the point, burst into tears and fled for her life. The other two behaved with great propriety. I gave them pennies, and the young lady suggested that her sister ought to have a penny too, so I sent the sister a penny." As for Joyce, he went around smiling for the rest of the day; "I could not even be severe enough in a private interview with the Emir this evening, who has 15 wives already, and yet insists on trying to grab other people's."

Gradually, as he got more and more involved in his new work, he lapsed into depression or anger far less. He had a project of converting oyster shells into lime, a worthwhile idea in a country whose soil tended to be acid because of the swampiness. Another goal was getting his house in order since its floors were so rotten that unless he stepped carefully, he'd put his foot through them. Both of these activities helped improve his state of mind, and he began taking more interest not only in the people but in the animal life around him, reporting to Gerty on the family of toads which lived under his bed and his pleasure at the birds that nested in the thatched roof of his house and were constantly singing and flying in and out of the doors. He was less keen on the abundant lizards and the hyenas that came and yelped in his doorway at night and stampeded the cows. "I understand now," he told Gerty, "how people in the Bastille made friends of mice and rats and toads. In some ways they are more satisfactory than human friends."

Even his views on Major Hamilton-Brown changed for the better. For instance, he wrote on September 27,

> Poor old Hammy has been starved for staff for years and now he has suddenly got four men under him. He is getting things done at last. If I go [Joyce was still occasionally being asked if he were fit for military service overseas], everything will be hung up. Not because my work is so important, so much as that someone else will then have to do it, and there will only be just enough men to go round. It is the one extra that matters — because he can do work that is not routine.

By the time the rainy season began at the end of September, Joyce was the happiest he had been since spending his 1916 leave with Gerty. The fact that the dirt floor of his house became a series of ponds, puddles, lakes, and rivers, with his bed set on one of the few major islands, and that his roof was half blown away by winds of nearly hurricane strength, hardly disturbed him. He was quite ready to console himself with the idea that the situation could be a good deal worse; after all, "The guard house was blown away altogether in the barracks so that I am perhaps not unlucky." A few months before, though, he would have been cursing the natives, the governor, and Lloyd George.

Possibly not all this apparent change of mood was real. Gerty, after all Joyce's talk of depressions and outbursts of temper in his letters of the spring and early summer, had again written him several times to urge him to look for work in England. Then he could be rid of such dreadful surroundings and loneliness, and they could be together for more than a few months every second year. Why couldn't he become a teacher, she suggested, as her brother-in-law was at Harrow. Mrs. Ogilvie also wrote to tell Joyce how unhappy Gerty seemed. Joyce tried his best to cheer his wife up, but as for the teaching job, he told her he simply did not have the qualifications and it was useless to think of trying for a place. Gerty was not prepared to accept this answer, either then or when he gave it so many times in the future.

So, whether he really meant it or whether it was to please

Gerty and at the same time rebut some of her arguments that he
must leave Nigeria, Joyce wrote increasingly cheerful letters in
the autumn of 1917.

Circumstances were improving, however. For instance, when
a new detachment of police arrived in mid-October, Joyce wrote
home,

> Do you remember a slight breeze I had here with a drunken
> corporal last June, whom I sent back to Hammy [Major Hamil-
> ton-Brown] with a stinker. It has had the most comical effect.
> All the police are terrified of me, especially the N.C.Os. The
> truth is that the police are run very slackly. It is wonderful how
> good they are considering. They are nearly always out in small
> detachments with political officers who either don't know any
> military training, or don't bother to import it. Add to this the
> tender heartedness which permits N.C.Os to keep their stripes
> when they are quite incompetent, and have forgotten everything
> they ever knew. This corporal must have spread awful reports
> about me. The next detachment trembled visibly at my voice,
> and the Sergeant's eyes bulged with anxiety. But we got on very
> well. Drill improved greatly, and with it general smartness and
> discipline. The Sergeant discovered what I wanted, and found
> that really he could quite approve of it.
>
> Now this new detachment just arrived is trembling and bulg-
> ing. . . . The Sergeant I knew of old — a little knock kneed old
> rascal, who thinks he can turn any white man round his finger —
> a master of eyewash, and I should fancy a heavy drinker. But he
> is smart enough — and he is so nervous of me just now that per-
> haps he will keep off the liquor.
>
> (22 October 1917)

Then on October 28 he received word he was to be relieved in
Borgu by another A.D.O., Percy Diggle. "I am told 'that in exi-
gencies of the public service etc etc one officer is to go on
leave,' " but he had no idea if he were to be that officer or if he'd
simply be transferred to another division. To get his hopes up
and then find out he was only going to be reassigned would be
very disappointing.

He turned his mind toward the more immediate subject, his first British visitor in Borgu. Half facetiously he commented,

> I wonder what Diggle will be like. I'm quite curious about my first visitor since May. I wonder have I got any eccentric tricks in these months. Perhaps I am not fit for society any more. . . .
>
> (30 October 1917)

Then on November 1 he heard from H. W. Cowper at Yelwa that *he* was coming to take over Borgu and that he believed Joyce was meant to go home on leave. Again Joyce tried to keep his hopes from soaring.

Joyce's most immediate task was to get all his records absolutely up to date and outline the various projects he had begun in Borgu, so that the new man — whoever it would be — could take over with no trouble. To add to his work, his cook came down with a temperature of 104.4, and Joyce had to put him to bed under a heap of blankets and give him fifteen grains of quinine to break the fever.

On November 15 new word arrived: Cowper was not coming, after all. But Diggle was. "So I don't know when I will get away. I am nerving myself for some sort of catastrophe probably unexpected." On the 21st, for whomever was coming, he gave himself his first haircut in months. "It had regular ringlets in it all over. I send you some," he told Gerty, "to show the state I was in. Now I look as if I had been eaten by rats."

Diggle did arrive, finally, on November 25, with the first definite news that Joyce was getting leave to go home to his seven-month-old son and the wife to whom he had been married a year and a half and whose company he had enjoyed for only two months.

19

LEAVE, 1918

JOYCE FAILED to get home in time for Christmas as he had hoped. He had not had a proper Christmas since he had been a student at Oxford, and he was looking forward to the turkey, the chestnut dressing, the plum pudding, and the festivity of it all. He loved family gatherings and rituals. The get-togethers in Donegal or at his Uncle Tristram's Cromwell House had been the happiest times of his childhood. And the food had been something to dream about during the months in Borgu, where the monotonous menu had driven him to this outburst:

> o how I *hate* and *loathe* the sight of the filthy food — meal after meal day after day — greasy soups, watery chickens, milk pudding with bad eggs in it [Almost every village Joyce went to gave him a present of all its eggs — for which they expected a return present of money — and since no A.D.O. had been in the country for a year, they had a prodigious number of old eggs to give him] — the only thing I eat that doesn't turn my stomach is the morning porridge. O for a potatoe! a piece of cold beef! vegetables! cheese! a glass of port. Sometimes I have a real longing for a glass of port. I'd give a good deal for a bottle of good port here.
>
> (24 September 1917)

The soup was inevitably a slop of water and peanuts, and the chicken was skinny, tough, and half wild. So the loss of a Christmas dinner at home meant a great deal, especially since it would have been his first with Gerty and Michael.

But to get home at all with Nigeria in its wartime under-staffed state was a bit of a miracle, and as he drew nearer to England his anticipation of seeing Gerty again replaced his disappointment.

Joyce arrived at Liverpool in weather which stayed cold, damp, and foggy until he reached London. He barely caught the train to Harrow Weald Station and when he arrived there, no cabs were to be had, so he left his luggage and walked to The Glade. When he was nearly there a runaway horse and wagon suddenly lunged out of the fog straight at him. The animal jumped the curb but veered enough so that Joyce was knocked flying but not run down. The wagon shaft missed him by two inches as it shot by, and then all of them — Joyce, horse, and wagon — crashed into a hedge.

It was another of those near tragedies; the amazing escapes that had happened so often to him were simply a case of sheer, blind luck. "What a pretty tragedy it would have been if the shaft had hit me instead of missing me by two inches," he wrote later to Gerty:

"Poor young man killed within a mile of home" Would you have been sad if I came home on a shutter. But I was born to escape this sort of thing — I shall not die a violent death. My insurance money will be wasted.

(5 February 1919)

After crawling out of the hedge and tidying his clothes, he hurried on to The Glade, rushing up into the hall where he was met by Mrs. Ogilvie and Elsie. After brief hello's he dashed up the stairs to the room where they said Gerty was waiting. "Then my first peep of Michael," he remembered, "with his nose in the pillow and a very grave quiet supper afterwards." [1]

The leave, lasting from February until the end of July (a compromise between the eight months he was owed and the three that were supposed to be the official wartime limit), was spent in a flurry of visits to the theater, to friends, to relatives, to the doctor, and to a nursing home for an operation on his nose, meant to correct the damage done years back at Clifton, when it had been broken at both boxing and football ("30 guineas spent to repair a kick on the nose from a 15/-boot," he wrote to Gerty). He hoped the operation would end the constant colds he had had on the last tour — and the asthma which they often triggered — especially on the boat going back to Nigeria. They had been one of the reasons for his low spirits and shortness of temper, he thought.

Joyce's 1918 leave was more hectic than the previous one, because this time he was in much better health. With his new interest in Borgu and his more serious attempts at writing, he had made up in the autumn for his ill health of early summer. Joyce and Gerty found time for another stay in the country, though, this time in Devon at Exeter, where they hiked, sat quietly on the shore, ate good country meals in whatever inn was handy on their walks, and slept soundly in the sea air.

Life at The Glade was almost as good, in between their frantic rushing about. Joyce played rough-and-tumble with Michael and carried him about like a satchel by the slack of his pinafore. Michael loved the game, but Gerty told Joyce he was too rough. There was a damper laid on life at The Glade, however, by Mrs. Ogilvie.

Her Calvinism and her strong-mindedness made living at such close quarters difficult at times. Joyce, with his agnosticism and love of pleasure and with his hopes of becoming a writer, might be acceptable to her as a son-in-law in wartime, but as one with whom she had to live, he was as irritating to her as she sometimes was to him. So there were tensions.

Pressures increased when Gerty found herself pregnant again. Some inevitable pattern seemed to be taking shape: Joyce would come home on leave, Gerty would become pregnant, Joyce would return to Nigeria, and Gerty would be left at home to have her baby and care for the other children. She urged him again to look for work in England, and her mother backed her. Joyce told her once more that there was nothing he could do. He must stay in Nigeria until he could support her and the two children from his writing, whenever that might be.

The outburst came at a theater party with Freddy. The running argument lasted through the first part of the play, ironically called "The Naughty Wife," when suddenly at the intermission Joyce exploded and verbally slapped her down. They went back to their seats, Gerty with her lips trembling and tears running down her cheeks through the rest of the comedy. Joyce was miserable, too, and damned himself for months afterward for making her so unhappy. They made up, but the reason for the fight remained.

Even with all its shortcomings and frantic pace, the leave was a great success. Joyce's only regret — aside from the fact that it slipped by so quickly — was that he had done very little writing, although he had come home with the best of intentions, planning to complete a novel at last. After all, the sooner he got something finished to his own satisfaction and sold it, the sooner the whole business of short leaves and long absences, with all their loneliness for them both, would be at an end.

In July he made the solitary trip back to Liverpool to board the *Burutu*. He was determined that during this tour he would finish a book and perhaps make it the last tour of all. He would see a novel through and then set about looking for a market. He had decided now that he would be a commercial writer, at least for the time being, until he had begun to establish himself. It was silly to have too many scruples and throw the best years of his and Gerty's lives away as a result.

On arriving in Liverpool he was unable to board his ship at once. A convoy had arrived at the port to discharge great numbers of American troops, and the *Burutu* had been ordered to leave the dockside and stand at anchor in the middle of the Mersey basin. Joyce had been quite upset by the Russian Revolutions of April and November, 1917, for they seemed to mean a lengthy prolonging of the war, continued suffering for everyone, and years more of short and infrequent leaves; thus, he was delighted at the sight in the harbor. "The Americans were a splendid looking crowd — thousands & thousands of them," he reported to Gerty when he was able to board his ship. "They say that their numbers have been purposely understated."

This sight lifted him out of the gloom he felt at leaving home. A swift ending of the war would have so many results. Jack Cary would be freed from his Turkish prison camp and shipped home. Heneage and Freddy Ogilvie would return from France, as would Duncan MacGregor and many other friends. Nigeria would be on a peacetime footing, which meant, he thought, not only longer and more frequent leaves but that a great many more young men would come into the Service and larger sums of money would be spent for the bridges and roads and agricultural improvements. The end of the war would have important consequences for Nigeria.

MAPPING BORGU

IN THE SUMMER of 1918 Germany, having knocked Russia out of the war, turned all her strength to the west, while at sea her U-boats were doing their worst, sinking an enormous tonnage of shipping. So the *Burutu* joined a convoy bound northwest, rather than coming down the coast of France, Spain, and Portugal. The result for Joyce, who had brought only summer clothes, was a cold in the head, despite the operation he had had that spring in a London nursing home. The cold lasted through the rest of the voyage and seemed to be almost gone one day only to be much worse the next. Joyce's temper, however salved it may have been by the sight of the American troops, grew raw, and he was especially irritated by one of the men at his table, a supercilious young Cambridge graduate, who confided to Joyce that he wrote poetry and whom Joyce, in writing to Gerty on August 3, called "an absurd fellow — with the drawl — the drooping eyelid — and the mock-original opinions one associates with his kind. He is a perfect specimen. I am treasuring him. But he would not do in a book. The thing is too hackneyed."

On their seventh day out, at dinner (another man at the table was Major Hamilton-Brown), the fellow made a few silly, mocking remarks while Joyce was speaking. Joyce jerked around to him, raging, and said, "Are you trying to be rude to me, P——, because if you are, I'll push your face through the back of your neck and bloody quick too!" There was a stunned silence from everyone at the table, while Joyce sat, unable to stop shaking with fury, staring at the other man.

After a moment the conversation, awkward and forced, was resumed, while Joyce's anger slowly gave way to embarrassment and silent self-condemnation. "I've not done such a thing for a long time now," Joyce mourned to Gerty that night, "& thought I had better control of myself." As he said earlier in this letter, "One reason why I am usually so careful of my tongue, is that if I do let it go, my temper goes too."

The young man, Joyce noted, "took occasion to talk sociably later on," but Joyce felt that he had made a fool of himself and would be talked about for the rest of the trip.

To add to his discomfort, he shared his small cabin, with its blacked-out, sealed porthole, with two men rather than one as last time (several of the Elder Dempster Line ships were torpedoed during the war, and shipping consequently was scarce). The cabin was so small that when one man wanted to dress, the others would have to crawl into their bunks or step out onto the deck to give him room. Now, as the *Burutu* reached mid-Atlantic and turned south for Africa, moving further and further into hot weather, one of Joyce's two cabin mates began drinking heavily (there was more drunkenness on the boats heading home, but it was out of good spirits; when a man drank on the way back to Africa it was because he was miserable). The cabin began to stink of sweat and stale liquor, and Joyce, when he could stand it no longer, took to sleeping on a corridor floor or out on deck, where the drafts made his continuing cold worse. But then so did the hot, fetid cabin, and at least he could get some sleep outside.

There was a good doctor on board (most of the ships' doctors, Joyce told Gerty, spent their trips dead drunk), and he eased Joyce's cold as much as he could, treating it with ammoniated quinine. But by the time Joyce reached Lagos on August 23, he was about done in from his cold, his consequent asthma, and his lack of sleep. The episode with the Cambridge man, however, had been forgotten so much that at Freetown, Sierra Leone, the fellow had run all Joyce's onshore errands for him.

The tour, though, was off to a bad start. Then at Lagos Joyce's cabin box, with his toilet kit and other necessary articles, was mislaid, so he couldn't wash or shave or even put on a clean, dry shirt. After a thoroughly miserable evening of hunting for the box and for his bed, also missing, and wondering where and how he was going to sleep, Joyce bumped into one of the oldest and best Nigerian hands, Jerry Ambrose, "the hardest old bushman in Africa, a famous pugilist, horseman, shot, raconteur & old bachelor," who took Joyce home with him, fed him good food and champagne, and next day sent his adjutant out with fourteen soldiers to find Joyce's belongings. Ambrose's good-heartedness bucked Joyce up a great deal and was just what he needed. Someone else, though, had worse luck, Joyce told Gerty: "By the way my drunken cabin mate ended by being robbed of everything by one of his boon companions, but I fear the thief has been arrested. . . ."

Joyce and Major Hamilton-Brown finally set out together for Kontagora with their long train of porters.

Along the way Hammy told his subordinate of a stroke of good luck. Since Joyce had done such an excellent job of collecting tax on the previous tour, more than doubling it, Hamilton-Brown had asked for an extra duty pay for his province, to be given to the officer in charge of Borgu Division. The major's request had been approved and meant a raise of £80 a year for Joyce. He also was to get a yearly war bonus of about £50. The news of an extra £130 was as good a way to start a tour as any; at the same time it increased Joyce's ties with the Nigerian Service, since the more money he made there, the less chance there was of his going to England to look for a job at which he would earn less.

Joyce went to Zuru, northwest of Yelwa, where he was to replace Cowper, who was going on leave. A few weeks later Joyce in turn would be relieved at Zuru by Diggle. All this shuffling around of staff meant Joyce would not be settled in Borgu until sometime in October; he would have to spend a total of three months traveling from the time he left The Glade to his final arrival at Bussa. He had meant to settle down from the very start of the tour to a strict writing regimen, but writing had been impossible on the *Burutu* and now all this shifting about meant further delays.

The Lieutenant-Governor of Northern Nigeria, H. S. Gold-

smith, had read Joyce's report on Borgu and had called it one of
the best he had seen, which perhaps facilitated the approval of
Joyce's duty pay and meant that he was starting in as a man
known for doing a fine job in a difficult area.

When Joyce arrived at Zuru to relieve Cowper, he was very
impressed by the man's garden with its "masses of flowers — just
huge clumps of colour — the sort of bed I like — not too carefully weeded or looking too much gardened." The brightness
and lushness made such a difference to Cowper's station that
Joyce decided he must have a garden at Bussa, and, after getting
an idea of the kinds of flowers that would grow in the climate, he
wrote to Gerty for seeds. A garden would make his Bussa house
seem more like a home.

The personal boy Joyce had hired at Lagos ran off during the
trek, so Joyce hired another, Sali, at Zuru. He also had a new
cook for this tour, a dapper fellow named Frederick, who was
able to fold napkins "like a restaurant waiter." Frederick, he
hoped, would prepare a better meal than his last cook had. The
trip to Zuru nearly left Joyce without any cook at all, though,
since it turned out that Frederick was not a good walker, however adept he was at folding napkins. Toward the end of the
trek he was barely able to stagger. But the new pair of servants
were agreeable, and because of their compatibility and because
of his idea for a garden, Joyce looked forward to the changes he
would make in Borgu this time.

Bussa came as a shock after all Joyce's plans, however. After
another year of rain, tornadoes, and birds nesting in the thatch,
the house was a disaster. Everything at the station was leaning,
falling, rotting into the mud.

He did not have time to do anything about the situation,
though, because a murderer had been caught at Kaiama and he
had to hurry off there to see about the trial as soon as he tended
to the most immediate problems in Bussa.

Kaiama was a surprise, too, but a very pleasant one. During
his eight months in Borgu, Diggle had moved his headquarters
from Bussa to Kaiama, which was on higher ground than Bussa
and about eighteen miles from the Niger River, thus providing

a far healthier climate and no swamps. Diggle had made a lot of improvements in the station there, such as planting a vegetable garden, where Joyce found artichokes, beets, tomatoes, and cucumbers. Fresh vegetables were a luxury Joyce had longed for on his last tour, and now, with Diggle's magnificent garden, he could have them.

And he could have bread that was neither soggy dough nor flint-hard lumps, since Gerty had taught him how to bake scones during his leave. With fresh vegetables and bread, his projected flower garden, and the climate of Kaiama, he could feel like a human being during this tour. Besides, Kaiama did not have the same associations for Joyce as Bussa did ("I remember too many lonely weeks in this place," he had said on October 8 before he left it for his new headquarters).

On his second day in Kaiama, October 17, he baked. He reported to Gerty,

> . . . this evening has seen my great triumph. I made some SCONES. . . . I ate one for dinner, and I assure you, darling, it was better than Mrs. Dalton's [the Ogilvies' cook], much better. It was a wonderfully good scone. I am delighted. Now I shall have good bread. What it is to be married, and have a wise wife. I should never have learnt if you hadn't taught me. I think of you every mouthful.

His abruptly happier state of mind is evident from the pile of work he took on, first planning a new Treasury House and prison in the town proper to make his surroundings even neater, "Then taking some tax. Then a murder trial. Writing in the afternoon, off to see the garden watered, baking scones when I came back and reading & writing since dinner." There was a vigor in his letters, a consistent hopefulness that had been apparent only on occasion during the last tour and hardly at all since he had come to Borgu.

The war news was increasingly good (the German offensive in France in July and August had been defeated and Ludendorff's armies were reeling back; Bulgaria had signed an armistice; Turkey was in a state of collapse), and the conflict looked as if it would soon be over after the four years of relative stalemate. While all these events were adding to Joyce's good spirits, he discovered that the ship he had come out on, the *Burutu,* "full of Service people going on leave after long tours," was torpedoed and sunk by a U-boat while it was on a trip to England. Joyce, who realized that many men whom he had met and known had gone down with the boat, was shaken but managed to maintain his new equanimity.

The Treasury House which he designed and had built was a novelty for Kaiama and even all of Borgu, for it was planned with a sense of aesthetics rather than as a purely functional mud heap. Its windows and doorways were Moorish in style, and he had a hard time getting the design across to the builders, even though he told them that what he wanted was like the windows of Istanbul. His explanation was meant to win their approval, since, as he explained to his wife, "Stamboul is for them the legendary capital of the world."

The workers' first attempts were unsatisfactory and had to be torn down, but once the job was properly under way, he had to get started on another trek into the countryside to survey the population and economy, and the geography as well. He unrolled the official maps of the country which he was to survey, an area fairly new to him, and found that although they were all "white, clean & new," they were completely useless:

> Towns abandoned for years are entered in large letters, generally by the wrong names — the towns that do exist aren't there — magnificent roads on the map are mere jungle in reality, and new important highways have been left out. Mountains are just put in with the eyes shut. I shall have to start mapping at once, as I have to send in maps with my reports.
>
> (23 October 1918).

During his last tour he might have despaired over the useless maps and cursed the men who made them and the government which issued them, but now he treated the whole affair as a joke as he saw its ridiculous aspects. Apparently the "wrong names" that he mentions were the same sort of mistake he used in his novel *Castle Corner,* when Cock Jarvis is mapping in Nigeria. They were the fault of the language barrier, for the natives who were questioned about the names of their towns and rivers and mountains simply didn't know what was going on. So onto the official maps of Nigeria went What Did He Say? River and the town of I Don't Know. In early November Joyce set out to draw up his own maps.

He regretted having to go off so soon, because he had hoped to be able to make a flying visit to Kontagora in November to see if he could get news there of the second baby. In Kaiama it would take a week longer to hear, perhaps even two, and once he was on route, longer still. He dreaded going through the same suspense he had experienced at Michael's birth, although now that Gerty had borne one child without complications, he hoped the second birth would go equally easily. On November 9 he set out touring.

On this trek he came to know the people of Borgu even better than he had during his first trip. Rather than simply collecting facts — counts of cattle, types and quantities of local crops, all the statistical sort of information which his report required — he looked around him at the way people lived and was impressed at what he saw:

> I find lonely men in lonely huts working hard all the year to support one old blind father, and a child — or chiefs in old age still cheerful and undaunted with nobody left in their tumble down hamlet but a leper or so, and one household. One old chief was talking, when his son, aged perhaps five, walked up to him and sat astride his knee, and stared at me as if to say, now we know where we are. They are all fond of their children here. I find as much virtue in these savages, who worship something not very much different from the Devil — and pretty much the same dutiful ideals — as in England. They respect and care for the old, they feed the sick and the poor — there are no cases here of people starved to death — they pet and spoil their children. What would be wrong with us, is wrong with them. It is true that many things which are wrong to us are not wrong to them, but it is a question whether they are essentials.
>
> (Bejera, 9 November 1918)

I suppose it is natural that I should like to see so many babies
every day. I look forward to the babies. The black babies are of
course delightful — incredibly grave, and fat and their faces are
not much different from those of European babies. They sit and
stare at me — all stark naked — or crawl over their mothers and
fathers — or stagger cheerfully about the open space in front of
my table, while I work — and I should like to play with them.
But I have to be careful not even to stare at them, in case I should
be thought to be giving them the Evil Eye — or something like
that. I managed to give one small child my old tobacco tin to-
day as I left the village, and the last I saw of him was a small
figure gazing at his first toy with more surprise than rapture. . . .

(Vera, 12 November 1918)

This country which had seemed as garish and two-dimen-
sional as a picture postcard in his letters a year and a half before
takes on a depth and a life in the letters of November and the
ones that follow. Of course it was not the country that had
changed but Joyce. There had been hints of his transformation
a year before, late in his first tour in Borgu, and now his new
attitude is fully realized. There is a singling out of examples,
faces, and individual problems, and a vitality in the writing.
Even his servants during the previous tour had been faceless,
often referred to by their jobs rather than their names. But now
Frederick and Sali in particular are shown to Gerty as real people, sometimes amusing, sometimes pathetic, even tragic, but
they are always real and almost always drawn with sympathy.

The change in Joyce's perception meant a great deal to him,
for he no longer felt himself to be the sole white man in a blur
of black faces but one human being among a great many others.
There was benefit in this for him and benefit for the natives of
Borgu as well, since responding to individuals who are forced to
cope with terrible problems yet still manage to keep up their
spirits is easier than reacting to an inarticulate mass.

The problems of the people of Borgu were increased exten-
sively that winter by the Spanish influenza epidemic that was
sweeping the world and now crept into Borgu. As there were no
doctors or hospitals accessible and no roads to bring in the most
rudimentary medicines, Borgu suffered terribly.

Joyce himself caught the flu that first month. Since he was not aware of the epidemic, he thought it was a cold, but by early November realized he had influenza. He did not treat the virus too seriously, though, and believed himself "quite well again" and "immune, I hope from a worse infection," he wrote on November 8. But on the 13th he told Gerty,

> I was just crawling into bed — I'm worn out — but I had a bad conscience that my letter this evening was so short — the trouble is, I am quite done — Its influenza, I think, and the people here are catching it, two dead yesterday in the village — but don't be afraid, as I'm getting better, though I have had aches and pains, sore eyes & running nose for ten days now — to-night my back is broken, but I had to write again, or you would be disappointed and I can't bear to think of your having been disappointed by me. This may reach you about Christmas — my darling Gertie — you know I wish you all the happiness you have deserved. . . .

Joyce's influenza dragged on right through the month of November, despite his constant protests that he was getting better. He and Sali and Frederick staggered about the house like a trio of drunks, dazed, bleary-eyed, and coughing (Joyce stopped smoking entirely and was pleased at that) until on the 29th he wrote,

> I got up this morning, after breakfast, in the regular sick-room way, as if I were at home. At least I never heard of an invalid who got up before breakfast. I am glad I did get up, because I believe by my symptoms to-day that another day in bed would have put me in the grave. I staggered here and there in the most comical way. I am rather unsteady now, but much better than I was.

The next day, with the aid of two canes, he was walking about the house, and on his birthday, December 7, he wrote, "To-day I smoked one pipe, the first for ten days. I was down town too, all the morning, counting and checking the people, and did not feel over-tired." From then on, except for one brief relapse, his health began to return. This time his illness left few aftereffects. Before, a series of head colds had dragged him down into misery. But now his spirits revived with surprising speed.

21

"THIS IS A LONELY SPOT"

JOYCE'S THIRTIETH BIRTHDAY that December, coming when he still was feeling groggy from influenza, made him rather melancholy. At thirty he no longer could regard himself or be regarded as a promising young man. Now the promise should be fulfilled. But with nothing published in ten years, nothing since *Verses* in 1908, he was very conscious of growing older:

> It is as if I came to a turn in the road, after ten years easy walking, and looked ahead a long way — not so easy — to the next turn, and that is at forty. I shall not stop now — there are no more turns — until I am in middle-age. At 20 I felt nothing of this. I did not look forward to 30 with the same feeling with which now I look towards 40. Darling, I am beginning to grow old. It is very little yet — a small bald patch — a little blind — a few wrinkles — a loose tooth or so — but it begins. Either one grows, or one grows old. I have been growing up till lately, now I shall grow old.

His writing, like the projects he had begun to envision for Borgu, was stopped by his illness and the disruption of his household and the town's life that the epidemic brought, so perhaps this added to his gloom about aging. But up to mid-November, he had made some steady progress at a novel.

In December his chief concern was Gerty. Since he had returned to Kaiama on November 16, he had expected to receive a cable any day about the baby. By the first of December he was

very worried and next day sent off a runner to Kontagora with a
telegraph message for Major Hamilton-Brown to send to the
Ogilvies. A week later, when there was still no word, he wrote,
"Oh darling I can't bear to think that every-thing is not well
with you . . . when next you have a baby, I must be at home,
for both our sakes. You must be out with me here for some of
the tour." Gerty undoubtedly said a strong amen to this. According to an earlier letter Joyce wrote, however, Gerty would
not have been allowed to come to Kaiama; women were only
permitted at stations where there was a doctor in residence.
Furthermore, a pregnant woman would be shipped home on
the next boat because of the tremendously high incidence of infant mortality (Joyce told Gerty of missionary wives who, because they were not in government service, stayed in Nigeria to
have their babies, with tragic results), and the two children
would have had to stay in England. So his suggestion that she
come out was merely wishful thinking.

But on December 18 he was able to write,

> Darling love, I've just had the GLORIOUS NEWS — this min-
> ute. I can hardly write straight I feel so excited. . . . Darling
> sweetheart — I hope you are glad it is a boy — I hope you won't
> be disappointed I'm not a bit. Its quite surprising because I
> thought up to five minutes I wanted a daughter very badly — but
> when I think of that great fellow Michael — I'm glad there'll be
> another like him. Think of the pair of 'em — the rascals — in a
> bath together — what a scene.

The baby, born two days after Joyce's own birthday, was
named Peter Joyce Cary. Joyce, remembering his own childhood with his younger brother, Jack, who would be coming
home any day from his imprisonment in Turkey now that the
war was over (if he had not arrived already), urged Gerty to
"Give Peter Jack and Freddy, two brave men, for godfathers,
and Elsie as godmother — thus his gifts will be courage and wisdom — he can't ask more — especially when he has you for his
mother."

If Joyce's writing had stopped for the moment, he still was

reading a great deal, especially during his illness when there was little else he could do. With so many aborted novels behind him, he increasingly read not just for pleasure but to study techniques, and he had a particular interest in the author's problems in handling a certain scene or character.

Some of the books he read were Thackeray's *Pendennis,* H. G. Wells's *Mister Britling Sees It Through* and *Marriage,* a book of Roy Flecker's poetry, Gilbert Cannan's *Mendel,* Paul Bourget's *The Blue Duchess* (which he praised to Gerty for its "lucid, unaffected style"), *The Autobiography of Benvenuto Cellini,* Cervantes's *Don Quixote* (a book he read and reread, always with pleasure), Thomas Hardy's *The Woodlanders* and *Jude the Obscure,* Stephen McKenna's *Sonia,* Motley's *The Rise of the Dutch Republic,* Thomas Love Peacock's *Headlong Hall* and *Nightmare Abbey,* Young's *Marching on Tanganyika* (for the account of the campaign in which he had wanted to participate), and Hazlitt's *Table-Talk.*

His letters home were full of comments on his reading, some rather technical and others wider ranging, such as these on Cannan and Wells:

> I was looking into Mendel again to-day. Did you read Mendel. It is at once very good, and very bad — a book written by a fine writer with some terrible holes in his experience. I am tired of the school who write always of unusual people, glorifying supposedly revolutionary deeds. Even Wells makes me fed up. Mr. Brittling is a dashing boring work. Wells is popular because he seems to be mind-improving — and all the classes and the masses, the mobs and the snobs are now trying to improve their minds. Of course they like to do it with as little trouble as possible, so they read Wells. They were awfully pleased when Wells produced a God too — how nice, an improved God quite easy to swallow. Wells is not worth Hardy's little finger, or Meredith's toe-nail — he's not even on the same plane as Arnold Bennet, in spite of that very bad book The Lion's share. Gilbert Cannan with all his faults is worth six Wellses — because he's a man with a heart liver lights etc. while Wells is a worm with the guts of a fish.
>
> (8 September 1917)

When Gerty asked him what he thought she should read (Joyce had told her that she had been too restricted in her reading by her mother) and how to set about it, he obviously was delighted at the idea of giving her lessons in literature and the chance of putting down his own pet theories:

> It is not so much what one reads, as the way it is read — that is to say — as long as one does not read mere trash. . . . One should not read passively. But think always. Not read the words alone, but the ideas. What is more, argue or rather discuss at least the ideas and if you care to go further, the way they are presented. . . . Why don't you take up the study of one author, his life, his writing, his letters, all about him. His style too, and try to imitate it, or at least see how he writes. . . . Lamb you know already, and his style was peculiar to himself alone, I mean as a genius, or almost so. Fielding had a varied life. Defoe too, tho' you needn't wade through his pamphlets. Swift had a very interesting life — many sided — & was a very interesting man. His style is splendid. You could scarcely choose better than Swift. Steele was in his way the most charming of men and writers.
>
> I think good novels, well-read, are as full of matter and more humane matter than most of the more specialized works. You should always read the Times Supplement leaders too — the front page. They are always worth reading, and take some thinking too. Don't be daunted by sentences you think you can't understand. Try 'em again. Try the whole article again. It takes me more than two readings to catch the full idea of some of them.

There is no better way of learning something than to try to teach it to someone else and be forced to answer his questions about it. So Gerty's obvious interest in Joyce's comments was a great boon, for it forced him to sharpen his critical faculties even more. This awareness also helped him to see what was wrong with his own work and what steps he should take to improve it.

So, despite the setback caused by influenza, Joyce ended 1918 well, with a greater appreciation for his surroundings, a greater sense of his powers as a writer, and a determination to get work done in both areas.

What he first needed to do in 1919 was finish the report he had been researching in November, "108 pages of close written foolscap — about 20 statistical tables — a map as big as this table — and a separate sheet, apart from the report, for every village." This was the first of seven such reports he had to draw up, one for each district of his division, and he agreed with the former governor, Lord Lugard (who retired in November, 1918, after a series of conflicts with the Colonial Office, and was replaced by Sir Hugh Clifford), that report making, with all its touring, interviewing, and observation, was the only way to learn how to properly run a division.

The report and the map making made Borgu his. Whatever was known about it was what he wrote. He corrected the position of its towns and roads and rivers on the map almost as if he had created them. What he saw and decided and said would determine the future of the region for years afterward, even after his own departure. His recommendations would help — or harm — its people for generations. The sense of this responsibility bolstered his already developed deep interest in Borgu and involved him increasingly in its life. He was an Olympian viewer no longer.

For instance, when the wife of one of his policemen died in childbirth at a village distant from Kaiama, Joyce was asked to break the news to the husband. Since it was not absolutely certain that the woman was in fact the wife of this particular policeman, Joyce and the police corporal worked together "to find out where the wife was without arousing the husband's suspicions. Then if it is true, I shall have to break it to him — a task I don't look forward to."

In the latter part of January he was off on another trek, heading east toward the Niger River to Bussa to handle problems that had arisen in its emirate, then westward to the Dahomey border to survey another of his seven districts. He did not return to Kaiama until March, as he was traveling six weeks except for the few days at Bussa. He saw more territory, met more people, and learned more of their ways and problems — at Kubli, for instance, he wrote,

This is a lonely spot. One man & woman living in a deserted village in the middle of the bush. They see perhaps one passer a week, with luck. In the rains they are isolated. Then too the elephants herd up this way — in fact more elephants use the road then, than men.

(20 February 1919)

Kenu, a town next to the Dahomey border he had visited a week earlier, held a different sort of interest for him. Its proximity to the boundary had made it a thieves' den, where fugitives from both colonies met and rival gangs lived in a state of truce. "I hope I won't be looted," Joyce wrote the day before he arrived there. "But I have my four police, with ten rounds apiece — and I have four cartridges in my revolver — so that I dread not any host." But the next day he wrote,

This den of thieves is very peaceable. A large deputation of brigands met me on the road and escorted me in. The old chief is blind — and came to me led by a small boy. He looked like Lear.

(19 February 1919)

So even here, in a place he might have damned, Joyce found himself interested and sympathetic.

At Babana, another border town, he found something that not only interested him but gave him ideas for the future:

In some ways this is more interesting route than most. It is a great trade road, and the traders are passing up and down all day long. Men coming north with huge loads of kola nuts, and men going South with cages of pigeons, cattle, and sheep. Just now in the dark, a herd of cattle have gone past. The moon is not up and it is pitch black. The cattle follow the herdsman, who gives a long cry every minute.

(18 February 1919)

Babana, with its trade roads, was as different from desolate Kubli (just ten miles away) as possible. It had vitality and prosperity, something to make life worth living, in contrast to the loneliness of Kubli and the passivity of its people, the two conditions that Joyce found in so many of the towns he had passed through. And the only difference between Babana and the other towns was a dirt road.

The answer seemed to be as simple as that. He had complained before about the lack of roads that prevented coconut oil from being shipped to the coastal ports and exported to Europe and America, thus denying parts of Nigeria a greater prosperity. But how much more Babana's road provided besides money. It brought a variety of goods and of people; it brought life.

He remembered Donegal and his grandmother's house at Clare, where every caller, whether a tinker, a poacher, or a relative come home, had been an event, and people flew to the windows when they heard the sound of a buggy or a cart on the road. A glimpse of a new face was exciting. And a visitor with news or new stories to tell was a major event. In fact, anything that broke the monotony of life was important and necessary. One of his aunts bought a bicycle once, when such vehicles were new and riding one was an adventure, and her life became ten times richer, for she could visit people whom she had seen only once or twice a year before. And she could ride the two miles into Moville to shop whenever she chose. The bicycle, constantly cleaned and oiled, stood in the hall in the place of honor it deserved.

The people of Borgu, whom Joyce had begun to see as no different from anyone anywhere, could get the same pleasure from roads. They could become part of a larger world instead of living stunted lives in backwater villages. And, of course, a road would bring greater prosperity.

But it would have to be a real road, not simply an enlarged trail winding through the bush. There would have to be bridges over Borgu's rivers, especially during flood season, and proper ditches to drain the road and make it passable in all seasons. Rest houses would have to be built in villages along the way so that travelers could sleep dry and be safe from the highwaymen who raided merchants on the bush paths. Joyce's new

idea would be a major project, the biggest one he had undertaken, yet it would have to be built with almost no money, since
he was not authorized to spend big sums on roads.

On March 2 he was back in Kaiama, where he ordered that
wells be dug for the town, since they would provide fresh water
free from guinea worm. And he planted the flower seeds Gerty
had sent him after his glimpse of Cowper's garden.

But on the 10th he was off on another trek, this time building
bridges as he went. One was built at Wowo and another at
Bussa, and four more were begun. Because there was no money
for them, Joyce had to improvise, using local materials entirely
and getting all the free labor he could from convicts, local
tribes, and the courts of the two emirates. As for design and
construction methods, he worked from memory and imagination, undoubtedly envying his father's knowledge of engineering — and the equipment and money Arthur Cary had at his
disposal. Joyce also had to use all his patience. This virtue,
though, was hard to come by now that he had a vision of what
Borgu could be with proper means of transportation.

At Bussa, for instance, he wrote,

> I went out to see my bridge this morning and found them mak-
> ing a botch of it. I was annoyed but it is no good being annoyed.
> These people are as God made 'em and nothing can teach them
> to take any pride in a job of work — not at any rate the chiefs.
> They have to do it all over again — but they will probably do it
> just as badly, and then do it a third time — feeling much injured.
> The Emir knowing this bridge was to be built and being within
> 12 miles of the bridge I wanted him to copy — was too slack to
> go and look at it. He sent a servant. This though he expresses
> the greatest anxiety to do the right thing.

The emir, rather than being "too slack," may have been inten-
tionally slipshod and careless in getting the Bussa bridge built.
He and the chiefs were much less eager than Joyce was to see
any new roads and bridges going through, because the more
their people were exposed to new ideas and other peoples, the
less rigidly could they be controlled. And the emir of Bussa,

with Borgu's history of revolt, was not anxious to see them made even more restive. The emir and the chiefs represented the establishment, and any change was a threat to their power and stability, as Joyce came to understand.

For all his setbacks, Joyce was getting the work done, and on April 21 he told Gerty,

> Borgu is really waking up. One road is now open all the year, with four new bridges, and four ferries — all put in in the last two years. Diggle started the ferries, I've made the bridges, and these other bridges will open another big road in the rains.

As for Kaiama, he reported that all the seeds Gerty had sent to him were sprouting and he was getting tomatoes from the plants Diggle had put in. His wells there were a source of pride, too:

> For 80 years since it was built Kaiama has had a water famine every year. Moreover 50% of the population get guinea-worm — a beast which lives in the legs and makes a temporary complete cripple of its victim. Then when he washes his sores, it lays its eggs in the water, which someone else drinks. So that in the farming season, half the farmers are laid up. So I have had four wells dug — people can't put their feet in a well, and we have found water in every one. Moreover the people are digging 5 more wells for themselves — they never thought of this before! Next year I hope there will be no guinea-worm.

These wells are still in use in Kaiama, nearly half a century later.[1]

On top of all this progress for which he was responsible, Joyce was feeling in the best of health, "sleeping like a top, as I expected, and getting quite fat and merry again."

22

"MY CHILDREN NEED NOT BE ASHAMED OF ME"

JOYCE DID HAVE one disappointment in January. The lieutenant-governor, after high praise of Joyce's work during the last tour, issued a directive to cut mail deliveries to Borgu from once a week to every other week. Depending so much on his letters from home, not just from Gerty but from all the family and the many friends who had now returned after the war, Joyce was extremely disappointed at this unexpected move. After all, with the war over, communications should have gotten better rather than worse. "I was in despair," he told Gerty:

It is rather hard when I am alone, to add to loneliness by cutting off my mails. Even now I know nothing of what goes on anywhere. I doubt if you can realise it. I don't even know what is happening in Nigeria, in Kontagora. . . . Hammy has come to my rescue to some extent in the matter of mails, by allowing me £3 a quarter for special mails. I can manage 3 mails a month on this. . . . However mails are not so slow now — Mum's letter is actually postmarked Cambridge the 9th so it took only a month and two days to come.

Yet what mail he did get was exciting, as it was full of news of what people were doing now that the war was over: what jobs they were taking, who was marrying whom, who was publishing what. He was pleased to hear that Jack and Gerty had met and liked each other and that his brother was getting his health back after the hardships of the Turkish camp. Jack had returned to

England with his digestive system in such poor condition that a
doctor ordered him to eat no meat except for fish, and even that
would be best if it were creamed. No liquor, either; beer at
most. Jack, who had dreamed of bountiful meals in England,
stood this abstinence as long as he could. Then one day he
charged into a restaurant and ordered a steak (which he immediately promoted to Acting Fish) and a whiskey (Acting Beer)
and found that he survived, so he abandoned the diet.[1]

Arthur Cary wrote to say that Jack had taken a fancy to a very
nice Irish girl, and he was trying to engineer a marriage between
the two. Joyce was all for the plan. He knew and liked the girl
and her family and especially favored the idea that they were
Irish, for less than altruistic reasons:

> I should like Jack to marry an Irishwoman — then we would go
> to Ireland to see them sometimes. I believe the F——s hunt — I
> might get some hunting, and that is one of my dreams. But all
> this is from a very personal point of view — and hardly consider-
> ate of Jack.

The news of Freddy Ogilvie was less happy. Gerty and Joyce
agreed that Freddy seemed bitter, perhaps as a consequence of
the war and his amputation. He was thinking of going into the
Church, to his brother-in-law's horror, because one clergyman in
the family was more than Joyce could stand. Instead Joyce
advocated marriage for Freddy to put him right again. Marriage, in fact, seems to have been his universal panacea for depression, bitterness, shyness — everything except, perhaps, the
common cold. The solution was usual enough for a young married man to suggest for the world's ills and probably pleasant for
his wife to read from time to time.

Freddy was at Balliol College, Oxford, trying to decide between a donship and the Church. Joyce hoped he would become a don at Oxford, because both he and Gerty were anxious
to get a home of their own and, after considering London, Ireland, and even the Channel Islands, they had pretty much decided on Oxford as the place where they wanted to settle. The

town was a good size and was full of theaters, concerts, bookshops, good talk — all the benefits of a large city, at least for
Joyce — yet it was not a sprawling, grimy metropolis. It was
near beautiful countryside, for the Cotswold Hills were just to
the west of the Thames, and it was an easy train journey to London, a ride of just over an hour. Duncan MacGregor and his
wife were settled there, and so was Tommy Higham. The prospect of Freddy's being there to stay, too, made it seem all the
more suited for their future home.

It was necessary to find a home, too. During Joyce's 1918
leave, he and Gerty had looked at houses and had found one in
London that pleased them, but Mr. and Mrs. Ogilvie had urged
them not to take it, since Gerty would then be on her own when
Joyce was away and might be unable to cope with a baby and a
house at the same time. There was plenty of room at The Glade
and, with all the other Ogilvies away, they loved and needed her
company.

At the end of 1918, however, they decided that The Glade was
too large a house to maintain for their diminished family, especially since servants continued to be scarce. So Gerty, with two
children now, had to take on the extra work and responsibility
of house hunting. Joyce regretted that he could do nothing, but
he could not be of any help in Nigeria, and this fact weighed on
him.

He had his own immediate problems, too. There was his oral
Hausa examination to prepare for that spring:

> I passed the written part in '17, but this is the colloquial, and as
> so few people here speak Hausa, and that bad Hausa I am rather
> nervous. I work at it every day when I come in — reading Hausa
> stories, but what I need of course is conversation lessons. If I fail
> it is quite possible they will stop my increments — that is my
> pay won't go on rising by £15 a year as it does now. . . . You
> are lucky — you have no exams after you leave school. Jack [who
> remained in the Royal Navy as a career officer] and I are always
> having 'em.
>
> (11 March 1919)

Meanwhile he was gone for all of May on another mapping
and census-taking trek, carrying with him the same enthusiasm,
the same sense of giving Borgu a good shaking up. He hoped
that there would be no repetition of what had taken place in
Kaiama during his last absence. For, as he had reported to
Gerty on April 24,

> I find that in my late absense a missionary popped into Kaiama
> — disappearing just before my return in a very peculiar manner.
> The Emir asked him to wait and see me, but he said he preferred
> to write, and hastened away. I don't know if this was accident or
> design. It seems unfair to impute design, but the ways of the mis-
> sionary are sometimes Machiavellian to an extraordinary degree.
> There are good and bad — but many of them seem to look upon
> the Service as their natural enemies — and many more are com-
> pletely ignorant of our principals of government, which they do
> not understand & try to thwart.

Missionaries too often attempted to wipe away native culture,
Joyce complained,

> and their language as well — turning them into the hybrids we
> see in the Coast towns — Europeanized natives who have too
> often all our vices and none of our virtues. . . . The Catholics
> have done best out here, and I think I should rather have a Cath-
> olic missionary than any other.
> But we will see what to do when the man writes. But we don't
> want any more bloodshed here. I have no intention of getting
> scuppered in a religious war.

Uganda, of course, had been the scene of a bloody religious war
between the converts to different branches of Christianity. But
Joyce's antipathy toward the clergy, together with the natural
resentment of many Nigerian Service hands toward missionaries
invading their territories, was probably the main reason for his
testiness.

Far more upsetting than the visit of the furtive missionary was
a letter Joyce received from Gerty on May 28. She had urged
him time after time to give up his post in Nigeria, and he had

told her as many times that he could not do so because the Service provided his only means of supporting a family. Now, seeing so many other couples reunited after the war's end, setting up homes and happy together, she was unable to bear Joyce's prolonged absence, especially since her father and mother were increasingly anxious to find a smaller house, one where there would be no room for her and the two boys. So she wrote to Joyce, not to urge him to quit Nigeria but to insist on it. Wasn't there *anything* he could do in England? Couldn't he try for something at Oxford, possibly a donship such as Freddy was getting? If Joyce would not agree to come home, she would not hold herself responsible for the future of their marriage.

Joyce was so upset, pulled in so many directions in the heat and anxiety of the moment, that he could not allow himself to answer the letter at once. Instead he waited two days before he replied:

> It comes to this — that you do not think I am justified in staying in this Service, and you are prepared to take the risks of my leaving it. So that if I stay, henceforward I must take the sole responsibility of the decision. I own darling that this has weighed pretty heavily on me for these days, and will I suppose never be much lighter. And last night at one time I was very nearly ready to say I would send in my papers, and risk all our future — it seemed to me that my position would otherwise be too difficult. You could scarcely help liking me less if I differed from you in such a fundamental point — and I did not think I could take *that* risk. But I remembered, too, later on, that you would learn to like me very much less, as a failure at home — embittered, struggling and hopeless.

An Oxford teaching post, he argued, was utterly out of the question for a man with a degree such as his. And a job in Ireland, which she had also suggested because of his fondness for the country, only brought back memories of his aborted attempt in 1913 under Sir Horace Plunkett. He went on,

> What are my special qualifications? None except the knowledge of my work here, a knowledge only useful here. And now espe-

cially when the market is crowded with ex-officers who are being trained for posts, and put into them all over the country, it would be impossible to hope for work — even clerical work of the poorest sort. . . . And I have done nearly a third of my time. In 18 years service, I have to spend 12 in Africa. In 3 months now I will have completed 4 years in the country. . . . Do you think I enjoy solitude here, when I have been with you? Do you think I don't feel, and feel bitterly, the difference between the happiness of my leaves, and the squalor and loneliness of this existence? You say you can see I am more reconciled to solitude. I doubt if you would think so if you had known how I felt last night — how strong the temptation to take advantage of you, and throw it all up.

After ranging from anger to self-condemnation at Gerty's insistence, Joyce ended the letter with a strong affirmation of his love and need of her and an emphasis on the importance of his work in Nigeria:

Nothing has steadied me but you and the children. I believe I might have made a failure of my life without you. And Dads affection for you is not a little based on the belief that you have steadied me. Now even if I never write a book worth reading, I know that I have done something in the world — work which can be respected, which is good, and has been good for others. My children need not be ashamed of me, if I am never more than an officer in this Service. Indeed as an author, even a great author, I might be less worthy of respect.

The next day, having been unable to sleep half the night from worry and still stewing over the issue, Joyce wrote again to remind her of the financial struggles of even the best writers. Hardy, Conrad, Gissing, Bennett, and Meredith, he told her, all had suffered and caused their families to suffer because of the precariousness of a writer's life. Some of them had endured actual starvation. He could not bear to bring her such unhappiness.

Then he sent off his letters by the mail runner, in the desperate hope they would work, that Gerty would understand his decision.

What made matters even more critical was a letter he had written Gerty nearly two months before — one that must have reached her just a few days after her own had been sent. In this letter Joyce had raised a subject as delicate and as vital as the question of whether or not he should stay in Nigeria. From what he said in the letter, it seems the problem had been with them from the start of their marriage yet he had never had the courage to broach it before. Now he burst out:

"When I married you dear," he began, "of course I found that you had learnt or been taught nothing of what (as I know from married men) other wives do know."

His letter went to the heart of their marriage, the whole question of sex and her attitude toward it and her response to him. It must have been an agonizing letter to write, because he knew it would hurt her deeply, yet obviously he felt the subject was crucial and had to be discussed. For he had to do his best at tearing away the shame and ignorance with which the subject of physical love had been treated in the Ogilvie household, whenever it was treated at all.

The fact that Mrs. Ogilvie had arranged their room at The Glade with two single beds in opposite corners of the room shows her attitude, a mixture of the Victorian and the Calvinistic. As late in her children's lives as she could manage, she had censored their reading in the strictest way, not only in matters of sex or religion but even in politics. No wonder that Gerty had entered marriage ignorant of what "other wives do know."

With sudden frankness Joyce told Gerty that their marriage as it stood was impossible, "because the very thought of such a situation [continuing] is horrible to me. . . ." Joyce felt he could speak so brutally and bluntly now because he had found, he said, means of changing matters in the future:

> As I say things were rather desperate from my point of view when I saw Marie Stopes books advertised and sent to Hatchards for them. They came in yesterday's mail, and I've read them, and they are exactly what ought to be explained to young married people *before* they marry.

The book by Miss Stopes* was *Married Love, and Wise Parenthood,* and Joyce urged Gerty to buy it and read it carefully.

In an appendage to his letter, Joyce breathed a sigh of relief at having stated his case at last:

> In fact darling I feel happy now with the sort of happiness of a man who has put up his stakes and has nothing to do but wait — at least he has decided something, and is not torn between conflicting questions and doubts and anxieties.

Her reply arrived on June 12, full of concern and agreement, just what he needed to hear to relieve his mind. Her expression of her own unhappiness that she too had been embarrassed to mention brought him joyous relief, and he replied,

> I love you, darling, and so far from having any disappointment, I cannot say how happy you have made me — how sweet it is to find that the woman one loved is always more loveable and dear.

He suggested they limit their family and have no more babies until their two small sons had grown to a more self-sufficient stage, an idea that must have relieved Gerty. It meant an end to that dreadful vision of one pregnancy and birth after another, with Joyce gone back to Nigeria each time. Perhaps it also made her a little less fearful of his plans to stay with the Nigerian Service.

Joyce had been relieved of one other worry at the time he received Gerty's ultimatum about his job. He had been concerned about a crisis at The Glade brought on by Mrs. Ogilvie, for she had let running the house wear her out and had laid the blame on Gerty and the two small children, who, to her mind, had turned the household upside down. Rather than saying anything to Gerty, she had spoken only to her husband, pouring out such a stream of grievances that Mr. Ogilvie felt compelled to write Joyce a letter, which he received early in 1919. It was a

---

* Marie Stopes Roe (1880–1958), a most remarkable woman, was an eminent paleontologist, suffragette, and author of poetry, plays, and commentaries on Japanese literature, as well as a pioneer in the fields of sexology and family planning.

shocker, for it blamed Joyce for all the problems at The Glade
and accused him of shifting his responsibilities onto other shoulders, particularly Mrs. Ogilvie's, while he lived a gay and carefree bachelor's life in the balmy climate of Borgu. Mrs. Ogilvie,
said her husband, "has had one family to bring up, and its
hardly fair to ask her to take charge of another."

Joyce had been hurt by Mr. Ogilvie's letter but had been diplomatic in his reply, blaming himself for Mrs. Ogilvie's state.
Yet he could not help feeling some resentment, since it had
been Mr. and Mrs. Ogilvie's pleas that had prevented his taking
a house during his 1918 leave.

When the Ogilvies sold The Glade in February and bought a
home on Addison Road, Joyce wrote to Gerty, "I'm glad M & F
have found a house they like especially one with a garden." It
was not until Mrs. Ogilvie got panicky at the idea of moving and
changed her mind about the sale two weeks after it was made,
insisting on staying at The Glade (Mr. Ogilvie bought the
house back but lost heavily on the affair) and on Gerty's staying
with them, that Joyce finally told his wife of Mr. Ogilvie's letter.
Even then he still urged Gerty, "don't let Father know I give
him away in this fashion. . . ."

The Ogilvies' decision to remain at The Glade took some of
the pressure off Joyce when he learned of it in April, but now
that Gerty's letter had come, although it could be explained
partly by the upheaval at The Glade, he had to do something
besides show her the dangers of his quitting the Nigerian Service
too soon. He had to demonstrate that he was attempting more
positive action. He had to prove himself with his writing.

But he had been trying to do this for almost three years, since
his arrival in Nigeria in the summer of 1916 after marrying
Gerty. He had told her at the beginning of this present tour, in
1918, that he was aiming at commercial success now, since it
would be selfish and even frivolous to set his standards too high
and aim for art rather than money. Although he had made
progress in his work in the year since then, he still had not made
a penny from it. Her letter now increased the pressure on him
immeasurably. He *had* to make a living from his pen or risk
seeing his whole world collapse.

23

NOVELS AND POTBOILERS

SINCE HE HAD SAILED from Liverpool in July, 1918, Joyce's writing had been done in fits and starts, constantly interrupted by his treks around the division. He was on the move continually. During the first four months of 1919, for example, he went out on surveys more than three quarters of the time, carrying his manuscripts around in green cloth saddlebags.

Although Joyce had developed the ability to write just about anywhere, at any time, and under any conditions, he still found it difficult to handle a novel while on the move. In April he explained to Gerty why he had not completed any single work:

> Partly this is because I have to write in little bits — forget my first scheme, and have to invent another. Also it is impossible to keep the papers properly when they have to be packed & jumbled together so often — when the table has to be cleared every time its wanted for something else.

It was discouraging to end up with a heap of separate scenes that, due to the interruptions of traveling, simply would not cohere.

Yet he felt the quality of his writing was improving all the time, so he began to think more and more of not only trying to sell his work but of other practical moves as well:

> There is one thing I must do next leave — learn typewriting. I have come to the conclusion it is absolutely necessary for my work

— my writing work. One can't tell what a thing looks like until it is typewritten. Also I must find a literary agent to sell my stuff — if he can. I daresay he won't be able because I have no illusions about its saleability.

(10 April 1919)

That spring, before the blow of Gerty's ultimatum, he worked with increasing intensity. He felt he was making up for the "great gap from 1912 to 1916 in which I must have forgotten much, as well as leant nothing." His April, 1919, letters dwell more on his writing than those of the whole preceding half year; he apparently had come to a milestone even before Gerty's letter arrived and was trying to come to terms with himself, get the measure of his talent, and justify his going on:

I write and learn, and learn and write. What I am at now I have been at, on and off, for many months. And so one loses the excitement of a first composition. This was my danger. I like to rush something down in enthusiasm and leave it when I tired — or rather I tire of it, take a dislike to it, and leave it because I think it a waste of time to go on — some better notion has carried me off. I have to learn to drudge at writing. . . . Mine is not work of genius — but sometimes I think it might be good work, worth reading, worth even preserving, in time, with hard toil, steady application and no faint heartedness. I face the difficulty that all face at a beginning — that until I have proved myself, I must be doubted. So that at my hardest time, when I have the first struggles, I can have no support but in myself. It is easy to doubt oneself. It will be easier when I do finish something, and begin the heart breaking task of finding a publisher. However I have had a long training. Dad never pretended to think the writing anything but a waste of time. . . . And then as you know I am sensitive — I can't help it, in all honesty — and when as once or twice I have shewn something to have it received with insincere praise, or polite kindness — then I have really been daunted. So I keep it to myself. You shall read it in typewriting, but noone else. And I fear even your reading, in case you do not like it. And in your heart you think like the rest — Joyce deceives himself — he will never do anything and if once I believed

that myself, then I should really fail, and in that failure, half my
life would go out. The unsaid disbelief of others — the eager-
ness to push me into some profession — the joy when I was found
able to make money like other people — these did not affect me
at bottom — but your disbelief might. . . . If you have faith in
me, it must be the faith — as someone said, which is the usual
kind — in what is incredible.

(20 April 1919)

The problem of keeping continuity in his writing while living
a life filled with chaos plagued him until, in mid-May, he decided that he must do something more than try to keep the plot
in his head, where it kept getting jounced loose. He must outline. He needed to write a thorough synopsis of the novel to
which he could refer whenever he sat down to write. Then there
would be no inconsistencies and no lack of continuity; he set at
the idea with a new enthusiasm:

> The first skeleton is nearly done (I put in there whole 13 hour
> days at it at Yashikera and four to-day — and already I find an
> advantage. I see weak points. I perceive the danger spots. A
> novel should have a plot but that plot should be told or rather
> tell itself through character. And that is where I fail so often.
> I make a plot — get the characters moving — get to know them
> — and then I find they are not evolving the plot — rather strug-
> gling with it. By this time (O how many times now) I hope to
> avoid this. I shall not plunge as usual into my tale before I see
> the end of it. I am going to work on that plan — pull it about —
> rewrite it — for a week yet at least. Pray for me. I am very weak.
> When I am full of a theme, I want to write — to write — to put
> down all the pictures and fancies that start up at once before me.
> But I shall have to walk this time before I begin to dance. . . .
> I have finished four or five short stories, and a short novel —
> or rather sketch of a short novel — but the latter will have to be
> rewritten, & the short stories are meant to be potboilers. I shall
> try and sell them.

(19 May 1919)

This letter is Joyce's first mention of any short stories to
Gerty, although he had told her he was trying some "fables"
along the lines of Tolstoi.

For the first time Joyce also broke his writing into two main lines: serious novels and "potboilers," short stories meant to make money. This innovation was his way of resolving the problem of whether he should write what he wanted to write or write what he thought would make money. Now he could do both, he hoped. By using separate forms for separate purposes, he would be better able to keep the commercial writing from undermining the serious.

On May 25, despite his intentions of keeping at the outline-drafting for a week, Joyce crowed, "I've written 82 pages of my new work." This output equaled a short story a day. Obviously the painstaking work of sticking to a detailed synopsis was not slowing down his productivity.

Then Gerty's letter arrived on the 28th, and for several days Joyce was in too much turmoil to keep on. There did not seem much point in writing, even if he could manage the concentration it required, if his whole world were going to collapse. Once he had resolved the question and sent off his reply, however, he was able to settle down again to the novel. On June 4 he wrote,

> I am at page 171, and sticking close to that famous scheme. This alone I find an immense advance. Formerly with my much rougher schemes — I used to allow myself to put in improvements & small changes as they suggested themselves. Then there would come an enforced break of a week — and when I started again I would look at the scheme and go on — forgetting some change. Thus later on — I would discover a hideous gap of inconsistency in the whole development — and noone who has not tried can believe the difficulty of alteration in *plan* of a book once it is nearly done.

By June 24 he had 390 pages of manuscript, the length of an average novel. Thus, the book represented the greatest amount of work he had ever done as a writer and proved that he *could* stick at a novel, even under nearly disastrous circumstances. He was delighted with himself and promised to show the novel to Gerty on his next leave. And she would see the scheme, the synopsis, as well. "What darling?" he asked. "Will you back me up? and say go on, Joyce — I've got an eye on you. You're pretty rotten at present, but you *may* improve."

He had a full head of steam, a sense of where he was going in his work, and a great pile of filled foolscap sheets to stow away each night when he put down his pen. He was getting somewhere now; the 390 pages were concrete evidence. He did not look on his apprenticeship as an insurmountable task or pretend that his writing was just a hobby. He felt that success was only a matter of time, patience, and work. But it was time that held him back. If only he could spend every minute writing. If only he could work unceasingly, without the interruptions of other necessary duties, then he could rush ahead to success.

Nevertheless, when he looked back on the past three years, he saw so much progress that he did not have to worry whether or not he was capable of improving his work. It *had* improved. He explained his feelings to Gerty:

> As a matter of fact, I have not even begun to find myself till this tour. Last tour was a re-beginning from the beginning and I burnt the whole batch. This tour I am beginning to find a definite plan — a surer intention — a better notion of how to set about the work. And it has been very productive. I shan't burn this years work. There are two unfinished novels I burn to get back to — I still take the keenest interest in them — and the one I am working at does not flag.
>
> (8 August 1919)

In June he caught a head cold that dragged on through July and August and brought on the inevitable asthma and insomnia. On other tours this combination of illness and sleeplessness had worn out both his body and his nerves, but this time it seems to have done neither. Perhaps he put on a brave face for Gerty's sake, so she would not have any more ammunition for her campaign against the Nigerian Service. But the amount of work he did under the circumstances shows that bravado was not his only reason. Obviously he was in a good mental state. Satisfaction with his writing and his work to improve Borgu were strong stimuli.

Even when bedded down amid soggy blankets with his nose

and eyes running, he wrote ten or a dozen pages a day. And when his cook, Frederick, broke one of Joyce's teeth, the work still did not stop. This incident occurred when Joyce, biting into a flint-hard scone (Joyce had taught Gerty's recipe to Frederick, but the cook either did not have his master's light touch or else had grown sloppy), cracked his tooth in half.

Frederick's cooking was not entirely to blame. Maggots had gotten into the flour supply. Joyce had tried one or two batches of scones soon after but found that although the maggots gave the scones a certain extra lightness, he really had no appetite for the bread. So he and Frederick resorted to native flour, particularly a heavy corn meal, and the scones grew harder and harder until the disaster with the tooth occurred. Joyce did his best to keep it from becoming infected or driving him into agonies of pain by slathering his mouth with disinfectant and pain-killer. These remedies seem to have worked well enough, and he kept on with his writing.

But after five months' work, the novel flagged. Joyce tried hard to revive it but finally gave up. He began on a new one at once, choosing from a dozen different themes that had gathered in his mind during the writing of the long work (he had drawn up outlines of several of them for future use). Again he completed an outline of the projected novel and plunged ahead with high spirits, as he wrote Gerty:

> I have my plot and am cheerfully writing away again. It makes all the difference in the world to me, especially when I have missed one mail, and must wait some time for another. I trot about all day when I'm not doing official work, chuckling over the situations I invent. I get much more fun out of my books than any reader ever will.
>
> (6 October 1919)

Shortly before this letter the last chimney of his kerosene lamp cracked. He watched the crack grow, the chimney's top break off, and then its stump fall off bit by bit until the lamp no longer could be used. There was nothing he could do about it. He had no more lamps, no more chimneys, and not even a candle, and he did not have glue or anything with which to mend the cracked chimney. Now his evenings were useless, for he could not write by moonlight or the flickering of an open fire.

This blow was far worse than the broken tooth or illness. As he wrote to Gerty before the chimney was totally gone,

> To sit in the dark full of ideas and unable to put 'em down would be maddening. And the evening is one of my best times, for while I go for my walk I invent my next chapter. Not to speak of all my letters which I write after dinner.

Added to these complications was his cold, which hung on into the autumn. He had been due for leave in August, since in 1918 his time had been cut shorter than usual, but instead the new governor, Sir Hugh Clifford, ordered still longer tours and shorter leaves. Joyce was stunned. He had hoped for better conditions with the war's end; instead, they were to be worse, hopelessly worse.

And to disrupt his life even more, Joyce received orders to leave Borgu in June in order to replace the man at Zuru. Borgu Division would be closed. This meant the area would fall into the state of war and chaos in which Joyce had found it in 1917. Everything that Joyce and Percy Diggle had accomplished would go to ruin. Borgu would be left as if Joyce had never set foot there. He was furious and told Gerty,

> Hammy is mad with rage, but he couldn't be madder than I am. I am abandoning everything, my work here, my garden, my mangoes, and my well earned peace during the wet season. Think of the garden alone. The gardener nearly wept when I went down this evening & found him bursting with pride at the shew of tomatoes, and everything else, and told him it had all to be left to go to ruin. Noone relieves me here. Borgu is to be abandoned for any length of time. Last time they abandoned it, they had a fight, and fifty people were murdered. But Lady R. (an amorous old woman as Hammy calls her — must have her husband).* Zuru

* The man Joyce was to relieve at Zuru had recently married the widow of a prominent British statesman and mother of a future prime minister. She had pulled strings to have her A.D.O. husband brought home, for even with a Spanish valet and other luxuries and the indulgence of the governor, he was not willing to stay at Zuru after his first few month there. But in retiring from the service, the man not only was forcing Joyce out of Borgu but was stealing Joyce's leave from him. Joyce had a right to be doubly outraged.

is a healthy place and the mails will come quicker & go to you quicker, so I suppose there are some good points. But meanwhile apart from everything else, I have a nice journey. I have 19 police, the whole of the office records, £2000 in cash (nine box fulls) and all my own things to take 10 days trek in the middle of the rains. . . . But I am sad for Borgu. All Diggle's and my work will be half wasted. It will mean beginning again. Hammy is almost incoherent with fury in his letter.

Joyce set out on June 28, heading for Zuru via Kontagora, with an immense caravan that included

Musa, the boys, Bawa the courier, Lafia the scribe, my fifty carriers & 8 hammock men, Musa's 8 carriers, 19 police with 27 carriers, four loads of office books, and ten of money . . . in all 132 people marching along in a row. I forgot three prisoners, which will make it 135. . . . I wish I could go to Zuru by bus.

After settling his affairs at Kontagora, Joyce was ready to head on for Zuru when, on July 13, a District Officer showed up at Kontagora, ready to take over duties at Zuru — and with orders that Joyce was to return to Borgu!

So Joyce turned around and went back the way he had come, arriving at Kaiama thoroughly disgusted with the Nigerian Service, Sir Hugh Clifford, and the Colonial Service, which was the department overseeing the Nigerian branch. He found his garden a weed-choked ruin. No one had taken care of it for five weeks, and it was a total loss. All the seeds Gerty had sent, all the fresh vegetables Joyce had hungered for, and all the flowers he had hoped would make the place seem homier were destroyed.

After exhausting himself with a series of invectives, he pulled himself together. At least he had the solace that some of his work in Borgu had not been wiped out. And, as a sort of consolation prize, he had been given a clerk from the coast to aid him in his work, a Mr. Graves, a Gold Coaster moved to Nigeria.

Mr. Graves would be something new for both Borgu and Joyce.

H

24

THE GRAND TRUNK ROAD

THE ADDITION of Mr. Graves to the staff at Kaiama meant a great relief to Joyce, since it would save him from the dullest and most time-consuming of all his jobs: copying.

Everything official that Joyce sent from his Kaiama office to any other post in Nigeria — all official letters, accounts, and memoranda — had to be copied. One copy went into Joyce's files and one (or even two or three sometimes) was sent on. With neither a typewriter nor carbon paper, Joyce had to spend hour after hour writing every copy out by hand (he was constantly blessing Gerty for her gift of a fountain pen), sometimes of the sheerest nonsense.

For instance, once Joyce came across a sack of money, which had been buried near the house and unearthed by his gardener. Joyce had no idea whether it was collected tax that had been buried during the Borgu uprising, or funds of one of the emirates, or even stolen money, but whatever it was, he was responsible, and he reported the finding. Immediately (at least as "immediately" as messages traveled back and forth in Borgu) he received a reply from the Treasury asking for details — in triplicate. Joyce wrote up all the particulars of the discovery, in triplicate. Then the Treasury demanded to know the original source of the money, in triplicate. Joyce told them everything he knew once again and sent off all the copies of his new report. Back and forth went the Treasury's questions and Joyce's replies, always in handwritten triplicate, until Joyce wished the money had never been found. Or that he'd just buried it again, or pocketed it, or spent it on roads and bridges, or even given it away.[1]

When he needed money, the Treasury would give him none. But now when he tried to give *them* money, he had to explain why over and over again, always in triplicate. He cursed the parasites and pen-pushers, the desk jockeys of the Treasury (who undoubtedly denounced him as a money-wasting bush savage who could not write a proper memorandum). A clerk, though, would save him most of this aggravation and perhaps a good deal of writer's cramp, for after a day of copying, his 2000–3000 words of fiction each evening was a physical ordeal, whatever it did to perk up his spirits.

When he met George Graves at Kaiama, Joyce was disappointed at his blessing from Heaven, for the clerk was "a long lanky youth in gold spectacles — Mr. Graves by name and look. He knows nothing, and I shall have to teach him, as well as do my own work. But he will save me some copying," Joyce said in a letter to Gerty. Graves, twenty-one, was an inexperienced new clerk, but he was a bear for work, and for this reason, as well as just for the company of someone else in the office, Joyce enjoyed his presence:

> Graves is a very serious youth, and turns up very early in the morning. My handwriting is troubling him, but he will get to learn it in time. I see him poring over a dictionary to find out what I mean. The world of a clerk is strange. Here he is as much a foreigner as I am. He has almost no intellectual interests, and will even miss out a line in a copy, from ignorance of or indifference to the sense. He is as near a vegetable as human creatures can get — a writing machine.

Joyce's bemusement and frustration at Graves gave way, though, because of a new episode. Musa, the Political Agent, was reported to have taken bribes. Joyce was outraged. Musa had accepted a bribe from Ilesha, "the biggest rascal among the District chiefs," to get him permission to have a ceremonial umbrella. An umbrella in Northern Nigeria was a symbol of such

authority that only emirs were allowed them. For anyone else
to have one, carried by an arm-weary retainer, was like parading
around with a bogus Victoria Cross or Congressional Medal of
Honor. What made Joyce furious with Musa was not so much
his getting sanction for the umbrella for Ilesha as his getting
Joyce to sign the authorization. Apparently Musa had given
Joyce the document among a pile of more innocuous official
papers for signing, and Joyce had given them just a cursory
glance. Musa must have known Joyce would find out what had
happened — the two emirs of Borgu would know of the umbrella and make protests to Joyce. So he must have felt that
Joyce would be too proud to admit having been gulled and
would do nothing to rescind the authorization.

Joyce, though, was not so pompous as Musa thought:

> But I haven't the least reluctance to explain in public that I
> have been taken in. I shall do it tomorrow morning in the great-
> est publicity possible. As for Musa, I'll comb his wool for him.
> I'll get him removed if I can, the ancient rascal. . . . What a
> grand row over a dashed old brolly. But the Indian Mutiny
> started in cartridge-grease.
>
> (19 August 1919)

While the case was not as ridiculous as it looked from a distance, neither was it as serious as Joyce felt at the moment. Bribery was an accepted convention in this part of the country —
in most of Nigeria, in fact. To take a bribe was no more a
moral issue than to accept Christmas gifts from business acquaintances or an apple from a pupil. The act only became
serious if the official who received the bribe allowed himself to
be biased as a result. Of course there was every indication that
Musa had done just that. But it was Musa's deceiving him that
made Joyce so angry.

The case of Rex versus Musa came up for trial at Kaiama on
November 4:

> I had a pleasant morning. I rarely have a head ache but I had
> one to-day, and the scene in the office while I tried the case of Rex

v. Musa, for corrupt practises, was not good for headaches. We were a strange party. I sat behind my enormous table with the patient air of the man who can't raise his voice because it hurts him; Musa sweated, literally poured with sweat, in his indignation and outraged virtue; the Chief of Ilesha, a witness said to have bribed Musa, who is over six feet high, of frightful emaciation, and a hideous cold protruding eye, with every line of his debauched countenance speaking his guile, treachery and folly, fluted in a high voice one contradiction after another, the mallam rolled his white eye in the background with a look of concentrated malice and venom difficult to imagine, and the Emir in the middle sat unmoved and calm, and probably half asleep.

Musa got off for lack of evidence. It is impossible to say whether he took the money. There's no doubt he combined with S. Ilesha, who is the worst ruling chief in Borgu, and a dangerous knave as well as a still more dangerous fool, to deceive me, but the consideration does not yet appear. The Emir and I together then tried the Chief of Okuta for an extraordinary piece of injustice. I said I wanted to turn him out. The Emir wants to give him another chance. I shall submit it to Hammy, and suggest that we take the Emir's advice, as tho' the fellow is useless, I want the people to see that the Emir is not a cypher. Neither do I want the Emir to feel that his advice is only a matter of form. The only way to make men do their work is to give them responsibility, and take the risk of a few failures by the way. And that is exactly our whole plan out here. To teach these people to rule, by letting them practice the art.

The ending to the affair was unsatisfactory, but Joyce had had more than two months to cool off before the trial so he accepted Musa's reprieve with fairly good grace and allowed him to continue in his job, although on quite a different footing from before.

A happier event was the creation of a Civil Service association by the Postmaster General of Nigeria, a man named Somerville. Somerville's association was prompted by the long history of mismanagement of the staff members of lower grade by the Administration. This already poor situation culminated with Sir Hugh Clifford's ruling for longer tours of duty and shorter leaves. The difference in policy was this: formerly travel time to and from Nigeria had been counted as neither leave nor duty but as a kind of limbo. Now it was to be counted as part of the leave. In other words, a month or two of each leave, spent in cramped quarters on a hot ship among a lot of drunken miners, was supposed to be as pleasurable as life in England. Joyce had not thought so, and neither had very many others. The affair of the new A.D.O. at Zuru and the special privileges he had gotten was just another bit of fat for the fire.

Joyce was elated and told Gerty,

> . . . there is one piece of great news. When next you drink fiz. give a silent health to Mr. J. Somerville, Postmaster General of Nigeria, and Chairman of our new association. He has issued his manifesto and it is good reading. I expect I may get £100 a year more pay, and a bigger pension.
>
> (28 August 1919)

The news of the association and the prospect of its benefits came only a week after Joyce had begun his biggest project of all in Borgu, his grand trunk southern road.

He had been pleased with the success of his bridges and Percy Diggle's ferries, which connected native trails and made them usable for the entire year. Now in August, 1919, he started surveying for a new road south which would link Kaiama with Lagos and the sea. It would bring to the heart of Borgu the same life and prosperity he had found in Babana that spring, he hoped.

"I'm going to train a roadman next week," he told Gerty on August 17, "and start him on a new main road cambered, with ditches, and straight. I have £60 to spend, a pound a mile, and I mean to get my money's worth." Five days later he told her,

> It has been surveyed for a mile. The ingenuous surprise of the people when I shewed them the way by compass was comical. They are quite sure they will never arrive — but are still driving a straight line through the bush. Perhaps they won't arrive, which will make a fool of me, what.

In six more days the road was surveyed another five miles. Joyce was using as his guide the pamphlet written by "A District Officer," his old chief, H. S. W. Edwardes, and as the project moved away from Kaiama he showed an increasing sympathy for the author's passion for roads. Joyce's new interest was an excellent complement to his writing, because it gave him not only an immediate satisfaction but immediate results. It provided a physical outlet, which he needed after the mess caused by the Zuru business and his upset over Gerty's letter of ultimatum. Each morning he went out with increasing pleasure to see the work and walk on *his* road:

> This morning I went to see my road, as it looked cleared. I galloped down and arrived before I was expected, and I was delighted. I cannot explain the pleasure of seeing a road which one has planned and surveyed in actual being, but it is a very unusually keen pleasure. My road is beautifully straight too. . . . I walked down again this evening to see how they were getting on with the ditch. I only make one ditch on the upper side, according to the rules laid down in a very good little pamphlet published mysteriously by a "D.O." who is actualy H.S.W.Edwardes, a twee mon. . . . The made part of my road is only 30 yds long at present but I am as proud of that bit as if it were as long as Watling Street. I shall take all my evening strolls down the road now.
>
> (9 September 1919)

He had some trouble getting the men working on the road to build it as he specified, but the problem was one of understanding rather than of lethargy or carelessness. The natives, unlike those at the Bussa bridge, were working under Joyce, not under either of the two emirs, and the difference was marked. The difficulty was getting them to camber the road so it would drain properly:

> The road goes better. They are beginning to understand what I want. . . . The curved surface to throw off the rain is their difficulty. I doubt if they grasp the reason of it now, for to-day much of the new part had been made flat topped. However, I

explain as much as possible, and someday one of them will graspe it and tell the rest, or the idea will begin slowly to spread among them.

(12 September 1919)

Joyce's feelings in this letter are quite different from his ferocious outburst, "But no black man on Gods Earth is reliable. . . . No black man is morally, or mentally, or even physically reliable. Not one can you trust," which he had written to Gerty almost exactly two years before, on September 24, 1917. Of course Joyce was feeling far better now than he had then. But he had also learned a lot and opened himself up to the realities of Nigeria and to the potentialities of its people.

The man who was in charge of the road crew especially earned his admiration. He caught on quickly to Joyce's ideas and carried them through well. Even better, he was quite capable of solving problems on his own. Joyce praised him highly to Gerty:

He is really a treasure. The road would have been impossible without him. He is the most precious of discoveries, a man who can do a job with a conscience — and a black man moreover with a straight eye.

(23 September 1919)

When the road came to "a bad place — a deep gully full of rocks" in early October, Joyce was afraid the project would be held up for some time and was surprised when he went out to inspect construction the next day that the crew had made real headway under the road chief:

The fellows have done better than I expected at the 3 bad places I pointed out yesterday. They are building stone causeways, and building them pretty well.

(4 October 1919)

As construction moved along and the road became something more than a vision or a small beginning, Joyce let his imagination wander into the future. He told Gerty of his dreams,

I thought as I walked along, alone because the Waziri [Vizier] had supposed I would not come on account of the rain, — this is as some Roman engineer felt when he strolled down the long reaches of Watling Street, and wondered how long he would be permitted to foretell the future of Britain — with one eye on the disturbances of Rome. Shall we all be recalled by the breaking of the Empire. And shall some Blackman in the year 4000 trace my road for a paper in the Kaiama Archeological Society, and debate learnedly the ancient greatness of Britain. It is certain. Nothing endures for ever. England will become little England again and Nigeria an Empire of the blacks — India of the browns. Unless indeed they conquer us. But that is not so likely as that we shall be ruled from Moscow or Berlin or perhaps New York.

(4 October 1919)

A month after work had begun the road moved along so rapidly that it was "too far now for daily inspection," Joyce explained to Gerty. He also told her of a piece of luck: "It seems that I am in the fashion. Clifford has issued a big circular about roads. Hammy will probably be pleased to have something for his annual report." For once he and official policy were in accord, even if he had begun work a month before the pamphlet was issued.

His plan was to accomplish so much work that no matter what happened, whoever subsequently was stationed in Borgu would have to continue the road through to its junction with the road from the coast. Then in ten years, he hoped, Borgu would be something more than a primitive backwater. It would be opened up to trade, prosperity, ideas, education, medical improvements, in fact, to everything that Europe and the world had to offer:

If Cowper or Diggle succeeds me here, or even a keen youngster, I hope to get it well begun, so that it can go on for another five or ten years until the whole Emirate is properly opened up, and can be run over on a motor bicycle. Theres no reason to prevent it. All my bridges are standing, and are in so much use, that in some cases the traffic has deviated fifty miles to use them. I haven't done anything here I am so proud of as my bridges. They've even saved lives, as there used to be a drowning every year. I only wish I could get a few steel girders, a pair of iron wheels, some good tackle, and a carpenter able to saw planks.

(3 October 1919)

This letter, with its reference to "Cowper or Diggle . . . or even a keen youngster," suggests that Joyce intended something more than a temporary replacement for him while he went on his now long overdue leave. He sounds as if he would not be returning to Nigeria, or at least not to Borgu. Possibly he meant the latter, for with the constant shuffling around of personnel in the country, he may have expected to be transferred to some other division in another province. But there is a ring of finality to his speculations all the same.

He was still writing the novel he had begun in September after the collapse of his long, careful summer plans forced him to give up the project. The new material was, much more than anything else he had written, aimed at the public, as he said:

> I want, between you and me, to serve God & Mammon, or rather, my art and the reader, at the same time. I want a plot with action & interest, to go off at once, to attract even the ordinary uncritical reader onwards to the very end, and yet to answer my own canons. It is very hard.

(30 September 1919)

That he was very intent on marketing this work is shown in a remark of three weeks later: "I'm right in the middle of a book which *must* be finished before I come, or it will never be done in the leave. I have just time by working every hour I can get."

But because of his anxiety about the road, his anticipation of leave, and his lingering cold and asthma, he felt "in such a restless state that I see its no good beginning any long piece of work. I shall write some short stories to pass the time." And the next day, November 14, he was launched:

> . . . I have at last managed to start writing again — a short story though it seems likely to reach 20,000 words. I must find out about the market for short stories — what length is favoured and

so on — and what is paid for them. I shan't waste time & thought
on them unless they pay. So far from being good practice for
novel-writing I believe they are bad. But if they pay, I daresay
I shall be able to sell some, for I can turn out the sort of plot required without much difficulty. So could you. The essentials
are a little sentiment, a little incident and a Surprise. The latter
must come at the end. But the end itself must be happy. Commercial art if you like, but it need not be bad if it is honestly
done. I must have a dozen plots in my bag, but I have been too
much preoccupied with novels to write 'em. I shall try and write
some on the way home.

Leave had come through in October, approved by Major
Hamilton-Brown, who had been disturbed at the state of his
friend's health when Joyce had been in Kontagora during the
Zuru transfer fiasco in July. Joyce had pressed for the leave
then, and Hammy had done his best to see that he got it.

It was generous of Hamilton-Brown to do this favor for Joyce,
because he too was due for leave and during this tour had had a
heart attack. It had not been severe, but a bad heart and the
terrific heat of Kontagora Province were not a very good combination. Provided nobody higher up than the major vetoed the
leave, Joyce expected to set out from Kaiama in November and
reach home in January. This time he made no comments about
missing Christmas dinner (although after more than three years
of marriage he had yet to have Christmas with Gerty and had
not been able to spend the holiday in England for nearly a decade); he was too pleased to be getting leave at all. "Bless
Hammy," he told Gerty:

My leave is APPROVED for the end of NOVEMBER. I danced
up and down the verandah when I saw it. But darling, should
this get to you, as it well may, before any cable remember that
it is not getting home to have a leave approved. Someone has to
relieve me. It seems that bating accidents they will do their best
for me.

(17 October 1919)

25

"I SHALL WRITE AN ENORMOUS BOOK"

WITH THE LEAVE APPROVED, Joyce plunged into work harder than ever, in order to advance his road and to finish as many short stories as he could before he arrived in England.

In his letters of that autumn, Joyce speaks often of a future in which he would be at home and writing, although he does not mention Gerty's most disturbing letter. He may have been thinking forward to the day when he would be able to retire on his pension. But he was not the sort of person who spends his time living in the future or even thinking about it except on special occasions such as birthdays. Although he speaks of his next tour, his letters about the future of Borgu when he would no longer be there also hint at early — in fact a forthcoming — retirement.

He wrote, for instance, of the help that Gerty could give him. When she suggested that even when he was at home, he would be spending most of his day away from her, shut up with his writing, he suggested that she work with him. If she really wanted to be a collaborator rather than a jealous rival, perhaps she could learn to typewrite.

The idea had been Gerty's originally, and Joyce was pleased that she suggested it and that she wanted to help. She could try, he said, but he reminded her, "typewriting is great drudgery." All the same, he said, if she *did* learn, her assistance would make him much more productive,

For often I am only prevented from writing all that I have thought of by the physical disabilities of time. I would have to correct a great deal, but I believe in writing the first draft very quickly and freely. The quicker I can write the better.

(30 June 1919)

A rapid writing of the first draft, he explained, helped him to get a sense of the novel as a whole, rather than as a collection of fragments, and brought the book alive far more than any outline could. But a marathon first draft also left him exhausted, and "Exhaustion is as dangerous in writing as in painting." So if Gerty were able to type, he could have a breather before tackling the difficult job of revision.

Furthermore, Joyce felt it was far easier to be objective about his work in typescript than when it was scrawled on foolscap: typing gave it far more the look of the printed page.

While he planned such practical activities as studying short story types, lengths, and markets and finding a literary agent, he also dreamed of The Book, a neverland of characters and themes and sheer words as ambitious and as long as his Grand Trunk Road:

Some day when I have a reputation and can afford to play tricks, I shall write an enormous book, with an enormous plot. Already I have to watch myself carefully, or I grow prosy. But in this book I shall prose to my heart's content. It will be a dense book. A forest of a book, full of good timber, and bad timber, and old bogs, and swamps, and rocks, and unexpected streams, and grateful springs and frightful blasted heaths, where the bones of countless readers bleach among barren wastes. I shall be damned for this book. And then countless champions will spring up to defend it. It will run through an edition once in every five or ten years. And in 2019, when Michael's great-children go to School they will be asked by the English master if they are any relation to the Cary who wrote The History of John Smith, and will reply that he was their great-great-grandfather, and there's a picture of him in the gun-room at home. And their great-great-grandmother who inspired that masterpiece hangs on

the other side of the fireplace in the extraordinary fashions of
1919. So short a time makes history — ancient history — of today.

(21 November 1919)

Joyce's reading, which always acted as an impetus to his writing, remained as catholic as ever. His list included Plutarch's
Moralia, Darwin's *Origin of Species,* Fanny Burney's *Evelina,*
Provençal poetry, plays by Ibsen and Björnson, the latest novels
of Conrad and Galsworthy and Compton MacKenzie, and a
book by his friend Alan Herbert, *The Secret Battle.* He was
pleased to see that Herbert (the husband of Gerty's friend
Gwen Quilter) had gotten a publisher and wrote Gerty to ask
her for a copy of the book. Joyce felt it was "a good book — far
better than I had thought by the reviews which pictured to me a
kind of Russian novel at second hand like so many books by
young men now who take themselves seriously."

There was another book he asked for in August, 1919. The
reviews he had read interested him, and perhaps he was intrigued by the author's name, too: "Its called 'Portrait of the
Author as a Young Man, by James Joyce." After reading the
book, Joyce's response was strong and clear:

> Joyce's is a little masterpiece. Wells I see says it is like Sterne,
> but I call that inept. It is not at all like Sterne. Sterne enjoys
> an equivocal word or phrase for its own sake. He likes to excite
> the giggle of the half-modest, or a blush of self-consciousness.
> But Joyce is honest, sincere, and so all that in Sterne which must
> always be half-contemptible, is in him artistic truth — and plain-
> ness. Sterne is the servant of a bad, or at least a shallow purpose,
> but Joyce aims high and straight, and takes all between.

(23 November 1919)

A Portrait of the Artist as a Young Man fascinated him as no
other novel had during his entire five and a half years in Africa.
Nothing else in his letters receives the praise that he gave this
work. Five days after his initial reaction, he wrote to Gerty,

> I return again to that book of James Joyce. I must get his other
> books. They are not expensive & there are only two. Will you

get them? I don't know why I can read bits of it again and again, though it is true I have a special interest in it, from its being about Irish people, and also for its style. It is a very novel and interesting style — much more so than one would think at first glance. I am very curious to see this man's other books, and to see what he will write next. Though I fancy I read somewhere that he is writing another book which is coming out in some paper by chapters.

I once began a book a little like the Portrait — though it was not a Portrait of one person, but of a family — I came across the beginnings of it the other day when I was sorting my M.S.S. It will have to wait for a long time. I have three or four books to write before I come to it.

Many associations and memories heightened Joyce's "special interest" in James Joyce. As he said, *A Portrait of the Artist* was "about Irish people." Its author's name was the same as those of Joyce's grandfather and his uncle (in fact, Jim Joyce of Donegal and James Joyce of Dublin even bore a certain physical resemblance), who had meant to be a writer until he lapsed into alcoholism. Both Joyce and James Joyce were from families that had come down in the world, and both were exiles from Ireland.

While Joyce's favorite stylistic device was the first person narrative, James Joyce used the third person. And he often did so for interior monologue, and this was similar to what Joyce had been attempting. James Joyce was far in advance of him, but Joyce recognized the finished product as a model which he hoped to emulate.

Hitherto Thomas Hardy and Joseph Conrad had been Joyce's heroes and, to some degree, his models. But Hardy was 79 and Conrad 62 in 1919 (besides, Joyce had been disappointed in Conrad's latest novel, *The Arrow of Gold*), whereas James Joyce, at 37, was a contemporary, only half a dozen years older than himself, and this made him far more of a touchstone than the two older writers.

Joyce's book, which was "a little like the Portrait," may have been an early version of either *Castle Corner*, or, more likely, *A*

222 Joyce Cary: A BIOGRAPHY

House of Children. Castle Corner is far more a description of a
family, but *A House of Children* bears greater similarities to *A
Portrait of the Artist* in its atmosphere and its subject matter,
the experience and growth of a young boy. The story is seen in
flashes by the boy, a device rather similar to James Joyce's
"epiphanies." So the novel of which Joyce speaks may be an
early version of *A House of Children*.

It may even have been an early version of both books, since
Joyce in at least one instance split one of his works into two parts.
Cock Jarvis, the hero who gave his name to one of Joyce's unpublished novels, surfaced again in both *Castle Corner* and *Not
Honour More*. In the former it is Cocky's military exploits and
humorous aspects that are used; in the latter it is Cocky's sense
of grievance and murderous paranoia that Joyce salvages.

In any case, Joyce had found a new master and a new inspiration in James Joyce. As his third tour in Nigeria drew to an
end, he returned repeatedly to *A Portrait of the Artist,* to read
passages from it and to study its techniques.

The last weeks of his tour were busy with writing, working on
the road, and preparing for the trek to Kontagora. By the
middle of November he had four miles of finished road to walk
along and take pride in, and many more miles of terrain had
been surveyed. He still hoped the road would be finished by
someone else:

> That is my cunning — I want my policy to go on. Therefore I
> shall leave a piece of work — a big piece — half done and the
> next man must carry on with it even if he swears. But Cowper
> likes work. He's a sound fellow, and a very good D.O., well worth
> the promotion he got last year. My famous moorish Treasury has
> stood the rains very well and I am much relieved. The critical
> eye of Cowper will fall upon it soon.
>
> (13 November 1919)

His leave was held up by a lack of boxes for the money he had
to transport. Major Hamilton-Brown had sent a shipment of
money to the Treasury in July and so was out of ammunition
boxes, but, after scouring the province, he got some together

and sent them on to Joyce. What he did not send, though, was Joyce's mail from home, and Joyce was maddened by this:

> My strokes of ill-luck fall with such even regularity that I begin not to care so much for them though I was angrier this morning than for a long time. In short the Hammies are keeping my mail for me in Kontagora in case it may miss me on the road. So they sent back the runner with nothing but a note to say so. I bet this is Mrs. Hammy's idea. I cannot believe Hammy would be so stupid — tho' indeed having committed one stupidity — the other follows. . . . Meanwhile they will keep everything including my birthday parcel if it has come. God damn them both. . . . She did a trick like it once before. She kept my mail for me, and so I got it 4 days later than I need have. She wishes my gratitude. . . .
>
> I cannot describe to you how utterly blank life seemed to me this morning, but I'm getting better.
>
> (27 November 1919)

The anticipation of his leave and his cold and asthma which dragged on for months were making him fidgety enough. Four days' delay in his life-giving letters from home, especially those from Gerty, seemed an unbearable eternity. But when the mail was delivered by the runner, Joyce's interest was restored. He told Gerty, "I feel ashamed of swearing at poor Hammy." He says nothing of Mrs. Hamilton-Brown, since even in his best humor he was not prepared to forgive her.

In fact Mrs. Hamilton-Brown had a permanent effect on not just Joyce but Gerty, too, for she caused Joyce to change his wife's name. Joyce could not abide the sound of "Gerty" as spoken by the major's wife, and, in the latter part of his tour, he tried out other names for her in his letters, one for each aspect of her character: for instance, Gertrude Margaret was the serious and prim wife; Peggy was the hoydenish girl he'd honeymooned with. And there was Trudy. Trudy suited both the wife and the girl, so it became the name that he called her for the rest of their lives.

In the tag end of the tour he finished off as many short stories as he could and counted and packed his fifteen boxes of money; he accepted the Hamilton-Browns' invitation to Christmas dinner while wondering how soon in the new year he should get a boat at Lagos for home. During his last period in Borgu he kept up with the literary news and came on one item which evoked the comment, "Do you see that rascal Middleton Murry I dug with at Oxford is Editor of the Athenaeum. But he was a brilliantly clever fellow. I think he might pay me the money he owes me now though."

On December 9 he wrote Gerty-Trudy — for the last time from Kaiama:

> The mail came in, darling, a big official mail as well as three letters from you, in the middle of my packing. I was counting and nailing up 15 boxes of money, while everyone in the country who wants to see me has of course chosen the last day to come. So it has been a wild day. I sit in a room like the debris of a fire. I may get away by tea-time to-morrow, and I may not.

And then he was off.

III

A RISING REPUTATION

26

12 PARKS ROAD

JOYCE BURNED most of his manuscripts before he left Kaiama, throwing them onto a bonfire near the house while Mr. Graves, his clerk, watched in astonishment.[1] Joyce salvaged only the short stories and perhaps one or two of the dozen or so novels he had worked on during the tour. He could save the stories because they were meant to make money, while the novels were for reputation and glory, and so far none had come up to his high standards. Better to burn them than work over bad material. He continued to labor over the short stories during the voyage of the *Appam* to Liverpool.

Trudy, together with her sister and her brother-in-law, the Carlisles, met him at the boat. The two boys, Michael and Peter, had been left with their nurse at The Glade. The two couples spent a quiet day together; then, as the evening came, Joyce and Trudy were left alone by the discreet Carlisles, who "threw heavy stones about in the rock garden" while Joyce talked to his wife.[2] He had a great deal to tell her, news he had saved until he saw her.

He was not going back to Nigeria. He did not have to now.

During the last months of his tour he had gotten in touch with a fellow he had known at Oxford, now established as a literary agent.[3] Joyce had sent him several short stories to see if the agent thought he had any chance in the field. His former classmate had assured him he did and rather than returning the stories, he had sent them off to the United States to *The Satur-*

day Evening Post. The editors of the *Post* liked them and
bought three at once.[4]

The news had come to Joyce not long before he was to leave
for England. Rather than writing of it to Trudy, he had saved it
until this moment. Still, such a wonderful secret had to be
shared with someone, so he had told Cowper, who was relieving
him in Borgu. Three stories that had taken Joyce only a few
weeks of work had earned him a good deal more money than the
Nigerian Service paid him for a year of drudgery, Joyce told
Cowper, so he was not coming back after this leave.[5] This success
combined with his slowly crumbling health made it evident that
there was little sense in returning for another tour. He was retiring.

The news must have overwhelmed Trudy. It was what she
had longed for and dreamed of ever since they had been married
and what Joyce had told her could not happen for years, perhaps
not until they were both in their forties. He told her of the sales
of his work and that one of the stories, "Lambrosine," was being
published that same month, just a few days hence, in the January 31 issue of *The Saturday Evening Post.*

The next day they went to London to break the news to
everyone: Joyce was a success as a writer and home to stay!
Then, as soon as they could get away, they were on the train to
Oxford to see about a house, because this city still remained
their choice for a home.

Now that so many couples were reunited and settling into
married life, houses were not easily available, but Joyce and
Trudy had good luck and found one that suited them on Parks
Road, just ten or twenty yards north of Keble College and opposite the University Parks. It was a bright, large, semidetached
Victorian house with a long garden. The sitting room was
rather small, but the location of the building was so good that
this seemed only a minor problem. Since the Parks were across
from them, living here would be almost as good as living at The
Glade with its lawns and ponds and privacy. There would be
more than enough space for the boys to play, as paths ran in all
directions. Some of the lawns were neatly mowed and others left

to grow to hay, tennis courts and trees of every sort abounded, and Joyce could teach the boys to pole a punt on the nearby Isis River. And the view from the house was magnificent, for it would never be obstructed. The location was perfect.

The house was also convenient to Freddy Ogilvie's flat, so they could all visit back and forth whenever they liked. It was close to the Bodleian Library, to the colleges, to the post office on the Broad Street, to shopping, and to almost anything they could want.

They took 12 Parks Road on a 99-year lease.

If Joyce's triumphal homecoming was delightful to Trudy, it must have been even more so for Joyce. Everything he had told Trudy must remain in the future, five, ten, or even more years away, he had now. He had proved himself. He was home with his wife and his two sons, they had a house of their own in the city they had chosen, and he had sold a trio of stories at excellent rates to a magazine whose editors wanted to see more of his work, every story he wrote in fact. He was among his friends again, some of whom he had known for a decade: Tommy Higham, who had been made Dean of their old college, Trinity, just the year before; Duncan MacGregor, looking fitter than Joyce had ever known him, and happily married, too;[6] Brierly, the man who had demolished Joyce's smugness about his theories of art in Joyce's freshman year at Trinity and whom Joyce in time had come to like and admire. It seemed a perfect life after Borgu, in truth a dream come true.

What he still lacked, however, was success as a novelist. Yet he was only thirty-one, and a reputation would come in time, without the struggle he had anticipated, it seemed, now that he was able to support his family so handsomely with his short stories and could spend all his working time writing. He could divide his days between the short stories and the novels, taking his time with the latter, thinking them out and polishing them until they were exactly as he had meant them.

In Joyce's mind the two forms were divorced absolutely — or as absolutely as possible — and once he was able to make a living from the novels, he could abandon short story writing and be

totally happy. He even had a different name for his short stories: they were signed "Thomas Joyce," while "Joyce Cary" was
reserved for the novels.

The Saturday Evening Post, which at this time ran five and
six stories a week together with one or two serialized novels, had
a voracious appetite for material, and Joyce's stories of life in the
Latin Quarter of Paris suited the taste of the magazine's editors.
They had run "Lambrosine" in the January 31 issue, and on
March 6 and 13 there appeared respectively "The Idealist" and
"The Springs of Youth." From then on the *Post* published
Joyce's stories at the rate of one a month, and even two in May,
"The Cure" and "The Reformation."

The stories were slick and slight, exactly the formula Joyce
had described to Trudy in his letter of November 14, "a little
sentiment, a little incident, and a Surprise." But they were
amusing and gave an honest glimpse into Joyce's Paris background. They were stories which would not shame him, even if
they were not the sort of work on which he wanted to base his
reputation.

To be able to sell one story a month at nearly £200 apiece
was remarkable, and there was always the prospect of even
higher rates as his reputation grew — or rather the reputation of
"Thomas Joyce." His fortune was astonishing, after all the despair he had felt in Borgu, particularly in the swelter of Bussa,
when he felt he would never finish anything and never have his
work in print. Now he would have an income three, four, and
five times higher than his pay from the Nigerian Service — and
even if the *Post* were to reject a story or two, he still had the
cushion of two family incomes.

The spring and summer of 1920 were idyllic. Trudy and he
played tennis in the Parks with the MacGregors and other
young couples. Joyce's tennis game was erratic, partly because
he could hardly spot the ball, due to his poor sight, so his partner often did not know if he were going to make a return or not;
he usually played net so he would have some idea of what his
adversaries were doing.[7] Mornings and afternoons he took long,
rapid walks along the paths, a habit he had formed in Borgu,

because a good walk stirred his blood and brain and gave him a chance to think about his writing before he sat down at his table. He could frame scenes and even murmur bits of dialogue to himself as he walked along so totally absorbed that he would sometimes pass his friends without even knowing they were there. They got to know this habit of his and did not feel snubbed. Joyce and Trudy saw Freddy Ogilvie almost every day for tea, either at his rooms or at 12 Parks Road. Freddy was a Fellow at Trinity, and now that both he and Tommy Higham were at the college, Joyce dined there often.

Trudy had stuck to her promise of learning to typewrite, because after nearly four years of reading Joyce's letters, she had become one of the few who could understand his handwriting without having to puzzle over half the words. Now Joyce's writing became more of a family affair, as she could read through the handwritten foolscap pages, make comments on what she liked or thought Joyce ought to change, and then type up the stories and send them to Joyce's agent in London.

During the summer they went out on the river often, Joyce poling along with his smooth stroke. A few times he went riding, for this was one of the few activities he missed from Nigeria — he especially wanted to play polo as he had at Nafada, and he wished the sport were not the exclusive domain of the rich that it was in England. He dreamed of getting together a group of friends and playing rough games, but the idea never came to anything.[8]

Then in the autumn he got a jolt. The *Post*'s editors were sorry, but the latest stories were just too literary and they returned them to Joyce's agent. Couldn't Joyce give them something that was more along the lines of the earlier stories, the ones they and their readers enjoyed so much?

Joyce tried, but he could not return to his previous form. However much he had meant to separate his stories from his novels, the left hand and the right were linked. As he worked on his novels that year, his writing improved and deepened in meaning as the style became more sure, but his stories were affected, too. A writer with the capacity for growth who is trying to grow cannot help but improve in every area. He can't develop his talent in the mornings and then smother it in the afternoons. So after the summer of 1920 *The Saturday Evening Post* never bought another of Joyce's stories.

Although disturbed at the loss of this very profitable market, Joyce was not too despressed. There were other outlets such as *Cosmopolitan* and *Colliers* and his agent could try them. But none of them was interested so he then tried some of the British magazines. The trouble was that they — *The Strand, Cornhill,* Middleton Murry's *Athenaeum, London Magazine* — paid so much less than the top American magazines. Their fee was only a fifth or even a tenth of what the *Post* paid, and the payment usually was at the time of publication rather than on acceptance. There could be a wait of three, four, or even six months before the check arrived.

Nineteen-twenty, a year which began with so much happiness and hope and prosperity and promise, the fulfillment of everything Trudy and Joyce wanted, ended in despair. Joyce had followed his star, and it had flickered and gone out. If his stories did not find an American market, he was finished. He could write for the British magazines (if they would take his stories), but he could not possibly duplicate or even come remotely near his income of 1920 with them. To do so, he would have to write five and ten stories a month, and, even if he could manage that and get most of them published, when would there be time for his novels, his most important work? Not only would it be impossible to match his 1920 pay, but even the equivalent of his Nigerian Service salary would be hard, for his expenses were far higher now, particularly with a big house to pay for and furnish.

There was even the chance that if no American magazines wanted his stories, a fact which was becoming increasingly evident, possibly the British magazines would not want them, and he would have no income at all except for the £500 that he and Trudy received each year from their families.

The thought was numbing for both of them. To Joyce it must have been ironic that for this uncertainty he had given up a secure and worthwhile job, one that in another few years would have allowed him to retire on a pension and do his writing with real security. Perhaps the Ogilvies and his father were right: he was just a rootless, foolish young man who would never amount to anything as a writer.

And Trudy must have felt a terrible sense of guilt. After all, if she had not insisted so strongly that Joyce abandon his job with the Nigerian Service and come home, they might not have come to this unhappy state. She had been selfish and foolish, making too many demands, insisting that Joyce give up so much just for her.

HUNGARY

WHATEVER JOYCE AND TRUDY FELT, he could not go back to the Nigerian Service. Even if he could be reinstated, he would lose his seniority, and that meant his pension would be even further off; if he did not lose those six years toward his pension, he would still remain an A.D.O., with only an A.D.O.'s salary. And it would be humiliating to take up his old occupation after crowing about his success as a writer.

It would be even worse to leave Trudy, Michael, and Peter, all his friends, the house, and the Parks after this great taste of happiness and contentment. A return to Borgu after spending 1920 in Oxford would be heartbreaking and might plunge him into the depression and despair he had felt in early 1917 or the sort of breakdown he had experienced in the late days of the Cameroons Campaign.

Besides, Michael was three and a half and Peter was two; they needed a father, now that they were past the toddler stage. Joyce, who had many pet theories, was particularly interested in their education; if he left, he would be a stranger to them, just a photograph on the mantelpiece.

Yet with no training, as he had told Trudy so many times in his letters, starting a new career at home at thirty-two was impossible.

He would have to hang on, trying the short stories, hoping they would make as much money as possible, and plug away at the novels which might eventually earn him some financial success. There were other possibilities. With friends at the various colleges, particularly at Trinity, he might get work of some kind. He had no hopes of getting any sort of regular position, but there were tutoring and coaching jobs to prepare students for entrance exams or to make foreign students more fluent in English. Joyce spread the word among his friends and hoped to get a little work this way.

So they struggled into 1921, tightening up the budget as much as they could, watching the hefty bank balance of 1920 begin to shrink, and wondering if they would be able to continue if matters did not improve. Joyce worked every day in the "Piggery," a little pantry off their sitting room, churning out the necessary short stories and trying to write a satisfactory novel, wondering sometimes if it would not be a good idea to combine his left and right hands and write a "popular" novel.

After all, one big windfall would solve everything for them. If he could write a novel that was a popular success, a good romance that moved along at a swift pace, he might make enough money to tide them over for the next five years, perhaps even the next decade. A successful novel in 1921 sold perhaps a hundred thousand copies. Wasn't it selfish to divide his life the way he did, stinting the present in hopes of making a respected name for himself as a serious novelist? Why not a good, fat, pot-boiling novel? Freddy Ogilvie for one urged that he should do just that.[1]

But this he could not do. He had kept the two lines of his writing separate in his mind for so long that he was unable to make this surrender, and Trudy did not want him to give in to monetary demands either. He had compromised enough by taking on the short stories.[2]

So he thought of a third field: drama. In Borgu he had been interested in playwriting; he had studied a book on the art of the drama and had thought of trying a play. He had had Trudy send him collections of Ibsen and Björnson in order to study their structure and methods.[3] One of his fortes was writing dialogue, so drama seemed a natural extension of his work.

A good comedy could earn an enormous amount of money.

George Bernard Shaw and Somerset Maugham had grown enormously rich on the theater, not just rich in comparison with
other writers, but rich enough to rank with business tycoons;
they were able to travel wherever they liked, to buy villas, wines,
paintings, virtually anything they wanted. A play was not much
longer than a short story, not anywhere near so ambitious a
project as a novel, at least in terms of time. One just had to dash
off a play, find a producer, and then sit back and watch the
money pour into the bank. At least so it seemed. So that summer of 1921 he made his first attempt.⁴

Trudy was away most of the summer. Mrs. Ogilvie had had a
severe heart attack in June; it had been so bad that Heneage,
who was sure she would not recover, summoned Freddy and
Trudy to London to see their mother before she died.⁵ Trudy
took Michael, now four, and left Peter at home with Joyce and
the nursemaid.⁶ But when Mrs. Ogilvie rallied and began to
improve, Trudy stayed on to run the household for her father
and to nurse her mother. When the Ogilvies went to Blair-
Atholl in Scotland (they still summered in Scotland but not at
Balmacara because it was too remote), Trudy accompanied
them, after a quick visit to Oxford to see Joyce. Both Peter and
Michael went along to Blair-Atholl, leaving Joyce in peace to
proceed with his projected play.⁷ The boys, after all, would enjoy the holiday, and if Joyce and Trudy could save some money
because of the month's free board and lodging, it was all to the
good. The play was vital and Joyce could use the quiet of an
empty house.

While Trudy was away, she and Joyce wrote daily, just as
when he had been in Nigeria. Joyce told her of the tennis games
he had played and the friends with whom he dined. He assured
her he was looking after the garden, too. He was doing some
painting again, mainly watercolor, and enjoying it so much that
"I must be careful to keep it for afternoons at most," or it would
interfere with writing.⁸ The gardening allowed his mind to
drift, particularly when he sat out on the lawn, digging up
weeds with a knife, creating new scenes and developing new
plots.⁹ When he painted he became so absorbed in the techni-

cal problems involved that his mind was shut off from thinking and worrying about bills and the future. Painting was more than a hobby; it was a temporary escape from his troubles.

He needed a diversion, too, because he could hardly keep from worries. When the local rates bill came, he had only nine pounds in the bank and had to let payment lapse until he received his share of the rents from the family properties in Ireland.[10] Debt was depressing. He had been in this circumstance before, in both Edinburgh and Oxford, but then it had not been so bad. He had been a young man with no responsibilities, his whole life ahead of him, and plenty of time to pay off obligations.

Now, with his income much reduced and no prospect of a change for the better and with his finances drifting further and further into the red, he could not help but worry. Debt, after all, had ruined the Carys and had driven them out of Ireland. If his grandfather had not lived beyond his means, Joyce and Trudy might be in Donegal, occupying the grand house overlooking Lough Foyle, where they could walk for miles before they came to the end of the Cary lands. Arthur Cary had spoken of all this often enough, and Joyce as a boy frequently had seen the melancholy look of loss on his Uncle Tristram's face. Now if his father knew how much he needed funds, he would be horrified. Joyce had gone to him for help before, but he could not now. In 1909 or 1912 he could assure his father it was only temporary, but who knew how long this present state of affairs would last. And he was too proud to appeal to Mr. Ogilvie. "Duns, to a proud man," Joyce said later, "are both infuriating and alarming." [11] They erode one's self-respect.

So he was dependent on his hobbies for peace of mind, and dependent on his friends for moral support, as he told Trudy:

> I dined again with Duncan. He has repaid your hospitality by being very good to me when I needed consolation. I have been very depressed on several occasions when he has come to the rescue with tennis or dinner. I don't know how I shall bridge the gap between his going and your return. I have to admit that I

am dependant on you, darling — I may be sometimes gloomy when you are at home, but I fall a thousand feet lower when you are away.

(August 1921)

His gloominess and depression did not slow up his writing, however. He sent off stories at the rate of one a week[12] and still found time for his novel and his big money-maker, the play, tentatively titled "Prue" or "Prudence." [13] The work had bogged down in June, perhaps because of the upset over Mrs. Ogilvie's illness, but then in July, with a new second act, it picked up once more.[14]

As the play grew, so did Joyce's enthusiasm, and he had to remind Trudy and himself of the harsh realities of the theater: "I can't believe she'll ever be acted. That would be fantastic — a first play accepted. But I hope she'll be good enough to invite encouragement." [15] He needed encouragement almost as much as money at this point. "Perhaps in another ten years," he told Trudy, "I shall see a play of mine on the stage. Meanwhile I suppose I may come to breaking stones." [16] All the same, he was heartened by his progress and anxious that Trudy should get it typed up when she came home, so that he could see how it looked in typescript.

Trudy had not mastered the typewriter yet, for Joyce said,

I miss my secretary — the piggers seems quite an empty room — I believe my mind works better to the accompaniment of "bother" and "dash," on the other side of the table. This is a remarkable example of adaptation.[17]

Trudy replied,

I am glad you miss me a wee bit darling — and that my bad language at the typewriter doesn't altogether keep you out of the piggers — but I am afraid for creative work you will find it difficult — and we shall have to transfer the typewriter somewhere.[18]

The typewriter was rented, since they had not bought one in

their flush days of 1920 and now the price of a new machine was beyond them. They rented one only when there was a big sheaf of manuscript to be typed; meanwhile they looked around to see if they could find an inexpensive used machine.[19]

Although Trudy returned to Oxford when the Ogilvies left Blair-Atholl at the end of the summer, she had to hurry back to London in the late autumn, when Mrs. Ogilvie had a stroke.[20] The Ogilvies had sold The Glade that spring and were living in a large flat at Queen Anne's Mansions in London (the sale of The Glade had been an unpleasant affair, since one of the family had collared many belongings promised to the others).[21]

Trudy hated leaving Joyce for a second time, especially since he had decided the play was a flop and was unable to finish it. With the dream of its success gone and deprived of escape from his worries through tennis and gardening by the change of season, Joyce was in a very bad state. He was deep in despair now, more depressed than Trudy had ever seen him, and continuously so. But again it looked as if her mother might not recover from her illness, and Trudy felt obligated to go to her.

Joyce's letters written during this absence have none of the hope and bounce of those written during the summer. He was absolutely at the end of his rope. Perhaps he even saw himself in the situation of the old artist he had met in France in 1904, painting for galleries that had become closed to his work. Joyce had been impressed very deeply by that meeting nearly twenty years before and remembered the man's plaints and his own indifference. But the old painter had had years of prosperity and acclaim before his crash came, whereas Joyce had been given only a few months of it, just enough to taste how sweet success could be.

Trudy took it on her own shoulders to make the big decision: they must leave 12 Parks Road, the big house overlooking the Parks, and face the facts of their failure. It had been she, after all, who had pressed Joyce to give up Nigeria and come home. She had sent him that ultimatum that he would be responsible for whatever happened if he did not give up the Nigerian Service; now she felt it was up to her to cope with the results of his retirement. So she wrote to him on November 23:

I

DEAREST, I have been thinking about your letters so much. I only wanted to try and comfort you when I was at home — I know what an awful strain you have been going through — and I feel most awfully worried about what you say about your physical [indecipherable] though I was awfully afraid you would have some kind of breakdown. Dearest I am afraid I have been a great coward about trying to face what I knew all the time must come — we must try & not think of the sadness of leaving Parkers & all it implies — but look forward to the time when we can perhaps go back feeling absolutely secure — and you darling having had the success I know you deserve. — As soon as Christmas is over we will begin to look for rooms or a flat.

Joyce was not prepared to leave the house and sublet it. That would make the break with the life they had begun in Oxford too sharp and final. It would be a surrender to a state of affairs he did not want to believe was permanent. It would only depress him in a different way to leave the house, so where was the sense of it? And in cramped quarters, writing would be more difficult, making a recouping of their finances that much harder.

Their second Christmas in Oxford passed gloomily, despite attempts to make it a happy occasion. It meant festivities, but it also meant bills, which they could not meet.

Although Joyce would not give up the house on Parks Road, they finally agreed upon a compromise; they would let the ground floor as a flat and live in the upper part of the house. Such an arrangement would bring in a fair bit of money and would mean they only were inconvenienced rather than dispossessed. They would still have the Parks Road house and almost all its advantages.[22]

The idea revived both of them, and they set about putting it in motion. Since they were so convenient to the colleges and the center of Oxford, they had no trouble finding occupants.

Then, in the summer of 1922 Tommy Higham came up with a treat for Joyce that would broaden his horizons and give him something to think about besides bills and writing and markets: a trip to Hungary, all expenses paid.[23]

In 1916, with the death of Franz Josef, the King-Emperor of Austria-Hungary, his grandnephew Karl succeeded to the throne of the Dual Monarchy, only to be deposed with the defeat of the Central Powers in 1918. In 1921 Karl made two attempts to overthrow the republican government of Hungary. During his second *putsch*, some Oxford undergraduates lit a bonfire in King Edward Street, just off the High Street, to demonstrate their sympathy with the pretender, Karl. As a result, a group of exiled Hungarian nobles and royalists, now living in England, invited some of these students to see the situation in Hungary caused by the peace treaty. On the return of this group, the same exiled Hungarians, gratified at the propaganda value of the students' visit, suggested that a larger party go to Hungary in the summer of 1922. They could see the crimes done to the country as a result of the peace. The exiles suggested that this time the group include several university dons, as well as students, in the hope that these influential visitors might return to England with the idea of demanding that the treaty be changed.

Tommy Higham was one of those invited. Fine, he told them, provided he could bring his friend Cary, a university graduate and very promising author. So the invitation was extended to Joyce as well, and he accepted. On his present income, it might be the only chance he had for travel on the continent for a long time to come.

The other dons in the group included C. R. S. Harris and Dermot M. M. Morrah, both of All Souls College, and Julian Huxley of New College. They and eleven students set out from London on July 22, 1922. All along the way they had glimpses of the remains and effects of the war: a Belgian railway station hung with German helmets in which flowers were growing; a mob of people fresh out of a political demonstration, still waving their banners and signs in the railway station at Passau, through which the Oxford group had to fight their way to get the train for Vienna; the great wads of kronen they got when they exchanged their money, the Austrian currency depreciating in value even during the two days they spent in that country (the krone slipped from 120,000 to 148,000 to the British pound).

Vienna seemed a dead city and not the lively place it was

reputed to be. It was shabby, and its people, with their dull eyes and hostile faces, appeared dispirited as they stood around on street corners. The party arrived at midnight on a Sunday and the next day Joyce wanted to take advantage of their brief stop-over by visiting the galleries. But the one Tommy Higham and he went to was closed on Mondays. However, after bribing the porter, they had a private tour. Joyce was delighted by both the paintings and the clandestine circumstances. The gallery was hung with fine works by Velázquez and Peter Brueghel, but some of the frames, they were surprised to see, were empty except for postcard replicas of the missing paintings. This, they were told, was because these particular paintings had been carried off as war booty by the victorious Italians. The postcards were a form of mute protest.

This irreverence added to their already dampened feelings about Vienna, and not even a dinner at one of Vienna's finest restaurants, a meal that included excellent champagne and still only cost them six shillings each, could shake their sense of depression. They wondered if Hungary would be as bad.

They also wondered if they would be spied on, since they were traveling at the expense of the Hungarian Government's enemies. Perhaps the Hungarians might have them trailed by a female spy, a Mata Hari. And what about spies, they wondered: were you supposed to tip them when you left the country?

At dinner some of the students, all primed for the trip next day to Hungary, were sporting white roses in their buttonholes, the symbol of their sponsoring organization in England, to demonstrate their sympathy with the monarchy. Joyce and Higham, for the sport, stuck red roses in their lapels and persuaded one student, who was less ardent than the rest, to wear both a white and a red rose to show his neutrality.

On Tuesday, July 25, they left Vienna on a Danube boat and were as disappointed in the river as they had been with Vienna. The only event that enlivened the first hour or two of the trip was a glimpse they got of a Czech soldier with bayoneted rifle on the north shore near Pozsony; in the town itself there were barbed-wire entanglements and earthworks at the Czech end of the bridge across the river. At another town, Komarno, the Czech end of the bridge had been destroyed, evidently dynamited by the Czechs themselves.

After being joined on the boat by their Hungarian host, who had been unable to meet them at Vienna because he could not get a visa, they arrived at Budapest, where a small delegation met them at the pier. The delegation, on seeing them, seemed quite disappointed; these British were not at all what they had expected. The greeting ceremony was saved only by the presence of Julian Huxley. As Higham noted in his diary of the trip, "Huxley's name goes a long way, and his beard was an asset to a party that must have seemed disappointingly young." It was Huxley who gave the reply to the speech of greeting, but in placating the Hungarians, he got his fellow travelers into an embarrassing situation by speaking of them all as "representatives of Oxford University."

Budapest was far more interesting than Vienna had been, partially because the group was feted but also because the city was livelier and, architecturally at least, a novelty. Their hotel, the Gellert, was in the old city of Buda, and Joyce and Tommy had a view from their rooms of the Danube and of Pest on the far side. The cleanliness and modernity of the city surprised them; its architecture combined very contemporary, western European building styles and decor with an exotic Byzantine or Turkish look. The Gellert itself was an example of this: it had thick pillars of brown marble and Byzantine domes and yet it also had a battery of push buttons in each room and loudspeakers that piped the music of the Gypsy orchestra that played for the roof gardens into each room. And the push buttons themselves were as cosmopolitan as possible, with pictures instead of names: a waiter on one button, a chambermaid on another, and so on.

Unfortunately, the knobs in the bathroom had no pictures, and the first thing Tommy Higham wanted to do once he and Joyce were settled in their room was to take a bath.

The trouble was, there were five knobs, two marked *Hildeg,* two marked *Meleg,* and an unmarked one. No pictures at all. So he tried a *Hildeg,* but with no result. Then he tried the

Meleg next to it and got a torrent of steaming hot water. He
tried the other *Meleg* and got even more hot water. Deciding
that the two *Melegs* were just for show, to give the tub a sense of
symmetry, he tried what obviously was the most important button of the five, the unmarked one, and suddenly hot water burst
from the ceiling, raining down on Higham and the tub and filling the room with steam. Higham, boiling away in the "one
good suit" he had brought for the trip, backed off and yelled for
help, and Joyce ran in with an umbrella, under which Higham
turned off the unmarked shower knob.

With Joyce for spiritual comfort and the umbrella for comfort of a more practical sort, he reached for the last remaining
knob, the second *Hildeg,* turned it, and cold water beat down on
the umbrella.

Eventually Higham found he had turned the anonymous
shower regulator too far in his desperation to get the hot rain
storm turned off, and now he turned it carefully to a neutral
position, and cold water calmly flowed from the tap under the
Meleg knob and hot from beneath one of the *Hildegs.* Although both he and his suit were pretty thoroughly doused, he
had his bath anyway, for it had now become a matter of prin-
ciple.

The next day was a round of official visiting, which took in
the Houses of Parliament, the Royal Palace, a museum, and tea
with the Prime Minister, Count Stefan Bethlen. Thursday was
the same, but Joyce managed a visit to an art gallery. On Fri-
day, everyone boarded a train to Balatonfüred, a spa on Lake
Balaton, from which they took a pilgrimage by boat to the old
monastery where King Karl had been imprisoned after his second *putsch* of 1921; however, the group was much less awed by
the pilgrimage than by the dancing at the country club near
Balatonfüred that night. They joined in the dancing until two
in the morning and did not get to bed until four. From then on
the tour of the "representatives of Oxford University" who were
going to weep at the sight of the poor Hungarians and then rush
home to rewrite the peace treaty became less and less an official
and solemn affair and more and more a holiday.

The one remaining official part of the visit that they enjoyed was a tour — fairly prolonged — of the State wine cellars at Budafok.

Before the group left Budapest for home, they took up a collection for The Cause, perhaps out of guilt at having enjoyed themselves so much. The take came to twenty-one pounds, five shillings (of which Joyce contributed two pounds). It was enough to have bought a couple of blankets and a hot water bottle for Karl, if he had still been in his monastery, but hardly enough to launch another *putsch*.

From Joyce's point of view, the two pounds were well spent, for he had had a two-week holiday in a first-class hotel, had had tea with a prime minister, and had viewed some excellent paintings. The experience might prove useful in a short story or two as well. And it had been a great relief to be able to forget about his empty bank account for a while and all those bills that dropped in the letter basket each morning with such frightful regularity. He went back to Oxford feeling happier than he had for months, ready to get into harness again.

28

COCK JARVIS

IT IS DIFFICULT to guess how many novels Joyce began during
the 1920's, but if his rate of production was anything like what it
had been in Borgu, where he had far less time for writing, he
must have made several dozen starts. One novel that out-
weighed all the others of the period, literally and figuratively,
was *Cock Jarvis*. Joyce wrote and rewrote this novel many
times, trying to cram into it as much of his Nigerian experience
as it would hold. But despite a tremendous amount of work, he
never was satisfied with the book and did not publish it.

Later he said that the main problem was that Jarvis, its hero,
was "a Conrad character, in a Kipling role." Joyce explained,

> He was sensitive, intelligent, and thoughtful, like Conrad's
> heroes, but he was a strong imperialist, like Kipling's. He had
> a high sense of honour and duty like Kipling's soldiers but he
> was also essentially liberal in sympathy. He believed in the Em-
> pire, in fact, as the only liberal civilization in the world, and he
> would say that the fall of the Roman Empire before the tribes of
> nationalist barbarians had wrecked civilization for a thousand
> years. And would do it again if they could smash the British
> Empire.[1]

Yet what kept Joyce from finishing the novel was not his conception of Jarvis so much as his conception of the world itself. A
clear idea of the nature of man's existence eluded him and this
made each attempt at *Cock Jarvis* end unsatisfactorily.

Cocky Jarvis is a fascinating character who incorporates bits of several Nigerian hands Joyce had known. Edwardes, Cowper, the cynical Fitzpatrick, even Lord Lugard and Joyce's father, as well, of course, as Joyce himself, all had a part in the drawing up of Cock Jarvis. The character created from these sources was a magnet that drew Joyce back time after time, perhaps over a period of twenty years, before he abandoned the novel for good. Although Joyce called the book a product of the 1920's there is evidence that he worked on it as late as 1935, and he may have begun it in Nigeria somewhere during the years 1916–1919, because a few pages of the existing manuscript are written on the same lined foolscap he used then, in the handwriting of that time and with the ink blurring as it used to during the Nigerian rainy season when the paper was sodden under his pen.

Cocky was a magnet because he is a truly tragic character, a great but flawed man. His greatness lies in the fact that he is a man of vision, creativity, and energy, capable of love, anger, and compassion, all on a grand scale. But he was born at the wrong time and is unable to adjust to the period in which he lives. Cocky is a nineteenth-century paternalistic imperialist trying to cope with the twentieth century. He has a strong sense of honor together with a total inability to understand the principles by which other people live when they differ from his own. Only Clerk Johnson of *Mister Johnson* and Gulley Jimson of *The Horse's Mouth* leave so lasting an impression as Jarvis.

The novel went through draft after draft, and even within a particular version one can find scenes rewritten several times. The manuscript, as it now exists, runs to about two thousand sheets, many of them written on both sides.[2] There are sketches of single characters and of whole scenes, handwritten drafts of complete chapters and finished sections of the book, handwritten and typed bits and pieces of dialogue, and, of course, finished rough drafts of the whole novel. The complete collection of manuscripts is a course in novel writing. Joyce returned to it frequently, hoping each time that he had the answer to its problems or that the answer would come of itself if he just worked a little longer. The result is a concentrated picture of his development as a novelist over a period of perhaps twenty years, from novice to the accomplished author who, however reluctantly, was able to see that the book never could become what he meant it to be and so discarded it.

Jarvis is an old man, at least old for service in Africa (in most versions he is fifty or thereabouts), and is Resident of "Daji, most western of the old Provinces" of Nigeria (sometimes he is only a D.O. in the province, having already been reduced to this rank from that of Resident). Daji Province is the most remote and primitive part of Nigeria, and its capital, Kura, is an island in the wilderness.

It was Cocky who captured the province for the empire, at a risk of war with the French, trekking through the arid country to the capital with a tiny army of native troops reduced almost to skeletons, then storming the town because to have turned back would have meant death from starvation and lack of water. The taking of Kura was an act of desperation, and so are most of Cocky's acts. After causing an international crisis and risking court-martial, Cocky left the army to join the Nigerian Service, and is made Resident of the province he has conquered. He had hoped this was the beginning of a brilliant career in the Service, but he is fifty when the book opens and remains Resident of Daji.

The major draft of the novel starts here, with Cocky's return from leave in England. At the provincial border he is met by the emir and his party, and as the triumphal march passes along "the peasants in the fields . . . dropped hoes and came scampering up and flung themselves on their faces at the roadside, throwing dust on their heads and shouting 'Lord, Lord, Lord of the world, God prolong your life, King of the World.'" This reception never fails to delight Jarvis, but it bores his young wife, Kate. (She is Nancy in some versions but will remain Kate here for clarity.) She knows the demonstration appeals to her husband's vanity and is annoyed that he should be so childish.

At Daji Station Jarvis is outraged to find that the new polo grounds have not been laid out and that Captain Parker, commander of the troops in this border area, has refused to loan soldiers for the project. Jarvis consoles himself for his failures by transforming Daji from a mud village into a Nigerian Versailles. One of his first acts as Resident of Daji had been

> to order from the public works department, a double decked bungalow, two thousand young fruit trees, several hundred pounds worth of flower, vegetable, and grass seeds, and thirty barrels of cement for an ornamental lake.

Instead, he was given only the bungalow; when he threatened to resign, they threw him a few mango trees and a dozen packets of seed.

> But every year since he had bought trees, seed, grass; and the station was kept like Versailles or Sans Souci, although, on account of the meanness of the Treasury grants, he could afford only three gardeners, of whom he paid two out of his own pocket.

The new polo grounds were to have been the latest addition to this Versailles, and Cocky rages at being balked on his home territory.

After telling Captain Parker to get out of Daji, Cocky goes on to his office to meet young Thompson, his protégé, whom he treats as a fellow conspirator against the administration of Nigeria. Thompson, during Jarvis's leave, has put the chaotic office into shape, by performing such tasks as making pigeonholes for the mess of official papers that used to lie about the office and whitewashing the walls. Cocky, to whom a chaotic office signifies that he is a man of action, is upset by this, too. But he pretends to admire Thompson's handiwork, despite his negative attitude toward any administrator who works behind a desk.

Jarvis's attitude toward administrators, especially those of the Treasury, is revealed in a letter he writes on learning that he has been refused money for a new ferry on the Mashi River:

> Daji.
> 2.9.07.
> SIR,
> With reference to your query about the over expenditure of one shilling and fourpence halfpenny on the vote for roads and

bridges. I have the honour to inform you that the sum will be refunded in this month's accounts. You will be glad to know that six persons have been drowned in the Mashi since Christmas. I understand that clerks in your office are allowed twopence a piece for the invention of queries, and I trust you will inform the gentleman responsible for the correspondence relating to the Mashi ferry, of his bag, which works out at something less than a farthing a head. Better results can be hoped for in the wet season. I offer to yourself, sir, such congratulations as are due to you for your share in a transaction so creditable to your department, and so useful to the real purposes of government.

> And have the honour to remain, sir,
> Your obedient servant.
> H.A. Jarvis.

This sort of letter, which Jarvis chronically fires off to the "desk jockeys" and "base barnacles," only serves to get him into a deeper and deeper hole. An increasing number of people all over Nigeria would be glad to kick the dirt in on Jarvis and bury him in that hole forever.

After the letter to the Treasury, Cocky writes another to demand Captain Parker's transfer from Daji. This request results in an official inquiry into Daji's administration, notorious throughout Nigeria as an example of maladministration.

The man sent out to investigate Daji, Mr. Lepper, is not after Cocky's hide; he regards himself as Jarvis's friend and intends to offer him one of the richest divisions in all Nigeria — one with a railway line being built through it to make it richer still. Such a division could hardly fail to make Jarvis look capable, for it virtually runs itself. Then in time Cocky might be given charge of another whole province and a far better one than Daji. As for Daji, it is to be divided among the adjacent provinces.

Lepper points out that Cocky, although he will retain the title of Resident, will in effect be D.O. of an arid, worthless division if he stays in Daji Station. If he accepts Lepper's offer, made in good faith, Jarvis will be saved from ruin.

Instead of accepting, Cocky does everything possible to insult Lepper, including having the guest house pulled down around the man's ears, with the excuse that it was not good enough for him and must be rebuilt. Lepper, spattered with rotting thatch and bird dung, resignedly begins his report. All his attempts to help are frustrated by Cocky's blatant perversity.

Kate, who has been cool to Jarvis since their return to Daji, sees him as the victim of his pride. But since he cannot rid himself of pride (which was one of the characteristics that first drew her to him) and since she sees it will be his downfall, she begins to warm to him again and urges him to accept Lepper's kindness, knowing that the investigator only wants to help.

Although he does not give in, Cocky is deeply moved and disturbed by Kate's plea, and that night he cannot sleep. He goes for a solitary walk in the bush to think and is astonished to hear himself say, "Yes, I shall have to shoot somebody."

Reluctantly Lepper files his report with the lieutenant-governor. Daji Province consequently is reduced to the level of a division annexed by Berewa Province. Cocky's staff move off to other posts and Captain Parker's troops are withdrawn to Berewa Station. The Resident of Berewa, Killick (who resembles Joyce's old Resident, Major Hamilton-Brown) attempts to treat Jarvis as an equal, but Cocky rebuffs this gesture with rudeness and insults. For he feels that everyone is plotting against him, even Killick. He becomes increasingly paranoid.

Kate, unable to make Cocky see reason, has grown ill from the climate and her unhappiness and asks him to let her return to England to recuperate. Although Cocky is shattered by his total defeat, he tells Kate she can go. She can join the caravan of troops, staff, and porters leaving for Berewa Station.

The evening before the caravan goes, Cocky gives a final dinner for his departing friends and subordinates, a grand banquet that costs him £50. At the dinner he seems his old bubbling, kind, and gracious self. Even enemies like Captain Parker are touched by his goodness and charm.

When the caravan leaves the next morning, the full realization of Cocky's ruin hits him. Should he simply cut his throat and be done with it? No, he decides; that would be folly. He will be given a new province in time, as soon as a residency is open. He just needs to hang on for a bit. Nobody wants to destroy him, he tells himself, and it's foolish to think so.

At this point the manuscript is muddled. Somehow Kate is still in Daji and tells Cocky that he has been passed over for promotion five times. She tells him to resign, rather than to continue living on false hopes. "What's the good of pretending," she says. "You know you'll never be promoted. But you're too proud to admit it. You might just as well resign." When he refuses, she breaks into sobs.

Again this draft breaks off and returns to what seems the original line. We find that Thompson, Cocky's protégé, has switched his allegiance to his new resident, Killick, because he has come to realize the mess his former superior has made of Daji. Thompson has made a great success of his new job in Shibi, "a pagan district, of swamps and islands, which had been neglected for years." Since their parting, Jarvis has embarrassed Thompson with a constant flow of gifts, such as whiskey, gin, and sacks of potatoes.

Shibi lies next to Daji, and there is constant friction between the two territories. Daji emirate tries to collect taxes in Shibi, and the Daji emir has kidnapped wives from Shibi. The latest kidnapping victim is the young daughter of Thompson's chief hunter. Thompson is furious and writes Cocky to say he is coming to talk with him.

He finds Daji in ruins. The gardens have been utterly overrun by jungle and the buildings are a shambles. There is a stench of rot about the place.

In the midst of this ruin sits Cock Jarvis, like Dickens's Miss Havisham in the ruins of her wedding glory. Thompson is disarmed when Cocky lavishes kindness on him, "not in an ironical or formal manner, but with that kind of nervous eager affection which might be seen in a father trying to reconcile a troublesome but much loved son." Thompson stays in the roofless rest house, resisting Cocky's invitation to the bungalow.

The sight of Kate Jarvis is even more shocking to Thompson than his first glimpse of Daji, for

She has become ugly, with hollow cheeks and a skin as white and dry as paper; thinness had changed the proportion of her features, making her mouth and eyes big, her nose pinched, her chin sharp.

Kate and Thompson had been in love at one time,* and Kate now wants to talk of this time. Thompson, though, changes the subject to Daji and suggests that Cocky retire. She agrees, but insists that despite what Cocky has done to Daji, he is still the finest man she has ever known. But she does not love him, she confesses; it is Thompson whom she has always loved. Yet she indicates she will stay with her husband in his defeat.

One day Cocky gives way to his bitterness and tells Thompson he must never attempt to be a leader; be a follower, he says — it's safer. Leaders are always betrayed. His own philosophy, he tells Thompson, is this:

Lay not up for yourself treasures on earth. He that seeks his life shall lose it — and that's to say, don't give a damn for anybody — and don't try to get anything for yourself. Christ knew the world, no man better. He knew there was no justice in it. He knew its damned ingratitude. He knew that more than half the people in it were animals no more responsible for their dirty work than hogs or snakes and you couldn't teach 'em better if you flayed 'em. Lord, forgive them, for they know not what they do — forgive, that's the secret. Why, you've got to. He saw that. If you don't forgive them, you're a fool. You're helping them. You're poisoning yourself — just what they want.

On and on Cocky raves, speaking of forgiveness and compassion, yet spitting the words out like a sputtering machine gun, while he chokes with rage and bitterness. He even flies at his native servant with a knife when Thompson's glass is not refilled promptly.

Meanwhile one of Thompson's constables has learned where

* In some versions Kate and Thompson were lovers in England and Jarvis married Kate when Thompson deserted her; sometimes Thompson, whom Kate loved, had ruined himself by gambling; in all cases Thompson is saved by Cocky, who gets him into the Nigerian Service.

the kidnapped girl is hidden. Thompson, aware that Cocky is
on the verge of a total breakdown, nevertheless asks for a
warrant to arrest the kidnapper. Cocky turns on him savagely,
accusing him of betrayal and of being one of the hyenas after his
hide. Thompson goes to the rest hut certain that Cocky is no
longer responsible for his actions or his words; the young officer
will have to act on his own. So, after outfitting himself, he joins
his police unit to rescue the girl.

She is found, but she has been badly beaten. Her kidnapper
is arrested, and Thompson returns to inform Cocky. Meanwhile
the emir has complained to Jarvis of Thompson's raid. Consequently when Thompson shows up, Cocky brushes aside his report and demands,

> How would you like it if Muma [the kidnapper] came into your
> house at two o'clock in the morning with a couple of police and
> carried you off to the town gaol because your cook had got a new
> whore in the kitchen.

He advises Thompson to free Muma, but the young officer refuses and returns to his hut to go to bed.

He is awakened and told that Muma has changed himself into
a bird and flown from the jail window, while the girl has been
carried off by a leopard. She is found, but she is dying, her en-
trails torn out. Muma then gives himself up. Cocky presides
over an inquest and declares, "A charge of murder should be
laid against persons unknown"; Muma is jailed for abduction
but escapes a second time that night.

Thompson seeks out the kidnapper and kills him when he
tries to flee. Thereupon he is delivered a letter from Cock Jarvis
that reads,

> I would perhaps have killed Muma in your place but techni-
> cally you've committed murder. I think I warned you not to
> shoot but if I had had any notion that you might do so, I should
> have made the warning stronger. I'm afraid there's no doubt
> about my own position. I must put you under arrest and report
> the circumstances to the Resident of the Province.

The next day, Kate, who has not spoken to Cocky for several days, visits Thompson in the rest house and stays there until after dark. She makes another visit the following day, returning home past midnight. Jarvis sees what she is doing and says nothing.

Killick tries Thompson and finds him

> guilty of insubordination, ignorance of the rules of the Service and the principles of indirect government, and a serious breach of law nearly amounting to a crime.

Killick says that only Cock Jarvis's intercession has saved Thompson from a worse verdict.

So Cocky now wants to play the role of compassionate Christ toward his assumed betrayer, Thompson. For Cocky is a religious man, frequently quoting (or misquoting) the Bible. His initials, C.J., however, are an inversion of Christ's, and thus Cocky is an inverted Christ, filled with rage, not love, racing toward his crucifixion.

Later that day Cocky finds Kate in the rest house with Thompson. He congratulates Thompson on his duplicity and asks if he means to steal Kate.

"She's dying of misery," Thompson retorts.

Jarvis states, "If I see you with my wife again I'll blow your face out of your back hair."

Killick begins an inquiry into the administration of Daji Division at Thompson's instigation (and backed by the perverse and self-destructive Jarvis). The emir and his court panic and accuse each other of crimes. Killick can only levy minimal punishments since so many are involved. But he tells Cocky that Daji is the worst administration he has ever seen, a disgrace to Nigeria, and recommends a further splintering of Daji and Cocky's demotion to Assistant District Officer, the lowest rank in the Service.

Cocky goes to Kate and tells her she must go home to England for her health, as the doctor has recommended. Furthermore, she must divorce him, he says, for he sees now he can only make her unhappy. She finally agrees to go and arranges to travel with a missionary's wife.

After she departs, Cocky packs enough supplies for a few days' trek and rides into the uninhabited bush country, thinking of suicide. Yet as he rides along he thinks,

> I might as well do something with life before I throw it away. At least I could murder someone, I could justify my existence. Yes, I'll make one gesture before I go, I'll be remembered, I'll teach 'em a lesson, I'll shew 'em that dirty work doesn't always pay. . . .

He races back to the station and follows Kate's trail. He discovers that she has gone with Thompson and decides to kill them both. He feels both exhilaration "and suddenly such tenderness, such affection for these two whom he had loved and to whom he had behaved nobly. . . ." He is surprised to find his revolver in his hand and tries to stuff it in his pocket as he approaches the hut where the couple have stopped for the night.

Kate runs out, followed by Thompson, who says that she is leaving him, too. Cocky grasps at sanity and tells himself that the only way to beat his enemies is to forgive them — Christ's way. They wouldn't be able to live with his forgiveness, for it, and not hatred, will shame them and poison their lives forever.

But the novel breaks off with Cocky's noble gesture, at least this draft of it. And no other draft goes further.

Evidently it was the novel's ending that posed the greatest problem, one that Joyce never was able to solve. To simply break off, as it did, would make the book an aesthetic and philosophical failure. Yet having Cocky kill himself, or kill Kate and Thompson, or, even worse, having all of them die would push the novel into melodrama unless with fantastic luck he were able to accomplish such an ending successfully. Probably all that blood would obscure any message he was trying to convey.

Even worse, Joyce simply was unsure himself what the message was, although the various drafts suggest that it was beginning to be apparent. He knew what questions he wanted to raise but was not sure of the answers. The central question, obviously, was the nature of injustice in the world.

Injustice was to be the theme of many of Joyce's novels. It is at the heart of his first trilogy, *Herself Surprised, To Be a Pilgrim,* and *The Horse's Mouth,* and in a less obvious way in his second trilogy, *Prisoner of Grace, Except the Lord,* and *Not Honour More,* for instance. It is a problem he was to write about until the end of his life; his last novel, *The Captive and the Free,* deals with the nature of God and whether or not He is a just God.

The fact of the matter is that injustice was central to Joyce's life and that of the whole Cary family. He had to ask himself why the Carys had been ruined in Ireland, why his grandfather had been dispossessed and had died of heartbreak; why his Great-Uncle Tristram had worn always a look of tragedy; why his own mother and stepmother had died and left him so bereft; why, for that matter, he had been made to suffer so much illness as a child and why he continued to suffer from his bad sight and occasional asthma attacks for the remainder of his life.

And he had to ask himself as well why he had been spared from death or at least serious injury so many times, what part luck or justice played in his and in everyone's lives. These were questions that his own experience forced him to ask, and *Cock Jarvis* is his first detailed attempt to answer them.

The conflict rages within Cocky himself; on the one hand, his Christian teachings say that the world is imperfect and without justice due to man's fall and consequent fallability; on the other, man demands justice, insists that he be dealt with fairly, and becomes bitter when he does not receive what he feels he deserves.

In fact, all the major characters of the book demand justice and feel they have not gotten it from the others. But what *is* the nature of justice or injustice, Joyce asked himself. Is it merely an abstraction? If so, then why do men pursue it so ardently? What is God's role in an unjust world? For that matter, what is God?

These were some of the questions on which *Cock Jarvis* foundered. In fact, all his books had similar problems, as he explained twenty-five years later:

> So I would start a book with a plan in my head; but before I had finished it, I would begin to question its significance. I could feel either it was trivial; or that it was dodging some final issue; that it was a fake. I had, from reading or talk, learnt something which made me dissatisfied with the plan, with the characters and their reactions. When I said that I was dissatisfied with my writing, at that time, in the twenties, I meant that I was dissatisfied with the meaning of my books; and that is, with every part of them, for style is part of meaning.
>
> . . . I finished several books before the first one that I published; but I never offered them to a publisher because, though they were complete in themselves, they all raised questions that I could not answer. . . .[3]

If he wanted to write a satisfactory book, he saw that he must educate himself properly. He had limped along with an education that was all shreds and patchwork for too long. He could live with its gaps and contradictions — most men do — but he could not use it as a foundation for his novels.

For that matter, he was unable really to use it as a basis for living, as his depressions proved. Perhaps with a solid education and a resultant philosophy of life, he would not be plunged into despair and led to wonder at the sense of living at all.

He needed a broader, more complete concept of the world, a metaphysic for his writing and himself, and he had to educate himself sufficiently to be able to form such a system.

A METAPHYSICAL CONSTRUCTION

IN THE 1920's Joyce was looking for a faith that was not to be found within the theological framework of any church at that time. He had scarcely a shred of respect for conventional religion, and he despised most of the clergy. During the war he had written to Trudy.

> I don't like parsons, and I never will like 'em. I always feel nervous when Mother says I might end up a parson etc. It shews how little mother knows of me. . . . One parson will damp a whole roomfull of men. The hypocrite atmosphere he carries about him in spite of himself, makes all the ordinary decent fellows shut up, and swear inside.

One of his in-laws was the sort of parson Joyce decried. At Harrow this man was known as "Creeping Jesus," and he barred Jewish boys from reading the lesson in chapel. He was the same fellow who had gone out of his way to be rude to Mrs. Ogilvie during the war because of her German birth.[1] Then in 1921, when Trudy was at Blair-Atholl, this parson talked on and on of his contacts in the publishing business yet never lifted a hand to help Joyce use those contacts.[2] Joyce — and Trudy — despised him.

When Freddy, after being wounded in the war, thought of going into the Church, Joyce had been very upset and was vastly relieved when his brother-in-law chose the academic life instead. One parson in the family was more than enough.

In a letter of July, 1917, he expressed what he despised about the clergy:

> I read an article yesterday as long as the ears of Balaams ass, in the Times on a magnificent piece of Christian work performed by a very great, a very wise, a very revered Divine. He had produced a work upon the question of what's to be done with the bread left after communion. It is considered of the first importance. In the same paper is a letter from Weldon, who's a Bishop I believe, suggesting that reprisals on the Germans are quite allowable and that they would have all the guilt, as they started. . . . If we are Christians we ought not to murder German women & children & civilians, even if Germans murder ours. . . .

Missionaries were as bad as the home clergy and often worse, as they were apt to be even more fanatical. He had heard enough about the missionaries in Nigeria to give him a negative attitude, and when the mysterious fellow crept into Kaiama in 1919, Joyce was upset at the prospect of having to live in the same station with one of the bigoted group.

The values Joyce tried to live by were love, duty, justice, and charity. Too few clergymen, he felt, believed in them. Instead they believed in ritual, power, and a long list of "Thou shalt not's." Joyce believed there was a greater proportion of worthy men outside the Church than in it — those in the Nigerian Service, for instance, who had left home to do some practical, material good works for people, making life possible where disease and starvation were rampant. Often they sacrificed their lives or at least their health in serving the people of Nigeria.

As he had no faith in an afterlife, Joyce did not believe in urging men to suffer gladly in this world in order to lie about in luxury in the next. Clean water, better and more abundant food, some rudimentary medical care, honest and just laws impartially administered, the end of slavery and looting, and a decent livelihood for oneself and hope of even better for one's children were what mattered in Borgu, and he believed they were what mattered anywhere.

Too often the Church, as part of the established order, stood in the way of progress. Too often it brought bloodshed, as in Uganda, rather than peace and prosperity. Too often it spent its time arguing "what's to be done with the bread left after communion" rather than working to put bread into the bellies of the starving.

So in trying to find what the world was all about, Joyce did not think in terms of faith and certainly did not intend to look for his particular truth in any church. Instead he sought it in philosophy, in systems of ethics, and in art, particularly in the works of such writers as Conrad, Hardy, and William Blake.

A great help in this search, its philosophic side at least, was John MacMurray, a philosophy don who had come to Oxford in 1921 and whom Joyce met at a party soon afterward. MacMurray, like Joyce and many other young men around Oxford in those days, had been in the war and had lost a great many of his friends in France and Belgium. Like Joyce, he was in search of answers to all the questions that the war and its bloodbath had raised or at least had made so much more pertinent than before.[3]

Joyce fell into the habit of calling on the MacMurrays on Sunday at teatime, staying on to talk, or, more often, to listen to his friend and whomever else happened to drop in. The talk ranged over many subjects: functional architecture and the philosophy behind it; politics and the need for a working world government, whether it be through the new League of Nations or through World Federalism; the historical process of political life; socialism, fascism, communism, and other political doctrines. Lord Lindsay, Master of Balliol, who was an ardent socialist, something of a Bergsonian, and an idealist whose beliefs in many instances were similar to Joyce's, was one of those who came most frequently.[4]

While MacMurray, Lindsay, and the others talked, Joyce sat by, appearing to take all the debate with a grain of salt, while drawing caricatures of the others. He was not an abstract talker or arguer, but he was a good listener. When he did enter the conversation it was with some practical instance out of his own experience that supported or contradicted a point someone else had made. He could draw on his knowledge of Ireland, Montenegro, or Nigeria when the talk centered on politics — Nigeria in particular was full of examples of racism, provincialism, or tribal nationalism, evidences of the difficulties of getting different peoples to work in some sort of harmony.[5]

He seldom spoke of his writing to his friends. He simply mentioned that he had come back from Nigeria to try his luck at it and was learning the trade now. He never spoke of how badly his work was going and how much the debts were piling up, nor did he talk of his dilemma with the novels, and the problem of finding an ideological substructure for them. He might show Trudy the depths of his depressions, but few others had any inkling of his state.[6]

Tommy Higham provided Joyce with one very inexpensive relief from his worries: the two of them took several walking tours together, one in France, a few in the Cotswolds, and several into other parts of England as well. Joyce was proficient at packing for these, as he was for any trips. If he were packing a trunk or a knapsack, everything had its special place and every niche was used. Then off he would go, forgetting his money or his train ticket, or some other essential. It was not his fault, he claimed; he was "an organized man in a chaotic world." The walking tours were good for his health as well as his morale, and his asthma virtually disappeared; this meant one less worry.

Joyce's biggest lift came from Mr. Ogilvie, however. Mrs. Ogilvie never fully recovered from her heart attack and stroke of 1921 and remained a semi-invalid. In July, 1923, sitting in her wheelchair in a shop in Bournemouth, she had a second attack. After lingering only a few days, she died. Mr. Ogilvie, nearing his seventy-first birthday, was not well himself, so he decided to give up his London flat and move to Oxford. He visited with the Carlisles, while Joyce, Trudy, Freddy, and Freddy's young wife decorated the house he had taken in Charlbury Road, toward the north end of Oxford. They painted and papered the walls, put down the carpets, and had the house completely arranged for Mr. Ogilvie when he arrived.[7]

Now that he lived only minutes from 12 Parks Road, Mr. Ogilvie could not help but get a general idea of Joyce's financial situation. He had always had a soft spot for Joyce and had been the only one in the family to encourage his son-in-law to keep after Trudy when the rest had thought he was a great pest to her. Now the Carys were struggling to keep their heads above water and, in a way, he seems to have felt it was his fault. He had backed Trudy's demands that Joyce come back from Nigeria. In 1919 he had burst out at Joyce for not setting Trudy up in a home of her own. Well, Joyce *had* come back and *had* gotten a place of his own, and he was suffering for it.

Now that his wife was gone, Mr. Ogilvie softened even more toward Joyce. He had been a struggling young man once himself, trying to become an engineer, and only a piece of luck and the generosity of relatives had gotten him into the import-export business. He had been called to Chile to relieve a cousin who wanted to go home to Scotland. When that cousin and then the cousin's brother died, he had inherited the business and made a small fortune at it. Luck, the benevolence of his relatives, and his own daring and hard work had made him a success. Now in his seventies, he could afford to be benevolent toward Trudy and Joyce. So, given Joyce's pride, he did what he could to bail the young Carys out and let them live with a few less worries.

In fact, Mr. Ogilvie did more than relive his youth vicariously through Joyce and Trudy. As a very young man he had fallen in love with a girl in Bristol, where he was working before the call to Chile and long before his marriage to Mary Wolff. He had wanted to marry Rotha Thomas but was too poor to ask her. When he got the chance to go to Chile, though, he decided he must marry her or lose her. So he proposed. Rotha told him she would marry him, but she did not want to go to Chile. It was Chile or marriage. But as an apprentice engineer, earning scarcely enough to live on himself, Mr. Ogilvie had to admit that marriage was impossible, so he left England.

Now, more than forty years later, he met Rotha Thomas again. She had never married. They seemed to fall in love for a second time, and at Easter he told his children that he and she were to be married that fall of 1924. That summer at Blair-Atholl, he suffered a bad heart attack and shortly afterward had a nervous breakdown. The children decided that the marriage would be good for him, since it would give him happiness and companionship in the few years of life he had left. So they urged him to marry Rotha Thomas despite his illness, and he did that autumn.[8]

Mr. Ogilvie, realizing as well as the children did that he had only a short while left to live, was all the more anxious to see Joyce and Trudy as happy and comfortable as they could be, and he was increasingly generous.

It was a great relief to Joyce not to have to worry so much about the economics of his writing and probably an even greater relief to Trudy. She no longer needed to feel guilty for her husband's dilemma. They could relax and enjoy life once again. They could stop worrying about the cost of the boys' education, a very pressing concern since Joyce did not want to stint on that and feel guilty for the rest of his life.

They even managed a holiday in Switzerland at the end of 1923. Both of them liked traveling, and Trudy had once hoped that if Joyce had stayed in Nigeria, she might have joined him for a few months of his tour. Traveling, though, had looked out of the question after the collapse of everything in the early 1920's, so the Swiss vacation was that much more of a treat, especially since there were just the two of them, as the boys were at home.

Their hotel was very quiet and out of the mainstream of Swiss tourism. They therefore had to travel from the railway station in a mail coach (the wheels had been replaced by runners for the winter) up twisting mountain roads, stopping every so often to get out and push. At one place, where there had been a small avalanche, the passengers had to dig a way for the coach to go through.[9]

The holiday was a delight. They skated on the hotel rink, and Joyce, equipped with a pair of Norwegian racing skis, went zooming down the mountains, having a grand time. Trudy, though, had to pray that he would not be killed, since, with his bad eyes and the swift skis, he scarcely could see where he was going and might easily slam into a tree or go shooting off a cliff into eternity.[10] It was the sort of risk that Joyce enjoyed, for he still believed in that special luck that would save him from a sudden, violent death.

They skated and skied by day and played bridge (Joyce hated cards as much as ever, but he had to be sociable and billiards, and they danced in the evenings, reminding each other that just two years ago they had considered giving up 12 Parks Road to move into a few rooms or a flat somewhere because of their financial difficulties. The vacation showed them how life could be, how luck could change if only they held on long enough. And it helped to convince them that they had made the right choice.

The financial strain had eased so much that Joyce, with a few pounds to spare, began buying a few shares of stock again. He had bought a fair number of investment stocks in 1916 at the time of their marriage rather than shares for speculation.[11] He wanted to invest, not to gamble. His career was too long-term for that.

Despite the new life that opened to them with the financial strain gone, Joyce was not entirely happy. Their new solvency was none of his own doing, and this rankled. He was past his thirty-fifth birthday now, halfway along that dreadful decade to forty that he had worried about in 1918. While others were getting ahead, he was getting nowhere. He was even unable to make ends meet through his own efforts. He staggered along, selling a few stories a year to English magazines at low rates, while Heneage Ogilvie was becoming a successful Harley Street surgeon with a growing practice, and Freddy, a rising young don, was appointed Professor of Political Economy at Edinburgh University in 1926, when he was only thirty-three. Everyone except him was getting somewhere it seemed.

He had spent years and years trying to write a novel that would be good enough to be published, yet sometimes it seemed he was no closer to that goal than when he had been sweating over his foolscap sheets in the Borgu bush. The Ogilvie broth-

ers had urged him ever since the end of his first success in 1921
to write a money-making novel, and they continued to do so.¹²
Only Trudy believed in him and tried to keep him on the right
track, however wrong that track seemed to the others.¹³

She worked with him, typing up the manuscripts and mailing
them off, making suggestions for improvements in the stories,
and encouraging and bolstering him when he flagged, wondering all the time what the use was. For instance, in 1925, when
he was off in Ireland visiting with his Aunt Netta and her husband, Peter Clark, at Castledawson, Northern Ireland, she wrote
this letter to him:

> DEAREST JOYCE — I know how you hate me praising your work
> and trying to give you any sympathy — and I know I should
> hate it in your place — but I only want to say this now — but I
> have so often spoken as if I didn't understand or know what a big
> thing this is for you — I was miserable last night in thinking
> about it — and what the disappointment of these five years must
> have meant to you. Darling I do understand — and there is noth-
> ing I long for more than for you to succeed — and I do think you
> will — My heart just aches for you sometimes — when I think
> how hard you have worked — against awful difficulties — and un-
> der the most impossible conditions in the house — which I think
> I should have made easier for you — From the financial point of
> view — I don't think you must worry now darling — I'm sure we
> will pull through with ease . . . but in any case perhaps you
> should have a room out — where I *cant* come and pester you.

Joyce, while he was in Ireland that spring (he got into the
habit of visiting Castledawson every Easter for a week or two,
sometimes with Trudy and their sons but more often alone),
investigated the possibilities of selling the family property there,
which was owned jointly by Joyce and Jack and their aunt, Mrs.
Beasley. He felt it would be wise, as the political situation continued to be so unsettled on the island. There was sporadic civil
war in the Free State, and I.R.A. raids across the border into
Northern Ireland on police stations, so who knew what might
happen? A burned-down house did not bring in much rent, and

Londonderry, practically encircled by the Free State, was a vulnerable place. Much of the Cary property was in the city.[14] If these properties were sold and the money reinvested in some solid stocks that paid a good dividend, there would be the same income and no rental agent's fees to pay. The money would be far more safe and sure.

He proposed the idea to Jack, who was at sea on H.M.S. *Endeavour,* and Jack agreed, although he said he did not think there was much chance of selling just then.[15] Joyce looked about for buyers and consulted with his aunt, but the whole venture fell through. Nobody wanted to risk his money any more than Joyce did. So the Carys and Beasleys remained minor Irish landlords.

Joyce, at "The Bungalow" in Castledawson, could see well enough what was going on. They did not live under a state of siege, of course, but people had to be careful. There was a nightly curfew, for example, and the newspapers constantly carried stories of violent acts. There were murders and dynamitings here and there. But a certain amount of amusement could be gotten out of the whole situation.

One agreeable institution was the "curfew dances." These began at nine o'clock, when the curfew went into effect and the streets were cleared, and they lasted until dawn or six in the morning, whatever the local regulation allowed. The Bungalow, with its large dining room cleared of furniture and a small orchestra settled at one end, was the scene of several of these curfew dances, as were a lot of the big country homes. Life went on as normally as possible, girls admired themselves in new dresses, and young men stammered out embarrassed proposals.[16]

There were plenty of stories for Joyce to hear, some of them tragic and some more humorous. There was a story of his two cousins at Castledawson, Toni and Cary Clark, for instance. One night they were being driven home, hurrying because the curfew hour had come, when they spotted a man standing against a hedge, watching them. Cary happened to have a "dog bomb" (a firecracker that exploded on impact, used by bicyclists to keep dogs from chasing them and snapping at their ankles), in his pocket, so he hurled it out the window at the pavement. It exploded and the furtive-looking man dived over the hedge, while the driver of the car, sure they were being shot at, ducked his head, shoved the accelerator to the floor, and sped them home. The episode made the papers, for the furtive man had been an innocent farmer, also caught after curfew, and he had sworn the car was packed with men of the I.R.A. taking pot shots at stragglers on the road.[17]

There had been another story in the papers that was just as much a joke. One evening two bodies of armed men had stumbled on each other in a corner of Northern Ireland and shooting had begun. It went on all night, while the people in the neighborhood huddled under tables and tunneled under beds or knelt on the floor and prayed that their lives would be spared. It was a ferocious battle, the papers said, and one man had been seen absolutely gushing blood.

It turned out that both groups were Unionists who were guarding against I.R.A. raids, and not a single one had been killed or even scratched during the battle. As for the man who gushed blood, he had had a thermos in his overcoat pocket because it was such a cold night, and when he flung himself on the ground as the shooting started, the thermos had burst and gushed tea.[18]

Still, even the jokes and the comic incidents proved the point that property in Londonderry was not much of an investment, either to prospective buyers or to Joyce, and he returned to Oxford feeling that his income was more precarious than ever. If the problem had been physical danger to himself, he could have stood it much better. In a battle he could protect himself, shoot at an enemy, and know that the fight would soon be over (he had told Trudy that a battle was not much worse than a rowing race, and he had been involved many times with both). But to live in a state of economic danger, with no tangible enemy or else one who was several hundred miles away, was eroding to the spirit. It wore down his resistance as much as the illness, asthma, and insomnia he had experienced in Nigeria.

MR. OGILVIE'S TRUST FUND

ALTHOUGH JOYCE'S FAILURE to make a living from writing sometimes sent him into a period of bleakness, there were plenty of
diversions in Oxford. There was good talk always and an abundance of sports: tennis, riding, boating, swimming, and skating
on the river when it flooded over Port Meadow and froze.

There were the fairly regular trips to Ireland and, in reciproc-
cation, Trudy and Joyce saw a good deal of Cary Clark when he
came to school at Radley, just outside Oxford, in 1920. Cary
was the eldest of Aunt Netta's children and thirteen when he
first arrived in Oxford.[1]

Radley was rather rough on new boys (one method of hazing
was to blindfold a boy, stand him on top of a row of lockers, and
stick him with compass points until he stumbled off the lockers
and fell to the floor below), and Cary, in his letters, hinted to
his parents of his misery. Netta Clark wrote to Joyce, who undoubtedly remembered his own unhappy start at Clifton and
spoke to Freddy Ogilvie about it. Together they planned an
inspection tour of Radley. The boy, when he found out, was
horrified. In desperation he talked them out of the visit. Joyce
then sent off a diplomatic letter to Castledawson to say that all
was well.

Cary's visits at Parks Road were always a pleasant event for
Joyce,[2] except one day in the summer when the boy trudged out
to the house, was let in, and halfway across the sitting room was
stopped by a shriek from Trudy. She pointed down at the

orange carpet. Cary had walked through some melted tar on his way and had left a trail of footprints to match the carpet's black border.

But in turn on a cold autumn day, when he and Joyce had been out walking, Cary got his comeuppance. They were by the Cherwell River near Summertown at Oxford's north end, and on their way home had to cross the river on a rope pull ferry. In drawing them across, Cary forgot to let go of the rope and went off the back end of the boat into freezing water up to his neck. He surfaced with his bowler hat clamped down over his ears, and Joyce laughed so hard at the sight he could hardly pull his cousin out again.

Perhaps it was just as well, because Trudy, when she saw his blue serge best suit sometime earlier, had remarked, "Well, I see you've had a good many lunches in *that* suit, Cary."

Joyce and his young cousin went for frequent walks together, either in the Parks or around Oxford, and once Joyce took him to a circus in the town and had an even better time than the boy did. He always liked excitement and got drawn into whatever was going on.

Like Joyce, Cary had had his nose broken more than once. The first time was when he was an infant, then when he was a small boy, and now at Radley it got broken again. His mother, after this last break, wanted the nose operated on to restore it to the proper Cary aquiline shape — and to enable her son to breathe through it, since the break had blocked the nasal passage. Joyce consulted Heneage, who in turn consulted a nose specialist, and Cary was sent to London to stay with his uncle, Arthur Cary; he was then put in a nursing hospital for the operation. But the operation failed to restore the use of his nose for breathing. So Cary was carried off to Edinburgh for a second try. There was a regular family reunion, with Carys and Clarks all staying in a private hotel in a body, where they debated what sort of nose Cary should be given, with Netta Clark leading the aquiline camp and Joyce all for leaving the shape of the nose as it was, rather battered but quite masculine, with only the breathing facilitated. While they talked at the hotel, Cary, feeling quite left out of things, went off to have the operation and, when he was released from the hospital (without the desired aquiline shape), the family threw a dance to celebrate.

In 1924, Cary left Oxford. Joyce had hoped his cousin would go to the university and had thought he had a good chance for a scholarship at Balliol College, but in 1924 there was a fire at the Clark linen works at Castledawson and Cary had to go home to take on much of the burden of restoring the business. Then, when his father died, he had to run the business entirely, and all hopes of Oxford had to be forgotten.

Although Cary Clark was gone, Joyce had his own sons to make life lively. He was good with children, and his storytelling ability came in handy at bedtimes. Working around two small boys was difficult, and sometimes he was irritated at the noise and running about. Trudy, doing all of Joyce's secretarial work, did not have much time for the children, who were left in the care of a series of generally incompetent nannies. Because of the financial strain, Joyce and Trudy were unable to afford the best nursemaids, and, living as they did under pressure all the time, they sometimes were harsh with the boys, especially their younger son, who was very much like Joyce as a youngster, quiet and shy.

In 1924, Michael turned seven and Peter six and, as they began school, the problem of their future bothered Joyce. Mr. Ogilvie's new generosity, now that he was in Oxford, provided buffer enough against the bills, but it was difficult to believe he would live much longer. When he died, it seemed likely that the bulk of his estate would go to his new wife and only a small portion to each of his five children. There would be little for the boys' education, and now that it was beginning, his financial dilemma hit Joyce with new force.

In 1925 Trudy became pregnant again.

It was an event that took some getting used to. Still, Joyce had hated missing the infancy of Michael and Peter, with all that accompanied it: the first step, the first tooth, the first words, all the stages of their rapid development. Now he would be able to share this with Trudy when the new baby was born. And they wanted a daughter so much that they had discussed only girls' names when they waited for Peter's birth. At the same time, the responsibility of a third child was daunting. Not only did it mean a further financial strain, but it meant disruptions of all kinds when Joyce was trying to get work done at home. The baby would consume much of Trudy's time, even with a nurse-maid on hand, and he badly needed her help. Without her, he could work at only half or two thirds of his present rate.

The baby, born in 1926, was quite definitely a boy, Tristram Ogilvie Cary. Joyce would have to wait still longer for the daughter who, he told Trudy, would grow up to pet and spoil him.[3] Still, a trio of boys could have great times together, just like the crew he had led in Donegal thirty years before.

The presence of a baby in the house, though, made it difficult to find a quiet place to write, so Joyce took up Trudy's suggestion and rented a room outside. He found a third-floor room on Rawlinson Road, out near Summertown, that a family named Campbell was letting.[4] Now every morning, instead of his walk through the Parks, he strode down Parks Road to Banbury Road and along five streets to Rawlinson. It was a nice, quiet area, and, in his room at the top of the house, he was able to concentrate and get a great deal of work done without any interruptions. It was like going to an office.

Previously Joyce had the problem that most writers have, particularly those who have not yet made a financial success: people refused to take his work seriously, since his professional habits differed so radically from theirs. His mind may have been functioning at a furious rate, constructing characters, scenes, even whole plots, but to anyone seeing him, he was doing nothing at all. Even Trudy, who knew how desperate he was to get his writing done, could not help interrupting him, and with children to see to, a household to run, and shopping to do, she was tempted to ask Joyce if he would run to the shop for something she had forgotten for the evening's dinner, or help her move a table, or answer the door since she was in the middle of this or that.

Since so much of the work went on in his head, any interruptions might destroy the whole line of development, thus any break not only used up time but occasionally cost him his ideas. So the room on Rawlinson Road was a great boon. He could work straight through for as long as he liked.

Mornings he might walk along with Michael and Peter, when they were at the Dragon School, and say good-bye to them at Bardwell Road, then go along to his own work. After completing the scheduled stint, he could drop in on the Highams, only a few streets away, before carrying home his sheaf of manuscript for Trudy to type or at least read and criticize.

When the General Strike broke out in 1926, Joyce was torn two ways, as a great many people were. He and Trudy had argued over the rights of workers to strike during wartime. Trudy, whose father was a big mercantile figure, was absolutely opposed to the idea; it seemed like treason to her. Joyce, though, argued that the owners of firms making war materials reaped a great profit without its being considered treasonable, so why shouldn't the workers get their fair share, and if they had to strike, well, that was the only real weapon they had. He told her,

You know, it seems as bad to me as to you that people can strike at this time, but I can understand it. You must put yourself in the place, let us say, of a porter or a miner of £2 or so a week, doing hard manual work at least 8 hours a day. Have you ever done hard manual work for eight hours, and gone on for some years, with only a few days in each year for holiday? I feel very bitter sometimes against the way I am treated, or we are treated by government — yet I am treated very well on the whole — suppose the govt. was more or less a private employer, and I had no pension to look forward to, and no regular rules of service — much less pay rising every year — I might be much more bitter. This doesn't affect my willingness to fight, and I expect these very railwaymen — in fact I know — they are very good soldiers at the front. They are ignorant of economy, they are told all sorts of lies all the time, they are often treated very tactlessly and then they strike. The fault is not all on one side, indeed like all social faults it is not on any particular side — it lies partly in the past, when these men were cheaply educated by cheap teachers — when they were allowed to see that they could die if they liked so long as dividends were paid. This is changed now — but the hatred and just hatred of the employer sown in labour during the last century, and especially the first half of it, will bear fruit now — just as surely as English misgovernment of Ireland in the 18th century produced a rebellion in 1916, for which there was now no reason. Nothing is more terrible than the saying that the children inherit the sins of the fathers — either in its original application — or politically.

Louis XVI was killed because Louis XIV was extravagant & Louis XV wicked — if there should be revolution in England, which I don't expect now however, it will not be for our faults, but the faults of our grandfathers — and then only in a small degree — for what could they have done by themselves. That is another awful truth — that individuals suffer for the faults of the whole nation — think of Russia, how many good men, innocent children, starved, outraged, murdered, for the faults of Russia and none of their own — simply because they were not strong enough individually to teach a nation in time, and alter its politics — absurd. A nation is like the body and one part must suffer innocently for the wrong doing or ignorance of the whole.

(14 November 1918*)

Now, during the General Strike, he sympathized with the strikers and yet realized that this strike might mean a general breakdown of society. As it dragged on, he volunteered to work among those who were keeping vital services going. He was assigned to the London docks to run a gang unloading meat from refrigerated ships. He went off to the railway station, dressed in a suit and his bowler hat, to be a laborer; Michael accompanied him as far as the corner, asking his father how long he would be away. "I don't know," Joyce replied cheerfully and was gone.[5]

To resolve the conflict in himself he looked on his new job as an adventure rather than as a crusade. In a way it was like being in Nigeria again, with the hard physical labor of moving sides of frozen beef, the comradeship of working among men, and the

* Although the war had ended three days earlier, Joyce believed it was still being fought. He only learned of the Armistice two days later, on the 16th.

good sleep at the end of a long day of doing something important and necessary. The strike provided Joyce with a chance to get away from writing and to become involved in a general crisis rather than worry about his own problems.

The following year Mr. Ogilvie died. His family had expected it, after his illness of the past few years. His life had been a full one and, on the whole, happy. He had made a fortune and he could take pride in his family, his sons and daughters. During the last months of his life he had the added happiness of his second marriage. Joyce owed him a great deal, both for his early encouragement during the courtship of Trudy and for the aid he had given them since his son-in-law's return from Nigeria, encouragement that Joyce and Trudy deeply appreciated.

Now that Irish politics were becoming a bit more settled, Joyce had been trying to sell his Londonderry properties, and once again his brother Jack was in full agreement, writing from his present ship, H.M.S. *Kellett,*

> Personally, I will leave it to you to do whatever you think best in the circumstances; certainly it would be very much more satisfactory to have perhaps a slightly smaller income and a safely invested one: as it is now as far as I can see, it is a bit of a gamble and you certainly know more about the chances than I do.
>
> (30 April 1927)

But either Joyce and Jack's aunt would not agree or else a buyer could not be found, for the properties remained in their hands.

Joyce had been putting every penny he could into solid stocks through an investment fund and hated being balked again. With Mr. Ogilvie's death, he would be able to invest Trudy's share of the estate and insure their future and the boys' education. However, Mr. Ogilvie left his estate in trust, with his new wife and the children to get a fixed income each year, and Freddy and Heneage Ogilvie were named as trustees.

Joyce appealed to them to have the trust broken, so Trudy and he could do as they liked with the money. With the trust intact, they would have a certain level of security, but their life would be more restricted than it had been for the past few years since Mr. Ogilvie had moved to Oxford. There would be no more gifts from him in especially tense situations. Instead there would be only a steady but small annual income to pool with their other incomes for the next ten or fifteen years.

By the end of 1940, Michael would be twenty-three and Peter twenty-two. In all likelihood they would have completed their studies at the university and would be earning livings of their own. Even Tristram, the youngest, would be fourteen, halfway through his education. By that time, surely, Joyce would be earning a decent living from his novels, so their income would be up and their costs reduced. They would have no need of money from the trust fund then. Now, 1927, was when they needed it.

But Heneage was not keen on breaking the trust, and Freddy was firmly against it. It was Freddy who had been the most insistent that Joyce write a money-making, potboiling novel, and now it was he, believing that Joyce had not acted responsibly, who was the firmest about not breaking the trust.[6]

The situation was not improved by the fact that Freddy and his wife Mary now lived in Edinburgh, so the whole affair had to be handled through letters, where misunderstandings were far more likely to arise than in conversation. The tone of voice in which something is said may make all the difference to the interpretation of a remark, and letters have only the tone that the reader assumes to be there.

Both Joyce and Freddy were strong-minded, and each believed he was right. Freddy, a successful don of economics, wanted to do the sound thing and could not help but believe Joyce was bent on a reckless course. Joyce, knowing that if only these recurrent pressures and crises were resolved he could get some solid work done and could abandon the bread-and-butter short stories, believed Freddy was being stuffy and narrow-minded. The result was a coldness between them that lasted nearly a decade, while the trust remainded intact.

Joyce was left with only his writing to buy him the peace of mind he needed.

31

LIBERTY VERSUS FREEDOM

In 1928 the Carys' fourth child was born. Again they had been anxious for a girl; among Joyce's papers is a pseudoscientific explanation of the conditions under which a girl can be conceived, which shows just how desperate they were for a daughter. The baby, a fourth son, George Anthony Cary, barely survived his birth. Trudy had caught German measles during her pregnancy (it wasn't until the 1930's that an Australian doctor discovered the link between German measles in the mother and damage to the child in the womb), and George suffered the results: he was born nearly blind and with a serious heart defect.

The tragedy of the baby's illness, along with the anticipation of future medical expenses due to it, could have been the final blow to the Carys after their series of disappointed hopes and frustrated plans. Yet Joyce seems to have reacted in exactly the opposite way. The new tragedy seems to have made him rally rather than despair. It had an air of crisis about it, and Joyce was able to bear a crisis better than a long, grinding series of disappointments. As for Trudy, if Joyce were on an even keel, so was she; her happiness depended on his.

Joyce set to work on a new novel soon after George's birth, a novel about Africa into which he intended to put the main elements of his beliefs.[1] The work, *Aissa Saved*, was essentially religious, as, in a way, all of Joyce's novels were to be. But they were to be "religious" in an extremely broad sense.

For to Joyce religion, politics, and love were fused together in the philosophy at which he had begun to arrive. This philosophy is very difficult to extract from his writings. Not only does it vary from book to book (or seem to), but when it is abstracted from the vitality and richness of his characters and their world, it loses much of its real meaning. Joyce was not an abstract thinker.[2] He thought in terms of individual people, not "the masses"; unless philosophy were couched in terms of human life it was likely to become a destructive force, he felt, rather than a creative one.

For Joyce's philosophy was based on creativity and love, forces which had to exist *in people* if they were to exist at all. In his view man's life is a series of meaningless experiences upon which some pattern must be imposed to give it significance. The pattern may be the individual's own creation or it may be formulated by society.

However, the pattern imposed from outside is never entirely satisfactory to an individual, Joyce felt, because the more creative a man is the more he feels oppressed by the rigidity of a structure, such as an established church, tribalism, nationalism, or the moral beliefs of a place and time.[3] So the best society or state is that which allows the individual the most freedom to create his own way of life.

Since each man creates his own world and since his creations cannot help but come into conflict with each other to some degree, society must act as a buffer that both constrains and protects. In other words, man must lose *some* of his freedom to have any at all. A state of anarchy, with no governmental restraint on freedom, might be an excellent abstraction, but to Joyce's mind it was an impossibility, since man needs the order and meaning of an *imposed* structure if he does not have the creativity to form his own. The other extreme, the totalitarian state, was even worse. He had seen this sort of government in the backcountry tribal life in Nigeria, and it crushed men.

Society must be poised somewhere between the two poles of anarchy and totalitarianism, necessarily in constant danger of verging toward either extreme. Governments must exist, but they must be challenged always in everything they do. Men must ask of each act of government and every law, "Does this give me more freedom or less?" They must demand still more freedom at every opportunity or they are in danger of losing all of it.

And it is freedom that they must demand, even more than liberty. For Joyce saw a distinct difference between the two words. Liberty was the absence of restraint; freedom was the provision of the means to self-fulfillment. For instance, as he wrote some years later, a painter in a democratic society has liberty to do what he chooses, but (and Joyce was writing during the Great Depression) he may not have the tools to paint with, a place to live, and food to eat. So his liberty is meaningless, at least so far as his painting goes. But a government grant, a WPA project, or some other aid would give him food, housing, paints, brushes, and canvases.[4] Liberty is "freedom from"; freedom, in Joyce's vocabulary, is "the opportunity to."

Of course he believed in both. He had seen absence of freedom in Nigeria and found such societies stultifying. The lonely men in the country's deserted border villages had liberty from tribal restraints, yet they had no freedom to enlarge their lives or those of their children.

He also saw the essential conflict between the two concepts. For the painter's government grant is paid out of taxes, and those taxes are imposed on someone else whose freedom thus is limited. A compromise must be established between the painter and the taxpayer. Thus, a government is necessary to work out this compromise between the two men's freedoms, and the existence of government and law in turn limits liberty.

So any complex society is riddled with compromises. The fact that this is so leaves man in a state of anxiety, which is heightened by the fact that these compromises are likely to be precarious. His very freedom, too, is a source of anxiety. The more complex the society, the more anxiety man must bear, and this is the burden of freedom. For freedom means choice, and the process of choosing is apt to be harrowing.

Joyce had seen this dilemma of choice which freedom brings upon man not just in Nigeria but in his own family, in the difference between the generations of his grandmothers and his aunts. For during their lifetime women had won a measure of freedom greater than ever before in history. He contrasted the two generations, looking first at that of his grandmothers:

> To woman was allotted a special function in society, as daughter, sister, wife, mother, and this function, like that of a priesthood, carried its own obligation and its own sacrifice. Nowadays women are horrified at what they call the Victorian subjection of their sex. It didn't feel like subjection then. Then, as now, the majority of women married, and the Victorian matron had formidable power in the home. She did not feel subjection, but duty, obligation to her task as a woman. And that was also a sacred vocation and a privilege.
>
> It was this sense of vocation, of privilege, that made so many women fight against the suffrage. I remember the gloomy prognostications of wise men that the emancipation of women would destroy that sense of vocation and bring down civilization itself. They were ludicrously wrong. Women nowadays emphasize their sex as never before. The modern mother is even too nervously concerned for her children. Human nature, the character of the sex, has proved much too strong for politics. Women are probably not happier. They are burdened by new problems of choice and responsibility, new conflicts. But no modern girl could endure the old life again; it is not happiness that matters to her, but power, freedom to act, richness of life. And that new richness is all our richness. The gain to general society is immense.[5]

This desire for freedom and the consequent enrichment of human life when freedom is won are central to Joyce's view of the world. "Man is condemned to be free," he said several times, for the desire for freedom is basic in man yet brings with it a terrible responsibility. More freedom equals more choice equals more anxiety.

At the heart of freedom is man's desire to create himself, but choosing from the variety of selves results in the greatest anxiety of all. Yet denial of this choice is far more fatal than is the freedom of choice.

Society is man's creation, and so are its various institutions.

These social institutions — the family, a religion, political forms and parties, morals, and even manners — are his tools of self-realization. They serve a positive function when they free him to become his fullest self. Once they have lost their meaning and vitality, however, these institutions cease to be tools and become constraints. Then they must be destroyed. Their vitality can be measured by their ability to exist dynamically in conflict with other, newer institutions, without resorting to artificial protections.

These artificial protections are coercive, usually laws enacted to preserve the dying institutions. Joyce did not oppose laws and their enforcement. But in his view, the value of laws, like that of governmental forms, was relative: those laws which preserved the individual's life, liberty, and freedom were good. Those which took away liberty and freedom were bad. It was as simple — and as complex — as that.

For it boils down to the old freedom-versus-security conflict. Obviously it is very difficult to judge whether some laws are good or bad and whether the measure of freedom or the measure of restraint which a law gives is greater. The result is an extremely pragmatic political structure, borrowing the best from all political systems, without regard for labels, and never lapsing into rigid doctrine. This form of government is a democratic pragmatism. But like other pragmatic systems, it is far more complex and difficult to follow than any simple, rigid creed.

This belief was to make Joyce a strong defender of political democracy and parliamentary government at a time when these beliefs were being challenged with great force from the Left and Right. The recurrence of scandal in parliamentary government, regarded by critics as evidence of its failure, was regarded by Joyce as a good. Parliamentary government's scandals were public affairs and the public could judge and check them. Scandals in a totalitarian regime were hidden and therefore went unchecked. As Joyce said,

> Everything gets publicized in a democracy and it is just in the
> most advanced and the freest kind of democracies that you get the

papers, of course, most full of every kind of crime, murder and divorce, and if there is any corruption going on anywhere, you hear all about it. Everything comes out and especially the bad things because the press likes sensation and they like a scandal.

Now in an autocratic state it is quite the other way — scandals are carefully hidden away and corruption is not seen. But this doesn't mean that there are no scandals or corruption in the autocracies — it's just the opposite. The history of the Fascist and Communist states is full of scandal, but of quite a different kind of scandal. Of course, certain kinds of corruption — you find them in all states, crimes like bribery, favoritism, jobbery, blackmail — you get them in all governments where anybody has got any power.

People must have power of any government. If they've got power they've got favours to give, and they can be bribed or blackmailed. You get it in business too, everywhere. But democracies have a special kind of corruption peculiar to themselves and that is misuse of the word. In an autocracy, on the other hand, the typical corruption is misuse of the law. You set the police to arrest your opponents on false charges; you have political prisons and at the worst, you murder the other people. The Russian trials of the 1930's were classic examples of corruption in an autocracy and both Stalin and Hitler used a great deal of murder. They murdered their opponents quite freely — and they believed in murder. They believed in the boss state, in authority at its very strongest and lots of Germans and Russians agreed with them.

Now that is a point I want to make: every state needs laws. You've got to have some authority even in a democracy, and in an autocracy you have to have some liberty. You have to allow people, for instance, to invent, or you wouldn't get any industrial progress. And everywhere in the world you find certain kinds of people who believe in authority. Also in a democracy you find people who believe in lots of law, stopping things by law. And you have also, of course, the people who believe in liberty, who trust in liberty, and want as much of it as possible. These are two different kinds of people, and most of politics in any state in the world is a fight between these two different kinds of people. Two different kinds of temperament.[6]

These "two different kinds of temperament" could be termed the preservers and the creators. The same person, at different stages of his life, may exhibit both the will to create and the desire to preserve.

For instance, a young painter may rebel against the conventions he is taught and which happen to be the established forms of the day. He says they are stifling and dead, and he creates new forms which have vitality and meaning for him and other young people. As he explores these new possibilities, he gradually becomes established. In time, his forms, once revolutionary, become the conventions. Since his forms are extensions of himself, when they are assailed by still younger artists, he must defend them, since an attack on them is in effect an attack on his mind, heart, and soul. Thus, the revolutionary is transformed into the conservative; the forms remain alive for him, although they stifle others.

Joyce's painting trip to France in 1904 was evidence of this inevitable process. The old painter he had met then had believed in what he painted. Young Joyce had believed in something entirely different. Both men found meaning in their separate beliefs, but one was a preserver and the other a rebel. In trying to keep intact a form that had meaning only for him, however, the old man was destroyed.

The only way to survive, then, was to be open to new experience, to be prepared to accept the new or reject it for its inherent worth. If the new were worthwhile, it should be welcomed, not because it was new but because it was creative. At the same time, if the new were not worthwhile, it should be rejected only on that basis.

Joyce felt that the most creative force was love. Love required an extension of self, a creative act both in a literal and figurative sense. Out of love a man and woman created a new pattern for their lives, established a family and a home and a posterity, in the most literal sense. They found a flat or a house and stocked it with furniture, they brought forth children, who caused them to further alter their lives.

In a figurative sense, too, love was creative since it required an act of imagination, a dream of the happiness and fulfillment that could come from a life with the beloved. It required an act of imagination to see in someone almost totally unknown the qualities that would complement oneself. Love offered opportunities for self-realization and for merging oneself with another in a larger creation.

Of course there are many kinds of love other than the love of a man and a woman for each other; there is love of one's parents, one's children, one's friends, or of one's country. Each of these acts of love is an opportunity for a further creation of and extension of oneself.

An episode in Joyce's own life in the early 1920's had helped to convince him of this:

> Just after the last war a young man was sent to me because he said that life wasn't worth living. He said he had no faith left in anything. I told him that this was an age of faith, I am speaking now of about 1924. Never, I said, was there so much faith about, chiefly political faith, in the Fabians, in the Russians, and all the rest of it. What's more, there was a girl very much in love with him who had actually sent him back to Oxford while she earned the money to keep him. So I pointed out that at any rate he could believe in love and in unselfish love. But he knew only the word and despised it. Nothing had any effect, and a few months later he shot himself. That boy had lost all power of receiving an intuition, everything had become conceptual for him, and the concepts were all of despair.[7]

Unable to respond to life on an emotional level, able to see it only in an intellectual and abstract way, the young man could not survive. An act of love or of faith was necessary.

Joyce's belief in his writing was such an act and however much it had made him suffer, it had also given his life meaning and direction. More important, Trudy had loved him and believed in him. Without her, he would have given way to the despair that preyed on him.

Joyce's belief in love, as well as his belief in kindness, honor, and duty, took him beyond the concept of the universe as purely material and mechanistic, as illustrated by the following two passages:

> If there is such a thing as unselfish love, if there is a single act of pure kindness, then the world cannot be entirely a machine, it must be at least partly a being that can love and feel beauty. If there is any love, any kindness anywhere in people it is in the being of the world. And as love cannot be conceived without someone to feel that love, this being is a personal being. Thus the world has personality, and that personality has goodness, has love, as a characteristic.
>
> ("The Duty of Love and the Duty of Reason")

And if you believe in goodness, you believe in God. You haven't any choice. What's more, this God is a personal God.

Einstein said that he believed in the Good, and the Beautiful, but not in a personal God.

But the good and the beautiful are feelings that cannot exist except in a personality. Probably Einstein imagined a personal God as a kind of man, a human person, and he was trying to dissociate himself from such a naive conception.

But the personal in this sense does not mean manlike; the actual nature of God is inconceivable to human minds. Just as such simple elementary functions of daily experience as space and time are insoluble mysteries. Either space goes on for ever without limits, which we cannot conceive; or it stops somewhere, and then we are obliged to ask what is outside space. For our minds are already hopelessly committed to a spacial imagination. We cannot think of being, of existence, except some*where* and some *when;* but the where and when both involve us in hopeless problems.

All we know of God, certainly, is that he is good, that he is love, that he is beauty, that he exists in the world, that is to say, in the universal nature of things as we know it and in ourselves. But of this, if we are not behaviourists, we are absolutely certain we have an unbreakable faith. No one is going to convince us that we never felt love, that sympathy never came to us.

And love and beauty are emotions and emotions do not exist except in personality. Can you imagine a feeling floating about by itself, without anyone to feel it? Love without a lover? The goodness, the love we find in the world is personal. That's why we know God as a person, and only a person.

("The Split Mind of the West")

Love, then, was the manifestation of God. This manifestation is only the corollary of the Biblical "God is love," of course, but it held special meaning for Joyce because he had arrived at it by his own route and through his own experience.

Joyce's reasoning was thus: since love is imperfect, God too must be imperfect. Thus the tragedies for which people curse a perfect and omnipotent God become possible. It is folly to curse God, since God is love and love is not omnipotent, for if God were perfect and omnipotent, man could have no freedom, and without freedom, he would not be man. Therefore, if man's nature is to exist as man, in a state of freedom ("condemned to be free," according to Joyce), then God cannot be omnipotent.

All this, of course, he postulated on the basis of his own — and man's — limitations, as quoted above. Since man's perceptions are limited, he can conceive of or create God only within those limitations. And this was the God that gave Joyce's life meaning and direction.

His faith gave him the ability, as he finally began to fuse his thoughts into a philosophy, to accept the tragedy of George's illness and the whole series of setbacks he and Trudy had suffered. It also inspired the essential idea from which he could finally create a finished novel which satisfied him.

Jane Cary, Joyce's grandmother

Arthur Pitt Chambers Cary

From the left, Joyce's mother, Charlotte Joyce; her sister, Bay Joyce;
and Memie Agar

Ravenscliffe, Donegal. Front row (from the left): Aunt Mab Cary, Joyce; middle row: Mrs and Mr James Joyce, Helen Beasley, Jack Cary; back row: Aunt Netta Cary, Uncle Jim Joyce, Aunt Bay Joyce Beasley

Joyce and Jack at Kitto Road, their first London home
Opposite, top. Jack, Aunt Netta, and Joyce
Opposite, bottom. Barney Magonegal and Joyce's Great Uncle Tristram with the dogs at Cromwell House

Tait's House, Clifton College. Joyce is in the third row from the bottom, centre. Heneage Ogilvie is in the top row, fourth from left

16. St. Bernard's
Edinburgh

My dear Dad,

I am very sorry
that I have made you
anxious about me.
Truly I realize the
importance of this
choice — and that is my
only excuse for delay.
I meant my last letter

Letter from Joyce to Arthur Cary, spring, 1909, declaring his intention to give up painting for a career as a writer

to tell you I leant
towards the Varsity.
and indeed, I have been
expecting your advice
on that project. So
many people — of
critical knowledge and
some literary standing-
advise me to write;
since I find I spend
most of my time thinking
about that kind of work,

whatever is going on, and
since I seem to be able
to labour at it without
tiring – as I have done
these weeks – I am
encouraged to decide
for it.   Will you then
tell me what you think?
my best love to you all,
        your affectionate son

                Joyce

P.S. The returns have arrived
thank you very much for
reading them on.

The crew of the racing boat *Torpid*, Trinity College, Oxford, 1911, including Joyce (standing, right) and Tommy Higham (seated, extreme left). Four members of the crew died in World War I

Trinity College garden, 1911. Seated (from left): Joyce, Tommy Higham, Willie McQueen, kneeling; John Middleton Murry, Count Bernstorff

Eights Week, Oxford, 1910, by the Cherwell. From the left, Magdalene Quilter, Joyce, Heneage Ogilvie, an unidentified friend, and Gerty Ogilvie

Gerty

The Ogilvies' home, The Glade

Mr and Mrs Ogilvie at Henley, 1914

Joyce in the Cameroons Campaign, c. 1915

The wedding, 1916

The University, Budapest, 1922. The first three members of the bottom row are, from the left, Tommy Higham, Julian Huxley, and Dermot Morrah. Joyce is in the back row, between the two windows

Trudy in the 1920s

Joyce in the 1920s

Joyce and his sons vacationing at Borta-y-Guest, 1935. From the left, Peter, Joyce, Tristram, George, and Michael

Joyce and Trudy on the steps of 12 Parks Road, in the late 1940s

Joyce in 1955

"LET'S ASK FOR IT IN ALL THE LIBRARIES"

THE NOVEL that developed from Joyce's philosophical conclusions, *Aissa Saved,* was begun sometime in 1928, but he was not able to finish the slim book (exactly 200 pages of text in the Carfax edition) until three years later. In the first place, at the beginning the ideas that went into it were not clearly enough formulated in Joyce's mind. He had glimpsed but not yet grasped them when he began. And on top of this he rewrote it many times, bringing in situations that bolstered the ideas set forth in the central plot and then cutting them as better sub-plots occurred to him.

All the while, too, he was working at other writing — he wrote fewer short stories perhaps, but he still had not entirely abandoned *Cock Jarvis,* and other ideas for novels sidetracked him when they appeared more fruitful than *Aissa Saved* or when it floundered and he was tempted to scrap it entirely.

As the basic idea developed, he was tempted to make it do more than it should have. As he said in the preface to the book twenty years later,

. . . when I had found answers to my own problems, I tried to put them in the book. Like anyone who has broken, with difficulty, out of a confused foggy disintegrated state of feeling and thought into moderately clear going, I wanted to tell everyone how to find the road. I did not realize that everyone has his own fog and therefore, needs a special map; that most of those who wanted a way out had found it for themselves, and that the rest would rather stay where they were; that is, different people needed different kinds of faith; "true" for them.

He was making the novel into a soapbox speech with characters meant only to convey his message. This was bad art, and therefore still further rewriting of the novel was required. Consequently, it was not published until 1932.

Meanwhile, the Carys' financial situation had again become serious. The New York Stock Exchange crash in the fall of 1929 hit them just as it hit millions of people everywhere. As the world plunged into the Great Depression, the stocks which were the bulk of Mr. Ogilvie's trust fund for his children sank to a fraction of their value, and companies ceased paying dividends, the dividends which provided a fair share of the Cary income. The stocks which Joyce had bought on his own also sank, and the income from the Irish properties declined as people were thrown out of work and could not pay their rent.

Joyce might gain some satisfaction from the knowledge that he had tried to break the trust fund, and if he had been successful, he might have had a lot more to show for it now than he did. But it was a hollow satisfaction, and whatever vindication he had was futile. What mattered was that Trudy and he were almost completely without money.

The one real blessing was the boys' ability to win scholarships (Michael and Peter were "the boys," while Tristram and George were called "the babies" until they were nearly ten, undoubtedly to their embarrassment[1]). First Michael won a scholarship to Eton, and then Peter got one to Rugby. In their turn Tristram and George also won scholarships to excellent schools. They all won university scholarships as well, so that Trudy and Joyce did not have anywhere near the financial burden that they had anticipated.

There was some additional consolation in the fact that this time they were not alone in their dilemma. Many of their friends who had seemed so comparatively secure a few years back were just as badly off now as Joyce and Trudy; living in debt, making do with clothes and furniture bought in better days, perhaps even having to leave their comfortable homes for ones smaller and much less cozy. The Depression reminded Joyce of the work he had done in the General Strike in 1926, for there was a similar sense of comradeship in the face of the crisis.

And Joyce did not have to blame himself for the state of affairs at home, nor did Trudy have to feel guilty. So neither one sank into gloom and depression this time. Besides, he had developed a set of beliefs, and he had the novel to sustain him, however many setbacks and rewritings it endured.

One of the Carys' new friends, James Boyd, who had lectured in German at Bristol University and came to Oxford in 1931 as Reader in German, was writing a book at the same time, *Goethe's Knowledge of English Literature.* On his way down to his workroom at Rawlinson Road, Joyce often met Boyd, who would be headed toward the university from his home on St. Margaret's Road. "How's your book going?" Boyd would call out when he saw Joyce.

"Mine's going well enough," Joyce would tell him cheerfully, since the novel was finally coming to its end. "How's yours?"

"Not so bad, not so bad," Boyd would reply happily, for the book on Goethe was his first.[2]

Trudy was especially drawn to the Boyds because of their love of music. She had kept up her music as much as possible. Joyce, in Borgu, had urged her to continue singing and even begin lessons again, because he had gotten so much pleasure from her voice at The Glade and had felt closest to her when she was singing. So in Oxford she had joined the Bach Choir. Now, because of the Boyds, she took up her cello playing again, and, with their violin and viola, together with a series of pianists, they rehearsed chamber music together.[3]

Their musical evenings provided a great diversion during the bleak days of the Depression. They were private affairs for their own fun since Trudy, although she was a matron with four sons, was too shy to play before a public audience. They played often in the sitting room at Parks Road while Joyce sat on a stool by the fireplace, his eyes shut supposedly so he could concentrate on the music; usually it was because he fell asleep during the playing. He had a great knack for waking up just at the right moment, though, and making some seemingly intelligent comment

on the work just completed. But Trudy, who knew her husband
and his tin ear well enough, was not fooled. And when Joyce sat
dozing next to the fire, in danger of falling into the fireplace, she
would sing out, "You're not taking a chill, are you, Joyce?" [4]

Joyce and Boyd both published their books in 1932, for Ernest Benn Limited, had accepted the African novel. However
few notices there were of *Aissa Saved* in the papers and magazines, there was a flurry in Oxford, because Trudy urged Mrs.
Boyd, when the book first came out, "Let's go to all the shops
and libraries and ask for it," hoping that they could spur the
bookstores to order it in great quantities and give it space in
their windows. [5]

But the book was a disaster at the stores. It sold a couple of
thousand copies and then was remaindered. In all, Joyce did
not get much more out of it than he had earned for one short
story for *The Saturday Evening Post* in 1920, and this after three
years' work and a tremendous amount of thought.

Worse in some respects was the way that the few critics who
did review the book misunderstood it. Several saw it as an attack on missionaries, for after all, didn't the converts in the
novel almost go to war against the pagans? Didn't Aissa, the
heroine, undergo terrible tortures as a result of her conversion
and die a most horrible death? Over fifteen years later, in 1949,
Joyce, in his preface to the Carfax edition of the novel, felt the
need to answer these critics, which shows how much their comments must have annoyed him:

> Some correspondents took the book for an attack on the Mis-
> sions. It is not so. African missions have done good work in
> bringing to Africa a far better faith than any native construc-
> tion. But it does try to show what can happen to the religious
> ideas of one region when they are imported into another.

Yet this is contradicted by what he wrote to Trudy thirty
years before, in 1919:

> Also I may have a missionary soon. That spy who was sent
> through the country in my absence, has apparently reported a
> good opening, and Hammy has been written to, by the Menonite

Brotherhood. These are the most narrow minded sect of all.
. . . In one tiny place I once found the D.O. and four missionaries. Of these three had never spoken to him, and refused all
his invitations. Why? Because he drank a whiskey and soda in
the evening, and smoked. The fourth, a Danish medical missionary, played tennis with him, and drank soda-water very ami-
cably afterwards, and dreadful to relate of so good a man, smoked
a pipe. But the others were adamant in righteousness. I may add
that the D.O. was a Christian and a very decent fellow, by any
standards, and by ours, one of the most popular men in the country. I hope I won't get anyone so righteous as those three American saints, but I fear it is possible.

This vitriolic letter hardly suggests a belief that the African
missions were doing good work, and, of course, Joyce when he
was in Borgu saw them as a disruptive force, staffed by narrow-
minded "saints" totally ignorant of African life and of what the
Nigerian Service was attempting to do.

Perhaps he meant what he said in 1949 about the African missions doing good work and had forgotten how much he had detested them years before, or perhaps his attitude had mellowed
and changed. More likely, though, he was trying to prevent new
readers from focusing too strongly on what he had intended as
purely a side issue. He wanted them to see what the religious
experience meant to Aissa and not what missionaries were doing
to Africa. The missionaries in the novel are meant to be a force
for change, not for good or evil. The impact of change on Aissa
as a creative force is the book's main concern.

He was working hard at his next novel, however, and could
tell himself that first novels proverbially sold badly. The first
book attracted some attention, so the second should do better.
An American Visitor dealt with the idea of conflict between the
worlds that various people created for themselves, together with
the difference between practical and abstract knowledge. One
of the main themes is the folly and even tragedy that can be
caused by well-meaning acts when they are based on theories
that have no roots in a real world, in this case the acts of the
American visitor to Nigeria, Marie Hasluck.

The novel was far better organized than the greatly rewritten

Aissa Saved, and the theme emerges much more clearly. In some ways it was a novel about matters of immediate importance to Joyce. He had met enough theorists who said of Africa, "The Government ought to do such-and-such," and then presented some obviously ruinous plan that was based on a conception of Africa out of Edgar Rice Burroughs's Tarzan books. He hated theorizers when their theories had no practical human application or no basis in reality. Cambridge philosophers like Bertrand Russell were among this group, playing games with semantics and abstractions that, however absorbing, had as much application and benefit to human affairs as a crossword puzzle.

Aldous Huxley was another theorist whom Joyce detested. He made fun of Huxley's pessimism because it was so unreal and of his subsequent mysticism:

> For the faith in God (I mean simply the direct conviction of God's existence & interest in the lives of people, tho of course he's not the God of the churches) is logically inescapable, and to me seems as simple and obvious as the lampposts. I know that the logical faith does not go very far. I suspect that the kind of faith which makes life both so rich in happiness & so black in grief is rooted in something far deeper than argument, in life itself, perhaps, whatever "life" is, in experience which is the activity of life. So that it is difficult for one man to advise another. But for what I mean by faith, a living faith, see any child enjoying itself on any muck heap. All that faith, in spite of defeatists like Huxley (who is really not very strong in the head) is perfectly sound and real. It exists as certainly, as really, as the muck heap, and has a good deal more effect in the world. The silly pessimist is just as deluded as the silly optimist — the Huxleys, I suspect, are escapists who dodge the troublesome job of moral and political decision by going up a rabbit hole & saying "All is darkness." The optimist blinds himself by gazing at the sun and says all is light, for just the same reason, to dodge the conscription of life.
>
> (Private letter, 16 November 1948)

> I hadn't read The Devils of Loudon and found it extraordinarily interesting. . . .
>
> And what an extraordinary picture you get of Huxley's mind. His oriental mysticism is about as oriental as the pagoda at Kew, and to his Brahman and Akoman I should have to add the gas-

man. His mind seems to dwell in abstractions so thin that the Indians themselves can make nothing of them. Brahma has almost disappeared from Indian Mythology. He is an old fashioned gush-box liberal anarchist who turned sour when it turned out that the world needed policemen as well as anarchists — & that anarchists turned into absolutists, by a very natural transition from heads to tails.

(Private letter, 30 December 1952)

Joyce, in *An American Visitor,* attempted to show the very real and extensive damage such modern theorists and abstractionists could do, in much the same way as Swift demolished their eighteenth-century equivalents in "A Modest Proposal."

When Ernest Benn published the book in the summer of 1933, it received much better notices than *Aissa Saved* had. Both *The Times Literary Supplement* and *John O'London's Weekly,* for instance, praised it highly. But it did not sell. It did not even match the sales of *Aissa Saved.* There were no royalties beyond the initial advance on either book. To be told he had written a fine book, his second at that, and then see it fail must have been crushing. And however gratifying a critical success may be, it does not pay the bills.

What the two books did do, however, was bring Joyce into contact with some of his old Nigerian acquaintances. He received a letter of praise, for instance, from his first D.O., H. S. W. Edwardes, to whom he replied:

DEAR EDWARDES,

I was delighted by your approval of the book. The critics were extremely kind but as you guessed, the public were cool, and my profit was small.

I have written another since which was even better received especially in the Times, but up to the present has sold no better. It is called "An American Visitor" and deals with a pagan tribe attacked by civilization in its two most insidious forms: social and religious.* It is a fuller book than the other; not so good technically but much richer in idea and detail. But my interest is not so much in the black man's mind as in everybody's mind, and

---

* This hardly agrees with his "African missions have done good work" of 1949.

tho' I have several other African books in various stages, my next
will probably deal with English tribes, pagans and witch doctors.

Joyce's mention of having "several other African books in various stages" indicates that he had already hit on the method he
was to use and develop for the rest of his career. It stemmed in
large part from his education as a painter and to a lesser degree
from the problem of writing books while on trek in Nigeria. He
would keep a dozen or more novels all going at the same time, in
various stages of development, just as a painter might work on
several canvases concurrently.

It was a painter's method because he began with a sketch or
two rather than the sort of outline he had tried during his last
tour in Nigeria. A character who struck Joyce might end up in
one of his pocket notebooks. Or a bit of interesting conversation he had overheard, an anecdote from a newspaper, perhaps a
few phrases created in his imagination — any of these might be
jotted down and put away somewhere in his desk or in a filing
box. Even a scene cut from a novel already under way might be
the sketch or embryo for a new novel.

As the sketches lay about, Joyce might pick one up and develop it a little bit. A scrap of dialogue might suggest a scene to
be roughed in or some confrontation between two characters: an
argument, a confession, perhaps.

As the scenes developed, two of them might seem related, and
out of that relationship might grow a basic theme. Constantly
filed away and constantly brought out again for additions, the
scenes would develop to the point where Joyce could begin to
block out a whole novel as a painter might block out a work on
the basis of a series of sketches and motifs.

Once a set of characters, a developed sketch, and a conception
of theme had suggested the form for a novel, the next step was
to outline the project and to try a few chapters to see if the idea
really would work. He might try the climaxes of the novel in
order to see if they could be handled or if they fell to pieces. He
sometimes tried the last few chapters of a book, because if he
could not end it properly, then there was no sense in beginning.

Many novels that start out in a promising way fall apart near the end, so the end was a good place to begin. Endings were perhaps the hardest part of a novel. If one worked out well, then he could try the beginning, or even the middle, whatever seemed to be the hardest, because if he were unable to handle the most difficult parts, he felt there was no sense in wasting time on the easy ones.[6]

Joyce had ten or a dozen novels at a time in some stage of development because of this system, and he had scraps of all sorts that could be developed into still more novels. "I don't think I've ever begun a novel as a novel right off, from scratch," he said, when he was asked about his method.[7] There was never any chance of his running dry of ideas.

Neither was there any real chance of his being stuck on one book, because he could always turn to another if he happened to bog down. He could channel all his creativity into production rather than frustration once he had begun to write this way. Instead of abandoning one novel after another because each one in its turn did not say quite what he wanted it to, he could keep all of them going at once, and if something he meant to say would not fit into this one, he could work it into one of the others. This unique juggling feat also provided him with a frequent change of pace, scene, and characters, so that he did not become bored with his work.

The result was a steady flow of writing, a very high rate of production, without any absence of quality. From 1932 — when *Aissa Saved* was published — until the end of his life, he turned out a book or a film a year.

33

CASTLEDAWSON

ALTHOUGH THE ADVANCES for both *Aissa Saved* and *An American Visitor* helped pay the worst or most immediate of the household bills, they were still too small to make a real change in the picture. By 1933 Joyce had sold the last of the stocks he had bought in the mid-1920's. The trust fund was paying nothing and the Irish properties were no gold mine, so he and Trudy had to resort to the desperate measure of ten years before: they let 12 Parks Road and went to live with relatives.[1]

Arthur Cary had bought a house in Somerset in 1929, when he retired from his profession. It was only a few miles, as it happened, from Castle Cary in eastern Somerset, which centuries back had been the family home before various members of the Cary family went to Ireland. And the River Cary flowed west to Bridgwater Bay, through Somerset, so the new home was almost as much family territory as Donegal had once been. Arthur Cary now lived in a comfortable old house with a walled garden that had a trout stream flowing through it, and two of the boys were sent to spend their vacation with him and his daughter Sheila.[2] Joyce went off to Castledawson, and Trudy and the other two boys went to her relatives.

At Castledawson, where he had often been before, Joyce slipped into a routine as regular as the one he had followed in Oxford: writing in the morning in the library-schoolroom, where he was left totally in peace, and no one, even if they wanted a book, knocked on the door or went into the room;

tennis every day in the afternoon unless the weather made it impossible; and in the evenings, usually, talking with his Aunt Netta and his cousins Cary and Toni.[3] What he liked best, though, was listening to his aunt reminisce about the old days of Castle Cary, Inishowen, and the London of Uncle Tristram and Poker Flat. He enjoyed the talk for itself, as it was a tie with the past and all its color, but he also was thinking of a novel — even a series of novels — about the family and its background, so everything his aunt told him had a special value.

Inevitably they talked politics, too, since politics and Ireland are inseparable. Joyce, a liberal, who had not lived through the breakup of the family in the 1880's and 1890's in the same way as Netta Clark had, could argue more objectively about the course of events and the necessity of many of the blows the Carys had suffered. He would present a sound, reasonable, logical argument to Aunt Netta. Then when he was through, she would simply say, "Yes, but you're *quite* wrong, Joyce." And that was that. Arthur Cary employed the same tactics. This, in fact, was known as "the Cary argument." Just one grand slam *non sequitur* and nothing more.[4]

When foul weather prevented tennis or when the courts behind the house were filled, Joyce liked to weed the big lawns. He would lie on the grass with a spike-like device and spend hours pulling up weeds. It was a nice, tranquil diversion which gave him ample time to think about his writing. Or he and Cary might walk along the river beyond the house and sometimes go out with rifles and take potshots at the rats that lived in the banks. Joyce, though, seldom hit anything; his brother, with a much better eye and more experience and patience than Joyce, did far better when he came over on leave from his ship.

Joyce's cousin, Toni, was a painter, and Joyce loved to get hold of her materials when he could and spend a whole series of afternoons working away at a canvas or talking of art with her. She found, however, that after he had spoken enthusiastically of a particular painter or school of painters as the only subject worth studying, she would read up on them as much as she could and examine their pictures, perhaps even try her hand at paint-

ing something similar, only to discover the next time he
dropped in unexpectedly at Castledawson, he had forgotten the
painter he had previously praised and was raving about a new
one. It was frustrating, yet with Joyce's constant enthusiasm,
she couldn't help but be encouraged to keep at her work and
enlarge her knowledge of the world of art. Some of Joyce's artistic enthusiasms bore less fruitful results, however. When he
came to The Bungalow in 1935 he decided that Aunt Netta had
all the paintings in her house hung the wrong way. He took all
of them down. But he never got around to hanging them the
way he intended. So all through his stay the pictures sat on the
floor, leaning against the walls. In fact it was months before they
were hung again, exactly as they were before Joyce had taken
them down.[5]

If he had to spend the spring and summer away from Oxford
and Trudy, there was nowhere Joyce would rather spend it than
Castledawson. His Aunt Netta had always been a second mother
to him, from the time she had come to look after Jack and him
when their own mother died. And he loved Ireland, too, in a
way that he never had England, however English he might feel
at times.

The Clark family linen mill was the source of another of
Joyce's enthusiasms. One day he decided that the Clark mill
could make a fortune turning out painters' canvas. He talked
over the idea with his cousin Cary every chance he got, asking
about all the technical points and problems that might be involved. He wanted to know everything that linen-making en-
tailed until Cary finally convinced him that it simply was not
practical to convert the mill — the amount of artists' canvas
bought a year was only a small fraction of the total linen output
of Northern Ireland, and new production would only glut the
market.[6]

This sort of enthusiasm for new ideas and information was
typical of Joyce. Jack Cary had experienced his brother's fervor
only a year or two before when Joyce visited him aboard the
ship he now commanded, H.M.S. *Brenda.* Joyce knew almost
nothing about ships, although he showed himself a sailing en-
thusiast whenever he had a chance. So he set out to educate

himself on ships and the way they were run, asking question after question of Jack — the length of the ship, the height of the funnels, problems of navigation — until Jack, overwhelmed by this thirst for facts, had to send for the ship's book and let Joyce read through it the way another person might read a murder mystery. Joyce was a glutton for facts, and nothing was unimportant.[7]

It wasn't just that he was a writer and thought that someday he might want the information for use in a book he was working on. The information itself was interesting, for it helped him see how the world ran. It rendered the world vivid and alive rather than allowing it to remain a flat backdrop or a gray mist through which he passed. Joyce was intrigued with all of life. His interest in people and their jobs made them open up to him and feel his sincerity. Out of curiosity and enthusiasm he talked with people of every possible sort — railway men, hotelkeepers, and fishermen.

Joyce was not interested only in people, however. Once when he was at his father's place in Somerset he became curious about Jack's hunting spaniel. Joyce had hated dogs ever since Nigeria, where dozens and dozens of them around Nafada and Kaiama used to bark and howl all night. As soon as they quieted down another dog off in the distance might let out a bark that would start off the others all over again for another hour of tumult. Suffering from insomnia as he did, Joyce came to dread the beasts and, when he was on trek, usually tried to make camp a good distance from any village so as to get some sleep for the next day's hike. Thus, it was surprising that he should take an interest in the spaniel. He watched it and wondered about it and asked Jack question after question: how did he train a dog, how could he get a dog to retrieve with a "soft mouth," how far would it range in retrieving, and so on until he knew as much about the spaniel as he did about H.M.S. *Brenda*.[8]

In the latter part of the summer of 1933 the family was together again in Oxford, a little better off because of the money made from renting the house. Joyce was back at work in the Piggery, and Trudy was typing for him.

Now that Joyce had published two novels under his own

name, a special kind of problem presented itself. Ten years before, on a walking trip with Tommy Higham in the Cotswolds,
Higham had signed the register in a small hotel for both of
them, "T. F. Higham and Joyce Cary." A few days later some
Trinity students had stopped at the same hotel for the night and
had noticed Higham's and Joyce's names together in the register. Soon after this, Higham found that the Trinity students
were plaguing him with questions about the theater, grinning
slyly all the while or looking so stony that he knew something
was wrong.[9] Miss Joyce Carey happened to be a very popular
and attractive London actress, with whom Leslie Howard had
made his dramatic debut.

When Higham realized the mistake the students had made, he
wangled an invitation for his hotel companion to speak to one of
the literary clubs of the college, and of course it was his friend
from 12 Parks Road who appeared. Higham cleared his reputation and Joyce got an honorary membership in the club at the
same time, however disappointed the students may have been
that there was no scandal.[10]

In the 1930's, Joyce began getting letters telling him what a
marvelous performance he had given, while Miss Carey received
notes saying that her latest book had given the reader a great
deal of pleasure or irritation. This happened so often over the
years that Joyce finally wrote to Miss Carey, who was performing
in Oxford, and invited her to Parks Road for tea. They spent an
afternoon soon after talking about books, the theater, families,
and especially about their mutual name.[11]

The publication of his first two novels also brought Joyce into
touch with a man whom he had once cursed, Lord Lugard, formerly the Governor General of Nigeria. Joyce took his son Michael to visit the old administrator one day and was struck by
the change in the man who had been almost omnipotent and
legendary twenty years before, a man so powerful that he had
sometimes acted independently of the government at Westminster. Now Lugard's era had passed and the man himself was almost forgotten. Joyce was touched, and as he and Michael
walked down the path from Lugard's cottage he could only comment, "A tiny man in a little house." [12]

Perhaps the visit to Lord Lugard prompted him to take out the abandoned manuscript of *Cock Jarvis* and work on it again, as a portion of the novel suggests that Joyce did more writing around 1935. But if he did make another start on the novel, he abandoned it after a short while, this time for good.

As he had told H. S. W. Edwardes in January, 1934, he wanted to try other works besides his African novels. For one reason, he did not want to be fitted into a slot; pigeonholing was one of his phobias, and he disliked the sort of mind that forced people, ideas, books, and everything else into predetermined categories. Besides, after more than a dozen years' absence from Africa, he was out of touch with the country and much closer to life in England. And he still had the idea for a book about the Cary family, set principally in the late nineteenth and early twentieth centuries but ranging over the entire three and a half centuries of the family's history.

As he developed the work it grew in his mind to trilogy length and became the great, long book he had told Trudy soon after their marriage that he meant to write one day. So besides his talk with his Aunt Netta, he asked his father and other members of the family about what they remembered and questioned them to ascertain the accuracy of his own recollections. His search for information must have included the smallest details, as the following letter from his father illustrates:

DEAR OLD BOY.

I really forgot all about the maids games with herring milts at Castlecary — they called them "melts" and they used to talk & laugh over the shapes which they took when thrown against the whitewashed wall — I think it was like "telling their cups" when the tea leaves grouped themselves in various patterns. — the little piece of herring is about 2½ inches long — thick as a match & tapered at both ends — and I presume quite impartial.

(22 April 1936)

Either he bogged down on the work or was diverted from it by another idea, because the next novel he published, *The African Witch,* was again situated in Nigeria. It introduces a new theme, the prejudices of some Britons in Africa, with regard to their racial views. In a way they are like the theorist of *An American Visitor,* Maria Hasluck, unable to see the real world around them, full of ideas of the noble savage; the westernized African hero of the novel is repugnant and even threatening to them because he has taken on their values, dress, speech, and education — in fact, as a university graduate, he is several steps above most of them. It was a phenomenon Joyce had witnessed often enough in Nigeria and which he for a time had shared — this belief that Africans should remain quaint and picturesque because then one could patronize them.

Despite their financial difficulties, Joyce and Trudy tried to take the children for a holiday each summer, usually to the seaside. They would pile into a train compartment or into their huge, ancient Humber, with Trudy at the wheel most of the time, and go off to Wales, either to the Pembrokeshire town of Saundersfoot or a resort, Borta-y-Guest, or some other fairly quiet place. Trudy drove most often simply because she was more capable at it than Joyce. His driving was even more "individual" than his dancing had been at Oxford, and being his passenger was no way to spend a vacation. Trudy, though, had a virtual instinct for driving and once, when the transmission gave out, she drove the car in reverse for twenty miles, almost as fast as in forward gear, until they came to a garage where the car could be repaired. Only once did her instinct completely fail her, and that was one day when she suddenly commented, "I didn't know there was a light under the bonnet." Joyce looked out at the hood of the car and told her, "That's no light! We're on fire!" [13]

Once they reached their vacation spot, the boys who were small enough were allowed to run around the beach naked, swimming, playing in the sand, and eating lunch. After his experiences in Nigeria of bathing on railway platforms and receiving petitioners in his bath and of having witnesses at trials calmly strip and dress themselves again, Joyce had lost any sense of prudishness on that score, especially when it came to children. If people objected, he was apt to give them a tongue-lashing, accusing them of having corrupt minds for thinking that the sight of naked four-year-olds was obscene.[14]

At the beach he played even harder than the children, helping them build sand castles, teaching them swimming, dashing into the water for some quick dips of his own, and exploring caves and coves and hills.[15]

As the boys grew older, each had his cakes and scones and his afternoon tea packed in a separate bag so he was free to go off by himself if he liked and still not be hungry. The boys were given plenty of independence. They could take a bicycle tour of a week or two, even to France if they wished. Tristram, for instance, traveled to St. Andrews in eastern Scotland all alone when he was fourteen.[16] All of the boys were good-sized and could take care of themselves. In fact, as they got their growth, each one towered over Joyce's five feet nine inches, George being the tallest at six feet five.[17]

One summer they spent the holiday at a farm, perhaps for the sake of saving money, perhaps because of Joyce's wish, expressed to Trudy in June, 1919, that they learn "gardening — how to swim — how to tell a cow from a bull — and how eggs are laid, and why." Joyce told the boys they must each choose a job on the farm and then stick to it for the entire holiday. They could choose any job as long as they saw it through. Perhaps he was trying to instill in them the persistence he had not shown as a boy and young man, a failing which had drawn him away from Store Street and writing in 1912 and had cost him six years of progress in his vocation.

Joyce had other ideas for the boys' education. For instance, he had written Trudy from Africa:

> There are two important parts of education which are worth a great many more unusual subjects — horsemanship and drawing. The one teaches courage, confidence, and a knowledge of animals, the other an original interest in environment, and perhaps taste. . . . The holidays is the most educative period, or should be, of a child.
>
> (24 October 1919)

He succeeded in teaching all four how to ride and even played a little catch-as-catch-can polo on Port Meadow with Michael from time to time,[18] but the boys turned out to have a great deal

more of the Ogilvie talent for music than the Cary bent for
painting. All four became quite proficient musically and played
duets and trios with Trudy, sometimes joining in the concerts
with the Boyds and other friends of the family.

Joyce also felt they should know something of their background:

> And they must have some family tradition too, which is why I
> want some family things. In a way, you know, to be connected,
> as it were, personally with history is a privilege of value. It en-
> larges the imagination. It can give a good sort of pride. And it
> should not make them snobs, because the Carys are not very dis-
> tinguished.
>
> (21 August 1919)

A sense of family had been extremely important to him, because
it had sustained all the Carys when they had had to leave Ireland.

He also taught his sons punting on the Cherwell and ice skating when the Thames was frozen over. And he told them
stories, especially serial stories that went on for week after week
in fifteen-minute or half-hour installments each night when the
boys were in bed. One concerned "Fishing-Rod Jim," a scamp
who fished whatever he wanted out of people's windows with
rod and line. Jim and his friends were constantly getting into
desperate circumstances yet always were saved at the final moment. Jim's inventiveness was his trademark. Once he rescued
a whole gang of boys from a swamp by getting them to take off
their shirts, then tying the sleeves together and letting them fill
up with marsh gas in a great balloon, which wafted the whole
group to safety. Another time, tied by villains and cast into the
sea to drown, Jim was rescued by a friendly swordfish, who cut
his bonds and let him swim away.[19]

Joyce did not teach his children religion, but one or another
of their succession of nannies did. Grace was always said at
meals in the nursery, and the family went to church at Christmas and Easter — "High days and holy days," as Joyce said.[20]

Michael, the eldest, was the most active son, going out for

games, playing the Wall Game at Eton and getting a half blue in lacrosse at Oxford; Peter was shy and sensitive as Joyce had been at Clifton; Tristram was the most carefree and rambunctious; George, whose sight improved somewhat but who remained unwell, was the scholar of the family.[21]

Joyce and Trudy enjoyed watching them grow up, but Joyce in particular was sorry that they could not stay infants, too. He complained at least once, "We've got no more babies!" To which Trudy replied, "If you want more, you'll have to get them yourself." [22]

Tristram and George, once they started at the Dragon School, to which their brothers had gone, brought the Carys into closer touch with Gwen and Alan Herbert, whose son John was also at the school.[23] Trudy and Gwen had been close friends once and had often gone to dances at Oxford together. Joyce enjoyed Alan's books and his company equally, and Alan gave Joyce his first introduction to practical politics in 1935.

In fact, 1935–1936 were good years in many ways for Joyce and Trudy, for *The African Witch,* his third novel, was published during this period and became the first of his books to make any real money.[24]

Because his first two books had done so badly, Joyce felt his publishers, Ernest Benn Limited, had not done enough to publicize and push his work.[25] For their part, the publishers felt that Joyce was not much of a money-maker. So Joyce and his agent looked for better prospects, and a contract was signed with Victor Gollancz for *The African Witch.*[26] When the novel appeared in 1935, it was made a Book Society choice, providing a great boost to its sales, which were to come to over 15,000 copies. Joyce's royalties amounted to over £1,000, the first financial success he had had in fifteen years, since the streak of luck in 1920.

34

A. P. HERBERT'S POLITICAL CAMPAIGN

IN 1935 ALAN HERBERT ASKED JOYCE, as a graduate of Oxford, to nominate him for the Oxford University seat in the House of Commons. Joyce asked him for what party he meant to stand as candidate, and Herbert replied, "I'm standing as a good chap." [1]

Joyce made the nomination, not sure just how serious Herbert was about the whole affair. Herbert was, after all, a humorist, a regular contributor to *Punch*. As an independent he did not stand much chance in the House of getting anything done, and, because of his slight stammer, he did not seem likely to sway vast crowds with spellbinding oratory. So Joyce was surprised when he found his friend running a very effective campaign for the seat, showing not only the wit he was famous for but answering seriously and knowledgeably all the questions put to him. Neither could he be faulted on his knowledge of government affairs, and anyone who has seen an Oxford Union debate knows the sharp-witted heckling a speaker can expect at the university if he is unsure of his subject. Herbert proved he knew what he was talking about, and he was elected.

Rather than sit in the House and wait until he could make a trivial and pleasant maiden speech, Herbert took the initiative and introduced a private member's bill. This was shock enough, but much more astounding was the bill's intent: to revise British divorce proceedings!

At the time Herbert had been married to Gwen Quilter for

more than twenty years and they seemed very happy. Why, then, some people asked, was he so eager to make divorce easier in England? Herbert's answer was that marriage is too good a relationship to be sullied by unions that have collapsed and yet cannot be dissolved because neither of the partners wants to be labeled an adulterer in public. Marriage was easy and divorce very difficult; Herbert felt to make sense it should be the other way around.

He had put much of his idea into a novel published in 1934, *Holy Deadlock,* the story of a married couple who simply have nothing in common anymore, who are pleasant and polite to each other but in love with two other people and want to be divorced. Neither is having an affair, but one must be arranged, so the husband is set up with a professional divorce corespondent for a weekend stay at Brighton. But this is not adultery; it is perjury, because, although he and the girl sleep together, sleeping is *all* they do. The judge before whom the divorce case is brought has begun a campaign of cracking down on proceedings involving sham adultery, and the case is thrown out. Then, believing she may never get divorced, the wife spends a night on a yacht with the man she loves, so now both husband and wife have committed adultery, one bogus, one real. No divorce can be had in this case, because according to British law only one partner in a marriage could claim to be the aggrieved party. Somehow or other, double adultery was supposed to equal a happy marriage. Now the husband must admit he is a perjurer if the divorce is to be obtained. He gets free of his wife but goes to jail. On and on the couple goes, tied together more and more inextricably by the red tape and narrowness of the law and less and less by any feeling for each other; they are caught in holy deadlock and can never be free to be happy.

It was an amusing book, and few people besides its author took it seriously. To Herbert the situation was amusing in some ways, but as a constant and real occurrence it was tragic. The book pictured marriage as a bad joke and the law as a grand process of torture and torment. Herbert's purpose in writing the novel was to bring about change.

Every chance he got, he was on his feet urging his divorce bill in the House and, because of his reputation as a writer, he got publicity for his speeches in the newspapers. Whether he convinced his fellow M.P.'s or simply wore them down, in 1938 Parliament finally enacted into law his bill as the Matrimonial Causes Act, the first revision in English divorce law in nearly a century and the only significant change of the twentieth century.[2]

It was an amazing feat, first that such a controversial bill should be passed at all, second that it should have taken only three years from its introduction to its enactment, and third that a private member who earned his livelihood as a writer of theatrical reviews, novels, and humorous pieces for *Punch* and who was a member of no political party and had no party's backing should have rammed it through. No one was more surprised than Joyce.

Joyce was fascinated by his introduction to practical politics in Herbert's campaign for the Oxford University seat and in watching the progress of his friend's bill from introduction to enactment. He always enjoyed being on the inside of a situation, seeing how it worked, and politics was one of his greatest interests. Like Herbert, Joyce belonged to no party. He leaned to the Liberals, but was more of a nineteenth-century Radical than anything else.[3]

After the successful campaign in 1935, though, he became a fairly frequent visitor to the House of Commons and lunched several times with Herbert together sometimes with other Members. In Nigeria he had been an absolutist — politicians should mean what they say and should pass many laws to prevent this or that abuse — but as he began to see how the government was really run and since he was no longer so directly under its thumb, he tempered his attitudes greatly. For instance, he said,

> I can never understand why parents, who handle so much politics in their own homes, are sometimes such narrow and blind critics of the political scene. But the answer, I suspect, is a double system of morality and divided minds. The same people who in their own homes, will do or say anything to conceal from a nervous sick child the danger of a necessary operation, who

persuade it for its own necessary good, that there will be no pain, abuse the statesman who tells a lie to hide from a nation the desperation of some crisis.

Both acts have the same justification, expediency, and those who are shocked by the word, practice the fact every day of their lives.

("Politics and Morals")

Joyce, like many other people, was concerned about what was happening in the political world of Europe. The outbreak of the Spanish Civil War and the weak attitude displayed by the Conservative Government toward it aroused a great many people in Britain. Both the Liberal and the Labour Parties took much stronger stands against the revolt of the Spanish generals and the aid which they were given by Hitler and Mussolini. The remilitarization of the Rhineland, the troubles in Austria that culminated finally in its annexation by Germany, and the failure of Britain, France, and other countries to give sufficient backing to the League of Nations' attempt to block Mussolini's war in Ethiopia were frightening to any attentive observer. But most Britons were far too interested in immediate peace at any price to give sufficient thought to the future and preferred to look on Hitler as a gentleman who kept his word rather than seeing him for what he really was.

But nearly thirty years earlier Joyce, in a letter to his wife, had expressed doubts that peace could continue, given the new shape of Europe:

> The whole of Europe seems to be breaking into small parts. History runs in comical circles. First parochialism, then nationalism, then Empires, and then nationalism again, and in the case of Russia, partly, parochialism.
>
> To think that there will be universal peace for ever with Europe full of small rival states is a dream. I see the Poles and the Ukraine are fighting already.
>
> There was least war in Europe under the Roman Empire, which included all, or nearly all. But nationalism is the most

dangerous of spirits, and it is strong everywhere. It rests on the best as well as the worst, and strongest of human nature — the love of home, the suspicion and therefore hatred of the stranger. On one hand admirable virtue, on the other, the evil ignorance & prejudice which attack an innocent person merely because he is foreign.

The theory is that all races should have their own land. But there is scarcely a land in Europe not of mixed race. It will have to go by majorities, and the boundaries will cause as much heart burning jealousy and bickering as any arbitrary division. Each country will have its Ireland.

(16 November 1918)

But Britain was diverted from international problems by the controversy over the marriage of Mrs. Simpson and Edward VIII, and Joyce and Trudy by another wedding, that of Joyce's cousin Toni Clark to Joe Thompson, at The Bungalow, Castle-dawson. Joyce took it on himself to help make the wedding as grand an occasion as possible and was particularly anxious that Cary buy the very best champagne. Toni's brother was determined not to fail, so he not only ordered the best but asked for half again as many bottles as the manager of the firm suggested.[4]

At the wedding, Joyce sipped dubiously, then his eyes lit up, and he gulped down the rest of the glassful and poured himself a second. Since Joyce was the most temperate of drinkers, averaging about one glass of wine a day, Cary felt relieved and the wedding went splendidly.[5]

The trouble was that after the wedding party, there was all that extra champagne to be consumed. Jack Cary hated to see his cousin in such a fix, so he volunteered his help and over the next five days Jack and Cary struggled stoically through bottle after bottle. When the last of it was drunk, they were feeling so wretched that they set out on a fourteen-mile walk to put their heads in shape, ending up at a friend's home, where they were invited to play tennis. They politely refused and were then offered tea. "No thanks," Jack said, "I never touch the stuff." He had his hands stuffed in his pockets to hide their shaking, and the idea of holding a cup of tea steady on a saucer seemed an impossible task. Fortunately, their host recognized the problem better than their hostess did and took the two men into his study for a whiskey to brace them for the long walk home.

That same year, 1936, Joyce had what seemed a stroke of good luck. After the success of *The African Witch,* his agent had placed the book with an American publisher, William Morrow. From his experience of 1920 with *The Saturday Evening Post,* Joyce knew how much money could be made in the States, and now he had another chance. But *The African Witch* was not to America's taste, and most of the edition ended up as so much wastepaper. It was a disaster.

There were other events to divert Joyce's attention from his novel's failure, however, for in 1936 Hitler and Mussolini entered into an alliance, the Spanish Civil War broke out, and Austria's independence was threatened by Hitler. Joyce became more and more concerned by the worsening of European affairs. He had written a satirical novel about the politics of the 1930's, *Arabella,* a modern *Candide* about a naïve young English girl who travels through Europe and America, meeting Communists, Nazis, anarchists, business tycoons, and technocrats, a novel he never published but must have had a grand time with.[6]

But now the situation had gone beyond humor, as the League of Nations was dying. So in 1937 he joined the embryonic Air Raid Precaution service. On October 13 he signed on as Number 931.[7] If there must be a war — and to him it was a matter of *when* the war came rather than *if* it should come — he wanted to help. With Hitler's Luftwaffe practicing on Barcelona, Madrid, and other Spanish cities, perfecting its dive-bombing and saturation-bombing techniques, much of the coming war seemed likely to be fought in the air. So protection against air raids was a prime concern.

In 1937 Arthur Cary died. He had been intermittently ill but lately had seemed well and was out playing a game of golf one day when, in the middle of the game, he had a heart attack.[8] The death, coming with such abruptness, was a great shock to his family.

Yet he had had a full life. He had done what he had set out to do: make a very respectable career for himself as a consulting engineer, raise a family of which he could be proud, and, in his first two brief marriages, find much happiness. Of his three sons, Jack commanded a ship in the Royal Navy, Joyce was a respected (if not terribly well-paid) novelist whose four sons would surely carry on the family line, and Tony, who was the son of his second wife and thus much younger than Joyce, was a farmer in South Africa.

Joyce was glad that he had been able to show his father some of the rewards of his own persistence and of the older man's forbearance, for his most successful novel to date had been published just the year before his father's death. But he regretted having seen him so seldom in the past few years. Somerset had been bad for his asthma so he had not gone down there very often. Arthur Cary, with his ups and downs of health, had done little traveling, so they seldom got together. As Joyce said to John Fischer when that man's father died,

> I know I did not realize till I lost mine, how much that special and unique relation means — a relation of interest as well as affection. There are very few people in the world at any time who take much concern in ones affairs and doings and none who take the same concern as ones parents. I know I am still saying to myself "I wish my father had lived long enough to know or hear so-and-so about me or the grandchildren. It would have given him so much pleasure."
>
> (24 May 1952)

The novel he was working on now, the first volume of the *Castle Corner* trilogy, might have brought his father pleasure as a reconstruction of the life at Castle Cary. This volume of the work, entitled *Castle Corner,* moved from the 1870's to the eve of the First World War and most closely paralleled the story of the Carys. It was an extremely ambitious novel, and the trilogy was even more so, tracing the lives of a number of characters over a half century of life in Ireland, England, Africa, and America, as the household broke up and the members of the family and its servants moved away to make new lives for themselves.

Castle Corner was published by Gollancz in 1938, but its reviews were not so good as those of his last two books and it sold less than 3,000 copies.[9] The result was that Joyce, dispirited and not very sure that Gollancz would be interested in the remaining two volumes of the trilogy, abandoned the project.[10] It seemed that his life only got better so it could go bad again. In nineteen years as a professional author, he had had only two successful years. But it was far too late now to give up. He turned fifty in December of that year.

The good reviews he had received for *An American Visitor* and *The African Witch* and the financial success he had had with the latter suggested that if he wanted any chance to make money again, he would have to stick with African novels, and in his next, *Mister Johnson,* he returned to the Nigerian setting. When the book was published in 1939, however, it had little more success than *Castle Corner.*[11]

Joyce and Trudy had scraped together £100 in order to buy some stocks to give Michael on his twenty-first birthday in 1937, and Joyce wanted to do the same for the other three boys.[12] But it seemed impossible to save that much. Michael's birthday had come when the royalties from *The African Witch* were coming in, and, however tight the budget was, that period had been the most secure since the middle 1920's.

Joyce felt very guilty that he was unable to give the boys the independence he had been given through his mother's legacy and looked about for ways of making money apart from his novels. Michael graduated in 1939 from Trinity College, Oxford, with a first in Mods and Greats. He then did very well on his examinations for the Home Civil Service so that he got a good position in the Ministry of Aviation.[13] So Joyce's eldest son did not have quite the need that the other boys did. However, Peter, now in university, and Tristram and George, who were thirteen and eleven respectively in 1939, could certainly use a bit of their own money.

So he put out feelers to see what sort of commission work he could get,[14] and he turned back to the idea he had toyed with back in 1921 — he would write a play.

35

AFRICAN NOVELS

WHEN HE BEGAN to devote all his time to writing in 1920, Cary had not fully digested his Nigerian experiences. Writing *Cock Jarvis* was a major step in their assimilation, but he used the external materials mainly — the settings — rather than attempting to render the African point of view. *Cock Jarvis* is concerned almost entirely with Britons in Africa rather than with the Africans themselves.

But his experiences in Borgu and in writing *Cock Jarvis* had begun a process of growth in him, in perception, intuition, and belief. Each of his four published African novels, *Aissa Saved, An American Visitor, The African Witch,* and *Mister Johnson,* is a further step in this development.

Another advance is evident in the four novels, and that is Cary's evolution as an artist and craftsman. *Aissa Saved* is a clumsy book that tries to do so much that little is done successfully, while the last of the four, *Mister Johnson,* is clean, engrossing, and powerful, a novel by a mature writer who knows exactly what he wants to say and is misunderstood only because of his readers' lack of perception.

Cary chose Nigeria as the setting for his novels not so much because it was exotic as because it allowed him to simplify his themes. In a primitive society, man emerged more clearly. Graham Greene's Major Scobie suggests the same idea in *The Heart of the Matter:*

Why . . . do I love this place so much? Is it because here human nature hasn't had time to disguise itself? Nobody here could ever talk about a heaven on earth. Heaven remained rigidly in its proper place on the other side of death, and on this side flourished the injustices, the cruelties, the meanness that elsewhere people so cleverly hushed up. Here you could love human beings nearly as God loved them, knowing the worst: you didn't love a pose, a pretty dress, a sentiment artfully assumed.[1]

However, many of Cary's readers mistook background for foreground, and Cary finally abandoned Nigeria as a setting for his novels not because he had run out of material but because he finally felt that an English setting might mislead fewer readers.[2]

Aissa Saved

In his preface to the Carfax edition of *Aissa Saved,* Cary wrote that he had been unhappy with his first attempts at the novel and had found it

clumsy and dull. As my own critic I rejected it and I fancied that publishers would do the same. And so I cut out the religious philosophising (chiefly between Bradgate and the Carrs) and rewrote the book several times in forms of increasing simplicity. That is why it took three years to finish.[3]

Even so, the novel in its final state remains far too complex for its length. Too many themes are introduced in too small a space. Consequently they cannot be carried through to a successful conclusion.

If the novel abounds in themes, it absolutely is crushed by its number of characters, as there are between seventy and eighty named, most of them Nigerian (it is hard to be sure of the exact number since the same names are sometimes given to two or three persons — there seem to be three Adamuses and Ganises, for instance — and occasionally characters are introduced by name and sometimes by title, so they may overlap). In a novel of two hundred pages, this means that a new character is introduced on almost every other page. The reader can not keep them straight.*

There are only nine or ten essential characters who fall into four basic categories:

1. The responsible men who attempt to keep the various religious fanaticisms from getting out of hand (Bradgate, the provincial resident, and Musa, headman of the pagan town of Kolu).

2. The religious moderates who are swept along to their fates by the frantic course of events (Harry Carr, Christian missionary at Shibi Station, and Owule, the old priest of the sacred grove at Ketemfe).

3. The fanatic leaders of the Christian and pagan groups (Ojo and Yerima, respectively), demagogues who bring about the religious warfare that leaves a wake of mutilated, burned, and butchered victims of hysteria.

4. The women who are both mothers and religious converts (Aissa, a former beer-hut girl, a wanton turned devout Christion; Ishe, the pagan woman whose baby is sacrificed to the goddess Oke; and Hilda Carr, wife of the Christian missionary).

It is the last group, the women, which is at the heart of the novel; they are torn between two passions: love of their respective gods and love of their sons. Two of them, Aissa and Hilda Carr, are shown to have been gay, carefree, and careless young women, but their conversions have overwhelmed and transformed them. Hilda Carr's conversion takes place before the novel begins, but the reader sees Aissa undergoing her second conversion. It resembles those recorded in the lives of saints or in William James's *The Varieties of Religious Experience,* for it is a true wrestling with God, an agonized experience in which Aissa's every secret place is pierced and ravished by faith. Having been portrayed as an extremely sensual woman, she experiences a sensual conversion.

---

* Professor M. M. Mahood, in her book *Joyce Cary's Africa* (Boston: Houghton Mifflin Company, 1964), points out that Cary used so many names that he had to borrow them from all over Nigeria rather than stick to names that would be found in the area of the book's setting. "For a Nigerian reader," Professor Mahood points out, "the result resembles a novel set in Stoke-on-Trent in which the characters are called Leonardo and Ivanovitch."

All three women sacrifice their children for their faith. Hilda Carr's child dies because she will not return to England either before or after its birth even though she knows the incidence of infant mortality is extremely high in western Nigeria; when the child dies, it is because Hilda is prepared to risk its life rather than leave the mission. As the book opens, the birth of her second child is near, and again she stays in the country, with the result that both she and her child die.

Aissa's and Ishe's sons are sacrificed in religious rites to bring rain that will end a famine in the region. One is a pagan rite, the other a paganized Christian rite.

The sacrifice of Aissa's son is portrayed starkly and brutally. The child, hungry for his mother's breast, lies in her arms when

> Ladije instantly cut off the child's head with a blow of his sword. The blood spurted on the ground short of the cross. "Hold it up," Kakoto shouted. Aissa let the body slide to the ground. Ladije snatched up the body and poured the blood on the branches.[4]

While this ritual takes place, Aissa, in ecstasy, sings the words of a hymn:

> All de tings I lak de mos
> I sacrifice dem to His blood.[5]

The death of Ishe's son is even more grotesque.

These two ritual murders so overwhelm the senses that the two mothers appear savage and brutal. The savage circumstances obscure the true importance of their sacrifices, and some readers may prefer to see the deaths as attacks on Africans and African life. But it must be remembered that the Christian missionary Hilda Carr sacrifices not one but *two* of her babies, as well as her own life, because of her faith. Furthermore, all three of these deaths occur offstage, reducing their horror and deemphasizing the link between Hilda and the other two women. A true reading of the novel is severely hindered by the violence it depicts.

Cary has failed to create a balance between these primary characters and episodes and furthermore has obscured their relationship by packing in too many subsidiary characters and episodes. Consequently the whole theme of the transformation of life through religion is muted.

But this is only one of a number of flaws in the work. The novel is an artistic failure because it is too ambitious. It is as if Cary *had* to put everything he had seen and known, together with his recently formed metaphysic, into one slim book. Even though a reader may salvage many fine bits of work from it, such as Ojo's rendering of the story of Christ in Chapter 9, the book remains a near chaos, with too many themes, too many characters, too many subplots, and too little balance and direction.

An American Visitor

Cary's second published novel, *An American Visitor,* was a distinct improvement over *Aissa Saved.* It has only a dozen characters, not seventy-odd, and most of them are European rather than Nigerian. Its thesis is much more apparent than that of *Aissa Saved.*

Cary used the Nigerian setting as a means of giving Marie Hasluck an almost completely free scope for her naïve simplification of moral and political values. Joseph Conrad employed West African settings similarly in *Heart of Darkness* as did Graham Greene in *The Heart of the Matter.*

Marie, a pseudoanthropologist, has all the hallmarks which Cary believed distinguished Americans as a people: idealism, impatience, romanticism, naïvety, suspicion of governments, ingenuousness, kindness. In fact she possesses those same qualities with which Henry James endowed his American characters. Rather than being an "almost incredible" character, as one critic recently called her,* Marie is a direct descendant of such Henry James figures as Isabel Archer, Milly Theale, and Christopher Newman.

* William Van O'Connor, *Joyce Cary,* Columbia Essays on Modern Writers (New York, 1966), p. 18.

Marie's idealism finds its outlet initially in an admiration for everything African, "African" to her meaning primitive. She is suspicious of government and empire, so at first she is an enemy of Eustace "Monkey" Bewsher, the local District Officer. When she learns that he too is against Western penetration of Birri District, she warms to him and writes in one of her articles for an American paper that he

> has preserved the primitive culture of the tribe both from the so-called education of the mission and the development of finance. The result is that the Birri are probably the happiest and wisest people in the world.[6]

But when the Birri turn against Bewsher and threaten not only him but the entire local European population and the mission's Christian converts, Marie is forced to give up her naïve belief in the noble savage. The Birri are as capable of duplicity as any other people in the world, riddled with suspicion, ambition, and all the rest of man's failings.

So she has to abandon her hopes of a worldly paradise to an uncertain belief in a heavenly one. Having thought religion just a mess of pottage for which man sold his birthright to a worldly Eden, Marie is forced to reexamine her beliefs in the light of events in Birri.

For Marie *must* have her paradise, her Utopia. She *must* believe. She cannot live without faith. And her faith is an American one, for the belief in a worldly Eden has been at the heart of the American dream since Crèvecoeur's *Letters from an American Farmer* in the eighteenth century.

"Monkey" Bewsher is harder to understand than Marie, perhaps because he is unable to understand either himself or his motives. He intends to unite the Birri into a single nation rather than a group of warring villages, so that they will present a common cultural front against the penetration of European traders, miners, and missionaries. The reasons for his plan are obscure, but generally they seem similar to those of Marie — he hopes to preserve a primitive way of life that he thinks right for Birri — but his romanticism is less articulated than Marie's.

For all his air of being a practical man, Bewsher is only slightly less ingenuous than Marie, and their mutual ingenuousness (aided by the Birri's ignorance and consequent suspicion of all strangers and strange ways) results in his death.

The result of Marie and Bewsher's naïvety is contained in the food box brought back to the station by Captain Stoker's patrol at the end of the novel:

> The coffin did contain Bewsher's smashed and mummified head, a horrible object whose bare-toothed grin made even Stoker feel uncomfortable, and a bagful of his finger joints. The other bones were probably Birri and one femur was certainly goat.[7]

So black and white, man and beast, come together in primitive harmony in the packing box, but only in death.

As for Bewsher's attempts to preserve Birri as a primitive society, their consequences are equally ironic. For the changes that come as a result of the Birri uprising (brought about by Marie and Bewsher's policies) are sudden, overwhelming, and devastating. Had Bewsher allowed gradual change in Birri, shaping and channeling the district's development, the best of Birri civilization might have been preserved and its society revitalized and strengthened. Instead, the Birri society is finished, the young men drift off to more prosperous territories, and the place sinks into "a state of social and political disintegration."[8]

An American Visitor is Cary's first clear statement on the inevitability of and need for change, which must, however, be tailored to local needs and given purposeful direction, together with the disaster that results from romanticists' attempts to stop it. Even so, the statement is not so clear as it might be. One reason is Marie's name, Hasluck. Marie has no luck, except in an ironic sense — she lives by "luck" or mysticism, rather than by real knowledge and the understanding and wisdom that result from it.

Some of the characters' racism is a misleading factor, too, that can result in an erroneous view of the novel. The theme is not racial prejudice itself; rather, an examination of the sort of mind that is capable of this kind of bias is Cary's concern. For that matter, it must be remembered that the racial prejudice Cary depicts is of two kinds: prejudice for and prejudice against. Marie loves the Birri *simply because they are African,* just as others hate and despise them for the same reason. Both views are simpleminded, depicting conditions as being far less complex than they really are. It is this oversimplification, this lack of ability to see the whole truth of a situation, that Cary has as his target in the novel.

Understanding this, one can see that Marie is not the novel's heroine, nor Bewsher its hero. Neither are they villains. They are simply credulous innocents whose ignorance brings chaos and death.

The African Witch

The African Witch contains almost as many characters as *Aissa Saved* and even more themes. That it exists as a unified work and presents its themes with greater clarity is indicative of how much Cary had grown as a novelist in the four years between the two novels.

The African Witch had existed in several forms before it assumed its final shape. As an early novel (*Aladé* or *The Black Prince*), it contained both the core of *The African Witch* and elements of *An American Visitor.* In one early version, Aladé, a young African prince, is a great friend of Foley, a D.O., but comes to believe the Briton has betrayed him. Aladé becomes a convert to African nationalism and racism. In some versions he is a Christian convert, an eloquent preacher and enemy of the Communist leader Haji. When he feels betrayed by Foley and the other British, he becomes Haji's ally.

In these versions Foley emerges as a comic self-portrait of Cary, of whom one character thinks, "Poor boy, with his moustache and eyeglass, fancying himself so grand and really he's a ridiculous object." Another character in the early version of the novel is Dorothy Brant, an extremely ingenuous American who foreshadows Marie Hasluck.

The problem with these early versions of the novel is the same as that of *Aissa Saved:* there is too much material. Even after sifting out part of it for *An American Visitor,* Cary still had more than enough for *The African Witch.*

In the final version he handled the world of juju, the relationship between colonial and native governments, the roles of the missionaries and local preachers, the necessity of education in Africa, love between men and women, Nigerian politics, and the communications gap between both individuals and cultures, as well as the basic Cary themes of preservation versus change and the necessity of finding or creating a system of belief for oneself in order to give life meaning.

A series of riots in Nigeria's Aba District in 1929, known as "the women's war," gave Cary the focus he needed. He stated in his preface that *The African Witch* was not based on the Aba riots, but this is belied by newspaper clippings and other items in his files that show his great interest in them. He added a second theme to that of the women's war: the imminent election of a new emir for Rimi. There are two prime candidates: Louis Aladai, educated at Oxford and a onetime Christian, and Salé, a Moslem.

Aladai is supported by the rabble-rousing preacher Selah Coker and by his own sister, Elizabeth, the high priestess of the local juju. Their support embarrasses him. He would far rather have the backing of the Resident, Burwash, whom he regards as sympathetic, enlightened, and intelligent. But Burwash is one of those people who wants to be above politics; he wants to be "fair." Yet the Resident's lack of commitment is understandable: having been disastrously outflanked early in his career due to his precipitate actions,* he has since built his life on a foundation of caution and neutrality.

Most of Rimi Station rejects Aladai because he is educated, friendly, ambitious for his people, eager for change, and European-oriented. Because he is no picturesque native, he is viewed as a "wog," a nigger in trousers or a climber, by the Britons. As he says when they snub him at the Birri race course,

* The man who outmaneuvered Burwash was Cock Jarvis; Cary finally brought Cocky into a published work.

If I had put on a turban, and three or four Hausa gowns, they'd have been delighted to see me. . . . Why do they not like me to wear their clothes — isn't it a compliment. But, of course, it looks as if I wanted to put myself on a level with them.[9]

His relationship with the British community is complicated by the presence at Rimi of Judy Coote, a former Oxford don whom he met as a student and who is engaged to Captain Jerry "Jockey" Rackham, the local D.O. Judy sympathizes with Aladai's ambitions for Rimi, and befriends him because of this and out of sympathy for the way the rest of the station snubs him. In turn, Rackham is jealous of Aladai because Judy likes the young prince, and the D.O. goes out of his way to insult and abuse him. Not that Rackham is a cruel man or a racist; he simply can't help himself, for he is an Ulsterman, and jealousy gets his Irish up.

The intolerance of most of the English and Burwash's caution throw Aladai step by step into the hands of Elizabeth and Coker, especially when Salé and his followers murder the ancient reigning emir and take over the palace. When Burwash takes no action against the murderers and does not reply to Aladai's letters (the Resident's early disaster was due to indiscretion in a letter, and since then he can commit himself to paper only after days of agony), the prince is finally convinced Burwash has betrayed him. Now he makes holy war against the British, a war that brings about his own death and those of Coker, the missionary Dr. Schlemm, the stupid English girl Dryas Honeywood, and many others.

Unfortunately the novel's essential theme can be misread as a simple statement on racism. But, as the use of Dryas Honeywood is meant to show, it is about a failure of imagination (Dryas, a visitor in the area, pities Aladai, who consequently feels she is his friend; but she pities him as she would a dog, for she cannot recognize him as a man). Racism is only a symptom and a result of this failure.

Most of the Britons at Rimi Station see Africans as picturesque creatures and can be fond of them in this role in the way they would be fond of a dog, a horse, or a favorite armchair.

Consequently Aladai's Europeanization confounds them. He challenges their stultified imaginations. His use of European clothes, his fine English, his education, and his ambitions for Rimi demand of them a recognition that Africa and her people are not merely scenery, views glimpsed on picture postcards, local color to amuse and divert. Africa is a country of human beings who must either grow or die.

Only Judy Coote can accept Aladai's challenge and see beyond the differences of color, clothes, housing, and ways to the essential humanity of the Africans. The rest fail to meet this challenge and disaster results.

But a number of critics and ordinary readers viewed the novel only as an attack on British colonialism and white racism (ignoring the fact that Coker and others are *black* racists and are condemned by Cary like the white racists). This reaction made Cary more determined than ever to abandon the Nigerian setting for one in either England or Ireland in his future novels and thus rid himself of the racial red herring.

Mister Johnson

After the failure of *Castle Corner,* Cary returned to Nigeria for the setting of *Mister Johnson.* But he used several devices to prevent the racial issue from dominating this novel. As in *Aissa Saved,* but much more clearly, white and black characters are paired off to show that conservatism, generosity, pettiness, imagination, sadism, in fact all the qualities of men, exist in both races. The virtues are not given to the blacks and the vices to the whites, nor is the reverse view presented.

For instance, Johnson's wife Bamu, who has lived all her life in an upcountry Nigerian village, is a complete conservative as is Celia, wife of the D.O., Harry Rudbeck. Bamu's family and Blore (another D.O.) also manifest the conservative point of view. These characters consider anything new, surprising, or foreign to be potentially dangerous. For instance, Bamu always refers to Johnson, who comes from the coast, as "the foreigner." She never uses his name because she never sees him as a real person, much less as her husband. She marries him only because her family can milk him of all his money and worldly goods. He is a gold mine, not a person. And she abandons Johnson whenever the going gets rough or he fails to meet his installment payments to her family after buying her as his wife.

Blore's attitude toward Johnson is the very same: Johnson is foreign, a Nigerian in European clothes, and therefore suspect. Blore wants Nigerians to *look* Nigerian, and by that he means as the natives looked when he first came to Nigeria, or, even more, as they looked in the books and missionaries' pictures of his childhood when he first formed his idea of Africans. His extreme conservatism, manifested in a love of the familiar and a desire to preserve the past, is perfectly illustrated by his attitude toward his old mosquito netting, which is a disaster of holes and darns. But he's owned it for years, perhaps since he came to Nigeria, so he must always have it. It is like the old rag of a blanket a small child carries around because it once warmed him in his cradle or wrapped him when he was held to his mother's breast and which thus contains for him the sense of being secure and loved. It is like the battered wooden horse that Cary slept with as a small child.

Both Blore and Bamu (Benjamin, the postal clerk, too — the three are tied by temperament and the alphabet) are preservers, conservatives in a literal sense. And the theme of *Mister Johnson* is the eternal conflict between the preservers and the creators of this world. It is through the building of the Fada road that this conflict and its consequences are best conveyed.

At the novel's start Rudbeck, A.D.O. for Fada, is a very conventional young man, a composite product of his home, his schooling, and his Nigerian Service training, just as Cary had been in 1914. Johnson, the new clerk at Fada Station, a youngster from the coast and stranger to Fada, is the catalyst that effects a change in Rudbeck, crystalizing his conflicting ideas into a harmonious whole.

Johnson, too, undergoes a transformation. Colonialism has given his life new meaning because it has provided him with fresh situations and food for his imagination, material that

Johnson must either incorporate into his life or reject. Since Johnson, temperamentally, is a creator, the new ideas afforded by British colonialism are a challenge which he accepts with delight. He is like a painter who has had to work with just one color and who suddenly is given a whole box of colors. Johnson splashes his canvas with different hues and is delighted.

When Rudbeck first begins to build his road, he does so under the influence of his first superior in Nigeria, Sturdie. For the D.O. has absorbed some of the mannerisms and ideas of all his former supervisors, however much they conflict, and Sturdie is a fanatic road builder. Many Nigerian hands (e.g. Blore) are against roads, against increasing trade, against the influences that result from both; in fact, they are opposed to change of any sort. The fact that Rudbeck follows Sturdie's example in the issue of roads suggests that he has a capacity for change within him but that it is in an embryonic state.

Rudbeck begins road building for no particular purpose except that it is something that one does. He never bothers to consider what the purpose of this activity may be or what impact it may have.

However, Johnson is inspired by the road, for it is a creation of his friend, Rudbeck, and anything that Rudbeck does or is interested in is of the utmost importance to Johnson. Rudbeck, however, is indifferent to his clerk. He doesn't care whether Johnson lives or dies, except for the paper work that would be involved and the necessity that would arise for breaking in a new man. Johnson is only a part of the local scene to Rudbeck, a black blob, nameless and faceless. As Johnson thrusts himself into Rudbeck's life, the D.O.'s perception of him deepens. First Johnson becomes an extension of Rudbeck's office, then a name, and finally a whole person rather than a bit of African scenery. Rudbeck's capacity to see an articulated human being is *forced* to develop, and it is Johnson's vitality and creativity that brings this evolution about.

Under Johnson's influence, Rudbeck's road building, at first only a whim or a duty, becomes a fanatic drive, but still without regard for its end result. As the clerk's capacity for creation increasingly infects his superior, however, the road begins to take on real meaning for him. He realizes it will open up Fada to trade, to prosperity, to education, to all sorts of opportunities.

In Cary's view these innovations are not strictly positive. For Fada as it stands has both vices and virtues. Although it is shown as squalid and backward and its people regularly suffer from famines and other hardships which they accept with stoicism, Fada offers a sense of community to its inhabitants. Each person is firmly established in the life of Fada and has a role to play, a clan to belong to, a pattern of life that is comfortingly sure. The harvest feast demonstrates the strong sense of community. Nobody needs to say what he feels; a glance, a moan, or a gesture is sufficient, for all are in communion. In many ways the people of Fada exist in a state of beautiful innocence; they are at peace with their environment.

But innocence is not synonymous with virtue. A state of "innocence" signifies ignorance of evil, while to possess "virtue" is to know both good and evil and thus be capable of choosing between them. So the Fada road may be likened to the fruit from the Edenic tree of the knowledge of good and evil. When the road is completed, the people of Fada will have a choice for the first time. Crime will come to Fada, but so will the knowledge to end the constant cycle of feast and famine.

The first truck which travels Fada road illustrates this dichotomy, for it makes a noise "between drumming and gunfire," [10] Cary says. Gunfire equals war, destruction, death; drumming in Nigeria means excitement, a triumphal procession, a feast. The road is both good and bad, because it will bring both benefit and bane to the town. Therefore it will bring the necessity for choice, and choice is a great burden. But it is a burden which man must assume if he is to create his own personality rather than have it molded by society. Cary felt it imperative that man utilize the former method for it alone would distinguish him from the other animals.

Cary wrote Johnson's story in the present tense. For Johnson lives in the present, where each moment is a blank canvas under his hand and, like Cary and many other artists, he is only interested in the immediate *act* of creation, the now, rather than in the finished creation, the past. So everything for Johnson is the present, or rather the present is everything.

Johnson's ultimate impact on Rudbeck is one of the novel's most often misunderstood aspects. Johnson has committed murder. Rudbeck, as A.D.O., must try him for it. Of course he cannot fail to find Johnson guilty; the case is open-and-shut. So Johnson is sentenced to hang. However, he asks instead that Rudbeck shoot him, thus placing his superior in the position of committing a personal act. In contrast, hanging would be an official act of the state.

Rudbeck resists Johnson's suggestion. He tries desperately to dehumanize the clerk, to turn him from a man into a thing again. This attempt is demonstrated in the scene in which the D.O. weighs Johnson in order to work out the length of rope needed for the hanging. Lacking a scale, he improvises one, balancing the prisoner against a box piled with shillings, sixpences, threepenny bits, and tins of flour and jam. This allows him not only to weigh Johnson but to transform him into the equivalent of these commodities or into a problem in arithmetic, thus making the task of execution less odious.

But Johnson has penetrated too deeply into Rudbeck's consciousness, especially when he asks his superior to shoot him and apologizes for causing him so much trouble. So Rudbeck cannot help but obey the man's request. He shoots Johnson dead in full view and hearing of Fada Station.

This is not the callous deed it may appear; it is a great sacrifice on Rudbeck's part. For in shooting Johnson, he has committed an act that officially will be regarded as murder. Hanging Johnson would have been perfectly legal; shooting him is not. Since Rudbeck has killed him in front of the whole station — police, clerks, traders, townspeople — even if he does not report it himself, stories will pass quickly to his superiors and there will be an investigation and a trial.* At the very least

* Cary was extremely careful about his facts. He checked them out both at the time of writing the novel and later, with legal experts including his next-door neighbor, Sir Donald Hurst, judge of the Oxford Circuit Court, to insure their accuracy.11

Rudbeck would be shunted out of the Nigerian Service, his career ruined, and any employment prospects in England made exceedingly dim. At the worst, Rudbeck would be found guilty of murder and hanged. Unless these aspects are understood and Rudbeck's sacrifice is acknowledged, many misunderstandings and false interpretations are possible, particularly the one that Johnson is a victim of imperialism and the novel is an anti-imperialist tract.

Cary was in favor of imperialism insofar as it offered opportunities to expand the lives of the colonialized peoples but not when it became an alternative oppression to the one they already suffered. Obviously Johnson's life *has* been enriched. Of course, it might have lasted much longer had he been left to live out his days in a primitive village. But it never would have been so rich.

Although *Mister Johnson* marked the end of Cary's series of Nigerian-based novels, it was the beginning of another genre as well, for it is the first of a series of picaresque novels, a genre-particularly suited to Cary's talents, materials, and themes. Cary uses a very loose, modified form of picaresque, incorporating into it whatever twentieth-century developments of narrative form would help him. It is not so much the picaresque device of the road as the roguish nature of its hero, the view of society, and the episodic quality of the narrative that Cary borrows from this particular literary tradition. It was a form that gave sufficient direction to his novels and their heroes, without cramping their styles.

A SECOND FLING AT THE THEATER

THE NEWLY FORMED Liberal Book Club came to Joyce in 1939
with a proposal that he should write a book for them. One of
their advisers, George Orwell, knew Joyce's novels and found
the political ideas expressed in them extremely interesting.
Joyce, he understood, was a liberal but was not affiliated with
any party and certainly not associated with the extreme Left.
Orwell, totally disillusioned with Communism after his experiences in the Spanish Civil War, which he related in *Homage
to Catalonia* in 1938, suggested that Joyce could offer an
alternative to either doctrinaire Left or nineteenth- and eighteenth-century Liberal ideas.[1]

So the offer was made by the Club: there would be a guaran-
teed sale through the Club together with a regular trade edition
of the book, and an advance of £100.[2] And Joyce would be
given absolute freedom to express opinions.

The offer of any sure money looked good to Joyce just then,
so he accepted. He saw his function primarily as that of the novelist, whose ideas were embodied in living characters and situations, and the opportunity to get a wider public for those ideas,
to do some proselitization, and at the same time make some
money attracted him.

He meant to call the book *Liberty and Freedom,* for it would
contrast those two ideas and attempt to bring liberal politics and
liberal theory into some sort of alignment.[3] For to Joyce, reality
and theory had been totally divorced ever since the late nine-

teenth century. "Liberty," in its classic sense, meant "freedom from" — freedom from governmental restraints, imposed religions, and oppression by another person or class. Joyce contrasted this with the idea of "freedom," by which he meant "freedom to" — to advance oneself, to educate oneself and one's children, and to realize the possibilities inherent in oneself.

John Stuart Mill had been the great theorist of the former concept:

> Mill — whose great book on liberty, published in 1859, is, with Rousseau's *Social Contract,* one of the rare classics of political thought — had the abstract conception of liberty as absence of restraint. . . . He imagined the state as keeping the ring in which men and minds, according to their private inclinations and characters, could fight their own battles. He laid down rules to stop encroachment by the state on the ring.
>
> This led him directly to the contradiction of saying, first, that the danger of democracy was stupidity in its rulers, and, secondly, that the civil service ought not to be made attractive to clever men at the expense of private business.
>
> Such contradiction is inevitable under the old idea and infects all the liberal thought of the past.
>
> Thus Mill and Spencer, and Gladstone himself, were suspicious of all state action. They looked upon it as an encroachment and restraint, and they could not solve the puzzle of legislation.[4]

This belief led to Lord Acton's famous remark, "That government governs best which governs least," and it also led to events such as the Great Famine in Ireland when, with the potato crop wiped out, millions starved or died of "plague fever," because the British Government believed so rigidly in a *laissez-faire* economic policy that it even criticized strongly and threatened with punishment the crews of Royal Navy ships who gave away their food to the starving populations of the port cities where they put in. According to the civil servants at Westminster, this action interfered with the legitimate profit-taking of shippers and grain merchants.[5] These civil servants were as compassionate as the next man, but their devout belief in this economic and political theory was completely at odds with reality, and theory won out, at the expense of millions. Joyce's great-grandfather, Reverend Anthony Cary, was among those who died of "plague fever" while tending the starving and ill members of his community.

It was a theory equally at odds with what Joyce had observed in Nigeria. He had been the government there and had interfered with trade, health, and social patterns and consequently had saved and enriched lives. He had seen then that the theory of Mill's *On Liberty* could not be taken as universal gospel. It had done its job and no longer had the same application as it once had, particularly with the introduction of universal adult suffrage, under which government ceased to be a separate entity from the population but an extension of that population.

The idea that a government that served the people was a bad government was blatantly untrue and silly. A welfare-state government was not evil, although it bred of necessity a large bureaucracy, which *could* work to the people's disadvantage. The answer to a too powerful bureaucracy, though, Joyce felt, was not less government but more power blocs or pressure groups within society to make the wishes of the people carry greater weight and force the government to keep the bureaucracy in check.

In the book he deals with the various forms of government in an attempt to show why a parliamentary organization is, in the long run, the most efficient, as well as the one which best insures the populace of the nation of liberty and freedom.

The book is written in simple, clear English, with vivid illustrations of his points, and could serve as a model for any scholar. It is a powerful book, too, ending with a strong affirmation of democratic government; and it came at a time when democracy was discredited by many and when totalitarianism seemed the wave of the future:

> How long can any new alliance of frightened autarchies hold back the march of the peoples, gathering power from every check, recoiling upon their enemies with the enormous blind violence of war and revolution?

Those who fight liberty set themselves against a power more subtle than thought; as secret as will; as persistent as nature, of which it is the life; as all-pervading as life, of which it is spirit; at a time when, throughout all countries of the world, it swells up towards the last phase of its revolutionary triumphs and the first of its world mastery.[6]

The book, which, despite Joyce's objections, was retitled *Power in Men*, was brought out in May by the Liberal Book Club and by Nicholson & Watson, Ltd., in the trade edition. It had been severely cut, without Joyce's approval, and he was very unhappy with the result, which he regarded as misnamed and botched in the editing.[7] Since he had been asked to express *his* political ideas, he wanted them *to be* his.

To make matters worse, Hitler grabbed off the remains of Czechoslovakia in mid-March, Mussolini invaded Albania in April, Germany and Italy signed a military alliance in May, the Russo-German nonaggression was signed in August, and Hitler's forces invaded Poland on September 1, opening the first battle of World War II.

It was a bad season for books on political theory. In its first six months *Power in Men* earned only £20 of the £100 advance Joyce had been paid and sold 1,600 copies, including those that had been taken by the Liberal Book Club.[8] All the renaming and editing in the world wouldn't have done much good, so the title and text might just as well have stayed as Joyce wanted them; at least then he might have had a book he could be pleased with.

Joyce's other experiment in 1939, besides his first nonfiction book, was a play set in Africa, *The King Is Dead, Long Live The King*. He had never lost entirely the dream of making a financial success on the stage, and now he decided to try again. Hoping to guarantee success, he invited an old friend, J. B. Priestley, to act as collaborator. As one of the most successful British playwrights of the century, Priestley would be an invaluable partner. His experience with the theater (not to mention the drawing power of his name) would be a great boon.

The plan was that Joyce should write the play and Priestley

then would doctor it — which suggests that Priestley was not
quite so enthusiastic as Joyce about the idea, perhaps because
the African material was alien to him or perhaps because he
really did not hold out a great deal of hope for the project.[9]

The play in its earlier versions was called *Happy Valley* and
concerns a film company attempting to shoot a script in an African location.[10] The film is falling to pieces because of a bad
script, the illness of the female star, and numerous romantic
complications. Into this situation comes a native preacher,
Mponyi, who is opposed by Captain Frick, the local D.O. Frick
is convinced that the preacher is stirring up the natives and
practicing juju. Mponyi blames the D.O. for the many deaths in
the area, telling him, "The people would not die if they had
faith. . . . They are dying of boredom — because they are not
free. They are shut into little ideas — little lives. Teach them
to live for something greater than cattle, make them know the
world where they live — how great and glorious are god's works,
and how strange and wonderful the thoughts of god in man."

In fact, Mponyi tells everyone in the film company the truth
about themselves. At first they refuse to admit he is right, but
then some of them, at least, learn to face the truth. The film
actress is cured by Mponyi, and Frick decides the film is a great
idea, as it brings liveliness and economic benefits to the country.
He realizes, though, that the chiefs of the area will have Mponyi
killed, for they feel he has become a bad influence on the people
by agitating them and causing them to shake off their misery.
But the director of the film helps Mponyi escape to bring salvation to others.

It is a very bad play, with cardboard characters, silly dialogue,
and an impossible set of circumstances. Mponyi represents a
wretched attempt to delineate a Christ figure. And the play's
theme adulterates and oversimplifies Joyce's ideas to the point of
absurdity.

Priestley begged off working on it because of a dose of hay
fever (although the play itself is enough to bring on an allergic
reaction). He told Joyce, though, that the line he had taken
seemed a dead end and advised him to go back and start fresh

with his original idea, putting the emphasis on Africa, not on the film people, because they had been treated in other plays, novels, and films. It was the African material that was fresh and gave the play promise.[11]

Following Priestley's suggestions, Joyce tried the play again that summer, to much better effect, but it still was unsatisfactory, although at least the second attempt was not ludicrous.[12] For the time being he gave up ideas of the theater, but the ambition to have a play of his produced someday still remained.

Earlier in 1939 Joyce had taken a trip to Italy to crowd in as many of the galleries at Florence and Rome and other cities as he could, because he knew the war was coming and was afraid that many of the masterpieces in Italian galleries would be destroyed before he had a chance to admire them.[13]

He worried about his boys, too. Michael and Peter were both of military age, and, should the war drag on for years, Tristram and George would also be eligible. The prospect of his sons' going to war bothered him far more than his own experiences ever had.

When the war did break out in September, he attempted to enlist at once. But in September, 1939, the army was not much interested in 50-year-old former lieutenants with bad sight, and he was turned down.[14] He was chagrined because his brother Jack, only three years younger and retired, went back into the navy with a job in the Admiralty. His son Michael was with the Ministry of Aviation and would shortly go into the navy, too, and be posted aboard an aircraft carrier. And Freddy Ogilvie, after four years as Vice-Chancellor of Queen's University, Belfast, had been appointed Director-General of the British Broadcasting Corporation in 1938. Running the BBC in wartime would be a tremendously important job. In contrast, Joyce was only an air raid warden in Oxford, and the Germans had not even begun to think of bombing at this time.

Besides, with the outbreak of war, all dividends from stocks were frozen for its duration, so the investments he had made, which had begun to show profit, were for the moment worthless, and he and Trudy were as poor as ever.

M

ARP POST B27, RHODES HOUSE

IN MAY, 1399, Joyce was offered a chance at a much more important role in British affairs. On a visit with Alan Herbert at the House of Commons he had been introduced to Harcourte Johnstone of the Liberal Central Association. A few days later Johnstone wrote to say, "I have been wondering . . . whether you would care to take an active part in Liberal politics as a Parliamentary Candidate?" [1]

Joyce's *Power in Men* had come out just a few days earlier so the question was not entirely a surprise. Barring a war, there would be a general election sometime that year or at least in 1940. The Liberal Party was at its lowest point. In the General Election of 1935 only seventeen Liberal candidates were elected to the House. Yet an autumn election in 1939 gave the party a chance of making real gains. It had opposed the governments of Baldwin and Chamberlain on the Spanish Civil War question, on defense policy and rearmament, and on other important issues. Now the world situation in May, 1939, vindicated them. War was a distinct threat, and Britain stood wretchedly equipped. The Spanish Republic had ceased to exist earlier that year and in March Franco had signed Hitler and Mussolini's Anti-Comintern Pact; Spanish iron ore and other raw materials were beginning to flow to German and Italian armament factories, partly as a result of the Conservatives' failure to aid the Republic or even maintain the sea blockade.

Given this situation, a great many voters might desert the

Conservative Party and some of them, timid about voting Labour, certainly would swing to the Liberals as a less extreme alternative. The Liberals might wind up with forty or fifty seats, and Joyce might have one of them.

Even if he were not elected, campaigning would be a unique experience. Joyce would be even more on the inside of politics than when he'd helped Alan Herbert in his Oxford campaign in 1935. Besides, it would be fine material for a book one day.

Thus tempted, he met with Johnstone in London for lunch a few days after receiving his letter. They ate and talked at the Central Committee Rooms in Gayfere Street, and Johnstone showed Joyce around the headquarters to give him some idea of the preparation for the expected election campaign.[2]

Then Joyce went home to talk to Trudy and think about the offer, flattered at being asked, intrigued by the idea of the campaign and even more at the remote possibility of his being elected and gaining a forum for his political ideas (being an M.P. would not do his book sales any harm, either). In fact, it was two weeks before he replied to Johnstone to say that he was sorry, but his present commitments would not allow him to be a candidate, at least not then.[3]

In a letter to H. S. W. Edwardes that August, Joyce passed off the whole incident:

> It was noble of you to join the club [the Liberal Book Club] — I'm afraid I didn't. I contributed only in kind. The liberals liked my book better than I expected. & asked me to stand for a constituency but I have neither time nor money to fly at politics. However, it was interesting to go to the central office and see how the wheels go round; & to attend one or two political parties in Oxford and see how politicians talk and think.

Yet it had been much more of a temptation that he indicated here, and he spoke several times years later of the episode, almost with regret.

There was no election in 1939, of course; the coming of the war prevented it, and the 1935 House of Commons sat until the

1945 General Election, when whatever small hopes the Liberals had in 1939 had long since vanished.

That fall, rather than making speeches and counting votes, Joyce spent Monday mornings and Wednesday afternoons at ARP Post B27, in Rhodes House on Parks Road, near his home, learning how to identify German planes and what to do in case of incendiary bombs. He was also working on a book about one aspect of war; the novel, *Charley Is My Darling,* is concerned with the evacuation of thousands of children from London, which was expected to be a prime target for the Luftwaffe.

The work is in some ways similar to *Mister Johnson,* for both novels are about boys (Johnson is eighteen and Charley fifteen) who are transported into unfamiliar worlds that offer them a variety of challenges, dangers, and opportunities. Each has to create his own world in the new environment and each has moments of glory but both, at the end of their particular stories, come to grief. With the publication of *Charley Is My Darling* in 1940, Joyce received praise, both by letter and in person, from a number of people involved in child welfare and child psychology, for the accuracy of his picture of the delinquent Charley.[4] Several of them asked how he had managed the feat. The question echoed one that a schoolmate of Michael's had asked years ago. Ruari McLean (who eventually married Trudy's niece, Toni Carlisle) asked Joyce how he managed to write so well about African tribes. "Oh," Joyce told him, "it's not hard. I just watch you boys at the Dragon School."[5] He could have said the same about his ability to capture juvenile delinquents on paper: "Oh, I just watched African tribes." Schoolboys, delinquents, tribal members, they all had their leaders, their pecking order, their codes and tabus, and the similarities, to Joyce, were far greater than their differences.

Charley Is My Darling was published by Michael Joseph Ltd., the third firm to put out Joyce's novels. The disappointing sales of both *Castle Corner* and *Mister Johnson,* together with the dim prospects for the Corner trilogy that had made Joyce abandon it, made him feel that Gollancz, like Benn, hadn't given him strong enough backing, especially after *The African Witch* had made the publisher a good profit.[6] It had been the Book Society that had made that book a success, more than his publishers. So during the late summer and autumn of 1939 he and his agent, Spencer Curtis Brown, looked around again for a publisher.

Macmillan showed interest, and so did Faber, but both preferred to wait until they saw Joyce's next book, *Charley Is My Darling,* before committing themselves. Michael Joseph, who had left the Curtis Brown agency to establish a publishing house, bid for the book sight unseen, having admired Joyce's work for some time.[7] Although a new publishing house was a risk, Joyce decided that he could not do much worse than he had previously, and it would be encouraging to have a publisher who had real faith in him, faith enough to buy his novels before they were finished. So he signed with Michael Joseph and remained with the company from then on.

It seemed a good decision, for *Charley Is My Darling* did quite well, almost as well as *The African Witch.*[8] The topicality of the novel probably had something to do with its success, as did the vitality of its protagonist, but having a publisher who admired him and felt honored to have him on his list certainly must have been a major factor. Since most of his and Trudy's small income was frozen by the war, the money was very welcome.

At the Rhodes House ARP station, when Sir Carleton Allen stepped down from the job of head warden, Joyce was given the job.[9] It was a frustrating job, though, because Rhodes House station was made up mostly of university buildings rather than houses, so recruiting staff was a constant problem. At the same time, it included the science area of the university, the most important sector of the city so far as the war effort was concerned.

Much of Oxford's science area was working on matters directly concerned with the war. Sir Henry Tizard, one of the developers of radar, was there, for instance. Radar was the single factor that enabled the vastly outnumbered Royal Air Force to cope effectively with the Luftwaffe, and its development was the most immediately vital in all of British science. Sir Howard

Florey, who won a Nobel Prize in 1945 for his work in developing penicillin, was not only at the university but on Joyce's ARP staff.

In fact, Oxford University, after the first months of the war, was almost totally geared to the military effort. Its student body soon consisted of people involved with science who had been exempted from military duty because their present work and future capacities were more vital, students who had been unfit physically for service, people who had had one year of university before war broke out and who were allowed to finish their degrees before being conscripted (most of these were gone by 1941, of course), and service cadets, first from the RAF, then from the army and navy as well, on six-month tours at the university as part-time students and part-time military trainees. By the end of the war the student body was almost entirely composed of science students and service cadets.

With so much military and medical research being conducted at the university, one solid raid on Joyce's area would have done the Germans more good than the destruction of several divisions of British troops.

Joyce's job was a large responsibility. After he got over the fact that he was going to have to remain a civilian for the war, he delighted in his duties, despite their frustrations. With the coming of the real war in 1940 and the fall of France, the Low Countries, Norway, and Denmark, then the threat of a German invasion of Britain and the beginning of the air war over the British Isles, Oxford saw wave after wave of enemy planes flying overhead on their way to Birmingham and Coventry to destroy Birmingham's industry and to make Coventry an example of what saturation bombing could do.

Oxford, however, was not hit. Almost every night there was an alert, and the wardens had to turn out to their posts. Even at times when there was no alert, a skeleton staff had to be on hand constantly so that if someone were ill or had to be out of town, Joyce had to find a replacement or else serve the extra duty himself.

Besides regular duty and turning out for the alerts that sometimes came two or three times a night and often lasted for hours, there were training sessions just outside Oxford or at Salisbury Plain. The latter were official; the former were not. Those at Salisbury Plain were largely bomb-recognition courses, an essential part of a warden's knowledge. At first glance a bombed house was just that; a more careful look might reveal it as something much more dangerous than a mess of leaning brick and plumbing and splintered beams. A large, delayed-action bomb which fell unexploded through a house could create as much destruction as an exploding smaller bomb. But the delayed-action bomb, if it were not recognized, might sit in the rubble for hours, days, or even weeks and destroy nearly a block of buildings together with rescue workers and equipment of all sorts — wardens, doctors, nurses, ambulances, and fire engines. So it was essential that wardens should learn to recognize the difference in the type of destruction each sort of bomb did when it fell as well as know what the bombs themselves looked like.

Joyce made himself the bomb expert of Rhodes House, attending almost all the courses offered by the army. He went because, not having a regular 9-to-5 job, he was freer than others, especially those doing essential research work. And he went because it was interesting, something new to be learned and new people to meet. Then he had to teach his staff what he had been taught.

The unofficial part of ARP training was done by the Home Guard, not the army. The ARP was supposed to be a noncombatant force, but in the late summer of 1940, with a real threat of German invasion, the ARP personnel wanted to have a part in the defense of their country, so they persuaded members of the newly formed Home Guard to train them in the use of weapons. Those who had never fired a rifle learned how to shoot. Those like Joyce who had used guns wanted to know how to use automatic weapons. With a shortage of arms and ammunition, the members of the ARP had to drill on the sly, a difficult task with automatic weapons.

As the air war progressed, Oxford remained untouched, except for a few stray bombs which fell on the fringes of town or in the farm country nearby. This made the problem of recruiting staff all the more difficult for Joyce, who had few enough people to draw on. As their job seemed less and less vital, wardens were apt to get discouraged. They might miss a duty round or fail to show up for an alert in the middle of the night after having done a full day's work. Digging into ruins and pulling people out to safety, or finding the dead, or identifying real bombs was one thing. But turning out night after night to sit about with a cup of tea and wait was another.

So the job of persuading people as to the importance of their jobs as wardens became increasingly difficult. It took all of Joyce's ingenuity. He invented the most interesting training problems he could think of. His lectures were as amusing, practical, and full of dramatic anecdotes as he could make them. He had to have enough enthusiasm to keep people concerned and at their posts each night. In a way it was like keeping the people of Borgu interested in building a bridge or digging a well when they simply were unable to see the reason for it. However frustrating the problem was, Joyce excelled at keeping up the people's spirit and interest as well as his own. He couldn't afford not to.

Trudy, too, had her share in Oxford wartime activities. She worked for the Housewife's Help Service, providing assistance to women who were working at wartime jobs and consequently could not take care of their homes and children or women with scads of young children and husbands off in the war. This responsibility brought her into contact with areas and people she had never met before. At The Glade her life had been terribly circumscribed, and Mrs. Ogilvie had kept a sharp eye on the young men who came to call. In Oxford, too, her life had been limited largely to academic circles. Now she was meeting barmaids and working-class wives, all sorts of new people, then coming home to tell Joyce about her latest adventure into other worlds, saying, "And really, you know, Joyce, she was *quite* a nice woman," while he tried to keep from grinning at his wife's awakening.[10]

She even began smoking cigarettes now and then, quite a

change from the time when, one war ago, she had tried to get Joyce to stop smoking his pipe.[11] She also painted the outside of the house herself, climbing out of windows and up ladders to get at window frames, pillars, and so on.[12]

She took on quite a load, for, besides her wartime duties, her house painting, and her secretarial work for Joyce (including typing everything from first to last drafts as well as a good quantity of letters, taking care of mailing material out, and helping her husband in the proofreading of books in process of publication), she also had to run a household without servants, with little money, with a husband whose ARP work made his hours a complete chaos, and with two and then three sons in the service who might drop in on leave at any time and in any condition, sometimes in desperate straits. Joyce noted in one case: "Tristram turned up suddenly on leave — with a roaring cough and cold due to living in wet boots — all his gear having been stolen." [13]

Joyce's life too had its surprises. In the middle of the air war Oxford suddenly went on full alert, with a massive German bombing raid expected any minute. It was one of the Luftwaffe's "Baedeker Raids," a series of bombings of places of historic importance that was meant to destroy British morale by demolishing as much as possible the people's heritage and links with the past. The German planes followed a radio beam that was crossed by a second beam. At the point where the two beams joined, the Germans were to let loose everything they had. The RAF had been able to detect these beams and learned soon enough their significance as site after site was plastered with bombs. Whenever they found the beams were on, all the intercepter planes available were massed near the obvious target, and all the fire fighting and medical equipment possible was rushed to the area, while all ARP personnel were put on full alert.

One day the intersection of the beams was detected over Oxford. Fire service vehicles and ambulances were sent in from all the surrounding area and mustered on the outskirts of the city. In the city as much scientific and other strategic equipment as could be moved was trucked out of the university buildings to places of safety. Rhodes House station and all the other ARP posts were fully staffed and ready for the attack that was expected.

Only it never came. For forty-eight hours the beams remained fixed over Oxford, while everyone who could participate in fire fighting, rescue work, lifesaving, and antiaircraft batteries waited impatiently, wondering why the Germans didn't come.

Then the beams went off. They never were aimed at Oxford again, and the city survived the war without a raid. Long after the expected attack, after the war had ended, the reason for the escape of the city finally was learned. The raid had been cancelled on the personal orders of Hitler, although ordered by Reichsmarschall Goering. Hitler had wanted no harm done to Oxford's ancient charm because, after conquering Britain, he meant to make Oxford his island headquarters and did not intend to set up house on top of a rubble heap. So the city was saved from a great deal of death and destruction by the Führer's dreams of glory. This was the closest Oxford came to the war, and after the incident events settled into their normal wartime routine again.

In late 1942 Joyce became involved in a different sort of war work: as a writer. The Ministry of Information was producing films to keep up morale and to rally the empire to the war effort. A young film director in the army, Thorold Dickinson, was given the assignment of turning a novel about combating sleeping sickness in East Africa into a film.[14] The picture's purpose was to show the benefits which Britain brought to primitive areas, even in wartime. Dickinson had the job of recruiting a film crew, a cast, transportation, sets, and a writer.

He sent his wife off to the library to find a writer who seemed to know his way around Africa. It had to be a man, since he would have to travel under rotten conditions and live with troops as well as camp out in East Africa with an all-male film crew (the novel's author was a woman). Mrs. Dickinson discovered a pamphlet Joyce had written recently for the "Searchlight on Africa" series published by Secker & Warburg. *The Case for*

African Freedom, which had been in print now for only a few months, was Number 11 in the series.

She gave Joyce's name to her husband, and he then gave it to the film's producer, John Sutro, who wrote to Joyce to see if he would agree to write a film script. Joyce failed to reply. After several weeks Sutro telephoned to Joyce to ask if he had received the letter and if so, was he willing to take on the assignment.

Joyce remembered that he *had* received a letter sometime around Christmas, but with the rush of events (he didn't mention his absentmindedness that allowed him to go off on trips around wartime Britain without his identity card or ration book) he had put it aside somewhere. Sutro invited Joyce to lunch with Dickinson and himself to at least talk over the project. Between the telephone call and the lunch, Joyce did find the letter: it was in the pocket of his dressing gown and had been there since he'd taken it out of the mail basket the morning it arrived.

The idea of going to Africa again, after having been away for twenty years, and of seeing the subsequent changes, which in a small way he had helped to bring about, intrigued Joyce. With so many of his friends and family involved in one wartime activity or another (even his half sister Sheila, who was in the Civil Nursing Service first at Bath and later at Axbridge, seemed more in the thick of things than he was[15]) and with the threatened Baedeker raid long since past and the threat of invasion utterly gone after the German defeats in North Africa and Stalingrad, he decided the assignment appealed to him. After talking with Sutro and Dickinson over lunch, he agreed to take part.

CHARLEY IS MY DARLING

CARY'S SIXTH novel, *Charley Is My Darling,* was published in 1940. It was the first set entirely in England and his first work of a topical interest. Yet it was no great departure from his African novels, particularly *Mister Johnson,* for it dealt with the impact of one culture on another, and Charley Brown's situation is very similar to Johnson's.

Both protagonists are adolescents and aliens, creating a world for themselves through their imaginations. Clerk Johnson, from the coast, finds himself among primitive, provincial people of different race, appearance, language, customs, and attitudes from his own. Charley, a wartime evacuee from London, finds himself among the people of a Somerset or Devon rural area, almost as different from him as the people of Fada are from Johnson.

Charley is further alienated from his new setting when he is found to be lousy. He must have his head shaved and his good clothes burned, which cuts him off from even his fellow evacuees:

> He comes out transformed, the bald skull, the green jersey which is too tight, and a pair of wide, cut-down trousers completely alter his proportions. His head seems absurdly small, the ears project like a dog's, his cheek-bones appear much higher, and his cheeks thinner, his body is shrunk by half. He is changed from a respectable looking young citizen in a brown suit, to something between the convict of history and the kind of street Arab represented in old comic papers.[1]

Charley's sudden isolation comes at a crucial point in his life, for he is on the verge of puberty and adult responsibility. His leadership and intelligence are evident in the way he handles all the problems of the evacuation, while the local officials at Burlsewood fumble:

> It was just this readiness to oblige that made him so useful to the distracted billeting officer, Miss Allchin, and her lieutenant, Phyllis Hawes, on the day before, evacuation day. They had soon discovered that Charley, though he had been thrown into the party at the last minute and was among strangers, knew more about its components and luggage than any member of it. Within five minutes of the train's arrival it was to Charley that both appealed when children disappeared, women inexplicably refused to enter motor cars, and two boys fought over the same suit-case with Cockney yells which neither could interpret.[2]

He might have taken a position of leadership among the evacuees, because his imagination makes him a natural leader. But his lousiness and ludicrous appearance cut him off totally from normal channels of self-expression and leadership. Instead of following him, the other adolescents abuse him with cries of "Lousy!" and "Baldy!" wherever he goes.

He displays his creativity in the help he gives Mrs. Allchin, the mother of the billeting officer, with her garden, creating a grotto from an abandoned air raid shelter, and in his drawing, especially his covert artistry on the tabletop, where he loses himself

> in concentration while he draws some new improvements to the scene on the table top, which has now, after a fortnight's work, covered two square feet of wood with every variety of naked savage, Wandle, dancing girl, man-tree, wild bull, rape and murder, the whole forming what seems at a first glance like a complicated forest of flowers, a tropical garden.
> . . . He is just drawing a shower of red rain falling from a black tree, with leaves shaped like hands, upon two little black figures, possessing only one leg apiece. . . .[3]

348 *Joyce Cary:* A BIOGRAPHY

Charley is an embryonic Gulley Jimson, making pictures of spilt milk just as the young Gulley draws with spilt ink, and he dreams of becoming "Sir Charles Brown, Royal Academy" and of giving a blue Rolls Royce, complete with driver, to his first patron, Lina Allchin.

Lomax, the art teacher, fails to recognize Charley's talent and believes that teaching only ruins a child's natural artistic gift, so Charley is thwarted. Old Mrs. Allchin becomes deathly ill, and the grotto is restored to an air raid shelter, so that too is a dead end. He can find outlet and significance only in the stories he tells the other children. These unending "histories of Diamond Eye, Jimmy the Chink, the dope doctor, or Ally the Phone" give him status in this alien society (Cary had earned status at Hurstleigh and Clifton in the same way).

But the stories are not enough. The other older boys, particularly Bill, remain hostile, and Charley must prove himself further by acting out the stories. First he steals beer, then releases a penned-up bull, and finally engineers the stealing of a car for a holiday in the nearby city of Twyport, during which he grabs a purse from a bicycle basket and spends the loot on gifts for his gang.

Once Charley has begun, he constantly has to feed the imagination of his followers, as all leaders must. So what the Twyport *Gazette* calls the "Tanborough gang" is launched in its series of housebreakings that culminates in the destruction of Burls House and Charley's imprisonment in a remand home.

All the time the gang is embarked on its housebreakings, Charley knows that the raids must stop, that he is sure to be caught, and that his crimes are absolute folly. Yet he cannot help himself. His feelings are shown when he steals a purse in Twyport:

> He is trembling with something more than fear; a kind of horror. He feels as if he were someone else; and as if this other person were feeling very sick and at the same time performing unaccountable feats.[4]

He feels the same horror during the second destructive raid on Burls House:

Charley was perfectly sane. He knew very well that he was not behaving sensibly, that he was taking absurd risks for very little return. He knew that Ginger's and Harry's criticisms were well founded, and that he was bound to end in the hands of the police, probably very soon. But he paid no attention to criticisms or common sense. He felt "that's all right if I was a different sort of chap." He smiled at good advice as an old rheumatic man smiles at an acrobat. It was as though a wall of glass stood between him and everything rational. He could look at reason, appreciate it, but he was obstinately prevented from making any use of it.[5]

This sense of schizophrenia depicted as a "wall of glass" that cuts him off from rationality also cuts him off from adult society.

All children are secretive — Cary likens them to a tribe that must keep its secrets from alien tribes; in Charley's case, this means all adults:

> . . . a tribal secret is not preserved by any deliberate taboo. Its only preservative is distrust of the foreigner. When the natives or the children forget natural distrust of intruders, whether anthropologists or adults, they chatter among themselves and everything is disclosed.[6]

But Charley, due to his imaginativeness and his alienation from normal society, is more secretive than most. Lina Allchin, who believes in freedom for children, a fine idea within bounds, does not give Charley the confessor he needs. The only one, in fact, who is prepared to accept Charley for himself, who does not need gifts or flattery or protestations of innocence, is Lizzie, the deaf and excluded girl whom Charley comes to love.

Lizzie, just reaching puberty herself, cannot give him security and counsel, because she too is cut off from society and too young to help him. All she can give him is love, and the only way they can communicate is physically. She recognizes Charley's sensitivity and need and gives him the only thing she has: herself. So,

> at night, when Charley creeps cautiously into her arms, she understands what he wants. As before she is at first startled, in-

stinctively begins to thrust him away, then feeling him daunted, as suddenly hastens to assist his awkward movements. Charley, she finds, in growing older, seems to grow more easily daunted, more shy and clumsy. She has to be quick to understand his difficulties, and bold to solve them for him.[7]

Lizzie, though, has come into Charley's life too late, since he is well launched in his criminal career. So he is caught and Lizzie is discovered to be pregnant. Lina Allchin turns on Charley for having betrayed Lizzie and, in effect, herself.

But Lina betrayed Charley all along the line. She didn't mean to; she liked him. But she betrayed him nonetheless, and if the novel has a villain, it is she. For she worked from theories rather than from compassion and love. It was Lina who ordered that Charley's head be shaved and his good brown suit burned, not seeing what this would do to his appearance and his morale. She has exercised no perception, no intuitive understanding, and when Charley is found to be the leader of the "Tanborough gang" and to have gotten Lizzie pregnant, this is her reaction:

> "I can't understand it," Lina says, but obviously she is sure that in this situation, at least, she can't be wrong. "I didn't think you were like that." [8]

Consequently Charley, rather than knuckling under, is made to feel completely cut off from society, from everyone, for "Since Lina had failed him he had lost confidence in all the world." [9] Now he wants only revenge against everything in sight.

He follows "Red" Toomer, the adolescent anarchist of the remand home, and decides to destroy the institution. His capacity for creation and for making order out of chaos has been transformed into its opposite, because society has betrayed him.

He is saved only by chance, a passing visit from Phyllis Hawes, the girl who shaved his head and burned his clothes at Lina's orders and who was aware that these acts might harm him. Now she sees Charley, delivers a message to him from Lizzie, and through these small kindnesses restores him to the human race. He now plans to escape, meet Lizzie, and run off with her to

America. He is caught again but there is the sense that Charley will hold on to life. The link reestablished with Lizzie will hold, and the realization that she loves him and suffers gladly for him will keep him sane.

Cary is concerned with three themes in the novel: the utter incapacity of humans to live whole, good, and creative lives without love; the destructiveness of those who base their acts on theory rather than love and reality (the theme of *An American Visitor*); and the nature of leadership.

This last theme is the most topical, for the novel was written in wartime (although the war itself scarcely enters the novel, except for the evacuation). Cary seems to be answering the question, what made people follow such shabby creatures as Mussolini and Hitler? He suggests that they both fed their peoples' imaginations just as Charley feeds the imagination of his gang. The dictators finally, out of both ambition and desperation, led their nations to war when they ran out of ideas, just as Charley had to go into crime to hold the attention and respect of his followers.

Both Hitler and Charley were frustrated artists, adolescents who dreamed grand dreams but could not realize them and consequently were embittered. But Charley is saved by one touch of understanding and affection. Love, Cary seems to say, is our only refuge from chaos and destruction.

39

IRISH NOVELS

CARY'S TWO IRISH NOVELS, *Castle Corner* and *A House of Children,* were published only three years apart (1938 and 1941 respectively), yet there is a world of difference between them. *Castle Corner* is a period novel, smacking of John Galsworthy's Forsyte or Mazo De La Roche's Jalna chronicles, while *A House of Children* is thoroughly modern, in the vein of James Joyce or Marcel Proust.

The difference between the two works is understandable when one looks at the novels that intervened, *Mister Johnson* and *Charley Is My Darling.* The characters of Cary's pre-*Johnson* novels are seen largely from the outside. They are actors on a stage, in danger of becoming merely mouthpieces. In *Mister Johnson* Cary moved inside his characters, giving them lives and, even more, *minds* of their own.

Castle Corner

Castle Corner was to have run to three or even four volumes rather than the single volume that was published.[1] It would have been extremely interesting to read the completed work to see how Cary would handle the tasks he set for himself. Yet it seems doubtful that he could have solved them all.

For *Castle Corner* is a staggeringly ambitious novel. It has three principal settings (western Ulster, Nigeria, and England), more than a dozen major characters (not to mention dozens of minor ones), and a variety of themes: the imperialist urge of

Victorian Britain, the political developments of Ireland from
the 1890's to about 1910, the question of moral responsibility in
business and personal relations, the nature of human ambition,
and the nature of motherhood, among others.

It seems impossible that Cary could compress all this material,
all these sites and characters and themes, into one novel, but he
does manage it for a time. There is much more unity at the
beginning of the novel than at the end, since the work deals
with an interlocking community that gradually breaks up and
scatters. The initial setting is the Donegal of 1890, specifically
the lands of the Corner family, where the life of the castle inhabitants is contrasted with the life of the tenant Irish. Meanwhile
James Slatter watches and waits and buys up bits of Corner
lands.

While Old John Corner lives, the Corner family remains
under one roof: his two sons John Charles (John Chas) and
John Felix together with their wives and Felix's eleven-year-old
son Cleeve. Slatter, their hanger-on, and his two daughters live
nearby as do Reverend Feenix and his son Philip. Young Harry
("Cocky") Jarvis also is on the scene. And in the castle kitchen
and the nearby tenant cottages all the Foys and Egans are
grouped.

But when Old John dies in 1891 the Corner family begins to
disperse as do the Foys. As each of these characters moves off
into a new world, he accumulates new friends and acquaintances, all of whom are thrust into the story. So the great juggling act gradually begins. But in attempting to maneuver all
these lives concurrently, Joyce failed. His ambition, he said
later, was to show "not only the lives of all the characters in the
first volume, but the revolutions of history during the period
1880–1935." [2] It is not surprising that this scheme was unsuccessful, considering how much he attempted. The real surprise
is that he held the book together as long as he did and managed,
at the same time, to create a great many memorable scenes along
the way.

For it is the individual episodes that one remembers. For instance, both the scene of old Mrs. Foy drumming out the news of

her family's eviction from their cottage and the scene of the eviction itself are brilliant. Cary wrote these situations in a cinematic manner, cutting back and forth from the castle to the lanes to the cottage, as in this excerpt:

> Mrs. Foy, who lived with her sons, was a woman of over sixty who had worked about Knockeen for fifty years. Her hard, withered flesh looked like a piece of the poor ground of her own farm and her face, as she beat her drum, had no more expression than the two twisted fists whirling the canes. She did not speak to the watchers or look at them. She stood high up in the blue air, beating the drum as if by that alone she could save her home, her sons and herself.
>
> Down below the lanes were blackened with the people hurrying towards the Foy holding; they pressed past the gates of the castle from whose white chimney stacks the new morning smoke, as blue as the washed sky, trickled into the cool air. A policeman lounged at the gates; but the main column was already at the Foys. It stood at the halt in the open rough ground before the cottage; picked out a mile away by its new straw thatch, glittering in its eastern facet like topaz. Three men in bowler hats and dark suits, bailiffs, approached its door, a fourth turned aside to the window, stooped to peer, but the glass was obscured with thick sacking.
>
> The brothers, taken by surprise, had stuffed sacking in the windows to hide their preparation for a siege. The cottage, lit only by the gleam of the holy lamp, one candle in a bottle and the glow of the fire, was like a cave full of excited gnomes. Con, the younger, small, long-armed, with long jutting chin, sprang from window to window, building them up behind the sacking with sods of turf. Each time he rammed in a sod he uttered a screaming curse against the police or the Corners.[3]

The counterpointing of the Foys' frenzied defenses with the lone policeman lounging at the castle gates while angry or curious tenants stream by is a well-drawn vignette of the social and political climate. An army of tenants is impotent to stop the eviction; a single, lounging policeman is sufficient to protect the Corners.

Other scenes stand out with equal effectiveness, particularly those set in Nigeria. The best of these are Felix Corner's arrival at the derelict station of the Mosi Company, the emir of Daji's raid on Laka and its aftermath, and Cocky Jarvis's assault on Daji,* when his starved, ragged, mutinous company beats off and then defeats the emir's massed army of cavalry and foot soldiers and shuffles into Daji, totally ignored by the market women.

The novel's theme goes deeper than "the revolutions of history" that Cary mentions; he is concerned with how individuals create and are formed by these revolutions. In effect, it is the problem of how individuals shape their worlds, creating them out of the materials at hand, and how these creations come into conflict.

Cary also deals with the importance of the individual imagination, for it is this power rather than the richness of one's environment that gives life meaning, as he demonstrates. One need only look at three characters, Felix Corner, Helen Pynsant, and Phil Feenix, to see this. Corner, sitting on the muddy bank of the Mosi by the native town of Laka, splattered with mud and dressed in rags, holding someone's baby in his arms, and watching a group of children and old men trapping fish, feels "that serene happiness of a man who recognizes a moment of complete satisfaction, not to be improved." [4] All his senses are alive to the world around him and he is happy.

Helen Pynsant, for all her money, finds little richness in her life. Instead she finds thrills in love affairs. But as she exhausts the limited delights of these affairs she must attempt new erotic experiments: she has two and three lovers (or potential lovers) as concurrent houseguests in order to watch their jealous maneuverings; she also tries to seduce Cobden Chorley, twenty years her junior, in a servant's bedroom so as to risk their being found in bed by her jealous but devoted husband.

Phil Feenix can find even less meaning for his existence. He looks for it outside himself, attempting to lose himself in the cause of Irish home rule and the work of the Land League. But he remains an outsider to both groups, which regard him as an

---

* This is Cary's first real use of material from *Cock Jarvis*.

enigmatic and possibly dangerous member of the ruling class.
He is unable to find a world into which he can fit because he
cannot find himself. All he can do is play roles. The Irish na-
tionalists reject him because he doesn't talk their language; he
only affects their accent to roar out a lot of slogans and clichés.
His inability to comprehend these people is demonstrated by
the extremely abstract language he uses in discussing politics
with people who only understand the concrete. Unable to at-
tach himself to life and find meaning for his existence, he finally
commits suicide. He is like the young man Cary met in 1924
who had to ask what reason there was for continuing to live.

Motherhood is one of the great generators of imagination, for
a mother is biologically compelled to create a world for herself
and her child, Cary says, and suggests that those mothers who
cannot, e.g. Helen Pynsant, are unnatural beings. His picture
of the Nigerian girl Bandy creating a home for herself and for
the two children in her care, survivors of the Daji raid, is an
excellent example of the creative force of motherhood:

> . . . she became a collected and responsible person, like one be-
> longing to an orderly household, with a head wife to give com-
> mands and a regular routine of duties.
>
> Yet she gave herself commands; she formed her own routine
> of duties, which were quite new and original. It was as though
> she needed only the notion of law, of order, to release her inven-
> tion.
>
> She began to devise schemes for feeding her family and shelter-
> ing them. . . .
>
> In three days Bandy had formed a household which was in min-
> iature the household of a Laka native; with cooking hut, sleeping
> hut, yam store, water pots, a heap of firewood; she herself like
> chief and junior wives in one, commanded, bustled, scolded like
> the head wife, pounded and cooked like a minor humble wife,
> gossiped and chattered like a daughter, from morning till night.[5]

One finishes the novel with a feeling of regret, wishing that
at least one more of the planned three volumes had been
written to follow the characters through another decade or so.

Yet it was impossible to keep up the juggling act as the number of characters and settings grew. The result could not have been an artistic success. And the investment of energy and invention required might have prevented Cary from writing his next two more important works, *Mister Johnson* and *Charley Is My Darling*.

A House of Children

Cary spoke of his second novel of Donegal and the Corners as "recollections," an autobiographical novel in which "names, places, and people are disguised, because [in 1951] many of the people are living," so it is of special interest from a biographical respect.

It is just as interesting from an aesthetic point of view, especially since it and *Castle Corner* deal with many of the same subjects, thus allowing the reader to easily judge the progress Cary had made between 1938 and 1941. Instead of an omniscient point of view, for instance, Cary now used one central consciousness. He also used the first-person narrator for the first time in a published novel (he had used it earlier, as his African letters show, in unpublished work). This device is a unifying force in a novel that is relatively without plot, so there is never the sense of things flying apart here that there is in *Castle Corner*.

Rather than a plot, the novel employs a series of revelations as its structure, similar to James Joyce's "epiphanies" in *A Portrait of the Artist as a Young Man*, the novel which Cary had admired so much.

In his preface Cary went on to say,

I have given myself an elder brother — why, I do not know. But I notice that this elder brother is also myself, and I suspect that I divided myself in this way because I realized by some instinct (it was certainly not by reason) that the two together as a single character would be too complex for the kind of book I needed to write; a book full of that clarity, the large skies, and wide sea views, which belongs to the vision of my childhood.[6]

A House of Children's two main characters, Evelyn and Harry, seem to represent two portraits of the artist as a young man, the passive and active aspects of the young Joyce Cary. Harry acts; Evelyn is acted upon. So Harry helps to bring about some of the experiences which precipitate Evelyn's epiphanies.

One of the major epiphanies comes out of the production of Harry's attempt at a play. It, together with the adults' production of *The Tempest,* destroys his interest in the theater. But the two plays don't discourage Evelyn; they simply open his eyes to the nature of reality and of his relations with others.

In fact, this is the novel's theme: Evelyn's changing relationship with the world and his discovery that words are the key to that world. Evelyn starts as an observer and ends as an observer-participator. In effect, he begins by seeing and ends by creating. For the creator is a combination of observer and participator, the man who is inside experience yet able to be outside it, giving it form and meaning.

The process of Evelyn's epiphanal progress toward art begins with two visions. The first is his father's sighting of a whale in Chapter 2:

> Once, when my father had taken us for a deep-sea bathe, just inside Sandy Point, and we were drying in the boat, he caught me and whirled me round. His bare arm shot out past my ear: "See, a whale . . . There you are — there he blows off steam — he's ocean bathing, too."
>
> . . . .
>
> But it was the phrase, "he's ocean bathing, too," which excited me. I felt the magnificence of sharing bathing-places with a whale. We both used an ocean. That whale still lives in my idea with his enormous beating heart and pumping veins, a torpedo of fiery life as big as a mountain, sliding through the small summer waves where we had bathed that morning.[7]

In Chapter 3 Evelyn has his second revelation when he is summoned by an underfed little girl and, peeking under a door with her, watches a drunken man chasing his two daughters:

> I therefore stooped down and looked, supporting myself by

grasping the girl round the waist. She, too, embraced me. We
were now tribal allies. . . .

The little girl muttered hoarsely next my ear. . . . I began to
turn my head round, to look at her. Several times I knocked my
nose against her ear or hard cheek-bone. I felt an intense curiosity in her, not as a girl, but as a being, a person. Perhaps this
was the first time that I realised another person. I studied her
as I might have a new species, and I began to feel very fond of
her. . . . It was, I suppose, as if one blade of grass should touch
another and feel it and think: "It is not me, but it is very close
to me." [8]

The phrase, "we were now tribal allies," and the image of them
as two blades of grass show Evelyn's epiphany clearly.

Into this life on a vegetable-animal-tribal level come the first
perceptions that each person is part of the whole yet separated
from it. But the sense of "otherness" both delights and disturbs
Evelyn. It threatens his security, for it means that people are
individuals with their own free wills. It means that he must
take an increasing interest in the adult world around him,
which he had viewed previously as only a forest of legs, an element in which he lived without awareness.

Seeing the world as composed of separate, articulated beings,
forces Evelyn to create a new unity from them, a unity far more
sophisticated than before. Harry's play impresses this upon him,
for it comes as a great blow to whatever security he still has.

The four children act out their roles in the play in which the
parts are hardly related to each other. Harry, acting a king-
general-prime minister, waves his sword and rants of battles
won and lost; Evelyn, a paper spyglass at his eye, is an ad-
miral*; Kathy is a nurse and sometimes Harry's wife; Anketel,
sometimes Kathy's son and sometimes a page carrying messages between the others, is the only real link between the
roles.

The disaster of the play, in which everything fails, makes

---

* Harry's sword and Evelyn's spyglass fit their respective temperaments of doer
and viewer.

Evelyn and Harry realize their fatuity. It is followed by Pinto
Freeman's staging of *The Tempest,* which has opposite effects
on Harry and Evelyn. It destroys all of Harry's artistic ambitions; the gap between his play and Shakespeare's is so total that
he channels his creativity into making a model stage, a handi-
craft that seems to presage a more practical way of life generally
for him (in his reading Harry is interested in facts, while Evelyn
reads for romance and adventure). For Evelyn, *The Tempest*
brings about the greatest epiphany of all. After the first hazy
sense of glory which follows the performance of the play, he
finally comprehends the power of words.

Evelyn thought himself quite a poet before this. His "The
Ant," appearing in the family magazine, received great praise
and prompted a successor, "The Microbe." He is shattered
when everyone calls it a repetition of his first poem. "After a
year at school," he says, "I thought of a poem as a subject treated
in verse, with rhymes." Now with *The Tempest,* all that is
changed:

> Not only words for feelings, like beauty, love, hate, had taken
> life and meaning for me; but also concrete substances like moun-
> tain, sea, thunder, star, boat, began to have new significances. Of
> his bones are coral made; it was a chord of strings, a sextet, each
> singing quietly in the ear of my soul; not only with music but
> souls of their own. A tune of lovely spirits . . . which fell for
> ever on the bright sea floor, made of itself the voice of creation.[9]

While Harry moves toward a practical and sober view of life,
Evelyn launches into

> a long poem about a magician who was wrecked on an island
> where he tamed a wild man to do his will. His name, I think, was
> Osferro, and he had a familiar spirit called Lario.[10]

He has learned a kind of magic and someday, perhaps, he will
use it to create his own structures rather than to imitate Shakespeare. For his life has been expanded through this magic, the
power of the word, true poetry.

In three successive novels Cary explored the origins of the creator: the eighteen-year-old Johnson, the fourteen-year-old Charley Brown, and now the ten-year-old Evelyn Corner. Consciously or not, Cary had gone to the root of the creative mind, as if he needed to probe it before launching out with his most ambitious vision of the artist, the trilogy on art which includes *The Horse's Mouth* and its portrait of Gulley Jimson.

40

KILIMANJARO AND EDINBURGH

JOYCE's AFRICAN film project for Thorold Dickinson got under way early in 1943.[1] The two men roughed out an outline of the script, titled *Men of Two Worlds,* got space aboard a troopship heading for Africa, and said good-bye to their wives. Four of the film's crew sailed from Glasgow in January aboard the Canadian Pacific ship *The Duchess of Richmond,* along with 4,000 troops heading around the Cape of Good Hope. *The Duchess* was a seagoing version of the Niger River craft *The Black Swan.* Just as *The Swan* had been rechristened *The Black Swine,* so Cary's troopship became *The Drunken Duchess* when, after she got out to sea, she began to stagger, reel, and pitch all over the Atlantic.

With sealed portholes and 4,000 jam-packed troops, a lot of them desperately seasick, the ship stank like a badly kept zoo, especially as she got further south. The troops wore woolen battle dress scarcely made for tropical comfort, so there were a good many complaints. Why couldn't they wear their summer dress of short-sleeved shirts and shorts, they grumbled, until a few soldiers broke regulations and tried it and came down with terrible sunburn that was far more uncomfortable than the scratchy battle dress.

Once the film crew had stowed its gear in the cabins (Joyce shared his with the cameraman, Desmond Dickinson, no relation to the director, Thorold), they all met on deck to begin developing the rough outline into a full shooting script.

Thorold, who had discovered he'd left his copy of the outline at home, said to Joyce, "I do hope you've brought your copy of the subject."

After the episode of the letter in Joyce's dressing-gown pocket, Dickinson should have known better. Very nonchalantly Joyce remarked, "Well, I was hoping you had *your* copy of the subject."

Nobody had a copy, it turned out, "Well," Joyce suggested, "let's start from scratch."

Their talk of films was a new world to Joyce, and he asked Desmond Dickinson who his favorite film star was. "Greta Garbo," the cameraman told him.

"Oh?" Joyce asked. "Who's she?"

The three others were staggered to find that not only did Joyce not know the name of one of the world's most famous film stars but that he had seen hardly any films in his life. To be sailing for Africa to make a film and suddenly find the script-writer was a blank page so far as the medium went came as quite a blow. But Joyce was willing to try anything and eager to learn, and his previous attempts at playwriting helped considerably.

The four men also took it on themselves to try to make what was turning out to be a wretched voyage a little more lively. They organized concerts, games, quizzes, and other entertainments for the soldiers. The project was not too different from Joyce's trying to raise the spirits of his ARP personnel, and the trip gradually became more bearable. Dickinson and Joyce even managed some work on the *Men of Two Worlds* script.

And in his spare time, what little of it he had, Joyce worked on a novel he had begun two months ago in November, 1942; this was *The Horse's Mouth,* the third volume of a trilogy which included *Herself Surprised* and *To Be A Pilgrim,* published in 1941 and 1942 respectively.

Nineteen-forty-one had been a banner year for Joyce. Besides his pamphlet *The Case for African Freedom,* he had also published two novels, *Herself Surprised* and *A House of Children,* the latter based on his own childhood in Donegal. *A*

House of Children won Joyce his first literary award, the James Tait Black Memorial Prize, as the best British novel of 1941.

Notice of the prize, Britain's most respected literary award for a novel, was given to Joyce in January, 1942. Joyce wrote to the judge, John Dover Wilson of Edinburgh University, to express his thanks:

> I must write to thank you for the great compliment which you have paid to my work. I discovered only yesterday that it was you who represented English at Edinburgh and it gave me the keenest pleasure to hear your name, so well known to me, and to know that it was on your recommendation that I was given the prize.
>
> This is a great encouragement to a writer who feels his own debt to scholarship. I should like, if you would like it, to send you a copy of the book with a piece of the M.S. and a drawing. That, for what it is worth, would make the copy unique.
>
> (31 January 1942)

Dover Wilson was, of course, delighted at Joyce's idea, and in February he received an autographed copy, a watercolor of a scene from the novel (three of the children in the boat, passing near the Red Man lighthouse outside Moville) on the flyleaf, and a page of the novel's manuscript. As a matter of fact, it was a page of two manuscripts, for Joyce had written *A House of Children* on the backs of pages from the manuscript of *The African Witch* and other of his books, due to the wartime paper shortage.[2]

The prize was, as he said to Dover Wilson, a great encouragement. During the past twenty years he had struggled for some sort of recognition and so many times he had had to resist the temptation to write for popularity and money. Numerous members of his family had urged him to get down off his high horse, so he had only Trudy and his own determination to keep him going on the right track. He and Trudy and the boys had had to endure a good deal because of his resolution to keep a high standard with his novels, and they had gone without many comforts. So to see his novel honored in this way vindicated him. It was justification of a kind he had never had up to now. If only Arthur Cary could have lived to see it. Surely this was one of those times that Joyce wished he could share with his father.

The prize helped fire him even more intensely with the desire to get on with his most ambitious work to date, his trilogy on art. Of course he had meant *Castle Corner* to be a trilogy but had abandoned it. This one, though, was to be of a different sort, for it was to express three different views of the world: the woman's, the conservator's, and the artist-creator's. At the time he received the prize, one of the novels, *Herself Surprised,* had been published and the second volume, *To Be A Pilgrim,* was nearing completion. He was almost ready for the third volume.

John Dover Wilson, in his reply to Joyce's letter of thanks, suggested that he come up to Edinburgh in the autumn to give an informal talk at the university. Joyce agreed at once:

> I have never lectured, in form, but I talk to university societies here. Sometimes on theory of freedom (real freedom) which would bore your students. In literature they might well lecture to me. But when I am next in Edinburgh I hope to have the pleasure of seeing you and then if we find anything on which you think I could speak to your pupils with profit to either of us, I shall gladly do so.
>
> I have some notions about the novel but they are probably as useless to others as a painters method to his students. Useless or dangerous and I have never thrown them into portable form.
>
> (11 February 1942)

Plans for the lecture went ahead, and Joyce finally decided on a subject: "Tolstoi on Art and Morals." The lecture was an excuse, really, to meet Dover Wilson and to savor the experience of returning to Edinburgh as an established, respected author. After all, it had been there that Joyce had decided to become a writer, the city from which he had set out thirty-four years earlier to build a literary career. Now, in November, 1942, it was a fitting place to enjoy a bit of triumph.

He and Trudy went to Edinburgh, and he gave his lecture,

met his new friend and a good many old ones, including Adam
Bruce Thomson, with whom he had wrestled on the grass outside the building that was now the Royal Scottish Academy,[3]
and G. M. Fisher, now Professor of Law at Edinburgh University. Fisher had helped teach Joyce football with the hairbrush
case in the dormitory of Tait's House at Clifton.[4] He showed
Trudy where he had studied and where he had lived. He had
told Dover Wilson in September,

> It is years since I have been in Edinburgh. I look forward
> very much to seeing it again, even tho I can no longer sit on the
> steps of the Mound, in a dirty painters blouse, and contemplate
> the passers, from that Bohemian other world which seemed to me
> then so much better furnished, for entertainment, than the
> Heavenly Mansions. But perhaps a student of music would have
> thought differently, especially if his studies had been in wind.
>
> (18 September 1942)

His memories of that period were revived enormously by the
trip, so much so that even on the way back to Oxford on an
unheated train it was as if he could see the past, smell the paint
and turpentine and feel the itch to draw and hold a brush. But
these feelings took quite a different turn from what they would
have thirty-four years earlier, as he told Dover Wilson in early
December:

> I was going to write to you when I had drawn in your book.
> [Joyce had promised Wilson a copy of *To Be a Pilgrim,* with a
> sketch of the narrator, Tom Wilcher, to match his earlier gift of
> *A House of Children.*] But to be honest, I had some ideas about
> a new book, in the train coming South & since then I have been
> throwing off scenes, characters, and dialogue at thousands of
> words a day. Most of it will be scrap but meanwhile, like Manet,
> as he painted his first drafts, I am learning the forms and neces-
> sary conjunctions of my matter, discovering its weaknesses before
> they are fatally included in some general plan, and getting to
> know my people by putting the question.
>
> (5 December 1942)

Of course the book was *The Horse's Mouth,* Joyce's novel of the painter Gulley Jimson, and the fact that he started it on the train back from Edinburgh, tired, cold, and wedged into a compartment full of soldiers, shows how deeply he had been affected by the memories of his own painting days in that city.

Joyce did not have the slightest idea that the book would be popular. In fact, *The Horse's Mouth* was to be the sort of long, rambling work he had told Trudy he dreamed of doing one day, and he expected it would be decidedly unpopular, for he went on to say,

> It will be a damn queer book but my agent told me to write what I damned well like & to hell with the publisher; & then the publisher smiled upon me and told me that whatever I write would receive his highest consideration or words to that effect. So I am going to give myself a fling. And then I shall write a classical and slow moving novel, what Trudy calls "a harvest of the quiet eye." Both these books have much material gathered. But in this last gay week, I have already cut the root stock of a book out of my new growth. God knows where it is among the heaps upon my desk. It will come to light at the next clean up. And the characters which are the very sap and spring of it are in my head already maturing and gathering experience.

The letter bounces with Joyce's pleasure at his new novel, and the vitality that he felt went into the book itself. He was reassured by the James Tait Black Prize, heartened by the success of *Herself Surprised* and *To Be a Pilgrim,* which made him feel he was reaching an audience with his message rather than writing into a void, and he was buoyed up immeasurably by his Edinburgh visit.

This was the manuscript he took with him aboard *The Drunken Duchess* in January, 1943. The trip gave him a bonus in his cabin mate, Desmond Dickinson, who not only was a Londoner but a cockney. Because of the character of its narrator, the painter Gulley Jimson, *The Horse's Mouth* uses London not just as a background but as a living presence in the story. Gulley is a Londoner through and through. He has to know his city just to survive, to know where he can find cheap food or canvas or hiding places. So having a cockney cabin mate, one who saw people and settings with a cameraman's eye, gave Joyce an immediate source of information together with a constant flow of idiom and accent that could not have been bettered. Like the Edinburgh trip, this encounter was a great piece of luck for the book and came at the best possible time.

The *Duchess* wallowed its way down to Africa and, as it rounded the hump, turned east to anchor off Freetown, Sierra Leone, a town Joyce had seen half a dozen times before. It was a quieter stop than he remembered because the ship didn't enter the harbor itself to be swarmed over by vendors and laundresses, and of course it didn't take on cargo nets full of passengers. Instead, it stopped only to drop off some passengers: the film crew. For Thorold Dickinson was told that they would have to be put ashore instead of staying with the ship to Tanganyika, which they had chosen for the film's setting. They and their kit were packed into a small boat, lowered to the water, and cast loose. Feeling like a cross between Robinson Crusoe and Captain Bligh, they rowed to shore.

Upon landing, they stacked their belongings on the beach and went in search of the local Information Officer, representative of the Ministry of Information, and told him they needed transportation to Tanganyika. All he could do for the moment was to find them quarters, and he did: two small tents in the middle of a deserted cricket field. When they asked where they were to eat, he pointed off in the distance at a small house on top of a hill. So, after dumping their gear in the tents, they set out to find food.

After struggling up the hill in the heat, they reached the house, the local officer's mess, and looked in. It was deserted. They poked through the lounge and the mess and found nobody. Finally Thorold Dickinson tried the door to the bar and poked his head in.

Joyce asked him, "Is there anyone there?"

"Yes," Dickinson said. "Yes, Graham Greene."

Joyce and the other two pushed past Dickinson to see if there really *was* anyone, and sure enough, there was Graham Greene.

Greene had been Security Officer in Freetown since early in the war and had been fighting a quiet battle to preserve his sanity in the godforsaken place, with its heat, dampness, and boredom, by working on a novel, *The Ministry of Fear*. Now he was about to get leave, he said, for England. He should be going off any day now.

After getting the parched, dusty feeling out of their mouths, the film people went to see what they could do about transportation on to Tanganyika. There might be a plane soon, they were told, and if there were room for them, they would be notified. So they waited and meantime found that there was nothing to drink in Freetown except what there was at the hilltop officer's mess, and that belonged to Greene, who had brought some cases of wine with him. They could have that if they wanted it, he told them, and they were quite willing to take it off his hands for a few pounds. Then Greene, his leave come at last, departed for home, while Joyce and the others settled down to wait for their plane.

When it did arrive they were told yes, there was space enough for them and they should be at the airport at such and such a time. They were there, all right, but the plane was not. It had jumped the schedule, they discovered, and was gone. All they could do was return to their tents and the officers' mess. After all their rush to leave England, they were three weeks in Freetown before they could get a plane out. Meanwhile Joyce sat in the officers' mess and worked at his novel.

Then by a hop, skip, and halfhearted jump they went from Freetown to Monrovia, Monrovia to Lagos, from Lagos on a very shaky plane to Khartoum, and finally on to Dar es Salaam in Tanganyika. Joyce had wanted to see Africa again, and the military authorities seemed to have done their best to give him the grand tour, two months of it. He became a real authority on the continent's airport waiting rooms.

When they finally reached Tanganyika, though, they were still unable to get to work, because Dickinson came down almost at once with a bad case of malaria.

The others took turns nursing Dickinson in his hotel room, and between duty rounds Joyce poked through Dar es Salaam to see what it was like and to contrast it with Lagos. He wrote to H. S. W. Edwardes, his old chief, who was sure to be interested in the trip:

Co. Secretariat
Dar es Salaam, Tanganyika

Actually I am at Moshi, just by Kilimanjaro. On a job for the M.O.I. We came out so quick, by convoy and plane across Africa that I barely had time to scrape a kit. Our job is to make a film, popular in story, but with a background showing the Empire at work. We chose this part to begin with.

Interesting to see Freetown (for the first time) and Lagos as it is, a great busy town which makes Dar on this side look like a seaside resort for retired colonels. Very pretty tho. The Germans have left real architecture all over the country; the Belgians and French are building it new; we are putting V.W.D. structures which look like lavatories of various importance. Amsha with a beautiful H.Q. (Boma) from German times, has, for the rest, a lot of shanties like a wild west settlement. The native cooperatives here (chaggas) wld. open your eyes. They opened mine. I wish you could have come with us on the trip.

(22 March 1943)

It wasn't quite like his return to Edinburgh, yet being in Africa and seeing the developments that had come since 1919 was a rewarding experience.

Less rewarding was the experience Thorold Dickinson was having back at his hotel, where his malarial fever was raging. When he had signed in he was told that because of the crowded wartime conditions in Dar es Salaam he could stay a maximum of three days and not one hour more. So on the morning of the third day he had a visitor, the officious lady assistant to the hotel manager. He must leave at once, she told him, because the room had to be made ready for the next guest. But he was sick, he explained. That didn't matter, she insisted. His three days were up and he was obligated to leave. He *must* leave! It was the rule!

"All right," Dickinson said, "I'll leave, but I can't walk, so you'll have to carry me."

Dickinson was about six feet two and, even with malaria, quite sturdy, so she decided against this and ran down to consult with the manager.

Meanwhile Joyce had got hold of a doctor, who took one look at Dickinson and at his temperature and then told the manager of the hotel that the film director could not be moved. If he were, then he, the doctor, would hold the manager personally responsible for the consequences. That settled it. Dickinson kept the room.

But the following day, Joyce burst into the sickroom and told him, "You'll *have* to get up tomorrow, because I've found her."

Besides scouting the city itself, Joyce had been keeping his eyes open for possible actors for the film. One of the hardest roles to fill was that of the sister of the film's principal character. The story focused on an East African who had been taken to Europe to develop his musical abilities and had been given a thorough training as a concert pianist. He had been torn between remaining in Britain and returning to his homeland to teach and to study native music. The film deals with whether he is to identify himself as a European or an African. His sister, characterized as a lovely, intelligent, and fairly well-educated girl, faces a similar problem: to which society does she belong? [5] It was a difficult part, requiring a sensitive and beautiful actress. Joyce, in wandering around the city, had found a girl with the requisite beauty. He had introduced himself and they had talked, so he found she had the intelligence and background for the role. He didn't know if she would be able to act but thought that with her perceptiveness, she should learn easily. He had explained what was expected of her, and she had agreed to meet Dickinson and Joyce at the hotel the next day. And, since as a native she was not permitted in the hotel, Dickinson would have to get up from his bed and walk right down the stairs and meet her.

41

"A DAMN QUEER BOOK"

THE MORNING AFTER Joyce's triumphal announcement to Thorold Dickinson that he had found the film's female lead, the director eased himself out of bed. He washed, shaved, dressed, and dragged his aching body down the stairs on Joyce's arm. Joyce talked a mile a minute about how perfect the girl was for the role. Just wait until Dickinson saw her.

The hotel was the city's best, very posh, and in 1943 restricted to whites only, for Dar es Salaam was segregated. Now, just as Joyce and Dickinson teetered out the front door and were about to start down the wide stairway to the street, a busload of pukka sahibs arrived and were disembarking at the bottom of those stairs. Just a few yards away beside a parked car stood a lovely African girl in a pretty yellow dress and hat. She waved to Joyce. Spotting her, he let out a whoop of pleasure and waved back furiously. "We're coming!" he cried. "We're coming!" The sahibs stared, their eyes popped, and they gaped like goldfish, while Joyce and Dickinson hurried down the stairs, greeted the girl warmly, then climbed into her car and shot off down the street.

Dickinson was pleased, the girl was pleased, the role was cast. This piece of good fortune spurred Dickinson's recovery and soon he and Joyce joined the rest of the crew to search for a good setting for the film. Finally they chose Moshi village, directly south of Mount Kilimanjaro, as the perfect spot. Now all they had to do was make arrangements with village and government officials for the next trip, when Dickinson would come out with a complete crew to film all the location scenes. When this requirement was fulfilled, they returned to the coast for a brief holiday before the trip back to England. If the trip were going to be anything like the one out, they could all use the vacation, especially Dickinson.

Whenever there was a crisis, such as Thorold's malaria, Joyce could always get the work done. He could nurse Dickinson, entertain the soldiers on *The Duchess,* or scour Dar es Salaam for a cast for the film. But when the crisis was over, he lapsed into his own private world, a world where, at 12 Parks Road, he had been decidedly pampered by Trudy.

On the way back to Dar es Salaam from Moshi, no crises were in sight, and Joyce therefore expected the indulgence which his wife had always shown him. Aboard the train he was chronically late for breakfast, leaving the others to wait politely for fifteen minutes or half an hour before he put in his appearance and they could begin eating. *And* he gobbled up all the fruit in sight. So one morning the others decided to fix him on both counts. When Joyce, as late as ever, sauntered in to breakfast, he found a gigantic stalk of bananas waiting for him, overflowing his plate and most of the table.

Joyce stared, his face rigid, while the other four sat straight-faced, holding back their laughter. Then in a cold voice he snapped, "I don't think that's very funny. I don't see much humor in that."

The others exploded. It was his icy briskness that did it. They howled with laughter as Joyce glared, until he had to admit that perhaps there was a small element of humor in the situation. Usually, though, he was not so reluctant to appreciate a joke and *could* laugh at himself. There was one such episode when they got to the Tanganyikan shore near Dar es Salaam.

Even in this country Joyce kept up his morning and afternoon marathon of constitutional walks. But because of the heat, he took them dressed only in a sun helmet and a pair of underpants. In Nigeria it had been believed that a red flannel pad on one's spine, under one's shirt, helped prevent sunstroke and that one should wear red underwear, too: red Aertex underpants like the bottom of a very brief bikini. However little time he'd had to get his kit ready before going to Glasgow to board *The Duchess,* Joyce had managed to take a few minutes to buy a new supply of red underpants, which he now used for swimming and his walks.

So one day, striding up the beach as if he were front man in a walking race, Joyce walked right into a picnic. Smack in the middle of his path were the Governor of Tanganyika and a large party of ladies wearing summer dresses and floppy hats and chattering away politely. There was nowhere for Joyce to go. He could swim around them, but it would be a great distance on that long, straight shore, or he could head inland and sneak back to base, dodging from bush to hedge to garden wall. Instead, he threw out his chest, and, arms pumping, strode on. He smiled, tipped his sun helmet, gave out a flow of "Good mornings," and breezed right through the momentarily silent ladies. As he strode on down the beach they still could spot the bobbing red underpants when he was half a mile away.

The trip back home was no trouble at all. There were many more half-empty planes leaving Africa than arriving there. However, when the entire film crew returned to film the picture's exterior scenes in October, Joyce remained in England.

There, however, when interior scenes were shot, he took in as much of the filming as he could, popping up all over the studio, talking to everyone and watching everything, and earning himself the nickname of "The Colonel." [1] The film studio was another new world to examine and try to understand.

There were numerous problems with the filming. For instance, it was to begin with a scene of the African pianist performing at the National Gallery at one of the noontime concerts organized by Dame Myra Hess during the war. When Dickinson approached Dame Myra about using the actual setting, she refused; she had permitted no black man to play at any of the concerts, she said, and would not permit one to play for the filming, even if it were for the government. So three replicas of the galleries of the National Gallery had to be set up on a sound stage. The problem of filming location shots when Phyllis Calvert, the actress who was to play a medical doctor, was refused permission to travel to Tanganyika because of safety regulations, had to be met, too. Joyce sat in on as much of the filming as he could, absorbing everything.

Meanwhile, all during the African trip, whether it was on board *The Duchess,* in the officers' mess at Freetown, in a hotel room waiting for Thorold Dickinson's fever to go down, or now in England, Joyce worked on *The Horse's Mouth.*

It was to be the cornerstone of the trilogy and the most complete expression of his theories of art and creation. He drew on his own experiences as a young man in Edinburgh, on his writing and all its problems, on the great gap between the artist's conception of a work and its actual rendering, and on his artist friends. Joyce had plenty of these, from such widely respected people as Augustus John, Henry Moore, and Sir Stanley Spencer and his brother, Gilbert, to others who could hardly get money together for a new tube of paint, artists who used to pinch from Joyce's mantelpiece at Parks Road the little carved Chinese ivory figures that he had begun to collect when he had a bit of money.[2] Even though the ivory carvings disappeared, Joyce had continued to invite the pilfering painters in, because he knew they needed the cash and were too proud to put the touch on him (he portrayed this pilfering in *The Horse's Mouth*). Sir Stanley, in particular, famous for his huge paintings of resurrection scenes ("Resurrection of the Soldiers" and "Resurrection at Cookham Dean," for example), his distortion of the human figure for the sake of the design of his works, and his flow of quotations from the Bible and William Blake, was a strong influence in the creation of Gulley Jimson.[3] James Joyce was an influence, too; the book, filled with stream of consciousness passages and word play, artistic epiphanies, and other stylistic devices, is really a portrait of the artist as an *old* man. James Joyce's Stephen Dedalus is at the threshold of his artistic career; Gulley Jimson is at the end of his, yet his creative urge is stronger than ever, enabling him to triumph over every setback.

Joyce put a great deal of himself into the book, not only his

376 Joyce Cary: A BIOGRAPHY

friends, his experiences (the old French painter Joyce had met when he was fifteen becomes Gulley's father), his philosophy, and his reading but the ordeal of constant setbacks that he had suffered through for more than twenty years before he found success. Only faith in his ability — faith on the part of both Trudy and himself — and stubbornness had kept him going and on the right track, and all that faith and stubbornness are portrayed in Gulley Jimson. The book is a statement of faith, Joyce's own, and, so far as he was able, that of all creators.

Because of the depth of *The Horse's Mouth,* the uniqueness of its central character, the great number of Blake quotations, and the fact that the hero dies at the end, Michael Joseph, Joyce's publisher, did not expect the book to have much success. He had never believed he would make much money from Joyce's novels, for that matter, and had published them for other reasons. Once, when Joyce had commiserated with Joseph over the relatively small profits the company made from him, the publisher told him, "I've got D—— to make money, and I've got you for prestige." [4]

Joseph was surprised to find that this novel provided both at once, for *The Horse's Mouth* was Joyce's most successful seller to date. Since its publication in Britain in 1944, it has been published in France, Germany, Sweden, the United States, and many other countries and languages. Finally it was made into a motion picture written by and featuring Sir Alec Guinness.

Now, at fifty-five, Joyce was popular with the general reader. For a long time he had been known only to a small but very important public, many of them authors themselves — novelists, poets, and critics, including John Dover Wilson, Edwin Muir, Arnold Kettle, Frank Swinnerton, Enid Starkie, Walter Allen, L. P. Hartley, Lord David Cecil, C. P. Snow, and Richard Hughes. In many ways the respect of his fellow authors meant more to Joyce than any general popularity could. He had aimed for the top rank when he set out to write. To be praised by those people who knew the difference between the truly worthwhile and the meretricious in literature meant that he had achieved his aim.

This coterie had not paid the bills, however. But now the success he was beginning to have with a much larger public brought him a good bit of money. It was no fortune, but it was enough to turn all the red ink to black and to allow Trudy and him many of the comforts they had lacked for two decades: fine books, paintings, old silver, new pieces of furniture, good china. It meant that they could do the traveling they had always wanted to do together — at least they could as soon as the war was over, because of course traveling and foreign exchange were under extremely rigid controls. Their dream would have to wait a while yet, but at least they now had the money for it.

Joyce could also set aside some money for his sons to give them the financial independence which he had once had when he was young. Three of them were in the services now: Michael and Tristram both were in the navy as radar officers, while Peter was an officer in the Oxford and Bucks Regiment in Italy. George, just sixteen, was too young for the war, and even if it lasted another few years, his eyes and heart would prevent his serving (at Eton he had suffered from a tubercular back and heart to further undermine his health).

Then in 1943 word came that Peter had been wounded. As a boy, Peter had been very fond of Freddy Ogilvie and had sometimes pretended that, like his uncle, he'd had his arm wounded, too, and wore an artificial hand. All the boys had enjoyed the fact that their Uncle Freddy wore first a hook and then an artificial hand. Trudy's brother had taken up his piano playing again and somehow managed chords with the hook on his left wrist. He even let the boys unscrew the hook and play a game of catch with it.[5] Peter, who also was a good pianist, had imitated Freddy's piano technique. Now it turned out that his wound, too, was in the arm. He was brought back to Oxford to the Radcliffe Infirmary for operations and recuperation. Here Trudy and Joyce could visit him often.

Michael was luckier than his brother. Because of his previous experience at the Ministry of Aviation, where he had been a junior private secretary to the Minister, working on Radio Direction Finding (RDF), an early form of radar, and his radar experience in the navy, he was called back into the Ministry for work in new technical developments.

Freddy Ogilvie, for that matter, had undergone a change of station because of the war. The tremendous job of running the BBC on a wartime footing, with a shortage of staff and equipment and constant new drains on both of these in order to cover the various battlefronts, had weakened his health. He had devoted himself to the job — even to the point of playing the organ for the BBC's Christmas concerts — and in 1942 he had to resign from his position as Director-General to take up less exhausting work. Then, in 1945, he was appointed Principal of Jesus College, Oxford, and he and his wife Mary, together with their sons, moved from London again.

And Joyce was interrupted in his writing by another assignment for the Ministry of Information.[6] *Men of Two Worlds,* although not a box-office success, had been received well by the film critics and a discriminating audience and had whetted Joyce's appetite for more scenario work and travel. This new project seemed to offer both.

The Viceroy of India, Field Marshall Lord Wavell, was trying to cope with an increasingly volatile situation in India. Dissatisfaction with British rule was reaching its high point. The Congress Party increasingly was agitating for self-rule and gaining a tremendous amount of support. Lord Wavell had seen a film Thorold Dickinson had made early in the war while he was still in the army. This was a propaganda film for home consumption and explained the need for the strict security regulations which the government had imposed. It was a very effective film, and Lord Wavell felt that if Dickinson could do such a convincing job on such an unpopular, even odious, subject, then perhaps he could do something to convince the Indian population of the benefits of British rule at a time when it was very important that India remain peaceful. The end of the war against Japan then looked very far in the future, however successfully the European effort was progressing.

The subject of the film was to be the irrigation works which the British had built in northern India. The area chosen had

experienced constant cycles of floods and droughts for centuries
— perhaps since the beginning of time. British engineers and
Indian labor had built a series of dams which controlled the annual flow of the rivers, preventing most of the floods and
droughts. The system was sufficient for most years, but an excessive amount of water would overflow the dams and an excessive
dry period would drain the reservoirs. What was needed — and
now was being planned — was a network of dams and reservoirs
that would take care of even these extremes. It would bring
great benefit to thousands, even millions of people, and Lord
Wavell, reasonably enough, wanted Britain to get full credit for
the project.

He asked Dickinson to come to India to see if the picture
could be made. Dickinson, in turn, wanted Joyce to handle the
script, so he had to come along to get some sort of rough outline
into shape if the possibilities looked good. The party, because of
the distance and the lack of sufficient traveling accommodations,
would have to be as small as possible, even smaller than the one
which went to Tanganyika on the first trip. Dickinson did manage to wangle a third travel permit for his wife, however. The
film would examine village and farm life in the areas where the
new dams were to be built, so the director insisted that there be
someone along who could penetrate purdah and talk with the
local women. The Ministry agreed that Mrs. Dickinson could
join her husband and Joyce.

FIRST TRILOGY

IN 1943, during a previous film trip to Africa, Joyce had worked furiously to complete *The Horse's Mouth*, the third novel of a series in which *Herself Surprised* was the first volume and *To Be a Pilgrim* the second. Eight years later, in a preface to the Carfax edition of the trilogy, Joyce summarized its intent: it "was designed to show three characters, not only in themselves but as seen by each other. The object was to get a three-dimensional depth and force of character." [1] At the same time, it obviously is a method of showing how each individual creates his own world and how these creations impinge on each other.

Cary had also intended to show three ways of looking at the art and history of an era. However, as he said,

> when I let Sara talk about art and history I found that she lost something of her quality and force; the essential Sara was diluted. . . . And in such a dilemma, whether to stick to my scheme, or to stick to character, the character as felt and known in the book, I stuck to my rule, which was character first. [2]

Yet concentrating on character did not detract from the book (a good deal would have been lost if Cary had used Sara only as a mouthpiece for a point of view alien to her), since character reflects the history of an era — Sara is a real period piece, as well as an eternal woman — and from character and history come a great deal of art.

Herself Surprised

Sara Monday is Cary's version of the essential woman, the wife, the mother, the homemaker, an eternal figure who keeps the world going when the men have all come to grief. She bucks them up, she sacrifices herself for them, she comforts them. Cary saw this combination not simply as the woman's role but her nature, and that Sara is not at all unique in this is suggested by the statues of Greek goddesses which stand in the gardens of Tolbrook Manor. As Sara says,

> When I saw them I knew why Gulley had called my figure good, for they had just such thick waists and wrists and ankles, and heavy chins. Not that I was so cocked up by that, for I had known a hundred country girls with the same limbs, and the boys used to call after us all: "Beef to the ankle." [3]

Sara's physical resemblance to the statues of the ancient goddesses, who embodied the essence of woman for their creators, suggests a resemblance in character and mind, as well as in body.

Reviewers compared Sara to other women in literature. Moll Flanders is the one most often cited, and Cary objected violently to this. As he wrote to Ruth Van Horn, a friend and student of his works,

> I am glad you jumped on the Defoe legend. Defoe has had no influence upon me whatsoever. The thing was invented by one of those stiff-minded persons who must find a pigeon-hole for a book before he can understand it; the sort of medieval sciolist who classifies a platypus as a bird because it lays eggs, and then condemns it as a degenerate bird because it has no wings. [4]

He claimed, in fact, that he had read very little of Defoe. [5] But this was belied by his reply in 1918 to his wife's request for a list of authors whom she should read, when he recommended Defoe, "tho' you needn't wade through his pamphlets." Either he was showing off to his wife after more than two years of marriage, or he knew the eighteenth-century writer quite well.

Whether or not Cary was conscious of a resemblance between Moll and Sara, it does exist. Both women are imbued with a zest for life, are strongly sensual, and possess a great capacity for rationalization. But Moll seems a conscious hypocrite. Sara's regret of her flawed morality seems much more sincere than Moll's ever does. Sara also resembles Chaucer's Wife of Bath or Shakespeare's Mistress Quickly of *Henry IV* and *Henry V* and certainly shares characteristics with Sean O'Casey's Juno and other of the Irish playwright's women. Sara springs from a long tradition, yet at the same time, as a character, she is unique rather than derivative.

For she is a West Country woman of the twentieth century, forced to face the special problems of this period while at the same time remaining true to her essential nature. As Cary said, "The essence of Sara is the revelation of Herself to herself — she is surprised at herself but also she is 'surprised' for us, in her nakedness, which is her naïve surprise." [6] In fact, Sara is the central character of the trilogy. Gulley Jimson, however much he dominates *The Horse's Mouth* and even parts of *Herself Surprised,* does not make more than a brief appearance in *To Be a Pilgrim.* And Tom Wilcher barely dominates his own story in the second book in the trilogy. But Sara figures in all three novels. Cary in his preface to *Herself Surprised* speaks of the three guises in which she appears in the trilogy:

> . . . as she sees herself (in this first book), the victim of mysterious events and her own soft heart; as Wilcher sees her (in *To Be a Pilgrim*), the devoted and unselfish servant and mistress; as Jimson sees her (in *The Horse's Mouth*), cunning, vain, lecherous, self-deceiving, a man-catcher, whose devotion is a cloak for her secret instinctive and everlasting design to build herself a nest somewhere in the world, even if she has to murder a man's soul to christen the foundations.[7]

Sara is torn by the conflict between her education, upbringing, and religion and her flesh. The old saying, "The spirit is willing but the flesh is weak," certainly applies to Sara, and so does the reverse: sometimes it is the flesh and all that it represents that is willing, but the spirit is weak. And this is what surprises Sara: that she intends to perform a particular act because it is either moral or conventional, but that, prompted by fleshly need, she is moved to act quite differently. Her whole long affair with Gulley, which is the core of her life, is just this sort of surprise. Gulley, she knows, is undependable, procrastinating, obstinate and perverse, even, at times, cruel, violent, and utterly improvident. But he is exciting. He loves her flesh, too, and is an ardent lover when the fit is on him. And he always needs his rips repaired and his buttons sewn on and his kitchen cleaned up and something put on the stove. Sara is wife, mother, mistress, patron, agent, model, and just about anything else that Gulley needs. Her tragedy, Cary wrote, was that "the only man she loved [Gulley] broke her nose and deserted her. He did not want to be looked after." [8]

Not that Sara's life is a tragedy, even though the story is told through the device of Sara's confessions to a reporter from the yellow press while she sits in prison for having pilfered from Tom Wilcher. For she is selling her story in order to send Gulley's son to school, and so even from her cell she is mothering, working, shaping. As Cary said,

> the everlasting enterprise which was her undoing was also her salvation. She was still making a world for herself, a home, a family, when she was cut off. As for the moral and aesthetic revolutions which had been tearing other people's worlds to pieces during her whole life, she was scarcely aware of them. Her morals were the elementary morals of a primitive woman, or nature herself, which do not change; and she was supremely indifferent to politics, religion, economics. She was a female artist who was always composing the same work in the same style, but it is a style which does not go out of fashion
>
> But all that had to be left out of the book when I chose to write it in the first person. In order to get the life of the character, Sara herself, I chose a means of presentation which, because that character was simple and had to be simple, active, unreflective, could not show the character in depth, as aware of itself, or its significance in the world.
>
> To do that I should have had to write the book in the third person, with a complex plot; to do, in fact, what I did in the second and published version of *The Moonlight*. Whether I was

right or wrong cannot be said as no other version of Sara was written, and it does not exist for comparison. That, in fact, is the kind of question which drives writers into an early grave — the technical problem. Every single method has its own advantages and its own limitations.[9]

Whatever Cary would have liked to have the novel include, his emphasis on character over and above theme succeeds, particularly with women readers, most of whom feel Sara is supremely realistic. The creation of a true woman in a contemporary novel by a man is a very rare event, and the book would be noteworthy for that alone. Sara never thinks out of character, and her allusions from a woman's world, particularly the culinary world (". . . and the sand so bright as deep-fried potatoes" or "Even the sky, I thought, was like church windows. I mean the plain ones with glass like tapioca") are always consistent with her character and her situation.

Sara's vitality matches that of Mister Johnson or Gulley Jimson and makes her, along with these two, a most memorable character and one who can hold her own with the best female creations in English literature.

To Be a Pilgrim

Gulley Jimson and Tom Wilcher personify respectively the contrasting psychologies of the revolutionary and the conservative. Tom loves tradition, manners, family, and mementos of the past; Gulley is the obsessed artist who is compelled to destroy the past in order to create the present.

Yet they have more in common than just their relationship with Sara. They are physically alike, as Sara indicates in her descriptions of Gulley:

Mr. Jimson was a little bald man with a flat nose and a big chin.[10]

and then Tom:

He was a little man with a bald head. . . . His nose was very
short, just like a baby's. . . .[11]

In fact Cary's sketch in John Dover Wilson's copy of *To Be a
Pilgrim* shows a Tom Wilcher very similar to his illustrations of
Gulley Jimson for the Rainbird Edition of *The Horse's Mouth*.

Wilcher and Jimson are passionate men who use Sara, even
contemplate marrying her, yet both finally let her down. And
Sara steals from Tom to support Gulley; Tom thus unintention-
ally plays a vital role in Gulley's life just as Gulley, as a representative of the world of art, plays a vital role in Tom's life,
since Tom lives for paintings, architecture, and interior design.

The two, as young men, working diligently in their respective
offices, would be hard to distinguish; they look and dress alike,
have the same ambitions, and appear sober and industrious. But
suddenly one is inspired, his imagination is given a tremendous
jolt, and he sloughs off all this life for art. Ink blots become
embryonic designs, his doodles are sketches for paintings, the
pictures in galleries hit him with electric shocks, and, ridden by
this new demon, he abandons his job, wife, children, security,
and reputation. Gulley truly becomes what Tom Wilcher always meant to be: a pilgrim. The snatch of the Bunyan hymn
that Wilcher quotes is an apt description of Gulley:

> No foes shall stay his might
> Though he with giants fight;
> He will make good his right
> To be a pilgrim.

Too late Tom Wilcher realizes that he should have foregone his
possessions (he does burn down one: his house at Craven Gardens) and gone on his pilgrimage; Gulley has wrestled with his
giant visions and huge paintings all his life, always moving forward no matter what.

Wilcher's problem is that he has let himself be tied to things.
Not that he is a materialist. It is the emotional significance of
his possessions that ties him to them. He has invested them with
life. For instance, there is the nursery table,

cut by knives and burnt by hot smoothing irons, stained with ink
and paint, [that] stood uncovered between the windows; and over
the mantelpiece, the old steel engraving of Raphael's Dresden
madonna. I stood waiting and listening.[12]

He stands listening and waiting for his dead sister and brothers
to come to him, for the table and picture are so heavy with associations that he can recapture the past and its memories through
them.

Things are at once his consolation and his torment, and he
says,

Possessions have been my curse. I ought to have been a wanderer,
too, a free soul. Yes, I was quite right to break off from this place.
Although I have loved it, I can never have peace till I leave it.
. . . "Yes, I must go." I thought. "I must move on — I must
be free." [13]

So he is possessed by material objects, held by their associations with persons, events, and whole eras of history that continue to live so long as the nursery table, or Tolbrook House's
Adam ceilings, or the Lovers' Lane live. In fact, Eliot's line
from *The Wasteland,* "These fragments I have shored against
my ruins," is the theme — or one theme to play off against that
of the pilgrimage — of Tom Wilcher's life. For that matter
Tom Wilcher is reminiscent of Eliot's J. Alfred Prufrock, another hollow man, fearful of the wasteland that seems to
threaten on every side. But he is more roundly shown than
Eliot's characters, more sympathetically portrayed in both *Herself Surprised* and *To Be a Pilgrim* than Prufrock. (However,
Gulley in *The Horse's Mouth* does leave Wilcher

. . . formulated, sprawling on a pin
. . . pinned and wriggling on the wall,

in his description of Wilcher as "Genus, Boorjwar; species,
Blackcoatius Begoggledus Ferocissimouse . . . ready to bite
himself for being so respectable." [14])

Wilcher has been an anxious man all his life, apprehensive of surprises, afraid of shocks, careful of money even as a child, "hiding [his] pennies under the chest of drawers, and down the crack in this very floor, in the bell trap, where for years afterwards, and even now, I like to keep a little change in silver." [15] His apprehensiveness was mocked then by his brothers Bill and Edward and his sister Lucy, and they made his life miserable at times with practical jokes even when the jokes were not aimed at him.

Yet Tom is capable of a real love of people. It is not only the dead who hold sway over him. The living have a great place in his life, although he cannot reach out to them; he cannot express his love. Sara remarks on this in the book, and Wilcher himself confesses it. In fact, the image of the islands in the lake at Tolbrook is a symbol of the way life is for Tom: each of the four young Wilchers has his own island. Tom Wilcher is like a man marooned on an island, hoping that someone will build a causeway out to him, and when they do, he is overjoyed. When the young Lucy visits Tom, who is ill with "measles or chicken pox," he feels a love that "seemed to expand and burst into a fit of laughter." [16] And when the between maid at Tolbrook seduces him (and he is desperately anxious to be seduced), he is so grateful that years later he says,

> I should have kissed her little red hands, swollen and glazed with washing soda, for that instinct of sympathy, like a bird's or a cat's, which perceived that I could not go back, and carried me so kindly and adroitly forward, even with compliments upon my manly powers, to the only possible solution of my deadlock. I wonder still at the goodness of that soul, so understanding, and ask how any can deny the love of God who have known, even in so trifling a passage, the unbought kindness of the poor and simple.[17]

The book begins with a crisis in Wilcher's life: his housekeeper Sara Monday has been found stealing from him and has been sent to prison. Wilcher, who proposes to marry her on her release, has been put under the care of his niece, Ann, a doctor.

His history of indecent exposure and suspected involvement in the fiery destruction of his London home make his family very apprehensive about him, and he is a virtual prisoner at Tolbrook Manor, just as he is an emotional prisoner of his niece there.

Wilcher's episodes of indecent exposure, which astonish and horrify him, obviously are a means of breaking out of his self-imposed prison, the counterparts of his actual escape from Tolbrook in Chapter 134 and his aiding in the burning-down of his home at 15 Craven Gardens (which seems an appropriately Bunyanesque address for the timid Wilcher). The only way he can break out is to do just that, *break out.*

But Tom Wilcher's breakings-out are only temporary. The real job of freeing him is a slow process in which his niece Ann and his nephew Robert, cousins, play a key role. For they marry and each brings new life to Tolbrook: Ann bears a child and Robert makes over the picturesque estate into a working farm. Another factor in his liberation is Ann's interest in her father, Tom's brother Edward, a turn-of-the-century Liberal politician whose cynicism and carelessness caused his political and marital ruin and his death. As Tom sees Ann becoming more and more absorbed by her past, he realizes that the past is dead, that it is death for her to be so absorbed by it, and that it has meant a lifetime of death for him to have been chained to it. This new view causes a gradual change in his attitude toward Ann, toward the innovations Robert is making at Tolbrook, and toward the modern world as a whole. It is in the changes that Robert makes at Tolbrook that this process of Tom's freeing himself is most vividly shown.

When he learns that the old Lover's Lane, lined with old trees and tangled hedges, has been destroyed so as to join two fields and make them over from scenic little plots into a workable area, Tom is physically ill and has a slight heart attack. "I had suffered a catastrophe far beyond Robert's imagination," [18] he says. But a few days later when Robert turns the elegant saloon of the house into a machine and tool shed, Tom's reaction is different:

But now I felt embittered against it. "Now you are crying out for help, too — you are jumping upon my back. And all your load of beauty is another burden. 'No,' I said, 'you can go to the devil. I have enough to do. If I can save this child's soul [Ann and Robert's son], if I can make his mother understand that he has a soul to be saved, then I shall have done quite as much as anyone could ask of me.' " [19]

But the real breakthrough comes near the end of the book, when Tom finds that Robert has installed a threshing machine in the saloon. His attitude is neither horror nor even stoicism but pleasure. He writes in his diary,

Tolbrook, so Jaffery [the estate agent] says, is losing value — it is already not much better than a farm house. But is it not a fall back from death to life.

Robert, I suspect, is more Brown than Wilcher, a peasant in grain. But he does not destroy Tolbrook, he takes it back into history, which changed it once before from priory into farm, from farm into manor, from manor . . . into a country house where young ladies danced and hunting men played billiards. . . . And after that, I suppose it was to have been a country hotel. . . . Robert has brought it back into the English stream and he himself has come with it. . . .[20]

Tom might add that he, too, has been brought into the stream after a lifetime of timid isolation, like Prufrock wearing white flannels on the beach and catching the voices of the mermaids but afraid to plunge into the destructive element. It is very late, but Tom Wilcher has given himself up to life at last.

The Horse's Mouth

Gulley Jimson, on the other hand, gave himself up to life when he was a very young man, and it has carried him along on its current ever since, like a piece of flotsam on a flood tide, tossed, pushed under, banged against all the rocks, and sometimes nearly smashed to bits but still going. Or perhaps not so much flotsam as a *voyageur*'s canoe, thrusting further and further into the wild and virgin lands.

Gulley is the true pilgrim. He has given up all his worldly goods for art. And he has become like a little child, too; he tells his disciple Nosy Barbon about himself,

> Why, you know what the critics said about his pictures in 1908 — that's thirty years ago. They said he was a nasty young man who didn't even know what art was but thought he could advertise himself by painting and drawing, worse than a child of six — and since then he's gone off a lot. As he's got older, he's got younger.[21]

For being an original artist requires that Gulley or anyone else see the world as a child does, with wonder, honesty, and imagination. However, it does not follow that he doesn't need to know the tools and techniques of his trade or that he should not give a great amount of thought to his work. Gulley ridicules Lady Beeder's idea that it's best not to think too much about painting:

> Oh God, these poor dears — and didn't Manet and Monet talk about their theories of art until the sky rained pink tears and the grass turned purple. . . .[22]

Art requires not simply the ability to see freshly, as a child, but the mastery of materials and techniques to render that fresh vision. Gulley stresses this point, and when he talks about art what he says is almost always what Cary believed.

The Horse's Mouth is a real portrait of the artist as an old man, an extension in many ways of James Joyce's novel. Jimson has lost a great many of the rough edges that marked Stephen Dedalus, but has compensated for this by exhibiting new ones. Stephen is a prig, an artistic snob who feels terribly superior to his companions much of the time. Gulley, on the other hand, is the complete democrat, enjoying such friends as Coker and Plant, and able to get along with Hickson, the collector, and Sir William and Lady Beeder as well. He can bed down at a doss house or a penthouse apartment. Of course he has to be democratic or he would not survive: he's as democratic as a bedbug, ready to put the bite on anyone.

This is Gulley's sharp edge — one of them at least: his predatory nature, sponging from such people as Hickson, the various "Ikeys" who own the secondhand shop, Coker and her mother, Sara, robbing them, cheating them, blackmailing and bullying them. Stephen would have been too proud for this, but Gulley, after half a century as an artist, has no pride of this sort. His pride is almost entirely in his ability to create (not so much in his finished creations). He cannot afford to have pride any more than he can carry a grudge or allow himself the luxury of a sense of grievance or injustice. This theme runs through the whole book: a grievance will hurt no one but Gulley himself. In Chapter 3, when he is just out of prison, with only a shilling or two in his pockets and no paints or brushes, he tells himself,

. . . I mustn't get up a grievance. Plays the deuce. I must keep calm. For the fact is, IT'S WISE TO BE WISE, especially for a born fool. I mustn't exaggerate. . . . So I have no reason to feel aggrieved and ought in fact to thank God I haven't got corns and bunions.[23]

And in the last chapter, 44, Gulley, although dying, tells Nosy,

There you go, getting up a grievance. Which is about the worst mistake anyone can make, especially if he has one. Get rid of that sense of justice, Nosy, or you'll feel sorry for yourself, and then you'll soon be dead — blind and deaf and rotten.[24]

When Gulley does lapse and allows himself to feel pride in his creations, he's almost always let down. Pride in his reputation is even more disastrous. The main instance occurs after his second bout in prison when he receives Professor Alabaster's letter about the proposed *Life and Works of Gulley Jimson, Master-Painter*. He savors the taste of fame and then finds that Alabaster is a threadbare fraud, as much on the make as Gulley is himself.

He finally realizes that it is the *act* of creation that is his real consolation and joy, for nothing can take that away from him. He realizes that truly original art is not accepted in its own time, because people must adjust to anything new. So the original artist must be prepared to see — as Gulley does — his paintings cut up and tarred over to patch a roof, whitewashed and gouged, or used to cover a screen in a barbershop. This idea that only the act of creation counts is carried to the ultimate when he begins his final painting, "The Creation," on a wall that he knows is soon to be destroyed.

He could rest on his laurels. Painting in the fashionable style of his "Sara Monday period" would pay, but he cannot do it. He has to move on. He has to go where his demon takes him. That path is indicated by the titles of the successive pictures he paints during the time span of the novel: "The Living God," "The Fall," "The Raising of Lazarus," and finally "The Creation."

The pattern is basically existential. Gulley describes "The Fall" as

> The curse of Adam . . . if he doesn't work, he doesn't get anything, even love. He just tumbles about in hell and bashes himself and burns himself and stabs himself. The fallen man — nobody's going to look after him. The poor bastard's free — a free and responsible citizen. The Fall into freedom. Yes, I might call it the Fall into Freedom. . . . Free to cut his bloody throat, if he likes, or understand the bloody world, if he likes, and cook his breakfast with hell-fire, if he likes, and construct for himself a little heaven of his own, if he likes. . . .[25]

The "Fall into Freedom," which is "The curse of Adam," is an existential state where man finds that a world is not created for him, but everything is in flux, amorphous, plastic, and therefore overwhelmingly frightening. Some men, such as Tom Wilcher, cannot face this state of freedom and crawl into a shell of pastness. Others, like Lazarus of Gulley's painting, emerge into this life-giving state, alive in every sense to it, and, out of this world in flux, create order, meaning, and even themselves. Out of this act of creation they achieve an ecstatic joy. As the nursing mother whale in Gulley's painting suggests by its great smile, women are born with a capacity for creation and self-fulfillment that men must search for and perhaps never really find.

So Gulley can begin "The Creation," knowing that it will be destroyed, because the finished painting means almost nothing at all; it is the act of creating it, conceiving it, and slapping paint on it that gives him joy and fulfillment. This act shows how vastly different Gulley Jimson's and Tom Wilcher's worlds are: Wilcher is a collector and preserver, living in the past until his final forced release; Jimson is a destroyer and creator, living in the moment and shrugging off past injuries as a necessary means to his freedom.

This type of contrast is the basic theme in Cary's later work and is taken to extremes in the first trilogy; a second pair of extremes is the subject of the political trilogy. In both, the woman, whether Sara Monday or Nina Nimmo/Latter, acts as mediator and buffer, a role absolutely necessary if the two extremes are to be kept from smashing into and killing each other.

43

"I HAVE BEEN WATCHING A LITTLE REVOLUTION"

TRUDY AND JOYCE had hoped that by 1945 they could do the traveling they had always meant to do when they had enough money. So Trudy was especially disappointed that she should not be able to go to India with Joyce. They'd had too many good-byes, too many absences from each other in the first years of their marriage. Then there had been the Hungarian trip and, much more recently, the trip to Tanganyika, both of which Joyce had taken alone. Now he was going off by himself again and would not return for weeks or even months. They were now in their fifties. There would not be that many more years left in which they could travel together and enjoy all the experiences of new places. When Joyce went off to meet the Dickinsons in early January, before the three of them left for India, he telephoned Trudy, who sat down almost at once to write,

Parkers,
Jan: 3rd.

DARLING,

I do feel I cannot bear many more separations, and I hope this will be our last. It was dear of you to remember to ring up . . . and I hope you will have a sleep before setting off at dawn. How I long to be with you — and even with the air sickness. . . .
GOD BLESS YOU DARLING, ALL MY LOVE — YOUR LOVING TRUDY.

Just before Joyce had gone they celebrated Christmas with their sons. The holiday was a real event in the Cary household, even with wartime shortages and a scarcity of gifts in the shops.

Joyce, who had missed so many English Christmases, almost all those from 1910 to 1919, liked the holiday to be a rousing affair that lasted for at least a week. All the family would gather together again. There would be dinner with all the trimmings. There would be the gift giving, the celebration of Boxing Day, and all the visits to friends and the welcoming of still others at home. There would be a family visit to services at St. Giles' Church, where Canon Diggle, the brother of Percy Diggle whom Joyce had known in Borgu, preached the Christmas sermon. And there would be an evening at the Christmas pantomime when chocolates and other treats would be handed around.[1] There might be family music provided by Trudy and the boys or perhaps some carol singing. Christmas was more than a festival for Joyce; it was a family ritual, and these were important to him. He had never forgotten the family gatherings and fun at his Great-Uncle Tristram's home, Cromwell House. Joyce wanted the same sense of a center and of tradition for his sons. And not even the disappointment of finding that Christmas in 1945 would be as full of scarcities as the worst of the wartime Christmases nor the fact that in a few days he must say good-bye to Trudy was allowed to dampen the festivities.

Soon after the holiday Mr. and Mrs. Dickinson and Joyce flew a zigzag course to India (though not quite so roundabout as the course to Tanganyika had been) and at once set about finding out just what their problems might be. They didn't have to look far, though. Problems were everywhere.

India seemed on the verge of total revolution; signs of unrest were all over the country. Joyce and the Dickinsons were dogged by bad luck almost from the day they arrived.

Thorold Dickinson was literally dogged, in fact. In one hotel where they stayed he was walking along the corridor to his room, so deep in conversation that he wasn't paying much attention to where he was going, when suddenly something stabbed him in the leg. He gave a yell and looked down to find that a big dog had sunk its teeth into his limb. The animal had been tied on a lead fastened to the handle of one of the doors along the corridor, a great, violent beast in a frenzy to do him more damage.

Just at that moment the dog's owner, an American Red Cross

official, happened along. Immediately he insisted on driving
Dickinson to a hospital to have the bite seen to. On the way he
explained that he'd tied the dog to the door so as to protect his
room — you never knew what might happen, with all these Indians around, he said.

When the bite had been treated and bandaged, the official
drove Dickinson back to the hotel, intending to have a check
made on the dog to make sure it wasn't rabid. But there was no
dog. The hotel staff had taken it away. Dickinson, they said,
was the second guest at the hotel who had been bitten by the
beast, so they had killed it and then gotten rid of the body.

When Dickinson told his doctor, the man said that with no
dog to make a test on, there was no way of knowing whether or
not the animal was rabid. So Dickinson *must* undergo the Pas-
teur treatment or he might very well die. Over the next fourteen days he had to have a series of daily inoculations into the
abdomen, an agonizing treatment that made him feel "as if walls
were bursting inside."

In Bombay Mrs. Dickinson became ill with some sort of food
poisoning, so ill that she had to be hospitalized and under constant care. Dickinson, though, had met some Indian film people
and, not yet realizing just how disastrous the political situation
was, hoped these contacts would prove useful if and when the
film got under way, so he was obliged to leave his wife in the
hospital to cultivate his new connections.

One day they invited him to a play in the center of the city
and he felt compelled to go. It turned out to be a piece of
violently anti-British propaganda.

Joyce, at their hotel, was watching the turmoil in the streets,
while Dickinson was busy with his friends. He wrote to Tommy
Higham in Oxford:

                                            Taj Hotel
                                            Bombay India
                                            17.2 46

DEAR TOMMY,
    I have been watching a little revolution this evening — it
seems to be a very small one. The sailors in the ships below my

windows have been singing & cheering & blowing the syrens, ringing bells, etc. There is some kind of mutiny in the Indian fleet. Meanwhile the life in this enormous and luxurious hotel goes on as if politics didn't exist. Indeed nothing is more interesting out here than to find among Indians whom we meet every day on friendly terms, how little politics affects the ordinary social round and its relations. Of course this does not prevent the big changes in the background — and it is a commonplace reflection that people living on a volcano continue to marry, eat, beget and argue about trifles. But it is true that personal relations between the Indians and the British are very good, and that there is respect for the English and that they respond to the ordinary politeness of social occasions with a hospitality which is almost embarrassing.

While Joyce was waxing philosophical at the hotel, Dickinson, at the play, went into the lobby during intermission and saw out in the street a great crowd running past the theater. People were carrying slogans and banners, and he saw one man carrying a unique flagpole: it had a Congress Party flag, a Moslem flag, and a Communist flag, all in a row, perhaps the first and last time all three were ever flown together.

Dickinson returned to the rest of the play, trying not to worry about what was going on outside or about his wife. Then, as soon as the performance was finished, he paid a flurry of compliments and hurried out to the street to get a taxi to the hospital. An Indian acquaintance managed to locate a surrey, but the driver, when he saw that his passenger was a Briton, refused to take him. The Indian friend argued with the driver and finally persuaded him to take Dickinson to the hospital.

As they moved slowly through the streets, pushing through the crowds who were hurrying to the government buildings, Dickinson became more and more concerned, especially when the surrey turned into the maidan and he saw the mass of angry people there. The driver stopped his horse and refused to take Dickinson any further. So the director jumped down and pushed through the crowd on foot.

He was grabbed by one of the Indian film people, who asked him where he was going. Dickinson told him.

"You can't go there!" the man protested. "There's shooting!"

"But I've got to go," Dickinson said. "My wife's in hospital. I've got to get to her."

After taking a look at the throng around them, the Indian turned back to Dickinson and said, "Then I'll go with you."

So they pushed across the maidan and finally got through.

At the door of the hospital, Dickinson's Indian Samaritan said good-bye. He wouldn't go in.

Dickinson rushed up to his wife's room. For a time the hospital itself was in danger of being invaded and perhaps sacked and destroyed, but gradually the crowds thinned out and by night, although there were still a great number of people in the streets, the danger had passed.

Dickinson realized that, so far as the film went, they'd had it. However polite the Indians might be, as Joyce had noted, the country as a whole was far too agitated for the film to be made, let alone for it to affect the people's attitude. The Indians didn't care about irrigation and flood control projects; they only wanted independence.

The Indian Navy was in a state of mutiny, and there were demonstrations and riots going on not just in Bombay but almost everywhere, and transportation and communication were disrupted. Fever spread even to the American troops stationed in India, who felt unjustly treated at not being shipped home, since the war had been over for half a year. In fact, they demonstrated in the city and carried big placards reading, "SEND US HOME!"

What good would a film do against all this? Even if India were still British by the time the film was shot and finished, why would anyone sit down and watch it?

So Dickinson reported to Lord Wavell that, in his opinion, the film was impossible. The three travelers, after leaving Bombay, had run into riots everywhere they went in the country. In fact, they'd run into the beginnings of riots so often that after a time a Reuters correspondent began following their car, believing they had inside information on the political situation and knew just where the next riot was about to break out. Dickinson reported all of this to Wavell, and both agreed that the project would have to be abandoned.

In a way it was too bad. The film was to have centered on one village in a valley in northern India where there was a religious shrine. The shrine was an outcrop of rock in the shape of a giant, erect penis, revered as symbolic of the source of life by people all over India. The village and valley would be flooded when the dams were built and the phallus with them. The idea of the film was how to deal with this situation.

Joyce, although he had gotten a slight touch of the food poisoning that had made Mrs. Dickinson so ill, enjoyed the trip far more than his companions. While Mrs. Dickinson was being hospitalized and Mr. Dickinson was suffering from mad dogs and unfriendly surrey drivers, Joyce relished most of the journey, except for one violent asthma attack.[2] As he said to Higham, in a letter,

> I have been . . . about a good deal — and shall be more so next week as I am flying to Madras on Monday to explore the South. I want to make the pilgrimage journey to Rames Masam a famous temple in the far South — but it will mean nearly a week in trains — local trains & by myself. Pray for me.
>
> Indian religion is highly difficult as owing to the system of avatars almost any god can take the attributes of another. But in its roots it is pessimist — not in the same sense that Christianity thinks badly of the world — but in the deeper sense that it thinks badly of life. Christianity invented Heaven to stick to its soul — Hinduism invented Moksha (liberation) to get rid of its personal self.
>
> (17 February 1946)

After his trip to the South, he was even more enthusiastic, as a letter to John Dover Wilson indicates:

New Delhi. 9.3.46

DEAR JOHN,

this is a fascinating country, especially at this time. Altho I must agree the fascination now has a certain demonic quality. I am not much interested in party politics but I am deeply inter-

o

ested in real politics — the actions and reactions of those mysterious forces which drive men and nations on their still darker courses. Here the nationalist process is now in full drive, down the middle of the stream — the interest is to see its effects — the eddies, the back wash, the wreckage stranded in creeks, squalid and hopeless creeks, the crumbling banks and the terror of the people, especially the millionaires, who have built their huts and palaces on them.

All Indians are nationalist — that is essential — but a pretty high proportion are fearful of the dark future — they tell you, "Our real enemies are not the British government but our own big business," and many of them from big business complain of the British government that it does not deal firmly with disorder.

I have been to the South to see the great temples — I don't know any building that gives so strong a sense of the numinous, in its most primitive and rich experience, as a great Indian temple at night. But one has to approach Indian religion by oneself — one doesn't get much real help from Hindus. Expositions are all soaked in 19th century Western liberalism — they do not explain — they explain away — and those who are still real Hindus in feeling do not explain.

Joyce was in the middle of two subjects that fascinated him: religion and politics. Besides these, he was also surrounded by a great deal of art. He was like a child turned loose in a candy store, surrounded on every side by pleasures. Hinduism, however, would never interest him except as a subject for study. Any religion that "thinks badly of life" could never have any hold on him. Only life and creativity mattered ultimately.

After the film was abandoned, Joyce and the Dickinsons returned to England with an idea for another picture, one set in England and the Near East which they would call *The Secret People.*[3] It was to be a commercial work, not sponsored by the Ministry of Information, a political film dealing with the process of revolutionary politics and the psychology of the professional revolutionary.

One draft of the scenario is set totally in England. It centers on the attempted assassination of Prince Arlberg, apparently a minister in the Austrian Government, by a group of English and European anarchists, whose base of operations is a cheap restaurant at 43 Sussex Street, run by a Hyde Park anarchist and his nonpolitical wife.[4] The plot, according to its registered synopsis, was this:

> Mary Brant, once mistress of Kelman, a terrorist, is asked to join a new plot. Mary, though now married, with a daughter, Nora, is persuaded by old loyalties. The bomb kills an innocent bystander. Mary horrified, threatens to denounce Kelman if he persists in such schemes. He does so. She denounces him but he escapes. The police change Mary's face by operation, to protect her.
>
> Years afterwards, she meets Kelman with Nora. She threatens his arrest if he drags Nora into murder. He refuses to give Nora up. Mary denounces him and he is arrested. But he stabs Mary to death.[5]

The film is set in the summer of 1914, when the threat of war hangs over Europe (one shot, for instance, shows a newsboy outside the theater where the bomb attempt is made, crying "Ultimatum to Servia. Latest"), although Joyce rearranges history a bit in his picture of the assault of the anarchist headquarters:

> Shot of artillery arriving. A gentleman is seen in a top hat, the Home Secretary, peering down the street. A volley from the house, and the hat flies off. Police etc rush to minister's assistance, he is smoking a cigar. He says
>
> MINIS. All right, get on with it.
>
> A gun is fired and the house is seen to be hit. A great cloud of dust rises from it — masonry falls into the street.[6]

The Home Secretary, with his cigar and top hat, obviously is young Winston Churchill at the famous "Assault on Sidney Street," the battle of police and troops against a group of anarchist assassins in 1910.

It is from this assault that the terrorist Kelman escapes, leaving his comrades to be killed or wounded in the battle and the survivors hanged or imprisoned. For Kelman's loyalties are not to his friends and comrades: they are to terror, revolution, and death. He only feels alive when he is destroying. He is Joyce's version of a truly evil man, a malignancy, a cancer cell in the social body.

At the end of the film, years afterward, when Kelman has involved Mary's daughter Nora in his plans for revolution, Mary confronts him:

MARY:　You never loved any one, Looee, you never had a friend, a comrade. You only use people, especially women, because they are made to be used by men like you.

KEL:　So much the better if they serve the revolution.

MARY:　Your revolution is yourself, your own power, your will, it is egotism and cruelty. You hate the whole world because it hasn't made you a leader. But that's the last thing you will admit.[7]

Kelman, then, is Joyce's *bête noire,* the man with a grievance, who feels the world has treated him unjustly, who has nursed and fed that feeling of injustice, bred it into hate and murder, and now only wants to destroy. Innocent bystanders mean nothing at all to him, or, if they do, they only mean that he has created terror, and that is all to the good. Although he doesn't say it, his belief is that of so many revolutionaries: "You have to break eggs to make an omelet." But he is far more interested in breaking than in making. He is the antithesis of the creator, the man who believes in life, goodness, love, and honor.

Joyce really could get his teeth into this story, but, despite trying several versions of it, he couldn't come up with a script that suited the producers — like his later stories to *The Saturday Evening Post* in the autumn of 1920, it was too literary. So, after a time, Joyce dropped out of the project entirely, although he remained interested in it. When *The Secret People* finally was filmed a few years later, he made several visits to the studio to watch and to meet the people involved — including a girl making her film debut as the daughter, Nora: Audrey Hepburn.

This was Joyce's last involvement in films. He turned from attempting to express his political ideas in that medium to a new project: a political trilogy.

IV
TRIUMPHS AND TRAGEDIES

44

"HOW SHE LOVED LIFE"

SOON AFTER his return to Oxford from India, Joyce received news that an American publisher was interested in one of his novels, particularly his latest one, *The Moonlight,* which had been published in Britain that year, 1946. *The Moonlight* was prompted by Leo Tolstoi's *The Kreutzer Sonata* and that author's interpretation of the female characters in the novel. Although Joyce admired the Russian writer greatly, he felt that Tolstoi had misunderstood and maligned women, so *The Moonlight* was intended as a rebuttal.[1] In many ways it was the type of book which Joyce had mentioned to Dover Wilson: "a classical and slow moving novel, what Trudy calls 'a harvest of the quiet eye.' "

The Moonlight is out of the mainstream of Joyce's novels and has a very specialized appeal — perhaps for that reason it is an unsatisfying work. Joyce's admirers, who come to the novel with certain preconceptions and expectations, are apt to be disappointed at its slow pace and its characters' relative lack of vitality.

Joyce himself felt it was the wrong book with which to reintroduce himself to the United States after the failure of *The African Witch* there in 1936. He felt that either *Herself Surprised* or *To Be a Pilgrim* would have been a much better choice.[2]

However, Elizabeth Lawrence of Harper and Brothers, the editor with whom the American branch of Curtis Brown was in contact, felt that *The Moonlight* would interest an American audience more than either of these or *The Horse's Mouth,* which Harper and several other publishers already had rejected (Harper had felt that *The Horse's Mouth* was "too English" [3]). So a contract was signed for *The Moonlight,* and it was scheduled to come out in 1947, eleven years after the disastrous appearance of *The African Witch.*

The $750 advance that Joyce received together with the prospect of further sales to Harper made Christmas of 1947 bright. Now that additional money was coming in, Trudy and Joyce would have more chance for traveling, as soon as the currency restrictions were relaxed. Peter was out of the army and back at Oxford, working on an English degree. After recovering from his wound, he had served in Cologne, getting the city's schools back in running order[4] (Peter and Michael had excellent commands of German, and Michael had won a prize for an essay in German at Eton, even though he was not a German specialist; Trudy and Joyce thought the award was due to favoritism on the part of the judge, Trudy's friend Professor Boyd, who insisted they were wrong and that Michael deserved the prize[5]). Tristram and George also were at school — George at Cambridge University, and Tristram at Trinity College of Music in London. So this new income could help them now and, when they married, the boys could do with something in the bank.

The Moonlight was not a success in the United States, however. Although a number of the critics liked it, it did not sell at all well — only 112 copies in the first week, for example — and Harper was hesitant about buying any more of Joyce's works for publication in the United States.[6] They were willing to see copies of *The Horse's Mouth* and *A House of Children,* but if they decided on any further novels of Joyce's, Miss Lawrence said, it probably would be new works rather than ones previously published in Britain. When another publisher, Knopf, showed interest in publishing Joyce, however, Harper picked up enthusiasm again. After a lot of debate, they decided on *Herself Surprised* in November, 1947, for publication the following year. It was one of the two novels Joyce had suggested in the first place.

But if the news was good from New York, at home there was disaster. Trudy, it was discovered, had cancer.

Through 1948 she was treated by doctors in Oxford. In June, 1948, she underwent an operation at Guy's Hospital in London, where her brother Heneage (since 1946 Sir Heneage, for his service to medicine; Freddy had been knighted in 1942 for his service in education and broadcasting) was chief surgeon.[7]

When she was able to travel that autumn, Joyce took Trudy to Switzerland for a quiet holiday. They went to the same hotel where they had gone in the 1920's and a few times in the 1930's. It had been a happy island of escape then, and Joyce wanted it to be so again now. He had their mail held in Oxford so that nothing should distract them or trouble Trudy. The trip must be a vacation in the true sense of the word for her sake. She *must* be made well again. She must have her chance for happiness, for the ease which their increased income meant and the travel which she had longed for.[8]

Harper, meantime, was wondering about the title *Herself Surprised;* a different appellation might help the sale of the book when it came out in the autumn of 1948. When Joyce received their letter, he replied,

> I've asked about the title of Herself Surprised but people here, including Curtis Brown, are much against a change.
> The point is that my titles are essential parts of the book. I don't forget for a moment that they appear at the top of each page. The essence of Sara is the revelation of Herself to herself — she is surprised at herself but also she is "surprised," for us, in her nakedness, which is her naive surprise. The essence of To be a Pilgrim is the sense of life as pilgrimage — and the whole background of the book is democratic history as a facet of the protestant evangelical mind. The book has been described as a "work impregnated with protestant feeling," and you remember that the title comes from Bunyan. And the Horses Mouth is not merely Gully, it is the mysterious injunction laid upon such as Gully to sacrifice their lives and their comforts for line and form and colour — and always new forms, new lines.
> These titles are so well established and understood here as parts

of the work that I think a change runs the danger of being misunderstood as a failure of comprehension.

(17 December 1947)

The change was not made, and Joyce took Trudy to Switzerland just after the novel was published in September, 1948.
Earlier in the year Joyce was delighted to find that there were
fringe benefits in having an American publisher and particularly in having an editor as interested in her writers as Miss
Lawrence seemed to be, for a parcel was delivered to Parks Road
on January 8. Joyce sat down at once to express his thanks:

> DEAR ELIZABETH LAWRENCE
> Your parcel arrived this morning and caused a sensation in the
> family, especially as we have had seven in the house for Christmas
> and they ate all our butter. Your butter therefore stood out like
> an ararat to the ark of our wandering appetites.

During the summer of 1948, when *Herself Surprised* was in
proof sheets, the editors of the *Ladies' Home Journal* expressed
interest in the book for either serial or one-shot, abridged publication. It would mean a great deal of money, and, fittingly, the
Journal was the sister publication of *The Saturday Evening
Post,* the other American magazine to publish Joyce's work. But
unfortunately the *Journal*'s editors, when they read the proofs
of the book, decided against it — perhaps because it was an
earthier sort of story than American women's magazines were
publishing in those days. All the same, their interest boded
well for the book's chances when it came out that September.

Joyce especially liked the illustration that Harper was using
on the dust jacket and wrote to find out the artist's name and to
see if he might have the original. Then he sent the artist, Alan
Haemer, an autographed copy of *The Horse's Mouth* and a
poem.

Another parcel arrived from Elizabeth Lawrence in June,
when Trudy was in the hospital and her niece, Toni Carlisle,
was taking care of the house for Joyce. Toni had recently married Ruari McLean, who had gone to the Dragon School with

Michael Cary twenty years before, and, when she had been a student at Oxford, she had often visited Parks Road. Yet there was a difference between visiting the house and running it, so the extra supplies of scarce foodstuffs came at a convenient time.[9]

That summer and autumn, until the trip to Switzerland, he was working on a novel that, like *The Moonlight,* was about a woman, but the new book was as different as possible from the earlier novel, for in many ways its heroine, Tabitha Baskett, was a feminine Mister Johnson or Gulley Jimson. It was a book about history and art, too, covering more than half a century in the rush of one life, from the Mauve Decade to post-World War II England. It was an extremely fast-paced novel, just as *The Horse's Mouth* had been, and it came with as much of a rush as the earlier novel. Even with the interruptions caused by Trudy's illness, Joyce had finished the 200,000-word first draft on January 22, 1948, the second draft in mid-April, and the third draft by the end of May, keeping his promise of January to Miss Lawrence:

> I'll give you a typescript of the Fearful Joy as soon as it is ready. I wrote the last word of the 1st draft to-day. Now the real work begins — it is for 1 thing about 200,000 words as it stands. I shall use everything, guns, dynamite, hatchets, bulldosers as well as chisels & knives. I have to murder at least 2 of my best characters they are making too much noise. Poor devils, they're going to get a shock — then I shall shoot the stage manager and cut down the band to 2 tubas and 1 oboe. Possibly I may throw in an ocharina for the 2nd ruffian.
>
> (22 January 1948)

But when Trudy's illness advanced more rapidly than expected, the operation took place, and she had to convalesce at home and in Switzerland; the book was suspended. They were greeted by a further blow upon their return from Switzerland.

Peter, whose wounded arm had never healed properly and thus still caused him suffering and whose career had suffered a major setback that summer, underwent a breakdown at The

Bungalow, Castledawson, where he was on holiday. Joyce, on getting the news, left as soon as possible for Ireland, and Trudy followed soon after, although she was extremely shaky. Joyce made a second trip to visit Peter in December, then returned to care for Trudy and to try to get some work done on the new novel.[10]

The sales of *Herself Surprised* in the United States vindicated Joyce's suggestion that it serve as his introduction there. For, while *The Moonlight* had sold only 112 copies during its first week of publication, *Herself Surprised* had an average sale of over 500 copies a week in its first eight weeks.[11] This was very far from a smash, but it was good enough to convince Harper that Joyce was a respectable property. It also meant that the hospital and doctor bills for Trudy and Peter would be met. Joyce was relieved, but he was too troubled to take any joy in his success. The food parcels which Elizabeth Lawrence and others at Harper sent meant more to him than the money did, since they gave variety to Trudy's meals and helped to overcome her failing appetite.

The following Easter, in the spring of 1949, all four of the Cary sons came to visit at Parks Road, and there was a small musical evening, for Professor and Mrs. Boyd joined them.[12] Trudy played her cello, the Boyds the violins, and one or another of her sons was at the piano or singing a solo. As one of the sons remarked to the Boyds, "It may be the last time we can play together." [13] It seemed obvious now that Trudy was dying.

She rallied time after time, however, as the doctors tried new and sometimes desperate treatments to halt the cancer's progress.[14] Through the summer and autumn of 1949 she grew more and more weak, and again their niece Toni Carlisle McLean came up to Oxford to see to the house.

Joyce spent as much time as possible with Trudy when she was awake. As she went about her jobs in the house, Toni could hear them talking hour after hour. Joyce sat on the edge of the bed beside Trudy, and it seemed as if he meant to keep her alive by recalling the past and talking of the present now that she was too weak to work with him on his manuscripts or even read through them. She could enjoy his new successes in the United States as much as he could, since she had been his partner in his work, not simply his wife. She had been editor, secretary, consolation, buffer between him and those who wanted him to turn his writing away from the goals he had aimed for from the start. Whatever achievement he had, she had a large share in it.

By the end of the summer Trudy was under around-the-clock care, and two nurses were attending her. Joyce wrote to Elizabeth Lawrence, "As you say, nurses are expensive but I am glad to find 2 such good ones to worry about the cost of them." [15]

In November a last remedy was tried, a medication similar in some ways to mustard gas that exploded inside Trudy in a final attempt to destroy the cancer.[16] She seemed to improve to a good degree and busied herself with the preparations for Christmas, signing and addressing cards to friends, worrying about gifts, reminding Joyce of the pantomime tickets.[17] She also wrote to Elizabeth Lawrence, asking that she buy Joyce a subscription to *The New Yorker* because he had seen the magazine and liked it. But her writing, never terribly legible, was so cramped because of her illness that Joyce had to add a note at the end of the letter to explain what it said.[18] Joyce, seeing her come round so well, now let himself hope that she might recover after all. But then she began to slip back again, and on December 13 she died.

She missed seeing the Christmas for which she'd prepared everything and had missed a concert on the 12th, too, one that would have meant a great deal to her. Tristram, after he had left the navy at the end of the war, had gone to London to study music, intending to become a composer; now Joyce wrote to Elizabeth Lawrence:

> Mrs. Cary died on the 13th & I can't even be sure that she understood how successful her 3rd son Tristram had been in his first composition played on the 12th at a London concert. She made a terrific fight for life — for the god knows she had suffered as much in the last 20 months as wld. have broken the spirit of most people, she still wanted to be with me and her sons. I never knew anyone with such a genius for life and love.

She had made Christmas ready for us, & so we are having her Christmas party — as she wld. have wished it.[19]

To John Dover Wilson, whom Joyce had tried to comfort when Wilson's son had died in the war and who now wrote to express his sympathy, Joyce said,

Poor Trudy fought to the last breath. I never knew so eager & passionate a spirit — how she loved life — in order to love us and serve us — 4 cures & 4 returns of the cancer, each time worse than the last, cld. not tame her or break her courage. The best of her will always be with me and the children.[20]

In one of the vest-pocket notebooks Joyce always carried with him, usually reserved for entries about his novels and short stories and in which the germs for many of them had first been jotted down, Joyce had written that spring before Trudy's death,

What is strange is that I got no pleasure in walking through the Parks and looking at the new leaves on the trees, at the buttercups which are just opening in crowds among the bright green grass. I used to think that looking at nature would always give me consolation in misery, but it did not do so today. The only thing that gave me comfort was simply a feeling for other people in misfortune and their need of love. I was made to feel, I suppose, for the first time, the *absolute need* of love to make life possible, and the continuous everlasting presence of love in the world. And so the fearful bitterness of this danger to T. and all our memories together, was mixed with the sense of something that can survive any loss, the power of love.[21]

Now she was dead. In the cold of December her four sons, her husband, and her friends stood in Wolvercote Cemetery by the open grave as her body was laid away. The service closed and Joyce turned abruptly to Professor and Mrs. Boyd. "Come along home," he urged them; he hated to go back to the empty house by himself.[22] Going back with the Boyds, with whom Trudy had spent so many happy evenings, would make the house seem less strange and might, for a time, make it seem that Trudy wasn't gone. He might feel her with him just a little longer.

He mailed the Christmas cards which she had signed and addressed. Christmas went ahead, with the dinner and the pantomime and the visit to St. Giles' Church. Enid Starkie, who had come to know Joyce since *A House of Children* was published in 1941, at very nearly the same time as the publication of her book, *A Lady's Child,* about her own childhood in Ireland, was one of the party who went with Joyce to the pantomime. She wrote of that evening,

> everything was carried through as if she were still there. There were programmes, one for each person, and chocolates, ices in the interval, and he laughed uproariously at all the jokes — even more than they warranted — crossing and uncrossing his legs, as was his habit at moments of excitement or nervous tension. When the performance was over, we went back to the house, and there was cold turkey, plum pudding, with all the trimmings, and champagne. But it was the saddest evening I have ever spent in my life! Later, when he saw me home, he said: "It has been a good Christmas!" The Christmas had been as his wife had always planned it so carefully, which was now his sole responsibility, and he was not going to "let down the side," even though his heart was breaking with grief.[23]

He celebrated Christmas as Trudy would have wanted and as she had arranged, but there were many things he could not do that they had planned. They would never travel together to America, to Africa, or to any of the places that they had hoped and for which they would now have had the money. They could not be together to watch their sons achieve success. It was especially tragic that Trudy, to whom music had always meant so much, should not have been able to attend or even comprehend the success of Tristram's debut as a composer.

Now Joyce was coming to his greatest success and fame, and she wasn't there to enjoy it, despite the fact that she had done so much to make it possible. In some ways he tried to keep her alive, to show his continued debt to her, for, as Enid Starkie recalled,

> even after her death, whenever he published a book, he always added a copy first to her own shelf of his works, because he wanted, he told me, her collection of his writings to be complete.[24]

She was gone, though. He would never have another of their furious (and often half mock) fights that inevitably ended in the sweetest sort of reconciliation nor doze by the fire while she and the Boyds and one or two others played César Franck and wake up to Trudy's amused, "Are you sure you're warm enough Joyce?" He wouldn't be able, in the middle of one of his arguments over the *real* nature of women with Enid Starkie, to shoot a swift glance at Trudy to catch the slight smile of amusement she gave them both.[25]

Instead he had to steep himself in life to keep from breaking entirely. And the life that was the best consolation, which had consoled him and given him hope in the very first days of their marriage when they had to be apart, was his writing of which she had been so vital a part. If he were to stay alive, really alive, he must begin to write again.

45

HONOR AND FORTUNE

DURING TRUDY'S ILLNESS, publication of his books had gone ahead steadily in Europe and the United States. Since Joyce was unable to finish *A Fearful Joy*, the editors of Harper and Brothers decided to undertake the publication of the second and third volumes of Joyce's trilogy; *To Be a Pilgrim* was scheduled for May, 1949, and *The Horse's Mouth*, for November or December of the same year.

Herself Surprised had a good sale and *To Be a Pilgrim* came near matching it. Then at the end of July Elizabeth Lawrence learned that the Book-of-the-Month Club was taking an interest in *The Horse's Mouth* and planned to have it on the agenda of its board's August meeting. She didn't tell Joyce, for fear that nothing would come of it, but did inform Alan Collins, who handled Joyce's novels at the New York office of the Curtis Brown agency. The meeting was held, and the novel was made a reserve selection of the Club. She cabled Joyce at once and sent an airmail letter the same day to explain that a Book-of-the-Month Club "reserve selection" meant that the Club would release the book to its members but that a date had not yet been selected. The fact that the book had been selected by the Club meant, she said, an additional sale that would give Joyce at least an extra $10,000 in royalties.[1]

The novel which Michael Joseph had published on faith alone, not believing in its sales capacity, and which Harper had rejected in 1946 as "too English" was surprising everyone once again.

In September, John Fischer, editor of *Harper's Magazine,* was in England and called at Parks Road. He wrote to Elizabeth Lawrence this glowing report:

> IIe is a wonderful man, bubbling with life, volubility, and ideas for new novels. He says he has parts of seventeen books already written, which he hopes to finish; and fragments of a dozen more he has abandoned. (One fragment, now in his attic, runs to nearly a million words.) There are countless others he hopes to write, but hasn't yet started. He lives almost as a recluse, and turns out two or three thousand words a day, all in long hand. His wife copies with a typewriter, and then revises. Nobody else can read his handwriting; she is desperately ill with cancer, and his current work therefore is handicapped. Cary is trying to learn to type, however. His wife is due for another operation as soon as she gets strength back from the first some six months ago. Cary talks as if he doesn't expect her to recover.
>
> Did you know that Cary is a fairly accomplished painter, too?
> . . . .
> He was pleased about the BOM news, because it will help with the doctor bills, but not in the least excited. Sales and income seem to be quite minor matters to him. What he really wants is for his wife to get well, and for him to have another fifty years of life in which to write all the things that are in his mind.
>
> For the first time in my life, I felt that maybe I had met a genuine 18-carat genius.
>
> (18 September 1949)

When Miss Lawrence learned from Fischer's letter just how ill Trudy was, she wrote to Joyce to suggest that Harper could pay the advance on *The Horse's Mouth* immediately rather than on the date of publication as the contract stipulated (a policy in effect since *Herself Surprised*), if he should need the money to meet medical expenses. He wrote, however, that a large advance from Michael Joseph had given him a hefty enough bank balance to meet all the bills.

Twelve days before Trudy's death Joyce had a letter from 10 Downing Street. It was from Prime Minister Clement Attlee's secretary and said that the Prime Minister wished to submit

Joyce's name to the King for the New Year's Honour List. Joyce, if he agreed, would receive the rank of Commander of the Order of the British Empire (CBE).

So that autumn and early winter Joyce had the news that *The Horse's Mouth*, due to its acceptance by the Book-of-the-Month Club, would be his widest-read and most profitable novel, earning in a few months more money than his writing of nearly fifteen years had earned him in the 1920's and early 1930's. He would have Tristram's concert debut. Now he had this honor offered by his King and his Prime Minister. All of this, and Trudy dying.

In fact 1949 had been filled with triumphs and tragedies. His Aunt Netta Clark, whom he had loved so much and who was one of his strongest links with the Cary past, died early in the year. Freddy Ogilvie, who had been a full professor in his thirties, Vice-Chancellor and Principal of Queen's University in Belfast, Director-General of the BBC, and Principal of Jesus College, knighted seven years before, had died of cancer, like his sister, that June, at the age of fifty-six.

He rejected the CBE. He replied to the Prime Minister's secretary,

> I take it that the honour proposed is for literary work, and not for my political books; and in that case I'm afraid I should be embarrassed by a distinction which seems to grade writers according to merit. But I am very sensible of the compliment paid to me personally & should like to express my warm thanks to the Prime Minister.
>
> (5 December 1949)

There are several reasons why he should have rejected the honor. As he said, it was a reward for literary merit and, as such, a passing of judgment on him and his work in relation to other writers. Was it really a government's job to do this?

Yet it is worth speculating on his reaction had he been offered a knighthood. His two brothers-in-law had been knighted. Perhaps he felt that, having worked so hard and faithfully and endured so much more than they had, accepting a lesser honor than theirs would be demeaning. It would show that he had come off second- or third-best and even at this late hour, would seem to vindicate their belief twenty-five years before that he was wrong.

Or perhaps it was just too late. He didn't need inspiration now. And Trudy would not be there to savor the honor. They had struggled along together with no one's encouragement, overcoming all the obstacles the world put in their way, so any award that came now would be a hollow recompense.

A few days later he had another letter from 10 Downing Street. The Prime Minister, it said, regretted Joyce's decision but understood his feelings. It is hardly likely that anyone really did.

Two weeks later, on January 6, 1950, when Trudy's death was still fresh in his mind, Joyce wrote to Elizabeth Lawrence,

> I am certainly lonely in this family house with a choice of seven bedrooms & all the family & my friends are wanting me to go away. But I have always had a better change in work, & as for loneliness I have spent a year at a time on the African frontier without seeing a white man or talking my own language.

Work had always been one of his salvations. Since the time in his childhood when he had run away from Clifton after his stepmother died, he had found that to overcome and forget unhappiness he must grab hold, plunge into life, and fight, work, and use what he had. Work, imagination, and love were his beliefs. The friends he had made at Clifton had helped him; Trudy's love had saved him. Imagination, the ability to create, had been the core of his career. So again he must work and create and look to his friends, his sons, and the rest of his family if he were going to be sustained.

He hired a houskeeper and a secretary, and even, at the age of sixty-one, attempted to learn to typewrite for himself; then he launched into a novel, one he had begun the previous April. It was the start of a second trilogy, the sort of project in which he could totally lose himself. *Prisoner of Grace* was to be the first of three novels on the world of politicians, *real* politicians, politicians that worked and sometimes got their hands dirty or had to tell a few lies in the process if they intended to get anything done. The trilogy was an attempt to deal with Radical government in Britain from the end of the nineteenth century to the 1930's.

If that were not an ambitious enough project, he had a third trilogy of novels in mind; it would deal with vital religion, the experience of faith and even fanaticism, rather than ceremonial churchgoing.[2]

Joyce had told John Fischer in the early autumn of the preceding year that he had seventeen novels in progress and ideas for a great many more. At sixty-one the completion of so many works was impossible, but Joyce intended to get as many of them on paper as he could in the years that were left to him. So his home had to be as organized as possible, his schedule strictly kept, and the typewriter constantly going; 12 Parks Road must be turned into a literary workshop. There was so much to say, so much he must get down on paper, and his pen could not move fast enough over the sheets of foolscap.

In February he wrote to Fischer to ask if he could order a British typewriter for Joyce as a "free gift" (the cost to be deducted from Joyce's account at Harper), since his old portable was breaking down. The government, trying to prevent the country from economic disaster, stuck "For Export Only" labels on almost everything, and, ironically, although they had offered him a CBE, they would not let him have a typewriter, however much money he brought into the country from his book sales abroad.

The loneliness of living at Parks Road increasingly oppressed him; the days were full enough, for he had his secretary and housekeeper, and friends dropped in, but the silent, empty evenings were so unbearable that sometimes he worked past midnight so as to blank them out. To alleviate his situation, he began to consider a trip to the United States. He had been urged to come by several of the people at Harper some time before and had wanted to take Trudy with him, but her illness

prevented anything of the sort, especially his going alone. Now
John Fischer and Elizabeth Lawrence repeated their invitation,
and he decided definitely that he would make the trip that August.[3]

Meanwhile *The Horse's Mouth,* rejected by seventeen American publishers in 1946, was on all the best-seller lists. Not only
was it selling in great quantities, but it was pulling up the sales
of the rest of his books which Harper had published and which
were still in print. It sold 1,998 copies in the first week of
March, for instance, more than either of his first two novels had
sold in their whole lifetimes in print. And now for the first time
in his life Joyce found he had an income-tax problem; he asked
if the Book-of-the-Month Club payment couldn't be made before April 1, so that he might spread it over the three previous
years during which he had paid the huge costs of Trudy's treatment and care.[4]

For all his anticipation of the American trip and his loneliness
at Parks Road, he hesitated about traveling and wrote to John
Fischer to make a suggestion:

> I have another project probably fanciful. The New York Uni-
> versity [Fischer learned after much effort and many false leads,
> that it was the City College of New York, not NYU] offered David
> Cecil a lectureship this spring which he couldn't accept because
> of other jobs here. But if they offered for September (one month
> only) I believe he'd come, partly to be with me. & I shld delight
> to have him there at the same time because contacts with critics
> & writers wld. be 10 times more fruitful & interesting if I cld.
> hear him deal with them also. He is one of our best critics, as
> you know, and quite the best talker I know, I mean really worth
> hearing — he never talks for effect and he is always on the point.

Joyce had never traveled such a distance alone since his Nigerian days. All his trips since then had been in company: to
Switzerland and Germany with Trudy, to France and just into
the Cotswolds with Tommy Higham, to Tanganyika with the
film crew, and to India with the Dickinsons. He was full of
techniques on traveling and, for example, insisted that his lug-

gage be packed in a special way, each item in the same place
every time. But when he came right down to it, he was a terrible traveler. During the war he had gone off many times without his ration book or, even worse, because without it he could
get arrested, his identity card.[5] He left things in hotel rooms.
He left train tickets at home. He would remember to pack his
tuxedo and forget clean socks and underwear. He might even
leave a partly completed manuscript in a railway carriage. His
excuse was, "I'm an orderly person in a world of chaos," but
now that he had to go on an extensive trip without someone to
shepherd him, he had cold feet.[6]

He was afraid of his reception in the United States, too. Acquaintances told him story after story of the hatred Americans
felt for the English until Joyce was afraid he might be walking
into a lion's den. He felt that if he could have Lord David with
him, he would have one friend, at least, to accompany him on
his trip into the savage American wilderness.

Lord David Cecil and Joyce had met at a sherry party at Oxford's Randolph Hotel early in the war; they had known each
other by name before that, but it was their first meeting.[7] Despite a great many differences in their points of view, especially
regarding religion (Lord David was high Anglican), they had
taken to each other from the start and dropped in at each other's
homes frequently. Joyce had, in fact, made a number of new
friends during or soon after the war: Lord David Cecil, Enid
Starkie, and Dan Davin of the Clarendon Press, whom he met
through the critic and novelist Walter Allen. Dan and Win
Davin were a young New Zealand couple who had come to settle
in Oxford and whom Joyce helped to make welcome. He hated
to feel bereft of them and of his other friends in the city, and
this was the reason for his brain wave that Lord David should
accompany him.

So, with that hope, he set about getting boat tickets and trying
to provide himself with some money for the trip, which involved
a fair amount of red tape since even five years after the war's
end, currency restrictions were still very rigid. He also tried to
arrange that his tour should include a visit to Los Angeles,

where his Aunt Mab's son, Lionel Stevenson, was in the UCLA Department of English.

Tentatively he planned to see New York, Washington, Chicago, San Francisco, and Los Angeles, "But you know," he added to Elizabeth Lawrence, "I'd like to see Des Moines, Houston and the rest if they can be fitted in." [8] The trip was to last only two months and would be filled with numerous lectures, cocktail parties, dinners, and a few moments of rest here and there, so his hope to see "Des Moines, Houston and the rest" suggests that, like a lot of Britons, he had little idea of the great distances of the United States. He might have seen them on a map, but they hadn't really sunk in.

Despite his attempts to get the household running smoothly so he could write, his new secretary did not have Trudy's touch with the battered family portable typewriter and Joyce, in trying to replace it, encountered more of the annoying red tape and frustration he had experienced previously. He wrote Fischer at *Harper's Magazine* on April 10,

> those nutts at the typewriter coy. misunderstood your letter & want to send me a portable when you told 'em my portable was breaking up under the work & also the curses of my secretary who hits the thing so hard in her rage that my thoughts have got as many holes in them as the argentine constitution — nothing will stand up to literature but an office machine — will you please confirm this to the company. . . . Another portable wld. of course be no good even when my secretary does not swear aloud, I *feel* her cursing and this causes electric disturbances in my receiver so that the message comes out full of stars & asterisks which have nothing to do with the dialogue.

In May the muddle was cleared up and Joyce — or at least his secretary — got the new typewriter and the work was able to go on.

Joyce began planning the talks he was to give on his American tour. He sketched out three basic lectures, with opportunities for some variation as the particular audience demanded. Essentially the talks would be the same as those he had given at various Oxford summer sessions to foreign students in the past few years and to gatherings of foreign professors at meetings sponsored by the British Council. He had to look up his references and the quotations he meant to include and also begin the rough drafts he would have to work over and over until they were as free-flowing as his novels.

Then on June 25, two months before Joyce was to leave, the Korean War broke out. Joyce, like people all around the globe, hoped it would not spread beyond Korea. Still, he felt he could not leave for America just then. As he wrote John Fischer,

> I was very sorry to change my plans. I hate changing plans and letting people down. Neither do I think there is much risk of a general war. Trumans & Achesons prompt and bold action has saved that position, so far as we can tell. Informed opinion here supports that view. But I cld not take even a small risk of an outbreak in Europe, even a limited action in the Balkans, while I was away. This home cld. be the chief refuge of daughters in law & grandchildren in case of evacuation, or even of new rationing difficulties in London, & I shld. have to be here to look after them.
>
> Also, as an old bomb officer of the last war, I may be needed by my corps. But I think that I shld. be able to come over in the Spring. I certainly count on it for I want very much to see you all, & the States.
>
> (27 July 1950)

Perhaps it was quixotic of him to think that he would be needed should the war explode out of Korea and actually reach England, for he was sixty-one now and, furthermore, there would be little use for wardens in an atomic war, if it came to that. And his sons were all grown — the two eldest in their thirties — and three were married, with the fourth, Peter, to marry that November. The two with children, Michael and George (who had just become a father that April), were better able than Joyce to look after his grandchildren. But Joyce was too much in the habit of doing what he could in an emergency, after three wars and a general strike, to be able to sail blithely away to New York just then.

However, the tour was rescheduled to begin in January, 1951, as soon as it became evident that the war would, after all, be confined to the Korean peninsula. Meantime he got back to his political trilogy, which was going badly.

In fact, everything was going badly at Parks Road. House-keepers came and went for one reason or another (one, a Scottish woman, found she couldn't bear to be in a place that did not have mountains, and Joyce was not prepared to build her a few[9]), and so did secretaries. Each new member of the household had to be told what to do and how to do it. Each secretary had to learn to read Joyce's handwriting, which made an already difficult job even more difficult. It was unbearably frustrating, when he had so much to write and so little time to do it.

But however much he fumed inside, he tried to get the house and the work moving smoothly and the trilogy begun.

46

TWO NOVELS OF WOMEN

AFTER HIS FIRST TRILOGY, Cary turned to two successive novels about women, *The Moonlight* (1946) and *A Fearful Joy* (1949). The former deals with the Caryesque theme of law and order versus personal freedom, as personified by two sisters, Rose and Ella Venn respectively. Through Ella's illegitimate daughter Amanda, Cary also tries (less successfully) to deal with the twentieth-century professional woman. In *A Fearful Joy*, he is much more concerned with character than with theme, and of the two books it is much the better. The difference between the works is in texture: there is far more life, more character, more event in *A Fearful Joy* than in *The Moonlight*, so while the latter seems to be a fabric stretched tautly over a framework of ideas which is always poking through, the former is rich, personal, eventful; it seems at first glance to have the aimlessness of life itself.

The Moonlight

Cary said in his preface to *The Moonlight* and in a broadcast with Lord David Cecil that the novel has two sources:

First of all, some years ago I heard, I can't remember exactly how I got in touch with it, but I heard of a case where three girls were left alone, their mother died and the eldest sister had to look after the other ones. They were a good deal younger. She gave her life up to these girls and her reward was to be rather disliked by both the others and to be hated by one of them. I felt profoundly the bitter injustice of this woman's position and of course, frankly, that also joined up with my general view of life, the fundamental and unavoidable injustice of life.[1]

The second source was

Tolstoy's Kreutzer Sonata. And I was so annoyed by Tolstoy's dense view of women, sort of dogmatic view of women, and his extraordinary misunderstanding of the whole situation of life, the dilemma, that I wrote immediately. I started right away and wrote a kind of Kreutzer in reverse.[2]

But the theme of the "unavoidable injustice of life" and the theme of a "Kreutzer in reverse" are not really fused into a single idea. It is the story of the three sisters, Rose, Ella, and Bessie Venn, that dominates, the story which deals with Rose's burden of responsibility. Many readers misunderstood the novel and condemned Rose as a Victorian tyrant who loved power and wielded it unmercifully over her sisters.[3] A careful reading indicates that it is Rose, not Ella, who is the ultimate victim. This is not because Ella murders her, for in fact Ella's administering of the extra sleeping drafts is an act of mercy from the point of view that Rose has been bowed down and crippled by responsibility.

If there is a tyrant, it is the sisters' father, Mr. Venn, who forced this responsibility on Rose. Mr. Venn wanted to be loved and adored, and Cary suggests that his unwillingness to discipline his children is a particularly cruel form of selfishness and neglect of duty. And duty had a high place in Cary's credo. Mr. Venn's shirking of his responsibility is shown in the episode in which Ella, as a child, burned Rose's wax doll and a good chunk of her sister's bedding. When Mrs. Venn proposes that Ella must be paddled for this outrageous action, he says,

"That will do very well, only take her well away. I never knew such a child for screaming."

"But my dear John, you don't propose that I should do the beating."

"Certainly, she is your daughter. Surely it's a mother's part to beat the girls."

Mrs. Venn gave her husband another glance. She understood completely this charming, selfish, sensitive husband, whose hypocrisies were so carelessly assumed that they sat on him like an additional grace.

"My dear, you made me slap Theo [their son] when he was rude to the Vicar."

"That was quite another thing. . . . Religious instruction, I should have thought, was in your province, at least while the children are in the nursery."

"I'm afraid we must do something, my dear, or nurse will give notice," with a nervous glance at the man who now, in the sulky drawl of a spoilt beauty, said, "Oh, if you're going to take that tone, there's no more to be said. I'll go and deal with the child."

Finally Mr. Venn suggests a "compromise": "Very well, if you will beat her, I shall talk to her," and he assumes "a heroic look." [4]

This sort of psychological bullying is hard enough on Mrs. Venn, but it is disastrous when Rose takes over running Florence Villa after her mother's death. Venn's absolute selfishness is well illustrated in the scene in which he uses Rose to persuade Bessie to marry James Groom, who had been Rose's love and fiancé until she renounced him in order to care for her "sickly" father. Cary manages to make this rank callousness seem so believable that many readers did not notice it, evidently, or they would not have been so hard on Rose.

It is these flashbacks of family history that are the successful part of the book, for they are filled with conflict and emotional peaks. It is the modern section, dealing with Ella's efforts to marry her daughter Amanda to the farmer Harry Dawbarn, that fails. Amanda drifts into an affair with Harry and then drifts out again. This is not a sufficiently strong theme to play off against the very rich one of the Venn family history. The one is alive, the other is flat.

The essential flaw in the plot centering around Amanda is Amanda herself. She is a type of character that Cary did not grasp sufficiently to use in a major role.[5] He had sufficient understanding of the type to use her as a minor figure (e.g. Tabitha Baskett's daughter-in-law, Kit), but he is far more at home with the late-Victorian woman, whom he could model on his aunts and his wife. Amanda lacks motivation partly because Cary meant her to and partly because she simply was beyond his scope.

It is possible Cary could have bolstered the Amanda plot by keeping Rose alive longer, but this would have thrown Amanda deeper into the shade. As it is, the novel as a whole is a failure, at least by Cary's standards, although its first two themes, the conflict between the Venn sisters and their emotional enslavement by their father, work well, and in the Amanda section the sale of Florence Villa (based on the sale of the Ogilvies' The Glade) and some of the farming scenes also succeed. But when one puts *The Moonlight* beside the novel it most closely parallels in theme, subject matter, and technique, *To Be a Pilgrim,* it seems second-rate Cary at best.

A Fearful Joy

Cary's next novel, *A Fearful Joy,* is one of the gayest romps through history ever written. It covers a great sweep, from the 1890's through the late 1940's, and deals with the manners, morals, wars, artistic revolts, industrialization, and a dozen more aspects of this period, yet none of the material is extraneous and nothing fails.

Tabitha Baskett, the novel's heroine, is a girl in a staid country town when she first meets Dick Bonser. That she has a capacity for great passion is shown clearly enough by the way she gives herself up to the piano or puritanism. At school, despite her tiny size, she overwhelms bigger and older girls by sheer force of will and emotion. And when she decides to give her life to music instead of foreign missions, she practices the piano six hours a day. As Cary says,

The idea of the Napoleonic soul which plans its career and carries it out with iron will and unshaken nerve had risen upon her
fancy, with all its powerful attraction for energetic minds.[6]

And yet the piano is not enough; she cries out, to her own surprise, "Oh-oh-oh, if only something would happen!" [7]

It does; Dick Bonser makes it happen. Bonser's name suggests
both "Bounder" and "Bouncer," and he is both. He is a liar and
a cheat and a seducer; at the same time, he adds tremendous
bounce to life and bounces Tabitha in particular into life. In a
letter Cary explained Bonser this way:

> In the F.J. it is true that the point of Bonser is not that he is a
> crook (tho he *is* a crook) but a man of imagination and so when
> Tabitha, getting bogged down in some sentimental or religious
> sandbank, is likely to stick there forever and die in her bed, he
> can always float her off. And so you see, the whole character of
> the book or world in which these people live is one of imagination
> (and the counter work of boredom) twin facets of life and death,
> of change and revolution (see the artists of the so called deca-
> dence) the inventors, the students, the Nazis and socialists — Hit-
> ler himself, shaking whole nations out of their rabbit holes. For
> the man of imagination has power for evil as well as good. . . .[8]

In fact, Bonser is a harbinger of that series of anti-heroes who
emerged in the 1950's and 1960's. But Cary sees him as extremely necessary, in one form or another, to society, simply to
get it out of the mud, the Slough of Despond, or "some senti-
mental or religious sandbank." The anti-hero was a type that
fascinated Cary, particularly when he was related to politics and
religion. He found the politicians especially interesting.

Churchill's Victorian hat and cigar, his siren suit, and fingers
held up in a V; Roosevelt and his cigarette holder and jaunty
grin; Stanley Baldwin and Joseph Stalin with their pipes — and
even Hitler with his Charlie Chaplin moustache and forelock
over the forehead — all these were appeals to the imagination,
necessary to their respective peoples. Whether they were called
"gimmicks," "packaging," or "style," they were recognizable

symbols of the particular man, marks of recognition to the crowd, gifts to the political cartoonists, and crystalizations of a distinct policy.

Cary uses two principal men of this sort in *A Fearful Joy,* both of them "confidence men" in the fullest sense of the term. One of them, Bonser, is exactly what we ordinarily mean by "confidence man": he is a swindler who even carries out the classic fraud of peddling a gold-painted brick to "a farmer who, knowing something of economics, has a deep distrust of banks." [9] He peddles bogus shares and anything else, but in the main he peddles himself to Tabitha and to the world. But he is not just a two-bit swindler. He builds an empire in rubber until it collapses in the slump after the First World War and is one of the first men to see the different social — and moral — life which the automobile brings into existence. He is a schemer and dreamer, a salesman of pie in the sky.

The other "confidence man" is Lord Gollan, Tabitha's first *legal* husband, a tycoon, inventor of the assembly line, promoter of the inexpensive automobile and the airplane, and organizer of British industry during World War I, when

> he has an immense reputation built up by the Ministry them-selves to reassure the public. The papers describe how he works ten or twelve hours a day. . . . His name, like Kitchener's, is one of those selected by a private committee of the cabinet and turned into magic which gives faith.[10]

When before the war Gollan's airplane venture collapses and the precarious structure which he has built seems destined for bankruptcy, Tabitha is prepared to retrench, firing servants, getting rid of cars, and cutting all household expenses drasti-cally. But Gollan spends, displays, entertains, and gives every indication he has not lost a penny, for as he says,

> ". . . we want to make the place look decent, or people will say we're broke. They're saying it now, trust 'em. Yes, they'd like to get me down; they've been counting me out for the last two years. . . .
> "Money — that's not the trouble; I can always get money." [11]

Rather than money, the problem is confidence. If one can inspire confidence, he can move the world, whether the political, the financial, or the religious world. So the two men are confidence men, two different levels of the breed, perhaps, but essentially the same, and they understand each other. Bonser indicates this when he tells his son,

> "You ask old Jim Gollan — he knows. Ask anyone who's got what it takes. You don't understand business, Johnny, it's an instinct." [12]

That John doesn't understand business — the confidence business — is indicated by the mess he makes of his life. John is a practical person, and his life is a dull ruin. After missing his true vocation, engineering, because it is not genteel enough, he goes to the university and experiences a conversion to relativism. But viewing everything in relative terms, seeing all sides to every question, he is crippled and unable to make decisions of any true sort. He takes a job at a new provincial university and is a failure; his marriage, too, is a mess because he cannot take a stand. His death in a mountaineering expedition is not even so positive as it sounds, for his wife urged him to undertake the excursion, since the exercise, she said, was good for him. In fact, John is that classic victim of circumstances, the "innocent bystander," as an episode during the war indicates. John, who is working under Lord Gollan in an essential job, gets involved with three girls and two soldiers, and they

> join a riot in the Circus, and in getting away manage to leave John in the hands of the police. He is tripped as he turns to fly and carried off to the cells. The police have no mercy for young civilians who make a nuisance of themselves; he is fined, and the magistrate makes some severe remarks about young men who if they are fit enough to break the law are also to be presumed fit to fight.[13]

John in fact is always left behind, always tripped up, and always shown no mercy. In failing to act, he must accept being acted upon.

P

The same is true of Tabitha's brother, Harry. His whole life
is a failure of the spirit, however good a doctor he has been.
When we see him last, as an old man, he has no rich memories
to draw on, no zest for life, only bleakness and timidity that
finally taper off into a merciful senility.

Tabitha, however, is both active and acted upon. Thus she
has her fear of the unknown but her joy from it, too, the fearful
joy of the novel's title. Her life is like a roller coaster and her
reaction to it is the same as the roller coaster's victim: intense
fear and intense delight and exhilaration. Her most active role
is that of mother. Once she has John, she dives into life, making
a home, a nest — protecting him, nursing him, building a faith
for him.

At the same time she devotes great energy to *The Bankside,*
the "decadent" review sponsored by her own "patron," Sturge,
and to bringing into being a salon that is as important to making Sturge feel a vital person as her going to bed with him is.

Thus Tabitha is that Cary archetypal woman, the homemaker. And she is "homemaker" in the same sense that Bonser
and Gollan are "confidence men." She builds a home for Sturge
in every sense, creating a whole world for him that includes sex,
solicitude, peace, excitement, a literary salon, *The Bankside,* in
fact everything necessary to make him feel alive and important.

With Gollan and Bonser, the other two men in her life, she is
more passive, since they are doers and actors, while Sturge is not.
With Sturge she must create a world; with them she merely has
to fit into a world which they have made and are constantly re-
making.

So Tabitha, between her various men, her son John and
brother Harry, and her granddaughter Nancy, lives the fullest of
lives as wife, mistress, mother, grandmother, editor, hotelkeeper,
party-giver, moral and religious mentor, buffer, bolsterer, victim, and mover. All of this takes place in the process of time or
history. And time is perhaps the most active character in the
novel. It acts on Tabitha perhaps even more than Bonser; it acts
on *The Bankside* and its contributors; it acts on Gollan.

For instance, Tabitha's cry, "Oh-oh-oh, if only something would happen!" when she is seventeen or eighteen (Cary seems not to be entirely consistent in his chronology in the novel, so it is difficult to be sure of people's ages) is a cry from a maturing body and mind that need excitement and sex. Her stubborn and unreasonable insistence that she bear her baby and not have it aborted is a result of time. The baby has been in her womb long enough for her to get used to it, long enough to make her feel a mother, and it is as if time said to her, "Look here, Tib, you've got a lot invested in this baby of yours, and anyway it's about time you were becoming a mother, so you hold onto it." That is to say, the idea and baby have both been ripening within her. The whole Gollan episode of her life is a history of change in time — the development of the automobile, the airplane, the assembly line, the development of small, pioneering companies into vast corporate bodies — and the consequent change of ideas.

The great change in Tabitha's life is shown in her dealings with her granddaughter Nancy, when Nancy, as an adolescent, is running — and sleeping — around. Tabitha is shocked, outraged, almost violent at Nancy's carryings-on, "And not yet eighteen — a child," she thinks in disgust. Yet Tabitha was pregnant by Bonser at seventeen, having run away from home twice with him, and at eighteen was sold off to Sturge as his mistress. The book comes full circle in time. Tabitha, once the breaker of all the proprieties, has now become the upholder of these proprieties, which her granddaughter Nancy now breaks. And Nancy, once she is pregnant and married, is seen on the same path of homemaker, mother, wife, and protector. Time tells Nancy exactly what it told Tabitha years before; her body, undergoing the changes of time, conditions her thoughts and her morality. It is not that they compromise or become hypocrites; it is just that their times have changed, and what is right or wrong is relevant to the age, whether the age of society or the age of the body.

The theme of the novel is summed up in Tabitha's thoughts immediately after reading the obituaries of Dick Bonser:

She remembers his robbery of some poor old widow in his Watling fraud, and says, "He was a wicked man; really capable of anything." But the very judgment throws her into the memory of some tenderness to herself, some charming piece of flattery devised to please her. She sees him again coming into her Urrsley flat, no doubt already bent on getting her money, and at once she thinks, "But where would I be if he had not come: an embittered old woman these last twenty-three years, a miserable useless old woman, and probably dead long ago. He brought me to life again; it was like a resurrection from the dead." And lost in this confusion of good and evil, as in a world, she gives up trying to form a judgment; she returns upon her loss, her solitude, and says to herself like thousands of widows, simply from the depth of their own feeling of loss, "The papers are right; there was something special about him." [14]

"It was like a resurrection from the dead": this idea is at the core of Cary's life and work, as central to him as the "epiphanies" are to James Joyce and his works. Life is a series of deaths which we may accept, allowing our lives to be crushed by something such as a dead creed or a moribund institution, or we may be resurrected (as Tabitha is by Bonser) or resurrect ourselves to life (as does Gulley Jimson).

47

CARFAX AND NEW YORK

In the autumn of 1950 Michael Joseph proposed that his firm publish a uniform edition of Joyce's novels, each of them with a preface in which the author should tell something of the sources and problems involved in writing the particular book.[1] After all, the novels of the 1930's were long since out of print, yet the expansion of Joyce's public had created some demand for the early books. The edition would not be a financial bonanza, perhaps, but Joseph had published Joyce from the start because he believed him to be a distinguished author whose work deserved a public and whose novels might well be read years after the money-makers had faded away entirely. So in part the uniform edition would be a gesture of Michael Joseph's respect.

It was a signal honor which few authors in Britain or America achieve. It meant that readers for years to come might be able to buy a complete set of Joyce's novels without having to put together a collection of secondhand copies and paperbacks. It meant that Michael Joseph expected the edition to find a market.

At the same time, it meant a good deal of work when work already was going slowly. In order to write the required prefaces, Joyce would have to go over novels composed so long ago that he had forgotten what they were about and could not even get their titles straight in his mind in some cases.[2] And of course it could not be a slapdash job; the point of the project was that readers and scholars should have a definitive edition, so the prefaces must be made to carry a lot of weight. The first volumes were scheduled to appear early in 1952, "So work seems to stretch out before me," Joyce commented.[3]

The American edition of *A Fearful Joy,* published in October, 1950, in the wake of the triumphant *The Horse's Mouth,* had an advance sale of 14,000 and moved along at a brisk pace following its publication date. In fact, the United States appeared to be much more appreciative of Joyce's work than Britain was. Various American magazines were interested in seeing his shorter pieces, including ones on his theories of the novel. Three of these appeared in 1950: "L'Art" and "A Novel Is a Novel Is a Novel" in the *New York Times Book Review* and "The Way a Novel Gets Written" in *Harper's.* Joyce, whose opinions on art and on the novel in particular were very definite, was gratified at having an audience for them.

At home, too, there was increasing recognition of his work. In the summer of 1950, Joyce had appeared on a BBC series about eminent authors, in which he was interviewed by Lord David Cecil. The transcript of this interview was to be included in a special issue of a little magazine, *Adam International Review,* which would focus entirely on Joyce and his work. Students at various universities were beginning to write theses on Joyce's novels, too. When universities, which seem so often to believe that the only good author is a dead author, began accepting him as a major literary figure, it seemed to Joyce that he had reached the position he had fought for.

In November the Chinese Army intervened in the Korean War, and Joyce again hesitated over the American trip, but, having put it off once, he decided not to delay a second time.

Before he could go, though, he had to celebrate the family Christmas and take care of all the elaborate preparations for it as Trudy always had, even in the weeks before her death. For the first time the holiday was entirely his responsibility, and he could not allow himself to botch it. He followed her ritual and gave up his work on *Prisoner of Grace* for the meanwhile; as he wrote to Elizabeth Lawrence,

I have the whole family for Christmas, eight grownups, 3 babies, 3 maids — and there will be nothing but festivity for at least a week — good for me but bad for books.

(3 December 1950)

Being surrounded by people again *was* good for him, too, after the loneliness of the past year and all its vexations. He bustled around the house, making sure everyone was comfortable, telling stories to the children, seeing that the food was prepared just right, talking, laughing, wishing the holiday did not have to come to an end. On New Year's Day, 1951, he wrote to John Fischer,

The last party my youngest George with his wife (who is half American) & their son, an enchanting baby of 8 months went off this morning in a snow storm and the house seems suddenly very large & quiet — & I myself rather melancholy. The trouble of a family gathering is that you miss it when it breaks up.

He was glad to have the American trip immediately before him, so he could turn his thoughts forward rather than back, and not have to knock about by himself in the "very large & quiet" old house. It was a wonderful place for a Christmas gathering but was too filled with memories for Joyce to live in alone.

Less than three weeks later he flew from London Airport and arrived at Idlewild Airport on the morning of January 21, full of advice, warnings, apprehensions, and mistaken notions of what he would face. Even the Americans whom he met had warned him of the country he was about to see. On board the plane, he had met an American couple who told him he would hate New York City, where he would be officially staying; if he wanted to see the *real* America, they said, it only began at the Ohio state line.[4] Joyce was to hear this same warning time and time again: the Midwest was not the *real* America — that was in the Northwest, or California, or the South, or New England, or wherever it was that the people he talked with had come from.

At his first New York party, a few days after he arrived, a woman said out of the blue, "Of course, I hate the British." But her remark was a kind of shibboleth with her, and, having gotten it out of the way, she was prepared to be completely cordial. As Joyce recalled, "We then sat down and had quite an amiable conversation about books." [5] That was about the extent of the anti-English feelings that Joyce encountered.

Then he was off on a swing through Virginia, Washington, upstate New York, and Connecticut, giving one or another of his three lectures to women's clubs, university students, and literary societies. Joyce's lecture technique appeared to be completely informal, almost slapdash. Enid Starkie described it in this way:

> Joyce Cary was a great craftsman in fiction, and I always enjoyed hearing him discourse on the technical aspects of his art and his way of solving the problems which arose. I liked it when he lectured on this subject, but he much preferred to deal with philosophical and abstract themes. On the whole, except when he referred to his own craft, I did not consider him a good lecturer, though not everyone agrees with me over this. His ideal of a lecture seemed to me mistaken. His novels were most carefully planned and plotted out, but he thought that a lecture should be impromptu — unscripted, as they say on the radio — couched in very colloquial language, and I have heard him say, in a set of lectures on the English novel at the University of Oxford, that some novelist had "fudged up" his material. He used to jot down the points he intended to make, on the outside of an airmail envelope which he had received from the United States — I never knew him to use anything else — and the quotations which were to serve as illustrations were scribbled in his illegible scrawl on little scraps of paper and stuffed into the envelope. Once, when he was lecturing at Cambridge, these had fallen out before he reached the platform, and he was obliged to invent his examples as he went along.[6]

This seemed a peculiar way to come armed for a two-month lecture tour: three tattered airmail envelopes each stuffed with a wad of quotations he could produce at appropriate moments — if he could sort them out.

But the procedure was not really what it seemed. Joyce liked to lecture in the same way as he punted on the Cherwell: he made it look easy but he would put in days and weeks of practice and preparation and a great deal of craft, not to mention craftiness. For Joyce liked to pull people's legs. Far from coming out to America with only a few notes on the backs of envelopes, he labored hard at his lectures.

First of all he wrote out a lecture in longhand, in "his illegible scrawl." Then this was typed up, and Joyce revised it and had it retyped. It might go through four, five, and six revisions and retypings. Then he sat down with a pair of scissors and cut out chunks here and there. With a pot of paste, he stuck together all the best parts from the various drafts to make up a final version. After it had been typed out, he began at last with his airmail envelopes. On these he printed out the key points of his talk as reminders. For by this time he had been over his material so many times that he knew it pretty much by heart. The envelopes and their jottings were memory-joggers, nothing more, and a handy holder for the quotations — usually typed, not scrawled — which he wanted to incorporate letter-perfect into the speech.[7]

Since he used the same talks a dozen or more times each, he had no trouble remembering what he meant to say, and the result of all this preparation was that he could do away with a bulky manuscript. Instead of reading from a script, which would inhibit his rapport with an audience, he would simply seem to talk off the top of his head. He didn't want to look at words; he wanted to look at the faces of those to whom he spoke and to make them feel he was *talking* to them rather than reeling off words like a phonograph.

As far as letting his academic friends such as Miss Starkie believe that he gave these talks to the most erudite audiences without any real preparation, well, that was for the spice of it, to make them feel, as the Ogilvies once had, that he was a bit of a buccaneer. And it may have been defensive, too. For if he had taken out a sheaf of manuscript and read it off, they might have gone super-critical, but how could they criticize a man who gave speeches off the backs of old envelopes?

On the first swing of his tour outside New York City (during which he made a few jumps back to his home base for interviews, lunches, and parties), he had one of the most exciting trips of his life: a drive from Burlington, Vermont, around Lake Champlain to Plattsburg, New York, through a blinding snowstorm and over roads thick with ice. The trip so thrilled Joyce that he wrote about it afterward:

> Four business men and myself, all with urgent affairs in Plattsburg [Joyce had a speaking date at Plattsburg State Teachers College that evening], proposed to hire a car. We phoned to various numbers, but had refusals everywhere — the weather was too bad that afternoon to risk a car along the lake road. At last we went out in a body to try persuasion at the garages. The first refused flat. At the second, where we caught the foreman in the doorway staring at the snow and surrounded him, we had at first the same head-shake. But when we pressed him, saying how important it was for us to get to Plattsburg before the roads were blocked with drifts, he said that he would go and ask his boss.
>
> This depressed us very much, we recognised a formula for getting rid of our importunity. But after five minutes the boss himself appeared, a large and prosperous looking man who would have passed anywhere for the President of a Wall Street bank, and said that he would take us himself. He then put on his sober Bank President's overcoat and hat, lit a cigar, and brought us out a car. This was the beginning of an experience that I would not have missed for anything in the world. What is more enchanting than the highest skill combined with perfect nerves. The boss was a master at this sort of winter driving. And he needed to be. No chains would hold on that road which was solid hard ice, ice which was full of ruts and large smooth lumps on which the car skated this way and that, sideways and even backwards, in enormous slides. And all the way the storm was beating, or rather exploding, against the wind screen, so fast that the wipers could not clear it before it was again blurred. . . . But the driver, sitting upright and intent, never made a mistake. He seemed to know by instinct, just how much to accelerate when we slithered, and where. I have never forgotten those skids. They were the largest, the most cockeyed, and strangely, the most deliberate, that I have ever felt. . . .

Our average speed throughout was under fifteen miles an hour; we were more than six hours on the road and arrived long after dark. The driver's concentrated attention did not falter throughout, but the only mark of tension I saw in him was his absolute immobility as he sat straight up holding the wheel, and his smoking — he smoked cigars the whole way without pause. But perhaps he always chain-smoked cigars. The price for this unforgettable affair, to me, was five dollars.[8]

Despite the constant danger of the car's skidding into a ditch and staying there until they were dug out by a snowplow or the possibility of it plunging off the edge of the road and down the bank to the frozen lake below, Joyce enjoyed the trip as he always enjoyed danger. Danger made him feel wholly alive and pushed all his senses to their extremes. And he always enjoyed seeing someone do anything really well, utilizing skill and concentration and achieving success with what seemed absolute ease. He hated the slipshod, the unprofessional, the indifferent, and this experience provided the very opposite.

In fact, he enjoyed almost all the trip, from the dangers to the delight of meeting new people and making new friends. He enjoyed being a celebrity and a "personality." For instance, in February he was guest of honor at a party Cass Canfield, Editor-in-Chief of Harper and Brothers, gave at his home, where the guests included Irita Van Doren, Belle Rosenbaum, and John Hutchens of the *New York Herald Tribune;* David Demsey, Harvey Breit, Orville Prescott and Charles Poore of the *New York Times;* Amy Loveman of the Book-of-the-Month Club; Max Gissen of *Time* magazine; Charles Rolo of the *Atlantic Monthly;* and the critic and essayist Clifton Fadiman. A few days later Joyce, John Fischer, and Cass Canfield lunched with the publisher of the *Times,* Arthur Hays Sulzberger, in his suite in the *Times* tower. Joyce enjoyed every minute of his being wined, dined, feted, interviewed, and shown off. It was exciting after the doldrums he had been in at home, and he hadn't time to be depressed or to feel lonely.

Then he was off west to Houston, Dallas, Los Angeles (where he saw his cousin), San Francisco, Salt Lake City, Denver, and

Chicago, a whirlwind trip of lectures, interviews, and appearances at bookshops, on radio, and on television. He had worried about being without his friends, but Harper and Brothers had given him great lists of people to look up and had written to friends and friends of friends to make sure Joyce felt welcome everywhere. He was not abandoned for a minute. The stacks of letters he dashed off to friends and family in England show his great exuberance.

More remarkable, he even managed to get some work done. Whenever there was a free moment, an hour or two in the morning, the afternoon, or in the evening alone at last in his hotel room, he would settle down to write. Or when he dropped in at the Harper office, as he did almost every day that he was in New York, he would find an empty desk and sit down to write, completely oblivious to clattering typewriters, people rushing about, the slam of filing cabinets, and hurried conversations.[9] It was like being on trek again in Borgu and writing while camp was set up about him. Despite the years of strict routine in Oxford, he had not lost the knack of working amid much noise and confusion. As he told the editors of *Holiday* magazine,

> I work at any time but my chief hours are in the morning. I use every method — long-hand, dictating, and I can write at any time, in planes, trains. I wrote half a chapter in pencil on the lower level at Grand Central when I missed a late train.
>
> (12 April 1954)

Peace and quiet might help him, but far more important was his need for stimulus, to feel in touch with life, and he had plenty of that during the tour.

There was a final flurry of parties and appearances in New York in March before Joyce left America — a chat with Eleanor Roosevelt on her television program, a dinner in his honor given by the New York chapter of PEN, the international writers' group, and many other activities. Then he flew home.

Immediately after his arrival, still bursting with the energy generated by the trip, he set to work to finish *Prisoner of Grace* and wrote to Elizabeth Lawrence at Harper,

You will be glad however to know that I find some bits of my book interesting & I am already working at it hard not only to get it finished but because it is interesting. & I need something to interest me for it *is* vacation time, all my friends are away & there is nothing to do but work, which I have always hated. I am a lazy man pursued by demons.

(15 April 1951)

Besides his own work, he was busying himself with the career of Gerald Wilde, a young painter whom he had met through the Davins. Joyce felt that Wilde's talent deserved to be fostered, but that the artist risked destroying it by his lack of self-discipline, a fault which he demonstrated the first time Joyce met him:

The first time I met Gerald Wilde was, I think, about '49, in Oxford, at the Davins. It was late in the evening. There was a crowd of people in the room, Ronnie Syme, the historian, was one, and I think Louis MacNeice was another, certainly I know I was sitting by the fire conversing on some historical matter with Father Gervase Matthews, when I heard a queer noise and saw in the middle of the room, a figure strange even in that gathering place of poets and professors; of dreamers in all dimensions.

At first glance, in the dim light, Wilde seemed like a spectre. His long, dead-white face with its hollow cheeks was like the mask of bleached skin on a skull, his arms seemed but bones, hanging loosely in the sleeves of an enormous coat whose crumpled folds gave no room for flesh. The arms, too, were extremely long, so that the bony hands almost touched the floor. It was as if this skeleton had but half risen from the grave.

All this figure was in violent and continuous agitation, and with a movement that seemed by itself preternatural. It was this quivering, shaking which more than anything gave, at the moment, the sense of visitation from another world. . . .

But how much more fearfully ghostly was this apparition that shook in every joint, whose enormous pale eyes were full of an excitement equally extravagant — whose very words sounded like the language of a world where meanings defeated any common syntax.

Startled, I began to get up. I could not make out what was

happening, or if Wilde was speaking to me, but he was staring at me and his stare was urgent. But at the same moment, he flung out his arms and plunged forward, knocking over the table of glasses and bottles with a crash which seemed to astonish and bewilder him. He stood gazing at the floor.

Win Davin then jumped up, touched his arm, and he went out with her. She came back in a moment, laughing, and said that Wilde had gone. The broken glass was swept up, the carpet mopped, and the party went on as if nothing had happened. . . .

I had been ready to think the man drunk, but afterwards, when I was going away, Win Davin assured me that he was stone sober. The stare, the trembling, the strange sounds which resembled speech to the ear but not the mind, were due simply to the shock of an unexpected event, and a clash of ideas all insisting on immediate expression.

Wilde was a painter who thought of himself as a Gully Jimson in the world, and seeing me unexpectedly, he had wanted to explain, all at once, his feelings about the book, about Gully, about the relations of artist and public.[10]

Gerald Wilde was not the only painter who saw himself as Gulley Jimson after the publication of *The Horse's Mouth;* more than one had announced himself as "the real Gulley Jimson" or accused Joyce of exploiting him in print; neither was Wilde the only artist in whom Joyce took the interest of a friend, admirer, and patron.[11] But he was the one to whom Joyce gave the most help and who caused Joyce the most trouble.

For a time Joyce gave him "loans," which were drunk up in the pubs of Oxford, London, and elsewhere. So Joyce tried setting up an account for Wilde at an artists' supply shop, but that plan failed, too.[12] Now, in 1951, he was trying, through the sculptor Henry Moore, to get Wilde an allowance from the Artists' Benevolent Fund; at the same time he was trying to bring him to the attention of dealers, critics, and the public at large.[13] He wrote an introduction to the catalogue of an exhibit of Wilde's paintings and attempted to get *Life* magazine to do a picture feature on the young painter.

Joyce was almost always sympathetic to struggling painters and writers. For instance, during the war his friends the Boyds learned that their dentist's secretary, a girl of seventeen or eighteen, was a great fan of Joyce's and a novice writer. She admired Joyce's work so much that sometimes she simply stood on the path across the street from 12 Parks Road to gaze at the house. Joyce, when he learned all this, invited the girl to have tea with Trudy and himself and followed up the invitation with several conferences in which he went over her stories as carefully as if they were his own.[14]

In the case of a frustrated and lonely young writer teaching in the American Midwest, Joyce carried on a lengthy correspondence to cheer him up and encourage him, recalling some of his own early experiences and talking of the problems he had had with his own writing and spirits.[15]

He knew what it was to be alone as a writer, without any real encouragement at the time when it is most vital — before publication. A published author had the encouragement of checks from magazines or publishers and the great satisfaction of seeing his work in print and knowing that somewhere someone was reading it. But the beginner, doubted by everyone and ridiculed by some, had only his own faltering faith in himself and could use every speck of encouragement he could get. Joyce gave it when he could, even at the expense of his own work and sometimes of his bank account.

Joyce also knew what it was to be without money and the independence that money could bring. He had regretted for years his failure to give his sons that independence. Now that he was earning a substantial income, he intended to remedy the situation. In 1951, when there was a prospect of Joyce's winning a major literary prize, he wrote to Elizabeth Lawrence that

> I shan't alter my life for any prize — but I'll enjoy the money because I shall be able to give some to the children who are just at that time of life, when they ought to have money. They can enjoy it. It always seems unfair to me that I inherited £300 a year when that was worth 6 or 700 to-day & they got nothing.
>
> (27 May 1951)

Although he was not given the prize, he did begin turning over to them the royalties from some of his books and the fees from shorter pieces.

He was writing more and more of these shorter works — short stories and articles — as the market for them opened up in the United States.

48

"THE COMEDY OF FREEDOM"

THE PROBLEM of running 12 Parks Road continued to plague
Joyce and interfere with his work, and the problem of loneliness
disturbed him often. So he was pleased when a family vacation
was planned for that summer. At the end of July he went to
France with a crowd of sisters-in-law, one son, nephews, nieces,
and other relatives. He taught the boys to gamble but warned
them, when they wanted to go off and try their new knowledge
at the local casinos, that they could never win at it. All the
same, they did try their luck, convinced that they had worked
out an infallible system, and they lost every penny in their pockets. "But they are STILL convinced," Joyce wrote, "that if they
had been allowed by Lady O. (my sister in l. and the mama of
the two boys [this was Lady Mary Ogilvie, Freddy's widow]) to
wake me up to borrow 4000 francs they would have broke the
bank." [1]

It was the sort of vacation Joyce liked, for he was with many
people and there was something going on every minute; even the
dangers were something to be savored:

I was swimming off a cliff and when I wanted to get back I had
to wait for the wave to lift me up on the ledge and it did lift me
up but with too much enthusiasm and it rammed the cliff with
my head on a mussel shell — it felt just as if it had gone into my
brain. And my son said my dear daddy you cant go up like
that — you are enough to frighten the girls into a fit you are simply all over blood. I liked this delicate thought for the ladies feelings — who shall say that chivalry is dead. [2]

Not long after, he went on another holiday, this one his annual trip to Stratford for the Shakespeare Festival. Joyce explained that he was going in the company of Lord David Cecil, since he would

> be able to tell me about them — I am shockingly ignorant of Shakespeare and most other things. I wish to God I had done more work at College — but perhaps if I had I should have turned out a philosopher and despised authorship and I have a ridiculous idea that I shouldn't have like this — ridiculous because of course I should have been perfectly happy despising every form of art provided I had been trained out of it.[3]

His comment about being ignorant of Shakespeare was nonsense. He had been to the plays at Stratford for years, and his friend, John Dover Wilson, was a great Shakespeare scholar whose books Joyce had read very carefully. In fact, the next summer, 1952, he wrote this letter to Dover Wilson:

> I've just had a wonderful week at Stratford — Coriolanus, MacBeth, As you like it, the Tempest & Volpone.
> Michael Hendern & [Anthony] Quayle did wonderful jobs.
> Quayle a very intelligent man suggested that "chuck" used by MacBeth to his piece is a term also of contempt (rather like piece) & expresses also the disgust of a thug with his wife when she has once had to doubt his nerve.
> I promised him a Shakespeare forgery by you. So will you please forge me one for him.*

> (29 August 1952)

A man who could sit down and discuss the nature of Shakespeare's language with an intelligent Shakespearian actor hardly seems "shockingly ignorant of Shakespeare" by most standards. He was pulling his friend's leg. In fact, it was almost a sign of friendship for him to do it, for Joyce was stiff and formal with

---

* This "Shakespeare forgery" was a facsimile of Shakespeare's signature. John Dover Wilson, who could do the signature perfectly, sometimes made these "forgeries" for his friends, often jotting it on the flyleaf of their collected Shakespeare — what could be better than a collection of the plays signed by Shakespeare himself? Dover Wilson had given copies to Joyce and one of his sons.

people he disliked and would only tease and joke with friends or strangers whom he took to.

That October *Mister Johnson* was published in the United States, the first of Joyce's four African novels to be put out by Harper and the first of them to appear in the United States since *The African Witch* disaster fifteen years before. Its advance sales were less than expected, but the book was reviewed on the front page of the *New York Times Book Review,* and Joyce received more than $3,000 in royalties in October alone. Joyce was more disturbed by the misunderstanding of the reviewer for the *Times* than he was pleased by the appearance of the review in such a prominent place. He decided to do something he had never done before. He would write a letter to the reviewer, Mark Schorer, to explain what *Mister Johnson* was about — in fact, what *all* the books were about.

In fact, Joyce's letter turned into a general preface to his novels as a unified body of work and perhaps helped him to prepare the prefaces to the individual novels which he was about to write for Michael Joseph's complete edition. Coming at a time when he was making himself familiar again with works written over a period of twenty years and when he had completed one trilogy and was embarked on his second, his comments have a perspective and authority which no other piece of writing had in his career to date:

Oxford 13.10.51

DEAR PROFESSOR SCHORER

I wanted to thank you for a very kind and interesting review and also I want to put a problem to you as a critic. My novels are all about one world — as much so as Blake's poetry is about his world, and I want, like him, to make people *feel* that world which might be described as that of *freedom.*

By freedom I don't mean the figment that politicians talk about — but *real* freedom — the active creative freedom which maintains the world in being — the activity which is most nearly described by theologians — the source of moral responsibility and of good and evil; but for me also of injustice and love, of a special comedy and a special tragic dilemma which can never be solved.

Some critics have perceived or partly perceived this — one or two some years ago who called me a metaphysical novelist (but the book was "The Pilgrim" which gave them an easy clue): and others lately (one especially in New Zealand) who called me a protestant novelist but of course my theme is far wider than any religious construction. It includes aesthetic and political freedom, the whole problem of the created symbol.

And like others (like Blake again) obsessed with a view of the world which seems to me so obvious, but to other people apparently so dark, I am very anxious to make my world understood and felt.

That is why, unlike Blake who invented his own mythology, to avoid the cliche of worn out definition, I use a quite different method of approach. I do not want to frighten people at the beginning by difficulties or by the idea of instruction. I do not want to start by saying "this novel is a metaphysical construction based on a comprehensive idea of life" or they will stop entering into my character's lives and instead treat the book, if they tackle it at all, as a kind of crossword-puzzle, asking what does this character stand for, — or that, — they will imagine an allegory. And I detest allegory — my people are real people in a real world or they are nothing.

In this book the dilemmas of Rudbeck, *making* his road — his wife creating her independent life (as she must do for his happiness as well as hers) Johnson creating his personal legend and the careerist making his career — all immersed in the world of creation — of free imagination — of injustice, or change — are those of actual souls faced with personal problems which are also universal ones.

Of course there are all the other elements to be considered to give a true picture — the "created" elements of society and convention — set-ups which have a temporary stability or rather a slower rate of decay ("The Horses Mouth" largely turns on such constructions of taste — "The Moonlight" with those of marriage and sex); the permanent characters of being itself — such as science examines — without which there would not be anything at all; and the derivative (which crop up in "The Fearful Joy" for instance, in the study of the refugees) such as the family and the social consequences of the family relation; and the sexual relation which obliges us to create with certain given materials.

Thus my problem of form tends to be complex. It is ultimately a moral problem (to give a true experience) — one can't put in the whole in a single book (nor in a hundred) one has to seek a balance. It is a special and difficult form forced upon me by my material.

An old friend who understood what I was at, was always pressing me to explain the position, but I have always been afraid of killing the books. I know how hard it is to make people enter into a new situation; how easily they push a book into a pigeon hole and turn your meaning into a cliche.

That is why I fought so long even against writing introductions and why, when I gave way, I made them so short and plain in the new edition.

But to you I can be frank. Ought I to go on as I am doing, presenting the books as yarns and letting a few people here and there find out by their own penetration what I am trying to do? Creating a homogeneous picture of the world as it is, as perpetual creation of the free soul with all its complex results in art and religion and its politics, its special tragedy and special morality: Mr. Johnson who simply forgets his grievance, who lives in creation, Gulley Jimpson who is aware of the dilemma and knows that he must not hate the injustice of the world, that he too must live in creation. Or ought I to write a general preface to the whole series under the head (which I once thought of using) "The Comedy of Freedom?" But what worries me is not the reviews of Mr. John but that such theses on my work as I have seen, even a very good job that came to me this week from a Norwegian scholar — are just as much at sea as most of the newspaper notices.

This man has discovered or sensed that the books are all part of one related scheme but he has no inkling of its nature. Perhaps such words as creation, freedom are so utterly worn out by fanatics and cranks, that they no longer carry any of their tremendous meaning.

Yours sincerely,
Joyce Cary

The letter was a polite way of telling the American critic that he had misinterpreted *Mister Johnson,* for Joyce had numerous friends at home who knew his work and what he meant to say in it far better than Mr. Schorer; there were, for instance, Lord

David Cecil, Enid Starkie, or, perhaps most sympathetic of all, Walter Allen, who, besides being a novelist and critic, had read most of Joyce's novels in manuscript for Michael Joseph. So he would be in a far better position to answer Joyce's question as to whether or not he "ought . . . to write a general preface to the whole series under the head . . . 'The Comedy of Freedom.' " The question, as it is posed in the letter, is purely rhetorical, an attempt (as is the entire letter) to get across the true nature of his work to a prominent critic, perhaps in the hope that the word might spread.

For Joyce was far more interested in being read and understood than in earning money on the basis of mistaken reviews. He had spent a decade resisting his family's attempts to get him to write for money alone. He wrote the novels because he had something to say in them, and to have his message misunderstood time and time again was utterly, damnably frustrating.

The collective title for his novels, "The Comedy of Freedom," although never publicly used, does help interpret them. "Comedy" was meant in both the classic sense and the modern sense, for the works are a celebration of man in a state of freedom and at the same time an invitation to the reader to enjoy and laugh at man. Freedom, a state into which man increasingly ventures, makes for a world of comedy, tragedy, and pratfalls. Man comes up smelling like a rose or, sometimes, with pie on his face. And Joyce did believe that man was increasingly free rather than increasingly conformist. In his 1952 essay, "The Mass Mind," for instance, he says that if those people who say our society is increasingly conformist could see the ultimate in conformist societies, the primitive tribe, as he had, they would utterly reject the idea that our society is becoming less individualistic. He felt that we enjoy more opportunities than any society ever had for self-expression and exploitation of our individuality, and we use these opportunities; we, unlike the people of the tribe, are forced to *choose*. Perhaps the majority would choose not to dare, but in most other societies even *that* choice is absent.

Man, in his developing state of freedom, can, in theory, develop himself to his ultimate but is threatened always by some one else — in fact by many someones — exercising *his* freedom. So man and society, or man and man, live in a constant state of tension, which, depending on the circumstances and the individual, may be exhilarating or frustrating but never so unbearably stultifying as the ritualized world of the tribe.

Since man does have this potential for great happiness or equally great frustration and tragedy, the world carries a mixture of tragedy and comedy for him. So, to Joyce's thinking, anyone who said the world was all one or all the other was a fool. Such a man was creating a fantasy world rather than a real one. The Aldous Huxleys were as much liars as the peddlers of sweetness and light. Dark glasses were as bad as rose-colored ones; both filtered out too much of the real world. In fact the gloom-mongers were even bigger liars, because they scoffed at the optimitists and pretended to be genuine realists and prophets of truth.

This was one of the major reasons for Joyce's slow achievement of success and a public; he had taken neither of these extreme and easy paths. He did not fall into the ranks of the postwar pessimists of the twenties or those of the social realists and proletarian optimists of the thirties who said that all would be well after the revolution or of the holocaust-oriented criers of doom of the post-World War II world. Since he did not bemoan the fate of Western society or point a damning finger at capitalism (or socialism) or screech that the individual was being crushed in a world of machines and faceless bureaucracy, he was not treated as a "serious" writer by those circles in which "serious" is equated with moans, groans, and continual damnation. On the other hand, since he did not say that everything was sunshine and roses, he was not apt to be a popular writer. Attempting to embrace the whole of reality, he offered no easy answers and would not be wedged into a small pigeonhole, so he was, ironically, confined to a small readership for years.

Even more ironic, now that he *was* beginning to reach more and more readers, he was increasingly thought by some circles to be a "popular" writer and therefore a lightweight. There is a

circle of critics, academicians, and lay intellectuals who see popularity and worth as being in inverse ratio: that which is read
cannot be good, and that which is good is not read. To take
their perverse reasoning and apply it to Joyce's writing — his
first books, which did not sell, are far better than his later ones,
which did — is an absurd idea.

That is why Joyce paid so little attention to the coteries of
contemporary writing. Only a few critics, those he felt truly understood what he was attempting and therefore were capable of
judging how much or how little he had succeeded in fulfilling
his goal in a particular novel, critics such as John Dover Wilson
or Walter Allen, interested him. The others he ignored most of
the time, but it galled him to be misunderstood by people who
were supposed to look clearly and closely at literature yet who
ended up trying to stuff his work into a confining category, or,
failing at this, threw it aside as insignificant.

These pigeonholing critics were like young Mister Johnson,
who filed a report on "tobacco, native" under "elephant poach-
ing in the Fada Kurmi" simply because his boss had once remarked that the native tobacco was green like elephant drop-
pings.[4] Joyce, who had published four novels at the time he
wrote *Mister Johnson,* may have had some of these critics in
mind when he wrote that scene.

However, writing letters or even prefaces did not do much
good. He continued to be misunderstood and could only end up
laughing at the critics who got him all wrong, as in this letter
to Elizabeth Lawrence about the reception of *Prisoner of Grace:*

> The reviews here are MIXED. the office boy at the times LIT
> SUP who usually interviews (I mean reviews — my mind is rather
> on interviews) modern authors (Since 1066 — before that they are
> done by real professors. Alfred the great could be sure of intelli-
> gent treatment) thinks I am a PUZZLE. the STAR THINKS i
> have too many brackets. But nina had a brackety mind so what
> could I do. Whats more she wouldn't have come over as nina
> without those brackets — but don't tell this to the crickets. It
> might give them brain fever.

(20 September 1952)

After getting back from the near-fatal holiday in France, when he bashed his head on the rock ledge, Joyce had continued writing *Prisoner of Grace,* part of a mass of work that he tackled that autumn, including three lectures scheduled for the winter term at the Cheltenham Festival and others at different schools and universities, two new prefaces for the collected edition (which Joyce had titled the "Carfax Edition," after the Carfax Tower which stands at the center of Oxford, the city where he had made his career. The title also pleased him because it alliterated well with his name: the Carfax Cary), and "about 50 letters" he had to answer — business letters, requests for talks, queries from students doing theses on his novels, and the occasional oddball (for instance, one woman wrote to ask about "the Indian way of making love" which he mentioned in one of his novels and which she was eager to learn; another felt she was his soul mate and offered him bed, board and herself — if he should ever be in Stockholm[5]).

The lectures were a necessary evil and required a good deal of work that kept him from his novels, as he explained to Elizabeth Lawrence,

> but I accept them (long before) because I know it is good for [me] to be routed out of my study and oxford and made to speak which always excites (especially if the audience heckles) and knocked up against some new people. I am too apt to sink into my thoughts and dreams and books and not see my friends — I see enid only once a week for a drink here and Cecil bless him digs me out. I adore friends but I am careless about keeping them and finding them. You are an old friend and I am grateful to you — I need friends always and treat them badly.
>
> (1 October 1951)

His comments on the lectures are not entirely true. Joyce enjoyed the talks themselves, especially the give and take with an alive and even argumentative audience, best of all an audience of students. They made him feel vigorous and offered him a real challenge.

49

"ANT MYTYPING GOOD"

As THE RUNNING of the house improved, Joyce was able to settle
into a routine of work. Mornings he handled his correspondence and wrote; he wrote and had his walk in the afternoons;
evenings he wrote again. But even Joyce, with his appetite for
work, could not stand such a rigid routine very long. He had
fewer and fewer amusements, fewer contacts with friends, and
although he told himself this was good for his work, it made him
edgy and irritable. The following letter to Elizabeth Lawrence,
although it starts out pleasantly, shows that his ability to shrug
off problems and irritations was not what it had been:

a good night for me is to wake between 5 and 6 and think what a
good day I had the day before and have some good ideas which I
write down in my notebook beside the bed. at that hour I have
my very best notions and answer my worst problems. Then I relaxed and got ready to have my morning sleep which is very important to tomorrow afternoon. And what is strange at night is
how time moves — this is due to the frightful activity of the
atoms in the head — I can't stop them rushing off on fancies and
all at once I heard the ½ hour on the dining room clock downstairs and say it cant be, and then 6 struck and soon after that I
went asleep till 7 and had some very good dreams. I prefer my
horse sleep to my baby sleep because it is a boon I dont rely on
and it always has good dreams. Then I had my papers at ½ past
7 and my letters at about 10 to 8 which gave me a fearful blow
with an enormous demand for tax. But then I saw it was a ramp

they had assessed me at 10000 which is more than twice what I made. It was a trick because my agent had not sent in my return — but a mean trick too. Only a pretty low type of blackguard goes in for tax collecting here and they bully you all the time. The spivs and frauds meanwhile get away with everything. I pay more tax than a butcher — writers are discriminated against or rather all people with unequal income they are not allowed to average 3 or 4 years income. One year one pays a huge super tax and then while one is finishing a book one lives on capital.

(26 October 1951)

This attack on bureaucracy and its "pretty low type of blackguard" and Joyce's sense of persecution are reminiscent of an earlier time. They recall the ill and exhausted Joyce of Bussa days, when he was surrounded by the Niger River swamps, lashing out in frenzy at the Nigerian Administration and the government at home (as for his complaints of tax collectors, he seems to forget that he was once one himself in Nigeria). In some ways the situation now was the same as it had been in Bussa. He was tiring himself out and feeling increasingly isolated and lonely, even though the isolation was largely self-imposed. He had no one to stir him up and get him off his mudbank. There was no Trudy with whom to argue and make up and no children to give life excitement. He was in danger of becoming crotchety and old.

Late in the autumn he became ill and was hospitalized by his doctor. Instead of making him even more gloomy, being ill seems to have pepped him up. Perhaps it was the change of routine, the other people about him, and the attention of nurses and doctors. Whatever it was, his letters grew more chipper, as shown by this one to Miss Lawrence on January 2, 1952:

Thank you 1000 times for that very well selected parcel — it was full of treasure for a man whose rations are for two persons and may have six to a meal any day of the week. I dont know if I told you I had been whizzed off to a hospital on suspicion of polio or osteo myelitis having a pain in my leg and a temperature. But it was a mysterious disease and I am nearly well again. I was

let out of bed in time for Christmas (or rather I got out) and had
a very good christmas with all the family but one grandson who
was with his granny. Now I am at work on your book which is
nearly done. . . .

What is your new years resolution — mine is to write a book —
a real book — a flawless work. Ive made that resolution several
times before — but at least it is an ambition — (interruption here
for a radio times man wanting an interview (Im broadcasting on
sunday 13th if they let me) nothing like fixing your typewriter
on a star.

Even a hospital trip made a break in the stultifying routine
growing up around him, and of course the family Christmas
party was the best remedy of all. His illness was diagnosed
finally as bursitis and, after a time, Joyce pretty much forgot
about it and had only an occasional twinge to remind him.

He finished *Prison of Grace* at last and was preparing to
send the manuscript off when his brother Jack fell ill at the
house in Somerset where he and Joyce's half sister Sheila lived,
the house which Arthur Cary had bought for his retirement.
Joyce hurried off to be with his brother, posting the manuscript
off to the United States on his way to the railway station. But
almost as soon as he arrived, he wrote to his editor at Harper and
Brothers,

No letters by request and this morning my poor secretary god
bless her for she needs it has sent me an effusion (the just word)
to say that probably the M.S. has a page missing. . . . Also she
says the last chapters are numbered wrong. I think *she* is wrong
(she is a muddle head) & I know *she* numbered the chapters
wrong once, but now I am worried and my sweet peace in this
lovely spot (a lovely little old house in an old fashioned garden
among apple trees with a clear trout stream running beside them
— the snowdrops & crocuses are out & a lively cocker bitch is waiting to take me for a walk) is utterly ruined. But I trust you, my
dear E. to see that the M.S. is coherent and the chapters right.

(24 February 1952)

But the page was missing and took almost a month and a half to find and send on. Joyce wrote a note of explanation and sent it with the page to New York:

> I do apologise most humbly for all these muddles in the MS it is the first time I have sent off an ms in such a state. the truth is that Mrs. Cary used to send them off for me and so the thing was properly done I had no idea it was so difficult.

Prisoner of Grace was the first novel Joyce had finished since Trudy's death more than two years before. The fouled-up manuscript was just another demonstration of how vital a part she had played in his life, not only as a wife but as a secretary-collaborator. Joyce was slipshod and absentminded, and Trudy had taken care of all the loose ends. Knowing what her husband meant to do in his books, she was able to edit and sort the manuscripts better than any secretary ever could. Joyce cursed his secretary, but the fault was to a large degree his own.

Working for a writer is exacting and exasperating, but to work for Joyce must have been particularly tough, since his handwriting was nearly impossible to read (it got worse as he grew older, and Cass Canfield at Harper had to get somebody else to read the letters he got from Joyce and then type up a translation) and he wrote such huge stacks of manuscripts each day. Furthermore, his carelessness with details did not help make the secretary's lonely job easier.

Joyce's attempt to remedy the situation was to learn typing himself, so he could either make a manuscript legible to his secretary or do away with having a secretary at all. The results were surprising:

> Ant mytyping good — if you could hear it you would know it is even scquiring RHYTHM. Soon I shall be abolr to type myself to sleep.
>
> (10 June 1952)

His friends were fascinated. Elizabeth Lawrence, for instance, suggested that his typing be set to music, and Robert Lusty, who handled most of Joyce's manuscripts at Michael Joseph, said he had never realized that Joyce had such an excessive number of fingers.[1] While it may have been a new art form, however, it did not serve for the typing-up of manuscripts.

So he still was saddled with the exasperation of having secretaries come and go, breaking in one only to have her leave or else bollix matters up so badly (with his aid) that she had to be dismissed. The problem slowed him down and disconcerted him when there was such a tremendous volume of work that he wanted to go ahead with.[2] He tried dictating to avoid the problem of someone's having to read his handwriting and even attempted, at the age of sixty-three, to alter his handwriting so as to make it more legible. But there seemed no perfect solution.

The mountain of work remained, not just the many novels he had under way but an increasing volume of articles and short stories, for which there continued to be a great demand. These meant good money, perhaps a thousand dollars each, and they involved a lot less work than any novel. He could write a dozen and more of the short pieces in the same amount of time as he could complete a book. And much of the money from them was earmarked for his sons, in place of the inheritance he had been unable to give them.

Between *Prisoner of Grace* and *Except the Lord,* the first and second volumes of his political trilogy, he worked especially hard on the short stories. The short story was a form he had handled very little since the 1920's, and he found himself enjoying the change to this genre:

> I have been working on several stories lately — I like this fine careful work to recover some precision before I begin another novel. But it is very slow and wasteful work — that is I cant afford to do too much of it at least this year when I have given away the book it takes too much time. I spent the whole of this morning on a story that has been in hand at least four years possibly eight by the writing and been rewritten half a dozen times at least and all I have done is changes in five places. Every word in one of these very short stories has to be weighed — and then weighed again after some weeks. I shall put these stories away for

now — I cannot tell if they are really finished until I can read them with a fresh eye.

(10 June 1952)

In the same letter, however, the strain of working under the conditions at Parks Road comes out again, despite the pleasure he felt in the short stories:

I need a holiday. I shall go to Stratford for 4 plays with friends. My trouble is that I ant used yet to taking *holidays* alone. Work is easy it fills its own time but not holiday pleasures.

After the stay at Stratford, he came home only to go off in the early autumn again, this time to Switzerland, where he stayed at the hotel to which he had taken Trudy the year before her death, when he could hope that she might recover.[3] He was considering another trip to the United States as well, to surround himself again with people.

At Parks Road he had begun to hold informal open house on Sunday evenings. This developed into a pleasant diversion for many authors, painters, university dons, and anyone else who wanted to come along. The Davins came often, and among others who might drop by were novelist Iris Murdoch, Gerald Wilde, or the Ostleres, both doctors working at Radcliffe Infirmary and living in a flat that overlooked Joyce's garden. Gordon Ostlere and Joyce had met through their mutual publisher, Michael Joseph, who was about to bring out Dr. Ostlere's first two books under the pen name of Richard Gordon.

There was plenty to drink at these get-togethers and a far more informal atmosphere than at most Oxford parties in those days and a lot less intellectual point-scoring. Joyce himself drank scarcely anything (a glass of wine was his usual, and sometimes a single sherry to last the evening*) but he could get as

---

* According to Ostlere (September, 1966), Joyce hardly ever sipped his sherry. When he was at the Ostleres' he would set his drink down somewhere without touching it. His host, seeing he was without a glass, would bring him another. This process continued throughout the party until, after everyone had left, the Ostleres would find a dozen glasses of sherry on window sills, buffets, and bookcase shelves, deposited absentmindedly by Joyce. They debated whether they should buy more glasses or simply stop inviting Joyce and decided on the former.

drunk on talk as other people could on several stiff whiskeys. Literature and painting were the usual subjects which delighted Joyce. To make sure nobody was left out of the conversation, he even had a special octagonal table built so all the guests could see each other.

If the talk trailed off into something that failed to keep his attention or if, as sometimes happened when his painter friends came by, the party got a bit rowdy, Joyce might disappear. One night, when his absence was noticed, someone went scouting and finally found him in the cellar, amusing himself with some old bound copies of *Punch*.[4] He let the parties run themselves and made his guests feel as much at ease as he could, so much so that as a friend recalled, "One felt if one wanted to stay all night, one could without being noticed." [5]

Joyce was particularly interested in the young writers who showed up at these Sunday evenings, just as he was interested in advancing the careers of young painters, and he was equally as liberal with his time and advice and money. Iris Murdoch, for instance, showed him the manuscript of her first novel, *Under the Net,* and they discussed it — and the novel form in general — at length, although in the end she found herself entirely in disagreement with his advice. As she said, "His ways were not my ways." [6]

An activity that cut into his time, at first pleasantly and then less and less so, was the constant string of interviews and requests for biographical information, which were necessary now that he was a well-known author. He was interviewed for a *Time* magazine cover story, an article in *John O'London's Weekly's* "Writers of Today" series, the BBC, and dozens of other magazines and newspapers. Going over the same material again and again was boring and time-consuming, so he welcomed fresh approaches, such as the *Paris Review* interview with John Burrows and Alex Hamilton or the request for information from his old friend Walter Allen, who was writing a pamphlet on Joyce and his novels for the British Council's "Writers and Their Work" series, because these had more depth than most interviews.

Reading his novels again for the Carfax prefaces and discussing his work and his background so many times made him increasingly conscious of the past. His short stories and articles written around this time are full of his past, for instance. These pieces include "Buying a Horse," which deals with his buying Satan, the pony he rode through much of the Cameroons Campaign; "A Child's Religion," telling of his old broken toy horse and his learning his first prayers from his mother; and "Christmas in Africa." There had been two autobiographical stories before this, "Bush River" and "Umaru," published respectively in 1945 and 1950. But this trickle of reminiscence now became a steady stream.

Along with the autobiographical stories, Joyce produced some others of a more upsetting nature. "Success Story," "Red Letter Day," and "Spring Song" are stories of pathetic old men who sit for lonely hours on park benches or pay unwanted visits to young relatives to whom they are a nuisance. It seems reasonable to conclude that Joyce either feared that this might happen to him or felt that it already was the case. Perhaps he had begun to see himself as old and alone.

So many of the people closest to him, those of his own generation, were dead: Trudy, Freddy Ogilvie, Flo Venables, Duncan MacGregor, and more. He saw less and less of those who still were living as their orbits, like his own, contracted. He felt the emptiness of the house and the loneliness and especially the absence of Trudy so that even a holiday was not a happy prospect since it would be made alone. Travel with friends and his escapes into the past in stories and articles were means of forgetting that, whatever acclaim he might have, there was no one with whom he really could share his life and his success.

Early in 1953 his son George, who had seemed so unlikely to live at the time of his birth and who had suffered so much illness as a boy, died of heart disease. George had been a brilliant student. He had won scholarships at Eton and Cambridge, and at the university he had earned a Double First in classics when he was just twenty. Then he had mastered Italian so well that the *Cambridge Review* said he easily could have become a university don.[7] Instead, he won a further scholarship and began post-

Q

graduate work on the medieval tradition of Alexander the Great, tracing that tradition's development as an indication of the changing temperament of those centuries. He won a Trinity fellowship with the resulting thesis.

Research for his paper led George to an interest in the Near East, particularly to Persian art and literature. The neglected state of Persian manuscripts and works of art made him decide that he would record as many of them as possible before they were destroyed by time and neglect. He studied the Persian language, the history of Persian art and literature, and photography, particularly color photography, the tools he would need in this grandly ambitious mission.

In 1949 he had made a brilliantly happy marriage to Meg Phipps, daughter of the British Ambassador to France, and they had a son now. Meg and George traveled to North Africa to do some preliminary work and had hoped to soon go to India (at the moment the state of hostility between Britain and the Mossadegh regime in Iran prevented an Iranian trip).

Now, at twenty-five, George was dead and all his plans and talent and knowledge, a brilliant start for a scholarly career, were gone.[8]

Joyce had taken great pleasure in George's successes, as he had in those of all his sons, and had been very pleased with the boy's marriage. In fact, he had visited George and Meg at their Cambridge home as often as he could. So his youngest son's death affected him deeply, although he kept most of what he felt to himself, as he always did with his sorrow. But he now became all the more restless, all the more eager to see new places and people rather than stay alone at 12 Parks Road.

He went down to London frequently to give lectures and radio talks, to make appearances on the BBC's "Brains Trust," or to see Michael and Tristram and their families. In London he often stayed overnight with Alan and Gwen Herbert in Hammersmith. He went to Dublin for the International PEN Congress in June and to the Glasgow PEN Club in January. In July he was in Edinburgh, where he was given an honorary Doctor of Laws degree, his first honorary degree. His state of mind is indicated by the fact that his speech of acceptance at Edinburgh (he spoke for all those who had received honorary degrees that day) was rambling and rather pointless, a disappointment to his listeners.[9] What should have been a triumph was slipshod and therefore spoiled.

Yet rather than taking stock and doing something to get out of his troubled state — taking a flat in Oxford, perhaps, so as to be out of the great lonely house, or moving to London, where two of his sons lived and where he would have far fewer memories around him — he took on even more work. He lectured on an average of once or twice a week and accepted an invitation to make a lecture tour of Sweden during the following year, 1953.

For a man of sixty-three who saw before him the completion of a trilogy of political novels, the launching of a trilogy of novels on religion, and a dozen and more other books as well, to be running all over the country giving lectures for only two or three pounds each time was utter folly. Writing a great quantity of articles made more sense, for they appeared in *Vogue, Esquire, Holiday,* and other high-paying magazines and earned the money he wanted to put aside for his sons and for George's widow and son. They made more sense than the glut of lectures, yet at the same time he was throwing away time and energy on them when he must have known he did not have much of either left.

Yet evidently they were not written just for the money. For in March, 1953, Joyce received a letter from T. R. Fyvel, the man who had edited the "Searchlight Books" series for which Joyce had written *The Case for African Freedom,* asking if he would be interested in writing a biography of Orde Wingate. Fyvel said that Mrs. Wingate, who was anxious that a biography of her husband be written, had asked especially that Joyce be approached to take on the job.[10]

It seems a perfect subject for Joyce to have tackled. Orde Wingate had made himself a legend, an unorthodox soldier in the line of Chinese Gordon and Lawrence of Arabia. When serving in the Sudan, he had spent a great deal of time exploring the desert in areas scarcely mapped. In Palestine he had led guerilla forces against the Arab revolt at the beginning of the war, and his work with the Zionists had made him one of their heroes and had almost gotten him court-martialed. And his famous force, "Wingate's Raiders," fighting a behind-the-lines campaign in Burma against the Japanese, had given him worldwide fame. All of this was climaxed by his death while leading the airborne force in the invasion of central Burma in March, 1944.

Wingate was the sort of brilliant and unorthodox person in whom Joyce delighted, a man of vision who plunged deeply into whatever world he had been quartered in. The combination of subject and author was a brilliant and natural one. There seems little doubt that the book would have been a success had it been written, as it could draw on the admirers of both men for its sales. Certainly it would have made Joyce as much money as his flood of articles and far more than his constant lectures. And of course he would have had the complete cooperation of Mrs. Wingate, since it was she who wanted him to do the book.

Yet Joyce refused.*

The challenge of a new form, biography, could not have been the deciding factor. After all, he had tried a dozen or more forms in his work: novels, short stories, autobiographical pieces, travel articles, essays on art and literature and religion, history, poetry, criticism, a book on political theory, talks and lectures, several plays and film scripts, and the children's stories he had made up for his sons and grandchildren.

Neither could it have been the time the book would have taken from his novels, for he was wasting weeks on his lectures. Nor could he have decided against the biography because facts would have precluded creativity and obscured his thesis, for he was handling factual materials in his articles.

Instead, the reason for his refusal seems to have been psychological: the job was too ambitious for his present restless state. The ordeal of sitting down and doing the research for the book, reading the papers and letters, writing to Wingate's friends and

* In 1959, Christopher Sykes' *Orde Wingate: A Biography* was published by World.

colleagues, and enduring the long, demanding job of writing the biography seem to have been beyond him. Instead he dashed off articles on the life of a typical Oxford don or the pleasures of Swiss holidaying, writing them on trains and in hotel rooms, cramming them into his schedule of lectures; he was writing from the saddle as he had done in Nigeria. Action seems to have been a substitute for life and a means of filling the void of his days.

He had published just one novel, *Prisoner of Grace,* since Trudy's death in 1949, one novel in three years, compared to the war years when he had published at the rate of nearly a novel a year (some of his very best work). He had been capable of nine books in seven years in addition to *Power in Men,* two versions of *The Case for African Freedom,* and *The Process of Real Freedom* — and these had been written while he was serving in the ARP and writing film scripts for the Ministry of Information.

One novel in three years indicated a tremendous falling-off in productivity for Joyce. Instead he occupied himself with busywork, a flurry of activity rather than the solid labor and craftsmanship he was capable of. The money it paid was more an excuse than a justification, for he was comfortably off and novels would pay more to his sons than the articles and talks ever would.

In refusing to face up to his real problem, his loneliness, and in feeling sorry for himself, as some of his stories indicate, Joyce was in danger of becoming the creature he had always scorned and feared, the man with a grievance.

50

NEW FRIENDS AND OLD

ONE OF Joyce's grievances was bureaucracy, especially that of
the Inland Revenue people. He was convinced that these income tax "blackguards" were out to get him. They were con-
spiring against him as they conspired against all creative
men.

There was the censorship plot, too, another windmill for
Joyce to fight. Of course any serious author sees any sort of censorship as a threat, and Joyce had opposed it for years. For instance, he had written to Trudy after they had been married a
year and a half,

> About books, I did not know you had been censored. I think it
> is unwise. Because of course the only reason was to prevent you
> knowing or wanting to know about sex matters. The result was
> that you thought a great deal more of 'em than you could have
> done otherwise. A locked room is fascinating to everyone, but
> especially a child — even though there be nothing inside. The
> act of generation is as natural and simple and commonplace as
> blowing one's nose or eating one's dinner, but such a mystery is
> made of its processes to children and young boys and girls that it
> has all the attraction of a deadly crime. It was first described to
> me by a boy at my private school. He described it all wrong and
> made it a disgusting secret. Luckily I was slow in physical devel-
> opment and forgot about it — at least did not worry about it.
> Noone ever told me about anything. You might say I should have
> guessed from the animals. As a matter of fact young people have

almost no power of drawing such parallels. All children should
be told simply and *plainly* in good unmistakable words (none of
the cowardly half terms — no child can understand 'em) before
the age of puberty. Of course they should also understand that
these matters are not subjects of every day conversation. As for
books of course they should read what they like — apart from
really dirty books. You'll find (as you suggest yourself) that they
will not care about the problem novel, and sex-situations will do
them no more harm than the Bible, even if they do read them,
which is not likely.

(18 November 1917)

He wanted no censorship even for the "really dirty books"
that he mentions above. Instead, as he said in an interview with
the Canadian critic Nathan Cohen, he hoped that whoever sold
such matter would not put it in his display windows and would
show some discretion in its distribution, keeping it out of the
hands of children at least.[1]

He had written often enough about sexual matters in his novels. Gulley Jimson, for example, was hardly a Calvinist, and
Charley of *Charley Is My Darling* masturbates and sleeps with
his Lizzie. There are more than half a dozen illegitimate children in the novels as well. Joyce had been criticized for this, and
some furious readers had written to him or to his publishers to
condemn his wickedness.[2] But of course he dealt with sex in a
way that offended only the cranks who would be insulted by the
pictures of bathing suits and underwear in mail-order cata-
logues.

But at this point in his life Joyce became obsessed with the
drive toward censorship. He felt that the cranks were gaining in
numbers, unity, and power to a frightening degree. There was
a strong attack on horror comic books by different parental and
religious groups, and Joyce saw this as the start of a general campaign of censorship that, if successful in this first area, would
grow in scope and power until it encompassed all written material and left no writer, good or bad, safe.

He began to fight against censorship, slipping mentions of it
into some of his articles, as for instance this paragraph in "A

Novelist and His Public," which was published in both British and American magazines:

> Half juvenile delinquency, that is, most of crime, starts in boredom. Boys and girls of twelve to eighteen have terrific energy and too little to do with it — they also have the most lively and eager imaginations, for which nothing is provided. If they show any imagination in dress for instance, like the Teddy boys, they are promptly marked down as rebels and nuisances. And respond very naturally by rebellion. If they show any interest in reading, it's odds on that the book will be labelled obscene and thrown on the fire. And then it is highly likely that they will stop reading altogether, and simply get on with gangsterism. Of course young criminals are found reading crime books, including detective stories. Just as parsons are discovered reading theology. But no one has asked whether the theory made the parson, or whether he reads it because he began with an interest in the subject.[3]

Joyce cut the last three sentences, because of their somewhat specious logic, out of the article. He was not always quite so discriminating.

Of course many of the points he raised were perfectly valid — in fact, almost all of them. And they were principles which he had believed in for years, as part of his faith in democracy, the necessity for each person to create his own world while at the same time making some attempt to prevent its impinging on the worlds which others created for themselves. He had always been against people whose only answer to any problem was, "There ought to be a law." For they lacked understanding of and, even more, respect for, their fellows.

He put the case against them clearly in his essay "Anti-Americanism, Anti-Britishism":

> Censorship in the Press of anything but libel is not only treachery to the very principles of democracy but a folly. Like all censorship, it does very much more harm than good. It conceals not only the facts of life, but it deceives a great many people, especially people in authority, about the nature of life, and of people. It is based ultimately on lack of faith. Its argument is, "Only I,

and people like me, middle-aged people who have seen everything and learnt everything, know what ought to be told to other people." They usually think of other people as the "masses," the "mob". And this policy of concealment not only seems successful, but it flatters the people who carry it out. Nothing can beat the self-satisfaction of the judge who is quite sure that the public must be prevented from reading the book which he has described as obscene because it offends his own prejudices. He is confident, of course, that it has done him no harm, but he is quite sure it will do the "public" harm. And he does not think of himself as a conceited person but merely a wise, experienced one.[4]

In several of the pieces, particularly in the flurry of letters he sent to the newspapers, there was a much more shrill note, one that had been absent from his work before this.

Part of the sharpness in the letters, where it was most pronounced, can be explained simply by the fact that these *were* letters rather than worked-over articles. Yet they were meant for print and Joyce never had let anything which was meant for publication leave his hands without much revision. So either he had dashed them off and dumped them in the postbox unrevised or he had lost the sense of proportion that was so important to him.

Besides the shrillness in much of his anti-censorship writings (he spoke often of "the censorship plot"), its sheer volume indicates an obsession. Gulley Jimson in *The Horse's Mouth* always reminds himself that he must not give way to anger. It is bad for his blood pressure and accomplishes nothing but self-harm. And Cock Jarvis reminds himself time and time again that he must not let go, he must not attack his enemies and let them have the satisfaction of knowing they have wounded him; if he attacked them he would be digging his own grave, but if he ignored them or, even better, forgave them, they would be impotent. But Joyce seemed to have forgotten this. He seemed to give way to an obsession and the only one hurt was himself. Instead of a serious novelist, he was in danger of becoming a chronic writer of letters to the editor.

Even trivialities seemed to bother him. For instance, when his telephone number of thirty years was changed, he felt it as a grievance. And he became extremely upset at a photograph of him which appeared on the dust jacket of one of his novels in the United States. He wrote to Michael Joseph,

> If you do see Cass in New York you can tell him that that horrible picture of me on the Harper's jacket has now got loose in Sweden. I thought I didn't care what the photographers did to me, but that picture by R—— did get under my skin. I did not mind coming out a lunatic by P——, but I rather hated the greasy ponce — a pansy ponce — that Harper's chose for the jacket.
>
> (11 January 1953)

Joyce had his vanities, but he had never made such a public issue of them before as in this letter. As for his other grievances, perhaps they were legitimate, but five or ten years before he would have let them rest rather than broadcast them as he was now doing. He had lost the reserve and tranquility that he had once possessed. Instead he was degenerating into the state of that young man at the captain's table of the *Burutu* who raged, "Are you trying to be rude to me, P——, because if you are, I'll push your face through the back of your neck and bloody quick, too!"

The American tour in the fall of 1953 got him out of an increasingly unhappy situation. It should have been a wearing trip, as it lasted from September through December and consisted of speech after speech, dozens of interviews, and travel that took him through the entire United States — East, Midwest, West Coast, the South. Yet Joyce thrived on the activity and the company, getting back all his good spirits.

Most of the talks this time were to university students, an audience he preferred to all others. He delighted in a group that was young, responsive, eager to learn and ready to argue, and they reacted with equal warmth to him. At the University of Chicago, for instance, after Joyce finished his talk the students crowded around him on the stage to ask questions, and the atmosphere was so friendly and informal that they automatically addressed him as "Joyce," as if he were a friend and an equal rather than an eminent foreign author in his sixties.[5] He loved this kind of response and was immensely stimulated by it.

Between legs of the tour Joyce worked at the Harper offices or relaxed at Edith Haggard's* apartment, where he liked to stretch out on the chaise longue and either talk or catnap. One afternoon Mrs. Haggard came home to find him napping and asked him why he was there when he had an engagement scheduled. He had forgotten, he told her. But didn't he have the schedule that had been made out for him? "Oh," he said, "I lost that weeks ago." Perhaps because he knew he could be exasperating or perhaps simply because he enjoyed puttering around, Joyce did some odd jobs at Mrs. Haggard's apartment. For instance, once when she was preparing for a small party and he was supposed to be sitting in the living room, he was prowling about and then called to her in the kitchen, "If you've got a screwdriver I'll fix the knobs on this chest." [6] He did and all of them but one still were tight when I covertly tried them in 1964.

In the middle of Joyce's tour in November, the second volume of his political trilogy, *Except the Lord,* was published in Britain and America. Joyce signed all the royalties over to his sons and Meg Cary, George's widow, as he had with *Prisoner of Grace* a year before. Now, in the midst of all the traveling and lecturing and partying, he began work on the third volume, *Not Honour More.*

Prisoner of Grace was the story of Nina Nimmo/Latter, told by herself, and the two men in her life, her soldier cousin and lover Jim Latter and her politician husband Chester Nimmo. In many ways Nina resembles Sara Monday of the first trilogy, the homemaker, devoting her life to the happiness of others, a task made deeply complex because of the quite different needs of her two men.

Except the Lord was Chester Nimmo's story of his childhood and youth as the son of an extremely poor miner, a childhood steeped in poverty and evangelicalism, an attempt on Joyce's part to show the protestant, evangelical background from which

* Mrs. Haggard was with the New York office of Curtis Brown.

radical British politics sprang. It was an attempt deeply misunderstood by many of his readers, even those who knew him and his work well; they could not make the link between the young and the mature Nimmo.

Not Honour More, the book Joyce now began, was Jim Latter's story. Jim, as a soldier, is a man who lives by rules and who wants others to do the same. The remedy for all human ills, he feels, is more rigidly enforced rules, legislation, more police, more control. He is an advocate of the police state and, although he fails to realize it, of fascism.

This third novel of the trilogy allowed Joyce to express almost all his strong feelings about the type of person who wants society to be rigidly controlled by laws, police, and power, the sort of man who advocates laws of censorship, for instance. It was a far healthier and more fruitful channel for his feelings than the letters to the newspapers. It transformed his grievance into art and gave him a sense of perspective and balance.

This new perspective is revealed in his portrayal of Jim Latter, who is not a villain but only a pathetic, crude, self-deceiving man. While the reader disagrees entirely with Jim, at the same time he is compelled to understand him. Walter Allen, who had read many of Joyce's novels for Michael Joseph, gave the treatment of Jim Latter high praise in his report on the book:

> I don't want to attempt to "place" this novel in relation to Cary's work as a whole. But taken together with *Except the Lord,* for me it is triumphant proof that its author is still growing, developing, experimenting, is still within the context of his view of life, unpredictable. *Except the Lord* had an absurdly silly press. It was evidence, I thought, that reviewers as a body were a long way behind Cary, still stuck somewhere about *The Horse's Mouth.* I suspect they will never quite catch up, that he will always be ahead, will always, with every successive book he writes, be compelling them to revise their opinions on his work as a whole. And if that is not being alive and creative I don't know what is.[7]

But the American tour did not get the restlessness out of

Joyce's system nor did the fact that he was well into the third volume of the trilogy. If 1953 had been chopped up with travel, lectures, and articles, 1954 was even worse. In March he went on a lecture tour of Italy; in June and July he toured West Germany and Berlin, speaking mainly at universities; in October he was in Paris; in November and December he was lecturing in Sweden, Finland, and Denmark. He was away on lecture tours almost half the year instead of finishing *Not Honour More.*

He seemed happy and well enough, but Enid Starkie, who met him in Paris in October, thought that he looked tired and that his right leg seemed to drag when he walked.[8] Evidently Joyce felt worse than he looked, because he went for a doctor's examination on his return to Oxford, but nothing of significance was noticed.

He went to Stratford as usual in September, 1954, this time with the John Fischers, who were in England for a visit. There had also been another significant visitor that year, in June.

For some time Joyce had been corresponding with John Middleton Murry. They had not seen each other or been in touch at all, except through each other's books, for more than forty years. Joyce, turning back to the past in his writings, now revived it in his exchange of letters with his old friend, and finally they arranged to meet. Joyce planned a dinner for Murry and his fourth wife, Mary, and invited Lord David Cecil and his wife, his sister-in-law Lady Mary Ogilvie, and the Dan Davins.

It was a gala evening, the two men getting on well despite all the years between this and their last meeting in 1912. Both had followed their particular stars, Joyce's the more steady one, and both had achieved a good measure of success. Murry's success — at least his literary success — had come earlier in his career. He had been a well-known writer and literary figure when Joyce still was trying to learn how to write in his ramshackle bungalow at Kaiama. Murry had been husband to Katherine Mansfield, friend to D. H. Lawrence, acquainted with the luminaries of Bloomsbury, and had published book after book when Joyce was throwing his manuscripts in the fire in despair. But while Joyce pushed steadily ahead with his writing, Murry had moved away from literature into politics, Christian communism, and pacifism, following this cause and that, losing touch, and being repudiated by many of his early admirers.

Now Joyce was a respected novelist, published and written about around the world, and Murry contrasted Joyce's position with his own. Joyce had been happily married and had raised four sons, and his reputation seemed to be growing even yet, while Murry had been married four times, the first three times unhappily, and his reputation was largely a thing of the past.

As one of the guests at the reunion dinner recalled, "Murry seemed a victim of the literary wars of the '20's and '30's. . . . It was a surprise to him that Joyce was the real genius. He [Murry] had a kind of battered dignity all the same." [9]

Then, finally, the evening came to an end and the Murrys returned to the Mitre Hotel, Murry having to be supported by one of the other guests, since in the convivial atmosphere he had drunk more than he thought. [10] Next morning the Murrys left Oxford. The two men had enjoyed their meeting but realized that, except for their memories, they had nothing in common. Their correspondence ebbed and they did not meet again.

Murry and his wife remarked to each other on the drive home how well Joyce looked, and how young, too. [11]

Nearly six months later, on the morning of January 16, 1955, Joyce, bound for a lecture tour of Greece and Cyprus, boarded a plane at London airport. There was a good deal of fog so the takeoff had to be based only on instruments. However, confused by the fog, the pilot taxied down the wrong runway. He headed his airplane down an old strip no longer in use, increasing speed; the wheels swished faster and faster along the wet pavement, and the plane was traveling at eighty miles an hour. Suddenly it jerked to one side, went into a violent swerve, and smashed into a steel barrier. Two of its four engines flew into the air, wrenched from the wings, and the remaining propellers snapped like willow twigs. The landing gear collapsed and the hulk of the plane skidded off the runway, coming to a stop on the wet ground. The fuel tanks, bursting open, spewed fuel over the wrecked plane. But it was kerosene and did not catch fire.

Ambulances, fire engines, and other emergency vehicles roared down the runway to the kerosene-drenched hulk. All passengers were removed to safety and none, it turned out, was injured, just badly shaken. The only victim was the pilot, who suffered back injuries.

Joyce, after he had been interviewed by reporters who crowded around the passengers in the terminal building, boarded the next flight to Greece, quite ready to begin his lecture tour as if nothing had happened, looking a bit tired but nothing more. Again it seemed he had been right when he had told Trudy, "I can't help seeing that a special Luck follows me everywhere," and when, after being knocked down by the runaway horse while on his way to The Glade in 1918, he had commented, "But I was born to escape this sort of thing — I shall not die a violent death. My insurance money will be wasted." He had escaped violent death at the explosion at Antivari, at the assault on Mount Mora, in the episode near The Glade, and now in the wreck of the aircraft.

Then, on his return from Greece, Joyce went to his doctor, feeling less than his best. After examining him, the doctor had him enter the hospital for a series of tests.[12]

51

SECOND TRILOGY

CARY'S SECOND TRILOGY, the political novels, does not succeed as well as his first as a unified work. The parts do not mesh entirely, the overall theme comes across less clearly, the chronology is too vast (*Except the Lord* is set mainly in the 1860's and 1870's, while *Not Honour More* is set in the 1920's), but most important is the problem of making Jim Latter and Chester Nimmo sympathetic characters.

Cary chose to concentrate on a fundamental issue: the ordinary person's prejudice against politicians who tell lies and his own prejudice against those whose answer to every political and moral crisis is, "There ought to be a law!"

He saw the dilemma of politicians as one of the key problems of democracy: if a politician tells the *whole* truth, he can do nothing; yet if he lies for the public good, he is denounced as a crook and demagogue. In the preface to *Prisoner of Grace* Cary comments,

[Sir Stafford] Cripps [Chancellor of the Exchequer under Prime Minister Clement Attlee] was one of the honestest men who ever went into politics, but when he was asked if it was proposed to devalue sterling, he answered that there was no immediate intention to do so. At that moment it was already arranged to devalue sterling within a few days.

Technically he did not tell a lie, but this is not the point, the point is that he had to deceive. Of course any mother will lie to a nervous child about the doctor or the dentist. She will say that a dangerous painful operation will prove a trifle, that the dentist won't hurt. She has to do so for the child's good.[1]

The point, Cary indicates, is that political morality, like any other morality, is not a matter of black and white. As the Cripps example shows, *some* means justify *some* ends, for in deceiving the reporters he prevented a panic, a coup on the part of currency speculators. The only ones he hurt were those who were prevented from making money at the nation's expense. On the other hand, Joyce gave a picture in *The Moonlight* of means which could not be justified by their ends.

In that novel, young Beal, the defender of the old-fashioned scientist Groom, is capable only of abstract and limited thought. One of his ideals is the Communist regime in Russia; he admires how it gets things done. When the stationmaster of a Russian town said that a train could not reach its destination on time, Beal recalls, he was shot. And the train kept its schedule. Beal thinks this great fun and excellent politics. The fact that a human being — a man with hopes, ideals, a family, who was only doing his best — was killed does not bother him because he sees the man as an abstraction. Beal is a moral failure because he has no imagination, and imagination is necessary to be sympathetic.

So the question is this:

> . . . how does a real politician, the handler, the manager of people, who is also a man of principle, keep his principles? How far do his ends justify his means? [2]

In other words, how can a politician achieve that elusive balance between morality and practicality? This is the trilogy's subject, yet it was obscure for many readers.

Prisoner of Grace

As in his first trilogy, Cary begins with the woman's point of view, Nina Nimmo/Latter's account of her relations with her two husbands, written to defend the first of them, Chester Nimmo. But what she says of Nimmo might also apply to Jim Latter:

> I am writing this book because I understand that "revelations" are soon to appear about that great man who was once my husband, attacking his character, and my own. And I am afraid that they will be believed simply because nowadays everyone believes the worst of a famous man. The greater his name, the worse the stories.[3]

For both her husbands were public men.

As Chester Nimmo's wife she is cast in the role of Caesar's wife, who must at least *seem* to lead an exemplary life. The same is true when she becomes Jim Latter's wife. And since both men are very religious, she also has the difficult job of justifying their lapses to herself and of persuading them they have not lapsed. As a wife, she has to support their rationalizations of their own actions because, as religious *and* public men, they cannot help but contradict themselves.

This is especially true of Nimmo. "Render unto Caesar that which is Caesar's, and unto God that which is God's" seems a simple creed, but it is extremely hard to obey, since the distinction between these two obligations is extremely hazy.

In making life possible for her two men, Nina risks making it impossible for herself and finally, of course, she is murdered by one of them. So in more than one sense she is a prisoner of grace. She is a prisoner of the sorts of grace represented by Nimmo and Latter; she is a prisoner of the graceful life she must lead as Nimmo's wife; she is a prisoner of her own state of grace as it concerns both men, for she *must* believe in them if she is to remain alive, sane, and functioning. She also is a prisoner of Aunt Latter's grace, absolute belief in Liberal politics and her conviction about what constitutes Nina's best interests. Thus Nina is forced into a life which allows no escape.

The primary state of grace to which she must cling is total belief in Nimmo, for if she does not believe in him, she is lost and her entire life will become meaningless. Her first crisis of belief comes at the start of Chapter 14, fairly early in the 126-chapter novel, soon after her marriage to Nimmo:

And these speeches, in Chester's "thrilling" voice, had a very strange effect on my nerves. . . . Chester's voice was one of his great gifts — it made him a power. And now when his voice shook, I felt myself shaking all through my body . . . so that I wanted to scream, "Stop, stop!" I would have done anything to stop this frightful quivering which seemed to shake my ideas and self-control to pieces. It seemed that I was two women, one of them quite furious still and watchful of every move by this cunning enemy, and one of them so close and sympathetic to him that she felt all his feelings like her own. . . . It seemed that I was being torn apart . . . yet when I felt his hand tremble as well as his voice this love seemed to fly all through me, so that I was all a tension of anger and pity at the same time, and all my arguments seemed to fall apart into dry dusty fragments which were quite contemptible.[4]

Nina is caught in the throes of what is essentially a religious conversion, and her description of it may be compared with spiritual phenomena described in William James's *The Varieties of Religious Experience*. In fact, her conversion is a condensed form of the one John Bunyan delineates in *Grace Abounding to the Chief of Sinners* (Bunyan was central to the first trilogy; his hymn "To Be a Pilgrim" provided that work's central theme). There is a strong element of sexuality in her religious conversion, just as there was in Aissa's.

Nina learns the power of the human voice and the power of the word from Nimmo. His thesis, he says, is, "A speech should never instruct; it should rouse people up." [5] This is the way of the demagogue, but it also is the way of the preacher, the author, and, for that matter, the statesman. Lincoln's Gettysburg Address, Churchill's pledge of "blood, sweat, toil and tears," and Roosevelt's "We have nothing to fear but fear itself" were all appeals to the people's emotions and not to their rationality.

So again Cary offers a complex truth in place of an oversimplified one. It is not the use of words which is evil. It is the purpose behind them and the results that ensue that are good or evil. One must ask, "This man has tremendous force, but what does he mean to do with this force? Who will it help and who will it harm? And what sort of man is he, anyway? What does he want?" Each case must be judged on its own merits, and this requires analysis and thought rather than prejudice.

Nina, however, is in no position to analyze Nimmo. She is too caught up in emotions and events. She is too close to him. She is not an analytical person; she reacts on an emotional level. And her emotions only come into harmony through Nimmo. Even then there is conflict because of her feelings for Jim and her children.

This conflict brings up another of the novel's themes, the politics of marriage. In his preface and elsewhere Cary argues that marriage is a political matter, made more complex by the presence of children and many in-laws. Anyone who grew up in a large family knows this is true. Cary carries it to an extreme in Nina's account of her marriage to Nimmo:

> All this time there was between Chester and myself a "situation." I mean, an unusual tension. There is, I suppose, always a "situation" between husband and wife . . . and "relations" which need the equivalent of "understandings" and "spheres of influence." . . . But with old married people who have a good "understanding," the spheres of influence are so well marked out that they can be very free with each other and argue quite indignantly and have "grave crises" without the least danger of an "incident." They are really quite comfortable with each other all the time, and their "situation" can only "deteriorate" if they show themselves "ill-disposed" or, of course, form a new "alignment." [6]

In this "politics of marriage," Nina serves as buffer, sustainer, and compromiser, a role she finds nearly impossible not only in itself but because it causes both Nimmo and Latter to suspect her. Neither man trusts her, finally. But that is the nature of her role and she is condemned to it. Her only way out is death. The final injustice for Nina is that she must die, like Sara Monday, at the hands of one of the men she protects.

*

Except the Lord

Chester Nimmo's memoirs of his childhood and youth are a great departure for Cary. They suggest John Bunyan, and Charles Dickens in his tragic and comic veins. The vigil the village adventists keep, awaiting the Second Coming and the world's end, suggests this blend. Having waited through the night, some of them in ordinary work clothes, some in their best, others in homemade heavenly roles, they pray and sing as the dawn approaches. Suddenly, Nimmo says,

a great sword of fiery light pierced through the hollow air.

The effect upon our congregation was incredible. I can still remember that sensation of mingled terror and elation which seemed, as they say, to turn my bones to water. . . . Several of our party fell on their knees, and one woman gave a loud sob. As that great sword flashed still higher to the very dome of the sky, our hymn ceased of itself and the minister shouted, "On our knees." But we were already on our knees — our legs had failed beneath us.[7]

But the "sword of fiery light" proves to be only a combination of the rising sun and the cloud formations. Nevertheless the minister prays on, and the congregation remains. As Nimmo says,

I do not know how long we knelt and how long the minister prayed. It was my father who first rose from his knees and lifted us to our feet. I know Ruth was so stiff and cold that she nearly fell, and we had to rub her legs to bring back the circulation. She fell asleep as soon as we put her back into the cart.[8]

These shabby few on Black Man Tor, believing that Christ would appear at this exact time and place (they had worked this out by mathematics) and that they alone of all the world's people are to be saved, are comic, pathetic, foolish, and inspired all at the same time. It is as if Shakespeare's rustics of *A Midsummer Night's Dream* had decided to act out the story of Moses and the Hebrew Children.

Their futile vigil can be looked at from a Marxist viewpoint: they are God addicts, fed on the opiate of religion and blinded

to their real needs and rights in this world. But such an interpretation would alter the meaning of the whole novel. Nimmo
attempts to deal with this Marxist sort of attack and other assaults on him when he says,

> My biographers are fond of dividing my life into three periods
> — that of the agitator, the preacher and the statesman, each of
> which, they say, led naturally to the next and contained all the
> former, so that they were rather chapters in a complete story than
> episodes in a broken career. The agitator who learnt the art of
> rabble-rousing from his father passed naturally into the revivalist
> preacher, the preacher with his extreme Protestant and dissenting
> creed naturally opposed himself to privilege and entered politics
> to achieve his ideal of equality. And then again he used the meth-
> ods of the demagogue. They quote my early speeches to show that
> I was one of the first "to dangle before the mob the offer of some-
> thing for nothing, pensions and doles, buying their votes with
> subsidies which must in the end ruin the national economy and
> confound poor and rich, industrious and lazy, the parasite and
> the worker, in one common disaster." [9]

He goes on to quote from an early letter to his wife in which he
had written,

> True religion centres in the family — for the Protestant, priest-
> hood resides in every parent responsible for a child's upbringing.
> That is why we are bound to stand for any state policy that can
> secure the family unit as a unit. For it is only in family life that
> the freedom and dignity of a responsible citizen accords with his
> religious duty, and who shall say that one, who knows the burden
> of authority over helpless dependants, is thereby weakened in re-
> sponsibility towards the state that is a father to its people. [10]

As Nimmo says, the labor agitator gave birth to the radical
preacher, and both radical preacher and labor agitator gave
birth to the Radical Liberal politician. What he does not ex-
plicitly state, but which the novel proves, is that at the core of all
three was the dissenting Christianity of his father, which conditioned Chester Nimmo's whole life. Even when he lost his faith
he acted on it, and his work in the unions (first the farm labor-

ers' union, then the dockers') was basically Christian work. Nimmo shows that the British unions were essentially Christian and that their early union cards were heavy with Biblical quotations.

In this novel Cary gets at the basic difference between British and European labor movements. British unions and unionists in general were based on Nonconformist Christianity, essentially groups that grew from the ground up. European unions and their consequent political parties often represented ideological structures imposed on the workers by intellectuals.

Cary contrasts the British unionists with the Europeanized Dr. Dolling:

> Born in France, son of a celebrated Greek scholar; became a student of philosophy; imprisoned by the Bourbons for an attack on the Press laws; released by the revolution of 1830, but at once arrested again by the agents of Louis Philippe; escaped to Germany, he took part in the revolution of '48 when for a short time he was Minister of Public Instruction at Hesse; seriously wounded in the suppression of their free government, he was deported to France; imprisoned by Napoleon for two years, and then exiled.[11]

There are three, perhaps four, clues in this passage to Dolling and the ideas he represents. One, he is an alien, an Englishman born in France among people and language not his own, and, to go even further, he takes part in the revolution of 1848, where he is even more alien. Two, he is a philosopher, a student of abstract systems. Three, he is the son of a scholar of Greek, a dead language. Finally, his background is completely bourgeois. In contrast, Nimmo is the laboring son of a farm worker and is steeped in his corner of England and its working class. He enters the union movement because he has experienced in himself and in his family the great economic ills of his time.

When the fourteen-year-old Nimmo hesitantly approaches the old revolutionary Dolling and finds himself lionized, he is amazed. However benign he seems, Dolling represents abstract thinking at its worst. He is an ideologue, cut off from human life, his perception flawed; he can reason only in terms of "the masses," because he is unable to conceive of, much less cope with, an individual human being.

Pring is another who thinks in ideological terms. He is "a convinced and consistent Marxist" who disdains the "muddle-heads" such as Nimmo's father or the members of the tin-mining union. It is Pring who orders that reluctant strikers be beaten up and their homes destroyed. The truth is that the strikers weaken in their resolve only when they see that their families are starving. Since individuals mean so little to Pring and he can destroy his strikers, he is striking for "The Cause," the abstraction.

Contrasted to Pring and Dolling are Chester Nimmo's father, who sacrifices peace, prosperity, and health for the tin miners and for his pastorate, and Chester's sister Georgina, who gives up freedom, marriage, a proper home of her own, and finally her life for her father and her brothers and sisters. They are concerned with individual *people,* not causes. They sacrifice themselves for others. And it is they whom Chester Nimmo finally realizes he must follow.

Believing in human beings and their welfare is much more difficult than believing in an abstract ideology, because the believer has no certain, fixed star to follow. He must solve each question as it comes up, basing his decisions partially on precedents, partially on the circumstances peculiar to each case. In assuming this responsibility, Nimmo follows the tradition of British political and legal thought, which has its basis in Common Law rather than in a fixed, formal constitution. And the tradition has its source in society, for Nimmo explains how he learned politics in the fabric of village life, where people lived so cheek by jowl that they had to learn the techniques of compromise and lobbying. As he says,

We had, too, our proportion, not large but momentous, among no more than two hundred persons living in closer quarters than many gaols, of drunkards, queer fish, touchy and quarrelsome people looking, as it is said, for trouble. And some degree of quiet and decency could only be maintained by a reciprocity of obligation and reprisal, a balance of powers in which true charity and fellow-feeling, conscience and self-respect — in short, Christian tradition and example, more or less recognized as such, was mingled with what I must call real politics, a system established over years of trial and error.[12]

He goes on to show how the community deals with the drunkard who lives next door to the Nimmos and delights in shouting blasphemies and obscenities all during Mr. Nimmo's Sunday religious services. The people's behavior is a vivid instance of how an issue may be dealt with in terms of practical, concrete politics.

Some people have complained that they can find no real connection between the young Chester Nimmo of *Except the Lord* and the middle-aged and then elderly politician of *Prisoner of Grace* and *Not Honour More*. The former, they say, is a sincere and dedicated young man; the latter is just a speechifying crook. But the elderly Nimmo, speechifying crook or not, still contains within him the idealistic young man. For that matter, the young man, who knows the *absolute necessity* of compromise in his household and his village, is learning the art of politics. He is learning, in fact, that it *is* an art that requires a subtle touch, the appreciation of the materials with which one is working, an understanding of what can be done with them, and a respect for intuition. For he knows that an attempt to solve political issues with rigid, abstract ideologies will end in failure.

Not Honour More

Jim Latter is the politician with laws and a gun, the absolutist run amuck.

The title of his novel of course is taken from "To Lucasta, On Going to the Wars," by Richard Lovelace (whom Jim always calls Colonel Lovelace):

> Tell me not, Sweet, I am unkind,
> That from the nunnery

> Of thy chaste breast and quiet mind
>   To war and arms I fly.
>
> True, a new mistress now I chase,
>   The first foe in the field;
> And with a stronger faith embrace
>   A sword, a horse, a shield.
>
> Yet this inconstancy is such
>   As you, too, shall adore;
> I could not love you, Dear, so much,
>   Loved I not honour more.

Jim makes the poem his motto, but he first strips it of all tenderness and love, distorting it terribly in the process.

But this is Jim's way. He is a brute and a liar, who, for all his ranting on and on about the lying politicians, the wordmongers and deceivers who run the country and who should be put out of office, cannot be trusted to tell the same story twice.

It is difficult to understand how many readers misinterpreted the book and sympathized with Jim as an honest man who has been driven to desperate measures; even more incomprehensible is that some took him for Cary's spokesman and assumed that his ideas were Cary's own. Nina, in *Prisoner of Grace,* prefigures Jim's capacity to hide the truth from himself when he wants or needs to (Nimmo does the same).

Jim gives himself away very early in the novel. He tells the story of his seduction of Nina three times, in Chapters 2, 12, and 13. In the Chapter 2 version, he torments Nina and drives her to such distraction that she agrees in desperation to have sex with him in order to find peace: he regards her as his victim. In Chapter 12 she is in a petulant mood and simply lets him have her to shush him: she acts like a slut. In Chapter 13 she practically seduces him, then ruins the act for him, leaving it without meaning or impact; she is almost sadistic, and he is *her* victim. It seems obvious from this that Cary wants it clearly understood that Jim is a liar. Not that he is meant as a hypocrite; he cannot help himself, and his talk of lying politicians is not cant but the sincere protesting of a sick mind.

For Jim is warped. Emotionally, he is still a child with the child's need for absolutes and a child's, or at least an adolescent's, view that all suggestions that life is complex and its problems cannot be solved in terms of yes and no are so much weaseling. Yet, like a child, he can lie and not even know it. All of this is shown in his distorting of Lovelace's poem and the telling and retelling of how he seduced (or was seduced by) Nina. Of course he wants no truck with lawyers, because a good one could twist Jim around his finger and tear him to pieces — not because the lawyer is a finagler but because Jim cannot tell the truth and cannot help contradicting himself.

And he is a fascist. His political feelings are more evident than his lying and are substantiated by Cary's explicit statement about him:

> Now the third book, which is causing all the fuss, came out this year and it is quite different. It is the statement of a man who believes in authority. He doesn't call himself a fascist and he hates fascism but he has a fascist mind; he has been a soldier and he asks why a country can't be run like a good regiment, by men who believe in duty and discipline and who don't grab all the money they can find for themselves. He says: "Why all this rottenness and corruption and lies which you get in a democracy?" He is a perfectly honest man and he is not a cruel man. He is just like those people who hate drink, which is a real evil, and who say why don't we stop it by law. That is to say people — they're people who want to make the world good by law. The only way is by education and by trusting them and giving them a sense of responsibility as free men to behave like good citizens and they won't have a sense of responsibility if you push them around by law.[13]

Actually, Cary is far easier on Jim here than he needed to be and much kindlier than he obviously was when he wrote the book. For not only is Jim a fascist and a liar, but he possesses other characteristics that Cary disliked.

For instance, in his role in Nigeria, where, as a political officer in Lugaland (obviously Cary was having fun with the name of his old governor, Lord Lugard), Jim is opposed to any changes to the economy or society. He is a noble-savage-worshipper. But his noble savages betray him. When several are brought to London in connection with Jim's campaign to prevent the opening up of Lugaland, they abandon Jim's cause and turn instead to those people who will invest in their country or bring education to their people, in fact all those whom Jim would keep out. The nasty brutes do not want to live in picturesque squalor and starve in heroic attitudes.

Jim's old-fashioned clothes that shock Nina when he comes home on leave during World War I, the clothes of an Edwardian dandy ten years out of date, reflect his childish conservatism. He is one of those who believe that all change is decadence, that even the new clothing styles are signs of social decay against which he must fight.

His utter disgust for those who are interested in making money is ironic, because Jim has been supported all his life. He cannot handle money. He ruins himself with debt, including huge gambling losses, and his family and Nimmo bail him out and set him on his feet again and again. Time after time he is saved by others. His house is an inheritance from the same brother whom he has despised. And during the 1920's it is Nimmo, through gifts to Nina, who keeps Jim fed and clothed.

Finally, there is his murder of Nina. This butchery is Jim's act of revenge because she has proved "unfaithful" to him. She has committed adultery. He fails to comprehend (or refuses to) that Nina has done this for him, in part, for her motives are fearfully complex. She allowed Nimmo to possess her because of his great need (Nimmo's great sexual drive, even in his seventies, is simply one manifestation of his drive for power), because the act prevents a real showdown, because it allows her to support Jim, and, among still more reasons, because her whole life is dedicated to giving. But Jim, with his narrow, childish mind, can see it only in the narrow terms of adultery, a breach of faith.

But Jim cannot admit that he is acting out of insane jealousy. He speaks of the act as an "execution." He ritualizes it into a symbolic protest against all the corruption he sees around him, corruption which is oozing out to smother the world with its putrefaction. He tries to make this paranoid murder an act of nobility. He goes on at length about "this great duty laid on me by a cruel fate":

I say I never loved this sweet woman so much as now when I knew she had to die. Because of the rottenness. Because of the corruption. Because all loyalty was a laugh and there was no more trust. Because marriage was turned into a skin game out of a nice time by safety first. Because of the word made dirt by hypocrites and cowards. Because there was no truth or justice anywhere any more. Because of the grabbers and tapeworms who were sucking the soul out of England.[14]

He draws out the moment of her death, savoring it, really, while at the same time trying to make it signify until

At last we heard a car in the drive. Grant coming back for his master [Nimmo, who is sitting, dead of a heart attack, on the toilet in the servants' bathroom]. I said we could not wait any more and did she want to pray. She knelt down but said she could not pray, she did not think it would help. But would I forgive her, because she had truly loved me.

I said it was for her to forgive me and I finished the thing in one stroke. She fell at once and did not struggle at all.[15]

Jim Latter's attempt to ritualize his murder of Nina, whom he professes to love, recalls the ending of *Mister Johnson*. There too Rudbeck had tried to ritualize his killing of Johnson. He had tried to turn Johnson into a thing, an inanimate object, equivalent to so many tins of jam and bags of sixpences, just as Jim Latter tries to turn his wife into a symbol of the corruption of the modern world. But Rudbeck is too big a man to go through with it; he accepts guilt and love, so he shoots Johnson and will pay the penalty for it. Jim Latter feels little guilt and is incapable of feeling love (the best he can feel is lust or possessiveness). While Rudbeck quietly accepts his fate, Jim keeps saying, "I don't care if they hang me," vaunting his bravery until it is seen for what it is: bravado and cant. Rudbeck acts out of love; Jim acts out of rage, brutality, and paranoia.

That so many readers, among them some usually perceptive critics, were deceived by Jim's story and sympathized with him, is an ironic tribute to Cary's art, for he has played Jim's role so well that his own feelings are almost totally disguised, and unless the reader looks carefully at the clues, he may be completely fooled.

Not that Cary meant to deceive; he felt that readers would be able to see through Jim. He was quite disturbed that they did not; he was even more disturbed that consequently they completely misunderstood the crucial point of the trilogy. As he said in a broadcast,

> People are accusing me of saying in a novel that I have just written that politicians have to be crooks, especially politicians in a democracy. Now I am very glad of the chance in this broadcast to deny this because actually it is just the opposite that I believe.

He clarifies his view of Nimmo in this same broadcast:

> Nimmo is meant to be like a real man with real thoughts. He often deceives himself about his own motives and that is pretty common among men of his type, that is to say men of action — spellbinders. They don't go in very much for self-criticism; they're too active; they are too interested in the world.[16]

Unless Jim Latter is understood and seen as Cary intended, Nimmo and Nina cannot be seen clearly, and the whole trilogy collapses into contradiction. If it fails as a unified work, it is not on this ground.

52

A NARROWING WORLD

JOYCE'S ILLNESS was not immediately diagnosed. He was in and out of doctors' examination rooms and hospitals in Oxford, Bristol, and London all through the spring and summer of 1955.

He had planned another trip to the United States that autumn, when he was to have taken part in a symposium at the Institute of Contemporary Arts in Washington, D.C., together with Dame Edith Sitwell and her brother Osbert, Stephen Spender, T. S. Eliot, Elizabeth Bowen, and Kenneth Clark. Joyce was looking forward to the trip because of this affair and because he had enjoyed his two previous visits so much. He felt completely at home in the Harper offices and had stayed with both John Fischer and Elizabeth Lawrence as an old friend rather than as a business colleague. Now the trip had to be put off, and he wrote to Miss Lawrence to express his disappointment:

> I shld. love to stay with you but the sad thing is, I'm not coming to the States this year. I had to cancel my tour on account of a mysterious illness. Some put it down to that plane crash in January, but now they say I had it beginning some time before — the crash only brought it out. I feel very well & do lots of work but I cant walk very far & I'm not allowed to get tired. I am missing my tour immensely, more than I expected. I have so many friends on your side and so enormously enjoyed all my visits.
>
> (8 August 1955)

He consulted Dr. Ritchie Russell, head of the Department of Neurology at Oxford's Radcliffe Infirmary, who treated him in September and attempted to narrow down the range of possibilities as to what the still-mysterious illness could be. In November Joyce was hospitalized again for three weeks, and the illness finally was diagnosed as disseminated neuritis, atrophy of the body's nervous system and muscles.

It is possible that the mysterious illness of December, 1951, the "suspicion of polio or osteo myelitis," was the first sign of the disease, and his "bursitis" was a further indication. But even if the true nature of the disorder had been diagnosed then, four years earlier, it would have done no good. There was no cure for it nor any means of checking its advance. Joyce was told the consequences of his illness: a gradual lessening of his coordination, a growing paralysis of his arms and legs and finally his whole body, possibly accompanied by intense pain, and in the end death. The illness could take a year or even four or five to do its fatal work.

In April his doctors had advised him to give up lecturing for several months. Yet Joyce did not follow their advice and had given talks to the Oxford University English Club, the Exeter University Literary Society, and a number of other groups in May. But as walking grew more difficult and the doctors' concern became greater, he accepted fewer engagements and even canceled some.

In the autumn, after learning the precise nature of his illness, he altered the whole pattern of his life. Now that he knew he was dying, he stopped running from whatever it was — the loneliness, lostness, and lack of direction in his art — that had pursued him for the six years since Trudy's death.

He was fortunate now in the people about him. That autumn he hired a new secretary, Edith Millen, who had trained to be a nurse but had given up that career and instead become a secretary. Joyce was her first employer, but she proved to be the best secretary he'd had in the past six years. Of course her nursing background was a godsend since Joyce was growing less able to look after himself. He had a new housekeeper, too, Mrs.

Nora Lightburne, recently widowed. This also was her first job. Both Miss Millen and Mrs. Lightburne stayed with him through the next year and a half, until his death.

After the full diagnosis of his illness, Joyce attempted to carry on his normal routine at home: his mail and the papers in bed after morning tea, then breakfast in the basement dining room. The rest of the morning he spent writing in his top-floor study which was filled with rows of files and had a special desk with pigeonholes for novels in progress. The study was an excellent workroom and had a view across Banbury Road to the west and overlooked the Victorian brickwork of Keble College to the south. After a morning's work he went down to the basement again for lunch and spent the afternoon in his sitting room. Dinner often was followed by more writing in the study or on Sunday by the regular gathering of friends for talk and drinks. The only activity missing from his days was the regular long walk through the University Parks at his usual furious pace.

One day, though, he took a terrible fall down the stairs and Edith Millen and Mrs. Lightburne urged him to work in the sitting room rather than his attic study. For the time being it was one of the few compromises he made with his illness.[1]

To help him get about he had a series of handles put along the walls and by the doorways of the house so he could drag himself around, and sometimes he pushed a chair in front of him, holding onto it for support like a child first learning to use ice skates.[2]

The knowledge of his illness and the fact that it would kill him only after weeks of paralysis and pain had a bolstering effect on Joyce's morale. Instead of going to pieces or sinking into apathy or despair, he gathered together his remaining resources as if he were determined to use to the limit what he had left. He had a fine example of courage: Trudy had fought bravely against her death, joining in life as long as she could. "Poor Trudy fought to the last breath," he had written. "The best of her will always be with me and the children." Now he must have the same courage as she had shown.[3]

He was reticent about telling anyone the extent of his illness

R

and its inevitable consequences, just as he had always kept his set-backs and ordeals to himself. He did write to Edith Haggard, who handled his short stories and articles for the Curtis Brown New York office, to ask if she would inquire about any new treatments for his illness which might have been developed in the United States. She went to her doctor and was referred to an important New York neurologist who, as it happened, was a great admirer of Joyce's novels. He told her that no new treatment had been developed. Her own doctor had said that with this particular illness Joyce would be very irritable due to the extreme pain. When she told him that this was not the case, the doctor said that Joyce must be an exceptional person, a great man.[4]

Meanwhile, at 12 Parks Road there was a great deal of work to be done. Joyce intended to finish the religious trilogy he had planned, although he could not be sure he would have time for it; the great many other novels which he had planned would now have to be forgotten. In addition to his own work, he was involved with two other projects: a dramatization of *Mister Johnson* which was undertaken by a young American poet and short story writer, Norman Rosten, and a book-length study of his novels being written by another American, Andrew Wright, whom he had met when he was in the United States.

Rosten, who had been deeply impressed by the vitality of *Mister Johnson* when he first read it, had envisioned the novel as a play and, although he had had no experience in drama, decided to tackle the project.[5] Early in 1954 he wrote to Joyce to ask permission to adapt the novel. Joyce did not reply until June, but when he did, it was to give Rosten permission. On his agent's advice, he said, he must have power of approval over the final script, but meanwhile Rosten could fire away with any questions that he had.[6]

The young writer sent Joyce a tentative script at the end of 1954 together with news that he had received a very favorable reaction when he had submitted it to a few producers in New York to see if they were interested.[7] Joyce was pleased with the script but at the same time said that certain points needed clari-

fication and some of the dialogue would need reworking, because it was too comic-British.[8] Instead of relying on Rosten to
handle the problems himself, Joyce set to work rewriting large
chunks of the play. He couldn't help himself.

After all, he had attempted in the 1920's and again in 1938–
1939 to become a playwright. Now he had a chance to try again,
with an excellent young collaborator, and producers who were
already interested; further, the play was based on one of his own
novels and drawn from his own experience. He could not have
kept his hands off the script if he'd had them tied behind his
back. Through the spring of 1955 he worked over the manuscript, making it over into his own, while Rosten, in Brooklyn,
wrestled to make the novelized manuscript back into a play
again. Joyce kept sending off changes, constantly assuring Rosten, "I am an old hand at dialogue."

He stressed one point about the play, a point he had empha-
sized in his letter to Mark Schorer: the story of Mister Johnson
must not be treated as an allegory:

> I think this would absolutely ruin it. The book is not allegory —
> not on your life. Allegory seems to me absolute poison in litera-
> ture or drama, because it destroys personality. Characters just
> become stock figures as in "Everyman." And you cease to sympa-
> thise with them as people. It is crude — you can't express any-
> thing but the crudest meanings in allegory. It is pretentious. It
> says $2 \times 2 = 4$ with more fuss than Einstein stated relativity. It
> is a champion bore.
>
>   I do very much hope you agree with me here. I'm sure the pro-
> ducer will agree. I speak from a pretty long experience of all
> kinds of writing.

>   (28 June 1955)

He also insisted in a letter to Edith Haggard that the shooting
of Johnson was murder, and as a result of this it was an act of
generosity, for Rudbeck *"has to pay* for it. If he doesn't have to
pay (as he would in life) what's the point? Tell Rosten."[9]
And he stressed this himself in a letter to Rosten to make sure it
was not missed.

In December, 1955, after returning from three weeks in the hospital, Joyce found Rosten had sent a new script, and he went over it with great care and pleasure as he saw the drama developing. His excitement is indicated by the fact that he dashed off four letters to Rosten during the following two weeks and even did some research that, at the time of writing the novel, he had not bothered with. Also, he asked his next-door neighbor, Sir Donald Hurst, about the shooting of Johnson: was it definitely murder on Rudbeck's part and was his falsified report an act of perjury? Sir Donald assured him about the murder aspect but said that it was dubious whether or not the false report was perjurous.[10]

Joyce made another point:

> The stuff about dressing for dinner in Africa is pure journalistic rubbish. At big stations one might dress for a big official dinner party, and, of course, soldiers change for mess at headquarters.
> But everyone changed for dinner simply because one needed a bath and clean clothes after the heat and dirt of the day. The usual, practically invariable, dinner dress was a clean white shirt without tie, and slacks; also, usually, mosquito boots, long soft legged boots, worn under the slacks.
>
> (7 February 1956)

His contributions, alterations, and suggestions continued to flow to Rosten through January and February, 1956; he took an interest in everything and worried particularly about the advertising layout that showed Johnson carrying an umbrella, since only chiefs and emirs had them in Nigeria (he had the case of Musa's subterfuge over an umbrella in mind). Then there was the tryout, and Rosten sent Joyce copies of the advance reviews. Joyce replied,

> Thank you for the reviews. I perfectly understand that you had no time to write before; I didn't expect to hear from you until things were more settled.
> Edith Haggard wrote and told me you were having a pretty hard time and I can well imagine it.
>
> . . . .

Don't take too many pills, and above all don't die yet; you might miss a really big success.

(19 March 1956)

With good advance notices and a fine actor, Earl Hyman, cast in the starring role, the play seemed to be going into New York with some luck. Joyce had written,

I hear that Hyman is very good and the reviews support that judgment. This was very good news for me because Hyman is the key of the piece. Do congratulate him for me on his efforts.

(19 March 1956)

When the play opened at the end of March, both it and Earl Hyman got excellent reviews. Reviewers from the *Daily News,* the *Post,* the *World Telegram,* the *Herald Tribune,* and the *Village Voice* all praised it highly. The critics thought Hyman was excellent as Johnson, and Vance Bourjaily felt sure, he said, that Hyman's was the best performance of the New York theater season. Only one reviewer, Brooks Atkinson of the *Times,* failed to praise the play, and even his reaction was not vehemently negative. It just was not his type of story.

But the play was a failure at the box office.

It was the same old story that Joyce had gone through with his early novels: excellent reviews and heartbreaking sales. Other writers had formed a small core of admirers during Joyce's early days, and now other actors were the greatest boosters of the play and its cast. Actors from most of the other plays in New York did all they could to give *Mister Johnson* the success they felt it deserved.[11] But they could not keep it alive. On May 5, just over a month after its New York opening, the play closed, and Joyce wrote to console Norman Rosten:

I can't say how sorry I am for you and for Hyman in this disaster which you so little deserved. As you say yourself the theatre is an extremely tricky business. Critics are always apt to criticize the wrong play; that is to say, they criticize a play of temperament and character for not being a thriller. Every original work of art runs up against this problem, that critics cannot understand or appreciate real originality; they are not used to it and when they see it they either try to fit it into some pigeon-hole of their own or damn it. You remember Chekhov's troubles in his beginning. He was considered one of the worst playwrights ever to attempt the stage.

I do hope very much the play will come over here where it might have a better chance; but, as you say, it would be necessary for Hyman to come with it. Do give him all my sympathy.

(9 March 1956)

It was an extremely kind letter under any circumstances, but especially so in this situation. Joyce was continuing to deteriorate physically. He was scarcely able to drag himself about and used a wheelchair much of the time. He had never complained of or even hinted at the presence of his illness to Rosten. Now the play had failed and his dream of a success in the theater, even a secondhand success, was denied him. Because, even if the play should be produced in England, it seemed unlikely that Joyce would live to see its production and know of its success — if it had a success.

Under the circumstances, Joyce might have blamed Rosten for the failure, lashing out at him for rejecting his rewritings and placing him among the "blackguards" and "plotters" of a few years before. But he had his bearings now, and he knew the writer had done a fine job of transforming the novel into a play and was at least as disappointed as Joyce was himself. Joyce was grateful for the months and years that Rosten had devoted to the project. He continued to try to cheer him up by investigating possible means of producing the play in England or even France. In December, 1956, when he was bedridden by his illness, he wrote,

I hope with all my heart Mr. Johnson will come on in London. Of course, I want it for myself, but chiefly because I feel so strongly that, after all your work and enthusiasm, you had a very raw deal in New York. I hope you will try to rub it in to the London producer that the play is not an expressionist lark, but something much more like that Orson Welles film about a family; I can't remember the name. That is to say, not a thriller, but the study of a situation where the character acting is all-important.

All good wishes for Christmas and the best of luck in the New Year.

The play was brought to London eventually and opened at the Lyric Opera House in September, 1960, again with excellent reviews and an excellent portrayal of Johnson (with Johnny Sekka in the title role) but with little more success than it had had in New York. It was Tristram Cary who went to the opening with Norman Rosten; Joyce had died three years before.

53

PLANS AND PROJECTS

ANDREW WRIGHT's projected study of Joyce's novels, the other project besides Rosten's play which demanded assistance from him, pleased Joyce. He was flattered by the idea, and he liked both Wright and his wife Gina, whom he had met before. He offered him all his assistance, just as he had done with Walter Allen and his "Writers and Their Work" pamphlet in 1952, and wrote,

> I should be delighted and most flattered that you should write a book about me, and if you want any material or references I should be eager to give them.
>
> . . . .
>
> As for biographical facts, ask me anything you like. I don't mean to write an autobiography, but there is a certain amount of reminiscence in books like the *House* of *Children*, and the short story Bush River is an account of actual fact.
>
> (15 March 1955)

Wright's book would offer Joyce an opportunity to dispel misunderstandings on the part of his readers, especially his critics, so he was pleased to cooperate. When Wright arrived in Oxford in April, 1956, Joyce gave him complete access to everything that he had ever written, from scribbled notebooks through finished drafts, including all the abandoned projects. Much of this material was in the attic study which Joyce had abandoned after his fall down the stairs the previous autumn, and there was more in the storeroom.[1]

Joyce also talked with complete candor about his writings, at least all of them that he remembered. Joyce had forgotten much of his past work, so Wright had to give him the names of characters and sometimes summarize a plot before Joyce had any recollection of a particular novel.[2] Because of Joyce's habit of concentrating only on the work immediately at hand or that which was planned for some future date, he had no real interest in his earlier writing. One work he especially had no interest in and which he regretted that Wright had discovered was *"Verses* by Arthur Cary," published in 1908 in Joyce's Edinburgh art-student days. He told Wright,

> As far as I remember, they were real trash; really very bad indeed for a boy of my age. But in Edinburgh I was moving in a peculiar atmosphere of sentimentalism, a kind of hangover of the greenery-yellery period or even earlier, late Rosetti.
> (9 October 1956)

Wright went to 12 Parks Road every day to dig through the material, sometimes with the help of the Davins' daughter Anna, and gave this account in his book, *Joyce Cary: A Preface to His Novels:*

> For nearly six months I went daily to his house in Parks Road. He gave me his study on the second floor to work in; he gave me permission to use anything I found. In the attic and in the study I found manuscripts of novels, short stories, essays, plays, poems, journals, letters. I found bills, memoranda, wallets, pistols, medals, trunks, boxes and bicycle tires. I have made a good deal of use of the literary and biographical materials which turned up; that I was able to use them freely is, I understand, not only unusual but almost unique: most people conceal or withhold some at least of the facts. Cary did not.[3]

Wright and his wife Gina also went along to several of Joyce's Sunday-night parties. Gina Wright was a bit intimidated at the prospect of sitting down with such prominent people as Enid Starkie, Sir Oliver Franks, W. H. Auden, Lord David Cecil, and

Helen Gardner, but Joyce seated her next to himself and immediately said, "Tell me about the hats in New York." [4] He meant it, too. He was as interested in women's fashions (Trudy had designed and made her own hats, and very good ones, too) as he was in the rest of the world — ships, hunting dogs, Venetian forts, and everything else.

Subsequently Andrew Wright became involved in another project besides his study of Joyce's novels. Ruari McLean, the husband of Trudy's niece, Toni Carlisle (who had run 12 Parks Road during Trudy's fatal illness), was in partnership with George Rainbird in a publishing firm which specialized in quality editions of books. In 1955 McLean proposed a special, limited-edition version of Joyce's most popular book, *The Horse's Mouth*. The edition would be illustrated, printed on rich paper, and beautifully bound. [5]

Joyce agreed to the edition and hoped it could include a long chapter entitled "The Old Strife at Plant's" which he had cut from the final version of the novel because he felt it was too digressive. It had been Trudy's favorite chapter in the novel and, when Joyce eliminated it from the book, she had urged him to get it into print in some other format. [6] So it had been published in *Harper's Magazine* as a short story with a note telling of its relation to *The Horse's Mouth*. But now Joyce was glad of the chance to have it within the same covers as the novel itself.

The edition was agreed upon, and work on it went ahead during the fall of 1955. Joyce proposed that Augustus John might be persuaded to do the illustrations, for "I have heard that he knows the book and has enjoyed it." [7] As a matter of fact, the book was very popular with artists on both sides of the Atlantic. But the idea to get John fell through, and finally it was decided that Joyce himself should do the illustrations, as a series of lithographs, together with a self-portrait for the front of the book.

The McLean-Rainbird firm would design and print the book, which then would be published by Michael Joseph in Britain and Harper in the United States. Two thousand numbered and signed copies would be published, half by Michael Joseph and half by Harper. As the project went ahead the plans became quite grand: the book would be printed on excellent Italian paper, it would include Joyce's illustrations, a preface by Andrew Wright, the text of *The Horse's Mouth* and of the previously omitted chapter "The Old Strife at Plant's," and a concordance of the William Blake quotations that larded Gulley Jimson's speech.

In November, 1956, Ruari McLean was all set to go to Oxford with two thousand blank sheets of the Italian paper for Joyce to sign (these would then be bound into the copies of the book) when bad news came. Spencer Curtis Brown told McLean, that, due to the idiosyncrasies of American copyright laws, if the printed copies of the book were imported from England into the United States, the American copyright on the novel would be void. Since it had been Joyce's most popular novel in the United States, the potential losses to Joyce, Harper, and Curtis Brown could be immense, for pirated hardbound and paperback editions would proliferate. The whole project seemed doomed, since Michael Joseph was not willing to underwrite the whole cost of the edition alone.

Eventually, after much negotiation, it was decided that the book should come out in Britain alone in an edition of fifteen hundred copies, published under the Rainbird imprint; a royalty of five shillings would be paid to Joyce rather than the original ten as planned, and the book would be sold at five guineas a copy. It was not to be an autographed edition, however, since by the time the deal was settled, Joyce was incapable of signing the sheets. He no longer had the strength for it.

In fact, he was only able to complete one of the planned lithographs for the edition, his self-portrait, and had to make pencil sketches do for the remaining illustrations, since this was less arduous. The paralysis was too far advanced for anything more.[8]

The edition, plagued with so many problems, limped to publication in 1957 and met its final defeat: it sold poorly and many copies had to be remaindered at a pound or so apiece. So this anticipated triumph, like the dramatization of *Mister Johnson*, ended in tragedy.

54

THE CAPTIVE AND THE FREE

CARY DID NOT LIVE to finish *The Captive and the Free,* a novel intended at one time to be developed into the religious trilogy. Its fragmentary manuscript was pieced together by Mrs. Dan Davin, his literary executrix, with the help of Edith Millen and Cary's own comments on it before he died. Putting together another person's novel, let alone one with such a deeply personal slant, is a harrowing job, but the published book is an entity. There are two gaps and a few loose ends such as the unexplained appearance of the American tycoon Laney in Chapter 62. But these could have been avoided only by a complete rewriting and, out of respect for Cary, Mrs. Davin chose to work entirely from his drafts.

The Captive and the Free can be understood best by looking at four of its characters: the faith-healing Missioner Preedy, the troubled Anglican curate Syson, the rationalist and atheist Lord Tinney, and the newspaper man-on-the-make Hooper. Preedy and Lord Tinney represent the most extreme positions, the former utterly convinced of God's omnipotence, and the latter equally convinced of God's nonexistence. Between these positions are the bewildered Syson, who has lost his simple faith in the Apostles' Creed and now is doggedly searching for the truth, and Hooper, who never had faith in God or belief in atheism, and who regards religion simply as a subject that will attract newspaper readers.

Although Syson violently condemns Preedy's mission and distributes anti-Preedy leaflets at its doors, the faith healer recognizes Syson as a fellow seeker after truth. "Yes," he says at their first real meeting,

> I believe you do want the truth above everything, and that's why you're getting into all this trouble with your vicar and your wife. You know, Syson, you're like me — you're a man who has to have the truth — at all costs. We're the last people who ought to quarrel — we ought to be friends.[1]

Syson, though, believes this is only a trick to make him drop his campaign against the mission. But Preedy's sincerity is evident when, thirty-eight chapters later, at the meeting where his chapel committee is trying to oust him, he announces,

> "I asked Mr. Syson to come in whenever he liked. After all, what he's got to say really matters. He's not one of your committee men, canting and wangling. He's interested in the truth and nothing but the truth." And, going to Syson, he shook hands and asked him to sit down. "I take it," he said, "the question between us is only in what sort of a God we believe in. You say that God cannot do a miracle, even of mercy, that he has no power at all in the world to cure all its miseries and cruelties, its fearful injustice." [2]

Although Preedy is interrupted before he can describe *his* concept of God, it seems obvious that He would be personal and omnipotent.

The other two, Hooper and Lord Tinney, also are related, for they both are involved in the *Morning Argus,* are masters at publicity-seeking, and love to debunk other people's beliefs. Hooper is a variation of Cary's promoter, in this case a newspaper man, the word-artist in print, who uses Preedy only to increase the paper's circulation and to aid his own progress in the world of journalism. Lord Tinney, too, is a familiar Cary type: the abstractionist, in this case a player of rational and semantic tricks, a lord, an ardent atheist mainly because this philosophical position allows him to demean other people's beliefs;

he is a publicity-seeker and self-promoter, a rationalist and pretender to the throne of radical conscience of the times, a "fanatic and anarchist." Hooper and Tinney are the comic villains of the novel.

The other characters, who are mostly women, are to a degree pawns of these four, and they include Alice Rodker, whom Preedy seduced when she was only fourteen before his conversion and who bore his illegitimate child, and who now desperately fights against loving Preedy and his God; Lady Kate Rideout, who also fights against believing in Preedy but succumbs to him, believes herself healed by him, and then dies of the cancer of which she had never been cured at all; Ada Rollright, a tubercular girl of twelve whose mother takes her to Preedy to be cured and who gives him a renewed sense of God's love when he needs it most, yet who dies after all; and Nona Clinch, a strong rationalist, who is cured of her paralysis by Preedy despite her total lack of faith in him. In addition to these there are assorted newspaper people who, like Hooper, are out for what they can get, and Preedy's chapel committee, most of whom are without real conviction, a bunch of sheep ready to abandon their shepherd whenever the going gets rough.

Cary's views are expressed through both Preedy and Syson, for they are the seekers after truth and wisdom. Instead of saying that Preedy has brought about the deaths of Lady Rideout and Ada Rollwright, Cary seems to suggest something quite different. As the novel opens, Lady Rideout has been hospitalized; she is abandoned by her friends and colleagues, lonely, despairing, feeling herself to be the victim of a conspiracy. Her doctors cannot find the nature of her illness or, if they can, will not tell her what it is. Preedy gives her the will to live, to take up her bed and walk, and she becomes a functioning human being again. So even if he has not cured her cancer, he has turned her from a dying vegetable into a woman who uses her last months to the full. Belief has given her life meaning. As for Ada Rollwright, her parents are at odds and are separated. Since emotional states are important in tuberculosis cases, perhaps it is this disharmony and lack of love which kills her, rather than the lack of medical attention.

Of the three persons Preedy treats, two of them, Nona Clinch and Ada, have maladies in which emotions play a significant part. One is cured, the other dies. The one who is cured is surrounded by love; the other lives amid discord. The suggestion is that love is a sustaining force (in the case of Lady Rideout) and sometimes a healing force (Nona Clinch), while its lack destroys human life (Ada Rollwright).

The novel's title, *The Captive and the Free,* seems ambiguous and perhaps was intended to be so. The words seem to have different meanings when associated with the different characters. The following interpretations are possible.

Kate Rideout, once she is "captured" by religion, is freed of the suspicion, doubt, and hopelessness she feels. Through becoming a captive of faith she is made free.

Lord Tinney is made captive by his own rationalism and tries to make others the captives of his own airless, sunless ideological cell; Preedy, though, is freed from egocentric, limited rationalism by his faith. Thus the captives and the free are contrasted.

Preedy, captivated by God, is freed from self. This kind of captivity *is* freedom.

Syson, having found himself a captive of the doctrines of the church, loses his faith and is thereby condemned to freedom, but in pursuing God, he is attempting to find a new haven of real captivity. He is thus free to search for his own personal and necessary form of captivity.

So the "captives" and the "free" may be different persons, the same person in different states, or concurrent and interlocking states in the same person. That the two words are not necessarily antithetical is suggested by Cary's phrase, "Man is condemned to freedom."

Yet this far-ranging and essential theme is reduced to a tawdry level by Hooper in the novel's last two paragraphs:

What did the *Dispatch* readers want, a piece of psychological analysis? A complicated story of mixed motives leaving them to make out their own judgments? It was crazy even to imagine it.

No, there was only one story here — the poor little girl seduced and ruined by a parson who then proceeds to murder her baby, who has such power over her still that he recalls her to his side and beats her up as a reward. And the poor little victim, besotted with love or terror, takes it. One could suggest perhaps that she likes being beaten; always a popular line. Really, whatever Joanna might think, there was no choice. And a good thing too. Yes, the story of the year.[3]

Hooper sticks a pin in the balloon of religious faith and presents the "exploded" myth to his readers in order to titillate them. This balloon has a buoying force similar to that of the real balloon fashioned by the rogue hero in Joyce's story to his sons. In the tale, that balloon lifted Jim and his band of boys out of the swamp and quicksand in which they had been caught. In *The Captive and the Free,* Lady Rideout, Nona Clinch, and in fact most of the novel's characters have been caught in a psychological or moral swamp. And it is the rogue hero Preedy who is able to lift some of them out.

Hooper and Tinney, though, refuse to be saved. Tinney, in fact, seems delighted that there is no escape and it is as if he called out, "Come on in, the quicksand's quite refreshing. Besides, this is all there is. That balloon's only full of hot air, you know. Be reasonable!" And Hooper fumes and grumbles, as if thinking to himself, "I wonder if there's a story in that balloon. If only it would crash. Yes. 'Thousands die in air disaster!' There might be a promotion for me if I got a scoop. Damn it, why haven't they sent me a photographer?"

Instead of saying that religious faith is fatuous, Cary indicates that it is a vital, life-giving force, and the characters in the novel who are most alive are those who are seeking earnestly for, or who have found, a faith. Their lives are enriched, even in the case of Syson, who loses wife and children, job and security, in his quest; but then he is a pilgrim and pilgrims must make sacrifices. Cary has ended where he began, for *Aissa Saved* dealt with transformation and transcendence through faith.

The Captive and the Free, despite its unfinished state, is a remarkable achievement, probing the complexity of the religious life with a great sharpness of vision. Although he was well read in the phenomenon of faith and particularly studied William James's *The Varieties of Religious Experience,* the ideas in his last work are his own. When one considers that the book was written by a dying man, its vitality is all the more remarkable. However much his body was failing, Cary's creativity and joy were undiminished.

55

DEATH

FOR THE FIRST TIME in six years Joyce had a smoothly running household due to Edith Millen and Nora Lightburne. When Joyce had first employed Mrs. Lightburne early in the autumn of 1955, he had told her he did not want to be consulted about the marketing. She would have a free hand in that as well as in most everything in the house. He gave her a list of the foods he disliked and left the rest of the marketing and cooking entirely up to her. Coconut, chocolate, and smoked herring were three foods he did not like, and chicken, too, for he'd had such a surfeit of it in Nigeria that he had not been able to stand it since.[1]

He left the marketing and meals entirely up to her, not because he didn't care what he ate; he loved good food and wine (his sons got the beginnings of a decent wine cellar when they married[2]). But he had so much to do and so little time to do all of it in that he was eager to have others take on as many of the day-to-day responsibilities as possible.

Not that he overloaded others with tasks. For weeks he went without his regular tea on Mrs. Lightburne's days off unless a friend dropped in and made it for him. His hands shook so much that he was afraid to prepare it and carry the tray himself in case he dropped everything. His friends and acquaintances learned this only by accident, for Joyce had not wanted to be a nuisance. Once the situation was known, someone always saw to it for him, whenever Mrs. Lightburne was unable to make the preparations herself.[3]

For the first few months only Mrs. Lightburne actually lived at Parks Road, while Milly (Joyce's affectionate name for Edith Millen), who left each day at six, would return to the house at nine to help put Joyce to bed. But eventually, as Joyce became increasingly helpless, Milly came to live at the house, too.

Some equipment was obtained from the therapy department of one of Oxford's hospitals to make life easier. There was a sling, for instance, that allowed Joyce to swing himself into his bed or his bath. He was able to feel he was less of a burden to Mrs. Lightburne and Milly because of these conveniences.

Christmas of 1955 was celebrated in the way Joyce liked. His sons and daughters-in-law and grandchildren swarmed into the house and imparted to it and Joyce new life and excitement. He was not yet bedridden or even confined to his wheelchair. The only sign of his illness, in fact, was his halting, shuffling walk, his having to hold onto furniture and the handles on the walls as he moved about, and a slight slurring of his speech. Soon after Christmas, though, he had to abandon walking and get around the house in his wheelchair.[4]

The writing went on. He was going ahead with the religious trilogy, as he had planned. But as his illness progressed and other matters interfered, he began thinking of it as a single book rather than the three volumes he had first intended it to be. It might be difficult to crowd into one volume all the thoughts he wanted to express in the work, but it was better than leaving the work unfinished, as he had with *Castle Corner*.

In 1952 he had given a series of three lectures at Oxford University which he had called "The Novel as Truth." He had used these lectures in digested form as a single speech, which he had given, along with a second one, "The Writer's World," on his second American tour and on his European tours of 1954–1955, continuously altering and improving the two lectures. Now he was asked to undertake a major project: the annual Clark Lectures at Trinity College, Cambridge.

The Clark Lectures, under the patronage of one of the two ancient English universities, were an excellent platform from which Joyce could deliver his theories on art, especially the art of writing. His aesthetics would be given a weight and a public that they otherwise might fail to achieve. So, despite the knowledge that he had just a short time to live, Joyce agreed. If he had not done the thinking, the research, and the frequent rewriting that he put into "The Novel as Truth," "The Writer's World," and other talks and articles, it seems unlikely that he could have tackled the job, or, if he had taken it on, that he could have finished it. As it was, he still had a tremendous task in tying his ideas together and expanding them to fit the needs of the lectures. In order to get the job done, he had to steal time from his religious novel, which already had suffered from the ebbing of his strength.

His world constricted more and more. First the outside world was cut off from him — the walks he enjoyed so much, which had consoled him so often except for that brief moment during Trudy's illness, and the visits to friends and to see his sons' families, especially the trips to America that had given him so much pleasure (for a time he still managed a few talks within a limited range of home, being literally picked up at his doorstep and being driven back to it afterward). He was confined to his house, or, in the early stages, his garden, which was overgrown now more than ever (and it had never been very tidy). After his fall down the stairs he was confined to the middle two floors of the house, then to just one floor. Finally, when he was bedridden at last, his world contracted to a single room.

But with Milly to help him and much work to be done, he kept on working, and the writing and the talk and laughter were as vital as they had ever been in his lifetime.

As his ability to walk diminished, it became impossible to keep the seriousness of his illness from his friends and from the outside world generally. He had to begin canceling speaking engagements and turned away new invitations from the United States, from Europe, and of course from the British Isles. Consequently throughout 1956 and early 1957 he was besieged with requests for interviews: what were his religious feelings now, did he believe in an afterlife, what was it like to know he was dying?

He gave in to many of the requests and answered many of the

written questions by letter, but it was not possible to respond to everything. Among the interviews that he gave were several to American magazines and a filmed discussion with Edwin Newman of NBC television for the "Today" program. He had loved his trips to the United States in 1951 and 1953 and had wanted to go on the one planned for 1955. There he had a great public which had given him the greater part of his financial success. He had many personal friends there, too. The television appearance would be a way of saying good-bye to all of them, so it was filmed in January, 1956, at his home.

The days were filled. There was the massive work of the novel, the Clark Lectures, and still more short stories and articles to finish. The interviews took time as did reading and answering all the letters to organizations which had requested him to speak: the English society of University College, London; the English Club, Cambridge University; Ruskin College, Oxford; the International Association of University Professors of English; a request from PEN that he deliver the 1956 Herman Ould Lecture, and others, so many of them from the sort of audience he liked best of all, students, scholars, and fellow writers.

There were friends to see, too. Lord David Cecil came in almost every day at six for a visit. Win Davin was in the house a great deal, helping him with his work, particularly with the putting-together of the Clark Lectures manuscript, and her daughters helped about the house. The Highams, his oldest friends in Oxford and Trudy's friends for years, came often. Sir Heneage Ogilvie, a friend for over fifty years, came up from London several times, as tall and straight as ever, although grown deaf. There were dozens of other visitors and Joyce was anxious to see them all. He had always relied on his friends, especially after Trudy's death. He still held his Sunday evenings at 12 Parks Road, from six to eight now rather than late into the evening, and Win Davin presided over them after Joyce could not be present himself.

On Wednesday and Sunday afternoons the three Davin girls and Joyce's eldest grandson, Lucius, Michael's boy, who was at the Dragon School, came in for stories. Joyce reeled off the same sort of serials as he had told the other boys after lights-out at Hurstleigh and Clifton and which he had later told to his four sons. His audience was as eager as ever. One day, for instance, when Mrs. Lightburne was in the kitchen and one of the Davin girls was trying to help, they both caught the murmur of Joyce's voice. "Oh!" the girl cried, dropping what she was doing. "Joyce is telling a story! I must go!" [5]

When Michael's first daughter was born, Joyce was full of the news. He remarked to Milly, to Mrs. Lightburne, and to anyone else he saw for the next few days that his granddaughter was the first girl born into the Cary family in fifty years. It was an extraordinary event, a wonderful event.

His son George's study of the legend of Alexander the Great during the Middle Ages was published posthumously as *The Medieval Alexander* and its success pleased Joyce greatly. He wrote to Andrew Wright,

> My son George's book on the Medieval Alexander, published by the Cambridge University Press, is practically sold out already; only 14 copies left out of 750. This is really a triumph for a learned work of such weight, selling at 52/6. I am so glad because I can feel that the poor boy's genius was not entirely wasted.
>
> (22 January 1957)

The proceeds from Joyce's writing now went almost entirely to his sons, so they would have the independence he had always meant them to have. He intended to have their inheritance as ready as possible for them in other respects as well. At his request Mrs. Lightburne sent the silver plate out for replating so that it would be at its best when it should become theirs in a few more months. And she worked at cleaning out the attic, so the boys would not have that job. It was full of the accumulated treasures and debris not only of thirty-five years of family life at Parks Road but of memorabilia going back to Joyce's university days and before: Joyce's medals from Montenegro and Nigeria, a trunk with "Milton Society" painted on it that was a souvenir of his student days, an academic gown grown green with age. Joyce had to check everything before it was taken care of, either thrown out or carefully put away. When Mrs. Lightburne showed him the student's gown, which she thought surely should be discarded, he told her that it must not be thrown away. "Oh no!" he told her. "I should be very proud to have one of my grandsons wear it as an Oxford scholar." [6]

In August, 1956, he wrote to the editors of *Holiday* magazine to say he was sorry, but he could not write any further articles for them, including two that were planned, because he had to devote his remaining time to his novel. *Holiday* had published seven of Joyce's articles in the past few years, for very generous fees, and had made the fewest possible changes in them; so few that his New York agent, Mrs. Haggard, had been surprised at how closely they kept to Joyce's original manuscripts. The most recent one, "The Most Exciting Sport in the World," not published until June, 1957, had been about the sort of scrub polo he had played with the others at Nafada station in 1916 and 1917 and had never forgotten — the same verve as was in his letters to Trudy pervades the article. But now even the opportunity to write about places and activities he loved and to be paid well for them had to be dismissed. Time was short, and he had his two main projects to finish.

Sir Donald Hurst, whom Joyce had consulted about the death of Mister Johnson, built a machine to make Joyce's writing much easier. It was a writing table which he could use on his bed, for it had an electric mechanism that allowed him to write despite his weakened arms. The device held a long roll of paper that moved down over the surface of the table when a switch was touched at the table's edge. This way Joyce did not have to lift up the sheets of paper and lay them aside when he had filled them. He needed to move only his forearm. Joyce used the writing table until only two or three weeks before his death.

He also dictated much of his work to Milly, and as Win Davin read him the typed manuscripts, he told her what corrections to make.

Then in November his voice failed. If he could no longer dictate, then neither of his projects, the novel and the Clark

Lectures, would be finished, for his laborious scrawling on the writing table would not let him write fast enough. But the doctor diagnosed the trouble as laryngitis which would clear up in a week or two.[7]

At about this time the family and the household learned that a cure for Joyce's illness had been discovered in the United States. The family and the doctors discussed its possible use. If it worked on Joyce, the best that it could do would be to prevent further deterioration. But he would remain a bedridden cripple. For a man who had been so vital and alive and active, who had enjoyed travel so much, such a life seemed an unnecessary torture. It was decided not to attempt the cure since Joyce was so terribly feeble now. He was not told of the discovery.[8]

Through December, once the laryngitis was gone, he dictated to Milly in a thin, slurred voice and scrawled through the rolls of paper fitted into his table, first in pen and ink, using a schoolboy's straight pen because it was lighter and easier to hold than a fountain pen, then changing to a pencil when he could no longer dip the pen in the inkwell at the table's edge.

Christmas came and the house was filled again or nearly so. Several of the youngest grandchildren were left at home or with other grandparents. Joyce, his voice nearly gone, his thin body inert and helpless, was the most cheerful member of the Christmas party. The good-byes were said earlier than usual, and he was left to his work again.[9]

He gave up the novel in December, realizing he had no chance of finishing both of his books, and determined that the Clark Lectures should be prepared for publication. His nephew, Robert Ogilvie, Freddy's son, would give the lectures in Joyce's place at Cambridge. Cambridge University Press would publish them, since it had published George's book and since Robert Lusty, Joyce's friend, had left Michael Joseph due to differences with Mr. Joseph. Since Joyce had strong ties with both Lusty and Joseph, and the lectures were given at Cambridge, this seemed the best course to avoid offending either friend.

In the next few weeks Joyce's voice gave way almost entirely, and his throat was in such a condition that he could not eat or drink. Instead he was fed intravenously. But he kept up a whisper of dictation through January and February and into March, not just for the Clark Lectures, which were to be published as *Art and Reality,* but for some short stories he was trying to finish, "Period Piece," which was finished in February and "The Sheep," which was completed on March 1.

At last he could barely whisper and was in such pain that he had to be under constant sedation. Up to then, his spirits had still been good. For instance, Enid Starkie remembered that "Even a short time before he died, when he could no longer speak, one could still make him laugh. . . ." [10] On March 18 Edith Millen wrote to Andrew Wright about Joyce's rapidly deteriorating state:

I know you will be very sad to hear that Mr. Cary's condition has deteriorated very rapidly in the last two or three days and the doctor feels that the end will be not much longer delayed. It is a good thing really as he has not been able to write and barely able to speak for the last couple of weeks and I'm afraid life has been very miserable for him. The ability to do even a little work every day was all that mattered to him and now that has gone. However, with the help of Win Davin, he managed to finish revising the Clark Lectures, and it was with great joy that I posted the typescripts off to the publishers last week. He hasn't done any work on the novel since before Christmas; I think he realised even then that he would never finish it. His courage has been heartbreaking to see.

Your letter with the revised first page of your preface for the Rainbird edition of *The Horse's Mouth* arrived to-day and I held it up for Mr. Cary to read; he just nodded his head so I think he is happy about it. Ruari McLean managed to get a dummy of *The Horse's Mouth* ready and to bring it down for Mr. Cary to see last week; it is good that he has been able to see it actually taking shape.

(18 March 1957)

Joyce lingered on for another week and a half. There were no last words, for he had no voice left for them, and all that he had meant to say was in his books and in the way he had faced death, accepting its challenge and matching the bravery that his wife had shown. Then on March 29 he died.

His son Michael wrote to Joyce's old friend, Tommy Higham,

> He had a fear that he might have lived on for weeks or even months in a state of complete helplessness; and as it was he died peacefully in his sleep, and had been able to recognize and to smile at Lucius only the evening before.

The funeral was from St. Giles' Church and was conducted by Canon Diggle. It was a very simple funeral, and Joyce was buried beside his wife in Wolvercote Cemetery just north of the city.

Lord David Cecil, one of Joyce's closest friends during his last twenty-five years, wrote a memorial for the *London Times,* which ended this way:

> But the man was as memorable as his work. He made a picturesque and exhilarating first impression. His elegant, virile handsomeness, his racy, vivid, appreciative talk, and something at once heroic and debonair in his whole personality, suggested a gentleman rider in the race of life, risking his skin for sport rather than for a prize, and looking on every crisis of existence as a hurdle to be surmounted gaily and gallantly, however many bruises and spills might be incurred in the process. This was a true impression but a partial one. The gentleman rider was also a sage and a saint.

Yet it could be said that Joyce wrote his own memorial. Enid Starkie remarked on his ability to enjoy a joke and to laugh, even when he no longer could speak. His laughter, even when he was voiceless, crippled, and dying, recalls Gulley Jimson's rejoinder at the very end of *The Horse's Mouth* when he is dying and being rushed to the hospital. The nun accompanying him tells him he shouldn't talk and laugh, not at a time when death is so near. She admonishes him to pray rather than to laugh.

Gulley's last words are, "Same thing, mother." They might have been Joyce's last words, too.

NOTES

SELECTED BIBLIOGRAPHY

INDEX

NOTES

*The bulk of Joyce Cary's letters are in the James Osborne
Collection of Joyce Cary's papers (referred to in
the Notes as the "Cary Collection"),
with the notable exceptions of those
to T. F. Higham, Norman Rosten,
and John Dover Wilson.*

CHAPTER 1
Inishowen

All information on the Cary family in Inishowen, unless otherwise indicated, is from Lionel Stevenson's *The Carys of Inishowen* (privately printed, 1963) and a genealogical chart in the possession of Cary Clark.

1. Misses Kane, Quigley's Point, Donegal, 1965.
2. Samuel Lewis, *A Topographical Dictionary of Ireland* (London, 1837), p. 398.
3. Cary Clark, Castledawson, Londonderry Co., 1964 and 1965.
4. *Ibid.*
5. *Ibid.*
6. *Ibid.*
7. Memie Wakeham, Wadeford, Somerset, 1964.
8. Sheila Cary, Wadeford, Somerset, 1964; Mrs. J. Thompson, Belfast, 1964.
9. Londonderry *Standard*, 17 August 1887.
10. *Ibid.*, 10 December 1888.

CHAPTER 2
Cromwell House

1. Cary Clark, Castledawson, Londonderry, 1964; Mrs. J. Thompson, Belfast, 1964.
2. Cary Clark, *op. cit.*
3. "Cromwell House," preliminary draft, Cary Collection.
4. *Ibid.*
5. Cary Clark, *op. cit.*
6. "Cromwell House," *op. cit.*
7. *Ibid.*
8. *Ibid.*
9. *Ibid.*
10. *Ibid.*
11. *Ibid.*

CHAPTER 3
Clare Cottage and Ravenscliffe

1. Records of the Londonderry City Cemetery.
2. "My Religious History," preliminary draft, Cary Collection.
3. *Ibid.*
4. "What Christ Has Taught Me," preliminary draft, Cary Collection.
5. "A Child's Religion," *Vogue,* December 1953.
6. Mrs. J. Thompson, Belfast, 1964.
7. Commander J. P. Cary, Wadeford, Somerset, 1964.
8. Cary Clark, Castledawson, Londonderry, 1964.
9. *Ibid.*
10. *Ibid.*
11. Mrs. Thompson, *op. cit.*
12. Cary Clark, *op. cit.*
13. Letter to Gertrude Cary (29 July 1917).
14. James Cochrane, Redcastle, Donegal, 1964.
15. Commander J. P. Cary, *op. cit.*
16. Cary Clark, *op. cit.*
17. Unused preface to *A House of Children,* Cary Collection.
18. Cary Clark, *op. cit.*
19. Manuscript entitled "Uncle J. gets drunk," Cary Collection.

CHAPTER 4
Hurstleigh and Clifton

1. Letter to Gertrude Cary (22 April 1919).
2. (24 May 1904).
3. Commander J. P. Cary, Wadeford, Somerset, 1964.
4. *Ibid.*
5. *Ibid.*
6. "My Religious History," Cary Collection.
7. *Ibid.*
8. Sir Heneage Ogilvie, Wimbledon, 1963.
9. Letter to Gertrude Cary (18 November 1917).
10. Commander Cary, *op. cit.;* Sir Heneage Ogilvie, *op. cit.;* Professor
    G. M. Fisher, Edinburgh, 1964.
11. Commander J. P. and Sheila Cary, Wadeford, Somerset, 1964.
12. Sir Heneage Ogilvie, *op. cit.*
13. Professor Fisher, *op. cit.*
14. Commander Cary, *op. cit.*
15. "Cheerful Protestant," *Time,* 20 October 1952.
16. *Ibid.;* "Preface," *The Horse's Mouth,* Carfax edition (London, 1951),
    pp. 9–10.
17. "My Religious History," Cary Collection.
18. "A Slight Case of Demolition," Cary Collection.

19. *Ibid.*

20. "My Religious History," Cary Collection.

21. Professor Fisher, *op. cit.*

22. "Cheerful Protestant," *op. cit.*

23. Professor Fisher, *op. cit.*

24. Letter to Arthur P. Cary (11 March 1906).

CHAPTER 5
Paris and Edinburgh

1. Letter to Gertrude Cary (8 January 1919).

2. A. Y. Jackson, *A Painter's Country* (Toronto, 1958), p. 8.

3. *Ibid,* p. 9.

4. Adam Bruce Thomson, Edinburgh, 1964.

5. Letter to John Dover Wilson (18 September 1942).

6. *Ibid.* (23 November 1942).

7. Thomson, *op. cit.*

8. Letter to Gertrude Cary (15 August 1919).

9. "Cheerful Protestant," *Time,* 20 October 1952.

10. Commander J. P. and Sheila Cary and Memie Wakeham, Wadeford, Somerset, 1964.

CHAPTER 6
Oxford

1. Letter to Arthur P. Cary (19 April 1909).

2. *Ibid.*

3. T. F. Higham, Oxford, 1963.

4. Quoted in F. A. Lea, *The Life of John Middleton Murry* (London, 1959), p. 15.

5. "Paris Diary, 1910–1911," Cary Collection. All material on Paris holiday, 1910–1911, is from this source.

6. F. A. Lea, *op. cit.,* p. 23.

7. John Middleton Murry to Joyce Cary (1 April 1911).

8. John Middleton Murry, *Between Two Worlds* (New York, 1936), p. 168.

9. *Ibid.,* pp. 182–183.

CHAPTER 7
The Ogilvies

1. Commander J. P. and Sheila Cary, Wadeford, Somerset, 1964; Lady Gwendolyn Herbert, Hammersmith, 1964; Sir Heneage Ogilvie, Wimbledon, 1963.

2. Letter to Gertrude Cary (10 November 1919).

3. T. F. Higham, Oxford, 1963.

4. "Cheerful Protestant," *Time,* 20 October 1952.

5. "A Slight Case of Demolition," Cary Collection.

6. *Ibid.*
7. Letter to Gertrude Cary (6 March 1919).
8. W. M. Ogilvie, *Reminiscences* (privately printed, 1926).
9. Joyce Cary's letters to his wife, 1916–1919; conversations with members of the Cary family, 1963–1965.
10. Cary Clark, Castledawson, Londonderry, 1964.
11. Arthur P. Cary to Joyce Cary (1 December 1911).
12. Letter to Gertrude Cary (14 September 1914).
13. Lady Gwendolyn Herbert, *op. cit.*
14. Letters to Gertrude Cary (28 November 1919 and 16 October 1917).
15. *Ibid.* (19 February 1917).

CHAPTER 8
Store Street and Antivari

1. Untitled essay, Cary Collection.
2. "Paris Diary, 1910–1911," Cary Collection.
3. Duncan MacGregor to Joyce Cary (undated, 1912); T. F. Higham, Oxford, 1963.
4. Lady Gwendolyn Herbert, Hammersmith, 1964.
5. Letter to Gertrude Cary (11 January 1917).
6. *Ibid.* (19 October 1916, 13 November 1916, and 2 March 1919).
7. *Ibid.* (5 March 1917).
8. *Ibid.* (19 October 1916).
9. *Ibid.* (11 January 1917 and 2 September 1917).
10. *Ibid.* (1 June 1919).
11. *Ibid.* (7 December 1916).
12. Sir Heneage Ogilvie, Wimbledon, 1963.
13. "Cheerful Protestant," *Time*, 20 October 1952.
14. *Memoirs of the Bobotes*, ed., James B. Meriwether (London, 1964). All material on the Montenegro campaign is from this source, unless otherwise indicated.
15. Alphonse Courlander, London *Daily Express*, 8 November 1912.
16. *Ibid.*
17. *Ibid.*
18. *Ibid.*
19. *Ibid.*
20. *Ibid.*
21. *Ibid.*
22. *Ibid.*

CHAPTER 9
Montenegro

1. Sir Heneage Ogilvie, Wimbledon, 1963.
2. *Memoirs of the Bobotes,* ed., James B. Meriwether (London, 1964) for this and the following information on the Montenegro campaign, unless otherwise indicated.

3. Mrs. J. Thompson, Belfast, 1964.
4. *Ibid.*
5. Letter to Arthur P. Cary (1 July 1913).
6. *Ibid.*
7. Cary Collection.
8. Letter to Gertrude Cary (30 May 1919).
9. Letter to Arthur P. Cary (30 April 1913).
10. Letter to Gertrude Cary (9 May 1919).
11. Percy Diggle and Sir John Patterson, Carlisle, 1964.

CHAPTER 10

A Steady Job

1. Sir Heneage Ogilvie, Wimbledon, 1963.
2. *Ibid.*, Commander J. P. and Sheila Cary, Wadeford, Somerset, 1964.
3. Letter to Gertrude Cary (8 January 1917).
4. M. M. Mahood, *Joyce Cary's Africa* (London, 1964), p. 10.
5. "Railway Camp," Cary Collection.
6. Mahood, p. 11.
7. *Ibid.*, p. 10.
8. Letter to Arthur P. Cary (June 1914).

CHAPTER 11

The Cameroons Campaign

1. This information can be found in almost every letter to his father and his friends at this time.
2. *A House of Children*, Carfax edition (London, 1951), p. 135.
3. M. M. Mahood, *Joyce Cary's Africa* (London, 1964), pp. 12–13.
4. *Ibid.*, p. 14.
5. Letter to H. S. W. Edwardes (2 September 1914).
6. M. M. Mahood, *op. cit.*, p. 15.
7. Commander J. P. Cary and Cary Clark provided this and subsequent information on Commander Cary's imprisonment in Turkey.
8. Commander J. P. Cary, Wadeford, Somerset, 1964.
9. "Bush River," *Spring Song*, ed., W. Davin (London, 1960), pp. 9–18.
10. "The Raft," manuscript in Cary Collection.
11. The account of the attacks on Mount Mora is from F. J. Moberly, *Military Operations, Togoland and the Cameroons, 1914–1916* (London, 1931), pp. 24–28.
12. Nathan Cohen, "A Conversation with Joyce Cary," *Tamarack Review*, Spring, 1957.
13. "Cheerful Protestant," *Time*, 20 October 1952.
14. *Ibid.*

CHAPTER 12

Leave, 1916

1. "Borgu Diary," Cary Collection.

2. *Ibid.*
3. Letter to Gertrude Cary (15 September 1917).
4. *Ibid.* (3 March 1917).
5. M. M. Mahood, *Joyce Cary's Africa* (London, 1964), pp. 22–23.
6. Letter to Gertrude Cary (24 September 1917).
7. Mrs. Rauri McLean, Blackheath, 1964.
8. Letter to Gertrude Cary (2 March 1919).
9. *Ibid.* (18 September 1919).
10. *Ibid.* (17 April 1917).
11. W. M. Ogilvie, *Reminiscences* (privately printed, 1926).
12. Letters to Gertrude Cary (28 December 1916, 2 March 1917, 20 September 1917, and 28 October 1918).
13. *Ibid.* (21 November 1918).
14. *Ibid.* (5 October 1917).
15. *Ibid.* (18 May 1919).
16. *Ibid.* (10 October 1916 and 24 February 1917).
17. *Ibid.* (10 October 1916).
18. Mrs. J. Thompson, Belfast, 1964.
19. Commander J. P. and Sheila Cary, Wadeford, Somerset, 1964.
20. Letters to Gertrude Cary (18 August 1916 and 11 January 1917).
21. *Ibid.* (2 March 1917).
22. *Ibid.* (17 July 1919).
23. Various letters of 1916 and 1917.

CHAPTER 13
The Nafada Polo Club

Information in this chapter is from Joyce Cary's daily letters to his wife, 1916–1917.

CHAPTER 14
Writing, 1916

Information in this chapter is from Joyce Cary's daily letters to his wife, 1916–1917.

CHAPTER 15
The Hausa Farewell

Information in this chapter is from Joyce Cary's daily letters to his wife, early 1917.

CHAPTER 16
"Oh To Be in Borgu, Now that April's Here!"

Information in this chapter is from Joyce Cary's daily letters to his wife, mid-1917, unless otherwise indicated.

1. Percy Diggle to M. M. Mahood (26 August 1962).
2. Percy Diggle, Carlisle, 1964.
3. Mrs. Rauri McLean, Blackheath, 1964.

CHAPTER 17
"Another Tornado Last Night"

Information in this chapter is from Joyce Cary's daily letters to his wife, mid-1917.

CHAPTER 18
"A Famous Accordion Soloist"

Information in this chapter is from Joyce Cary's daily letters to his wife, July-December 1917, unless otherwise indicated.
1. Percy Diggle, Carlisle, 1964.

CHAPTER 19
Leave, 1918

Information in this chapter is from Joyce Cary's daily letters to his wife, July-December 1918, unless otherwise indicated.
1. Letter to Gertrude Cary (27 July 1919).

CHAPTER 20
Mapping Borgu

Information in this chapter is from Joyce Cary's daily letters to his wife, July-December 1918.

CHAPTER 21
"This Is a Lonely Spot"

Information in this chapter is from Joyce Cary's daily letters to his wife, December 1918-April 1919, unless otherwise indicated.
1. M. M. Mahood, Oxford, 1963.

CHAPTER 22
"My Children Need Not Be Ashamed of Me"

Information in this chapter is from Joyce Cary's daily letters to his wife, 1918–1919, unless otherwise indicated.
1. Cary Clark, Castledawson, Londonderry, 1964.

CHAPTER 23
Novels and Potboilers

Information in this chapter is from Joyce Cary's daily letters to his wife, 1918–1919.

CHAPTER 24
The Grand Trunk Road

Information in this chapter is from Joyce Cary's daily letters to his wife, August-November 1919, unless otherwise indicated.
1. Cary Clark, Castledawson, Londonderry, 1964; Mrs. J. Thompson, Belfast, 1964.

CHAPTER 25
"I Shall Write an Enormous Book"
Information in this chapter is from Joyce Cary's daily letters to his wife, 1918–1919.

CHAPTER 26
12 Parks Road

1. George Graves to Colonel Moody (27 June 1962).
2. Letter to Gertrude Cary (August 1921).
3. M. M. Mahood, *Joyce Cary's Africa* (London, 1964), p. 61.
4. H. W. Cowper to Colonel Moody (27 February 1962).
5. *Ibid.*
6. T. F. Higham, Oxford, 1963.
7. Cary Clark, Castledawson, Londonderry, 1964.
8. "The Most Exciting Sport in the World," *Holiday,* June, 1957.

CHAPTER 27
Hungary

1. Commander J. P. and Sheila Cary, Wadeford, Somerset, 1964; Lady Gwendolyn Herbert, Hammersmith, 1964; Sir Heneage Ogilvie, Wimbledon, 1963.
2. "Cheerful Protestant," *Time,* 20 October 1952.
3. Letters to Gertrude Cary (27 December 1918 and 19 March 1919).
4. Various letters to Gertrude Cary (July-August 1919).
5. W. M. Ogilvie, *Reminiscences* (privately printed, 1926).
6. Letter to Gertrude Cary (4 June 1921).
7. Letters to Michael and Peter Cary (August 1921).
8. Letter to Gertrude Cary (June 1921).
9. Cary Clark, Castledawson, Londonderry, 1964.
10. Letter to Gertrude Cary (20 June 1921).
11. *The Captive and the Free,* Carfax edition (London, 1963), p. 271.
12. Letters to Gertrude Cary (June 1921).
13. *Ibid.*
14. *Ibid.* (summer, 1921).
15. *Ibid.* (undated, 1921).
16. *Ibid.* (undated, 1921).
17. *Ibid.* (4 June 1921).
18. *Ibid.* (undated, 1921).
19. *Ibid.* (undated, 1921).
20. W. M. Ogilvie, *op. cit.*
21. Mrs. Rauri McLean, Blackheath, 1964.
22. Lady Mary Ogilvie, Oxford, 1964.
23. Information on Cary's trip to Hungary is from the diary, in both notes and finished manuscript, of T. F. Higham for that trip, together with letters from Mr. Higham to his wife, other documents in his possession, and a conversation with him at Oxford, 1963.

CHAPTER 28
Cock Jarvis

1. Preliminary draft of "Unfinished Novels," Cary Collection.
2. All references to *Cock Jarvis* are based on manuscripts in the Cary Collection.
3. Letter to Elizabeth Lawrence (21 June 1949).

CHAPTER 29
A Metaphysical Construction

1. Sir Heneage Ogilvie, Wimbledon, 1963.
2. Letter to Gertrude Cary (August 1921).
3. Professor John MacMurray, Beaconsfield, 1964.
4. *Ibid.*
5. *Ibid.*
6. Professor and Mrs. James Boyd, Oxford, 1964; T. F. Higham, Oxford, 1963; Professor John MacMurray, *op. cit.*
7. W. M. Ogilvie, *Reminiscences* (privately printed, 1926).
8. *Ibid.*
9. Preliminary draft of "Switzerland," Cary Collection. Subsequent references to Cary's Swiss vacations of 1922 and 1923 are to this article.
10. Tristram Cary, Fressingfield, Norfolk, 1963.
11. Receipts from Cary Collection.
12. Commander J. P. and Sheila Cary, Wadeford, Somerset, 1964; Sir Heneage Ogilvie, *op. cit.*
13. "Cheerful Protestant," *Time,* 20 October 1952.
14. Statements from his property agents in Londonderry, in Cary Collection.
15. Commander J. P. Cary to Joyce Cary (6 September 1925).
16. Cary Clark, Castledawson, Londonderry, 1964; Mrs. J. Thompson, Belfast, 1964.
17. Cary Clark, *op. cit.*
18. *Ibid.*

CHAPTER 30
Mr. Ogilvie's Trust Fund

1. Information on Cary Clark is from conversations with him, Castledawson, Londonderry, 1964 and 1965.
2. Letter to Gertrude Cary (summer, 1921).
3. Joyce Cary's daily letters to his wife from Nigeria.
4. Mrs. William Belcher, Oxford, 1964.
5. Sir Michael Cary, Blackheath, 1964.
6. Commander J. P. and Sheila Cary, Wadeford, Somerset, 1964; Sir Heneage Ogilvie, Wimbledon, 1963.

CHAPTER 31
Liberty Versus Freedom

1. "Preface," *Aissa Saved,* Carfax edition (London, 1952), p. 9.
2. Lord David Cecil, Oxford, 1963 and 1964; Professor John MacMurray, Beaconsfield, 1964.
3. Joyce felt such structures were a barrier to man's "creative imagination," and he used the term often in his writing and conversation.
4. *Power in Men* (Seattle, 1963), pp. 89–91.
5. "The Revolution of the Women," *Vogue,* 15 March 1951.
6. *Power in Men, op. cit.,* p. 178.
7. Preliminary draft of "The Death of Symbol," Cary Collection.

CHAPTER 32
"Let's Ask for It in All the Libraries"

1. Sir Michael Cary, Blackheath, 1964; Tristram Cary, Fressingfield, Norfolk, 1963.
2. Professor James Boyd, Oxford, 1964.
3. Professor and Mrs. James Boyd, *op. cit.*
4. *Ibid.*
5. *Ibid.*
6. "The Novelist at Work," *Adam International Review,* XVIII, 1950; "The Way a Novel Gets Written," *Harper's,* February 1950; Enid Starkie, "Joyce Cary: A Personal Portrait," *Virginia Quarterly Review,* Winter, 1961.
7. Letter to Elizabeth Lawrence (21 June 1949).

CHAPTER 33
Castledawson

1. Mrs. J. Thompson, Belfast, 1964.
2. *Ibid.*
3. Cary Clark, Castledawson, Londonderry, 1964; Mrs. Thompson, *op. cit.*
4. *Ibid.*
5. Mrs. Thompson, *op. cit.*
6. Cary Clark, *op. cit.*
7. Commander J. P. Cary, Wadeford, Somerset, 1964.
8. *Ibid.*
9. T. F. Higham, Oxford, 1963.
10. *Ibid.*
11. Miss Joyce Carey to the author (31 July 1964).
12. Sir Michael Cary, Blackheath, 1964.
13. Tristram Cary, Fressingfield, Norfolk, 1963.
14. *Ibid.*
15. *Ibid.*
16. *Ibid.*

17. Peter Cary, Cambridge, 1965.
18. Sir Michael Cary, *op. cit.*
19. Tristram Cary, *op. cit.*
20. *Ibid.*
21. Various members of the Cary family, 1963–1964.
22. Professor and Mrs. James Boyd, Oxford, 1964.
23. Lady Gwendolyn Herbert, Hammersmith, 1964.
24. "Cheerful Protestant," *Time,* 20 October 1952.
25. Spencer Curtis Brown, London, 1964.
26. *Ibid.*

CHAPTER 34
A. P. Herbert's Political Campaign

1. "Cheerful Protestant," *Time,* 20 October 1952.
2. Preliminary drafts of "Profile" of A. P. Herbert for *Time,* in Cary Collection.
3. Sir Michael Cary, Blackheath, 1964.
4. Information on Toni Clark Thompson's wedding and its aftermath is from Cary Clark, Castledawson, Londonderry, 1964–1965.
5. Mrs. Nora Lightburne, St. Andrews, 1964.
6. *Arabella* manuscripts are in the Cary Collection.
7. Records of Civil Defence Service, Oxford.
8. Commander J. P. and Sheila Cary, Wadeford, Somerset, 1964.
9. "Cheerful Protestant," *op. cit.*
10. Spencer Curtis Brown, London, 1964.
11. "Cheerful Protestant," *op. cit.;* royalty statement from Victor Gollancz Ltd. (3 August 1939).
12. Sir Michael Cary, *op. cit.*
13. *Ibid.*
14. E.g., Spencer Curtis Brown to Joyce Cary (13 June 1939).

CHAPTER 35
African Novels

1. Graham Greene, *The Heart of the Matter* (London, 1948), pp. 33–34.
2. Letter to H. S. W. Edwardes (25 August 1936).
3. *Aissa Saved,* Carfax edition (London, 1952), p. 11.
4. *Ibid.,* p. 209.
5. *Ibid.*
6. *An American Visitor,* Carfax edition (London, 1952), p. 66.
7. *Ibid.,* p. 233.
8. *Ibid.,* p. 232.
9. *The African Witch,* Carfax edition (London, 1951), p. 23.
10. *Mister Johnson,* Carfax edition (London, 1952), p. 163.
11. Letters of Joyce Cary to Norman Rosten, 1955, and Sir Donald Hurst to the author, September 1966.

CHAPTER 36
A Second Fling at the Theater

1. Donald Barr, "A Careful and Profound Thinker," *Adam International Review,* XVIII, 1950.
2. Spencer Curtis Brown to Joyce Cary (9 May 1939).
3. Andrew Wright, note in *Handlist* to Cary Collection.
4. *Power in Men* (Seattle, 1963), pp. 27–28.
5. See Cecil Woodham-Smith's *The Great Hunger* (New York: Harper and Row, 1963).
6. *Power in Men, op. cit.,* pp. 242–243.
7. Wright, *op. cit.*
8. Royalty statement, Nicholson & Watson, Ltd. (7 November 1939).
9. J. B. Priestley to Joyce Cary, several letters (1939).
10. Manuscript in Cary Collection.
11. J. B. Priestley to Joyce Cary (13 July 1939).
12. Manuscript in Cary Collection.
13. Tristram Cary, Fressingfield, Norfolk, 1963.
14. *Ibid.*

CHAPTER 37
ARP Post B27, Rhodes House

1. (25 May 1939).
2. Harcourte Johnstone to Joyce Cary (19 June 1939).
3. Letter to Harcourte Johnstone (14 June 1939).
4. "Preface," *Charley Is My Darling,* Carfax edition (London, 1951), p. 5.
5. Rauri McLean, Blackheath, 1964.
6. Spencer Curtis Brown, London, 1964.
7. Spencer Curtis Brown to Joyce Cary (10 November 1939).
8. "Cheerful Protestant," *Time,* 20 October 1952.
9. This and other information on Cary's ARP activities is from Cary's wartime superior, E. H. F. Smith, unless otherwise indicated.
10. Sir Michael Cary, Blackheath, 1964.
11. Tristram Cary, Fressingfield, Norfolk, 1963.
12. Professor and Mrs. James Boyd, Oxford, 1964.
13. Letter to T. F. Higham (13 December 1944).
14. This and other information on *Men of Two Worlds* is from Thorold Dickinson unless otherwise indicated.
15. Sheila Cary, Wadeford, Somerset, 1964.

CHAPTER 38
Charley Is My Darling

1. *Charley Is My Darling,* Carfax edition (London, 1951), p. 15.
2. *Ibid.*
3. *Ibid.,* p. 185.

4. *Ibid.*, p. 82.
5. *Ibid.*, p. 255.
6. *Ibid.*, p. 306.
7. *Ibid.*, p. 298.
8. *Ibid.*, p. 323.
9. *Ibid.*, p. 349.

CHAPTER 39
Irish Novels

1. *Castle Corner*, Carfax edition (London, 1952), p. 5.
2. *Ibid.*
3. *Ibid.*, p. 15.
4. *Ibid.*, p. 243.
5. *Ibid.*, p. 266.
6. *A House of Children*, Carfax edition (London, 1951), pp. 7–8.
7. *Ibid.*, p. 11.
8. *Ibid.*, pp. 14–15.
9. *Ibid.*, p. 234.
10. *Ibid.*, p. 235.

CHAPTER 40
Kilimanjaro and Edinburgh

1. This and other information on the *Men of Two Worlds* project is from conversations with Thorold Dickinson, London, 1965, unless otherwise indicated.
2. This copy is in the Scottish National Library, Edinburgh.
3. Adam Bruce Thomson, Edinburgh, 1964.
4. Professor G. M. Fisher, Edinburgh, 1964.
5. Script of *Men of Two Worlds*, Cary Collection.

CHAPTER 41
"A Damn Queer Book"

1. Tristram Cary, Fressingfield, Norfolk, 1963.
2. Professor and Mrs. James Boyd, Oxford, 1964.
3. Sir Michael Cary, Blackheath, 1964.
4. *Ibid.*
5. Boyds, *op. cit.*
6. This and other information on the India film trip is from conversations with Thorold Dickinson, London, 1965, unless otherwise indicated.

CHAPTER 42
First Trilogy

1. *Herself Surprised*, Carfax edition (London, 1951), p. 7.
2. *Ibid.*, pp. 7–8.

3. *Ibid.*, p. 140.
4. Letter to Ruth Van Horn (17 June 1953).
5. Lord David Cecil, Oxford, 1964.
6. Letter to Elizabeth Lawrence (24 February 1948).
7. *Herself Surprised, op. cit.*, p. 8.
8. "The Way a Novel Gets Written," *Harper's*, February 1950.
9. *Ibid.*
10. *Herself Surprised, op. cit.*, p. 41.
11. *Ibid.*, p. 142.
12. *To Be a Pilgrim,* Carfax edition (London, 1951), p. 14.
13. *Ibid.*, p. 16.
14. *The Horse's Mouth,* Carfax edition (London, 1951), p. 183.
15. *To Be a Pilgrim, op. cit.*, p. 38.
16. *Ibid.*, p. 47.
17. *Ibid.*, p. 77.
18. *Ibid.*, p. 118.
19. *Ibid.*, pp. 128–129.
20. *Ibid.*, p. 328.
21. *The Horse's Mouth, op. cit.*, p. 25.
22. *Ibid.*, p. 153.
23. *Ibid.*, p. 16.
24. *Ibid.*, p. 296.
25. *Ibid.*, p. 174.

CHAPTER 43
"I Have Been Watching a Little Revolution"

All information on the India film trip is from conversations with Thorold Dickinson, London, 1965, unless otherwise indicated.

1. Tristram Cary, Fressingfield, Norfolk, 1963; Enid Starkie, Oxford, 1964.
2. Commander J. P. and Sheila Cary, Wadeford, Somerset, 1964.
3. This and other information on *The Secret People* is from conversations with Thorold Dickinson, London, 1965, unless otherwise indicated.
4. Scenario #3, *The Secret People* (17 August 1946).
5. "Synopsis for Registration" (25 June 1946).
6. Scenario #2, *The Secret People* (undated).
7. Scenario #3, *op. cit.*

CHAPTER 44
"How She Loved Life"

1. "The Novelist at Work," *Adam International Review*, XVIII, 1950.
2. Letter to Elizabeth Lawrence (25 July 1947).
3. Elizabeth Lawrence to Alan Collins (11 October 1946).
4. Tristram Cary, Fressingfield, Norfolk, 1963.
5. Professor and Mrs. James Boyd, Oxford, 1964.

Notes

537

6. Elizabeth Lawrence to Frieda Spiller (16 June 1947).
7. Lady Gwendolyn Herbert, Hammersmith, 1964.
8. Letter to Elizabeth Lawrence (14 September 1953).
9. Mrs. Rauri McLean, Blackheath, 1964.
10. Joyce Cary's letters of this period; Cary Clark, Castledawson, Londonderry, 1965.
11. Elizabeth Lawrence to Joyce Cary (12 November 1948).
12. Boyds, *op. cit.*
13. *Ibid.*
14. Mrs. McLean, *op. cit.*
15. Letter to Elizabeth Lawrence (8 November 1949).
16. Mrs. McLean, *op. cit.*
17. Enid Starkie, "Joyce Cary: A Personal Portrait," *Virginia Quarterly Review*, Winter, 1961.
18. Letter to Elizabeth Lawrence (22 November 1949).
19. *Ibid.* (22 December 1949).
20. Letter to John Dover Wilson (20 December 1949).
21. Starkie, *op. cit.*
22. Boyds, *op. cit.*
23. Starkie, *op. cit.*
24. *Ibid.*
25. Enid Starkie, Oxford, 1964.

CHAPTER 45
Honor and Fortune

1. Elizabeth Lawrence to Joyce Cary (19 August 1949).
2. Winifred Davin, "Joyce Cary," *Encyclopaedia Britannica* (Chicago, 1966), v. 5, p. 6.
3. Letter to Elizabeth Lawrence (5 February 1950).
4. *Ibid.*
5. Mrs. Rauri McLean, Blackheath, 1964.
6. Professor and Mrs. James Boyd, Oxford, 1964.
7. Lord David Cecil, Oxford, 1964.
8. Letter to John Fischer (1 April 1950).
9. Letter to Elizabeth Lawrence (8 March 1950).

CHAPTER 46
Two Novels of Women

1. "The Novelist at Work," *Adam International Review*, XVIII, 1950.
2. *Ibid.*
3. *The Moonlight,* Carfax edition (London, 1952), p. 2.
4. *Ibid.,* p. 33.
5. Enid Starkie, "Joyce Cary: A Personal Portrait," *Virginia Quarterly Review*, Winter 1961.
6. *A Fearful Joy,* Carfax edition (London, 1952), p. 13.

7. *Ibid.,* p. 14.
8. Letter to Elizabeth Lawrence (5 February 1950).
9. *A Fearful Joy, op. cit.,* p. 23.
10. *Ibid.,* p. 199.
11. *Ibid.,* pp. 185–186.
12. *Ibid.,* p. 221.
13. *Ibid.,* p. 213.
14. *Ibid.,* p. 359

CHAPTER 47
Carfax and New York

1. Letter to Elizabeth Lawrence (4 October 1950).
2. Andrew Wright, *Joyce Cary: A Preface to His Novels* (New York, 1958), p. 8.
3. Letter to Elizabeth Lawrence (4 October 1950).
4. "Party of One," *Holiday,* November, 1954.
5. *Ibid.*
6. Enid Starkie, "Joyce Cary: A Personal Portrait," *Virginia Quarterly Review,* Winter, 1961.
7. A number of these are in the Cary Collection.
8. Manuscript in Cary Collection.
9. Elizabeth Lawrence, New York, 1964.
10. "Gerald Wilde," *Nimbus,* winter, 1955.
11. Mr. and Mrs. Dan Davin, Oxford, 1963.
12. *Ibid.*
13. Letter to Mrs. Brian Robb (19 October 1951).
14. Professor and Mrs. James Boyd, Oxford, 1964.
15. Letters to Mr. Ackroyd (1946–1947).

CHAPTER 48
"The Comedy of Freedom"

1. Letter to Elizabeth Lawrence (8 October 1951).
2. *Ibid.*
3. *Ibid.*
4. *Mister Johnson,* Carfax edition (London, 1952), p. 54.
5. Cary Collection.

CHAPTER 49
"Ant mytyping good"

1. Robert Lusty to Joyce Cary (6 March 1952).
2. Professor and Mrs. James Boyd, Oxford, 1964.
3. Letter to Rosa Wells (26 August 1952).
4. Dan Davin, Oxford, 1963.
5. Iris Murdoch, Oxford, 1964.
6. *Ibid.*

7. (14 February 1953).
8. *Ibid.*
9. Professor G. M. Fisher, Edinburgh, 1964.
10. (10 March 1953).

CHAPTER 50
New Friends and Old

1. *Tamarack Review,* Spring, 1957.
2. Cary Collection.
3. *Ibid.*
4. *Ibid.*
5. Austin Wright, Cincinnati, 1963.
6. Mrs. Edith Haggard, New York, 1964.
7. Cary Collection.
8. Enid Starkie, Oxford, 1964.
9. Dan Davin, Oxford, 1963.
10. F. A. Lea, *The Life of John Middleton Murry* (London, 1959), pp. 337–338.
11. Mary M. Murry, *To Keep Faith* (London, 1959), pp. 170–172.
12. Letter to Elizabeth Lawrence (18 May 1955).

CHAPTER 51
Second Trilogy

1. *Prisoner of Grace,* Carfax edition (London, 1954), p. 5.
2. *Ibid.*
3. *Ibid.,* p. 9.
4. *Ibid.,* p. 44.
5. *Ibid.,* p. 35.
6. *Ibid.,* p. 286.
7. *Except the Lord* (London, 1953), p. 119.
8. *Ibid.,* p. 120.
9. *Ibid.,* pp. 103–104.
10. *Ibid.,* p. 104.
11. *Ibid.,* p. 145.
12. *Ibid.,* p. 24.
13. "The Political Novel," broadcast on the BBC series "Window on the World," July 1955.
14. *Not Honour More* (London, 1955), p. 220.
15. *Ibid.,* p. 223.
16. "Political Novel," *op. cit.*

CHAPTER 52
A Narrowing World

1. Mrs. Nora Lightburne, St. Andrews, 1964.
2. Tristram Cary, Fressingfield, Norfolk, 1963.

3. Mrs. Rauri McLean, Blackheath, 1964.
4. Mrs. Edith Haggard, New York, 1964.
5. Norman Rosten to the author (18 April 1964).
6. Letter to Norman Rosten (11 June 1954).
7. *Ibid.* (11 January 1955).
8. *Ibid.* (15 January 1955).
9. Letter to Mrs. Edith Haggard (28 November 1955).
10. Sir Donald Hurst to the author (14 July 1966).
11. Mrs. Haggard, *op. cit.*

CHAPTER 53
Plans and Projects

1. Andrew Wright, *Joyce Cary: A Preface to His Novels* (New York, 1958), pp. 7–8.
2. *Ibid.*, p. 8.
3. *Ibid.*, pp. 7–8.
4. Andrew Wright to the author (June 1966).
5. Rauri McLean, Blackheath, 1964.
6. Letter to Elizabeth Lawrence (6 January 1950).
7. Letter to Rauri McLean (6 December 1955).
8. Mrs. Nora Lightburne, St. Andrews, 1964.

CHAPTER 54
The Captive and the Free

1. *The Captive and the Free,* Carfax edition (London, 1963), p. 108.
2. *Ibid.*, p. 280.
3. *Ibid.*, pp. 316–317.

CHAPTER 55
Death

1. Mrs. Nora Lightburne, St. Andrews, 1964.
2. Tristram Cary, Fressingfield, Norfolk, 1963.
3. Mrs. Lightburne, *op. cit.*
4. *Ibid.*
5. *Ibid.*
6. *Ibid.*
7. Edith Millen to Andrew Wright (12 November 1956).
8. Mrs. Lightburne, *op. cit.*
9. *Ibid.*
10. Enid Starkie, "Joyce Cary: A Personal Portrait," *Virginia Quarterly Review,* Winter, 1961.

SELECTED BIBLIOGRAPHY

NOTE: This bibliography contains only those editions of Joyce Cary's own books, together with books and periodicals about Cary's work, most readily available to readers. In the case of Cary's novels, for instance, the list includes only the Carfax Edition published by Michael Joseph Ltd. in Britain and the edition published by Harper & Row in the United States.

FICTION

In order of original publication:

Aissa Saved. London, 1952; New York, 1963.

An American Visitor. London, 1952; New York, 1962.

The African Witch. London, 1951; New York, 1962.

Castle Corner. London, 1952; New York, 1963.

Mister Johnson. London, 1952; New York, 1951.

Charley Is My Darling. London, 1951; New York, 1960.

A House of Children. London, 1951; New York, 1956.

Herself Surprised. London, 1951; New York, 1948. (Published, together with *To Be a Pilgrim* and *The Horse's Mouth*, as *First Trilogy*. New York, 1958.)

To Be a Pilgrim. London, 1951; New York, 1949.

The Horse's Mouth. London, 1951; New York, 1950.

The Moonlight. London, 1952; New York, 1947.

A Fearful Joy. London, 1952; New York, 1950.

Prisoner of Grace. London, 1954; New York, 1952.

Except the Lord. London, 1953; New York, 1953.

Not Honour More. London, 1955; New York, 1955.

The Captive and the Free. Ed. Winifred Davin. London, 1959; New York, 1959.

Spring Song and Other Stories. Ed. Winifred Davin. London, 1960.

NONFICTION

Art and Reality (the Clark Lectures 1956). Cambridge: Cambridge University Press, 1957; New York: Harper, 1958.

Britain and West Africa. London: Longmans, Green, 1946; revised edition, 1947; published with *The Case for African Freedom,* Austin: University of Texas Press, 1961.

The Case for African Freedom. London: Secker & Warburg, 1941.

Memoirs of the Bobotes. Ed. James B. Meriwether. Austin: University of Texas Press, 1962; London: Michael Joseph, 1964.

Power in Men. London: Nicholson & Watson, 1939 (Ed. Hazard Adams) Seattle: University of Washington Press, 1963.

Process of Real Freedom. London: Michael Joseph, 1943.

SECONDARY SOURCES

Adam International Review (Joyce Cary special issue), Nos. 212–213 (November–December 1950).
   "The Novelist at Work: A Conversation between Joyce Cary and Lord David Cecil" is particularly interesting in illuminating Cary's techniques.

Allen, Walter. *Joyce Cary.* Writers and Their Work: No. 41. London: Longmans, Green, 1953; revised editions, 1954 and 1956.
   The pioneer study of Joyce Cary's work and still the best concise criticism, by a critic whom Cary aided and respected.

Bloom, Robert. *The Indeterminate World: A Study of the Novels of Joyce Cary.* Philadelphia: University of Pennsylvania Press, 1962.
   A study in which the author's conclusions seem unrelated to his evidence.

Hoffmann, Charles G. *Joyce Cary: The Comedy of Freedom.* Pittsburgh: University of Pittsburgh Press, 1964.
   An excellent detailed study of Cary's novels, always pertinent and thought-provoking.

Mahood, M. M. *Joyce Cary's Africa.* London: Methuen, 1964; Boston: Houghton Mifflin, 1964.
   A perceptive study of the relationship between Cary's years in Africa and his African writings, written while the author resided in Nigeria.

Modern Fiction Studies (Joyce Cary special issue), IX, no. 3 (Autumn 1963).
   A survey of Cary's work and detailed examination of some specific works, by a broad variety of authors.

O'Connor, Willian Van. *Joyce Cary.* Columbia Essays on Modern Writers: No. 16. New York and London: Columbia University Press, 1966.
   The biographical portion abounds in errors, while the critical portion is less than adequate.

Wright, Andrew. *Joyce Cary: A Preface to His Novels.* London: Chatto & Windus, 1958; New York: Harper, 1958.
   As its subtitle suggests, a valuable initial approach to Cary's novels, better on broad themes than on single works.

INDEX

Abasso, 116 f.

Accidents, 169, 447, 476–77

Acheson, Dean, 423

Acton, Lord, 331

Adam International Review, 436

Africa, Cary's ideas on, 124
  see also Nigeria, and names of specific areas

African Witch, The, 301–2, 305, 311, 313 f., 338 f., 364
  American publication of, 311, 405 f., 449
  summary of, 321–24

Agar, Miss Memie, 12, 46–47

Air Raid Precautions (ARP), 110, 311, 335, 338 ff., 467

Aissa Saved, 277, 287, 290, 292 f., 295 f., 314, 322, 324, 481, 510
  Carfax Edition, 287, 290, 315
  summary of, 315–18

Aladé, 321

Allen, Sir Carleton, 339

Allen, Walter, 376, 421, 452, 454, 462, 474, 502

Ambrose, Jerry, 175

American publications:
  African Witch, The, 311, 405 f., 449
  articles, 436, 446, 465, 470, 515, 517
  Except the Lord, 473
  Fearful Joy, A, 409, 436
  Herself Surprised, 405 ff., 410, 415 f.

Horse's Mouth, The, 406, 415 ff., 420, 436, 504–5
  Rainbird Edition, 385, 504–5
  Mister Johnson, 449
  Moonlight, The, 405–6, 410
  short stories, 446, 504
  see also Saturday Evening Post
  To Be a Pilgrim, 415

American trip, 1951, 419 ff., 436, 437–38, 440–42
  1953, 461, 472–73, 513
  1955 (planned), 493

American Visitor, An, 99, 291–92, 293, 296, 302, 313 f., 321 f., 351
  summary of, 318–21

Animals, 136–37, 164, 299

"Anti-Americanism, Anti-British-ism," 470

Antivari, 71–76, 151, 477

Appam, 227

"Apprentice Boy" of Londonderry, 12

Arabella, 311

Arrow of Gold, The, 221

Arrowsmith's, 49

Art, 60, 261, 375, 380, 390
  student in Edinburgh, 40–43
  student in Paris, 38–40
  see also Drawing, Painting

L'Art, 436

Art and Reality, 519

Artists' Benevolent Fund, 444

O'Doherty clan, 4 f., 22
Ogilvie, Elsie, 58, 111, 113, 148, 169, 183, 227, 262
Ogilvie, Florence, 58, 113
Ogilvie, Sir Frederick, 58, 61, 63, 66, 69, 86, 170, 183, 235 f.
death of, 417, 463
at Edinburgh University, 265
knighted, 407
in Oxford, 192, 229, 231, 262, 269
and trust fund, 275–76
and World War I, 110 ff., 172, 192, 259, 377
and World War II—BBC, 335, 378
Ogilvie, Gertrude, *see* Cary, Gertrude, Ogilvie
Ogilvie, Sir Heneage, 36, 58 f., 63, 128, 236, 265, 270, 515
at Guy's Hospital, 69, 78, 85 f., 136
knighted, 407
and trust fund, 275–76
and World War I, 110 f., 113, 172
Ogilvie, Lady Mary, 276, 447, 475
Ogilvie, Mr. William Maxwell, 62 f., 69, 86, 110 ff., 140, 193, 198–99
generosity of, 262 ff., 271
remarriage of, 263–64
and trust fund, 275–76, 288
Ogilvie, Mrs. William (Mary Wolff), 62 f., 69, 85, 110 ff., 165, 193, 259, 263
illness of, 236, 238 f., 262
strictness of, 148, 169 f., 197, 198–99, 342
Ogilvie, Robert, 518
"Old Strife at Plant's, The," 504 f.
On Liberty, 332
Orwell, George, 330
O'Shea, Kitty, 12, 24
Ostlere, Gordon, 461
Ould, Herman, lecture, 515
Owen, Wilfred, 81
Oxford, England, settling in, 192–93, 228 ff.

see also Parks Road, Rawlinson Road
Oxford and Bucks Regiment, 377
Oxford Union, 306
Oxford University, 45 ff., 48–57, 58–61, 63–66, 67–68, 155, 192, 305
colleges: All Souls, 241
Balliol, 192, 261, 271
Brasenose, 50 f.
Keble, 228, 495
Jesus, 378, 417
New, 241
Ruskin, 515
Trinity, 48 f., 65, 229, 231, 313
Freshman Wine Party, 49–50
lectures at, 423, 438, 513
societies, 59
Elizabethan Club, 59
English Club, 494
Gryphon Club, 59
Milton Society, 59, 516
Petronius Club, 59
in World War II, 339–40
Painters, 279, 443–44, 462
Painting, 32–33, 36, 236–37, 283, 294, 297–98, 416
Paris, 38–40, 52 ff., 130, 154–55, 230, 475
Closerie des Lilas, 39, 52, 54
Paris Review, 462
Parks Road, 228–29, 239–40, 296
after Trudy's death, 419, 424, 447, 461
musical evenings at, 289, 410, 414
"Piggery," 235, 299
Sunday evening open house, 461–62, 503–4, 515
Parnell, Charles Stewart, 3, 7 f., 12, 24
Paterson, Graeme, 36, 70
PEN, 442, 464, 515
"Period Piece," 519
Philosophical conclusions, 256–58, 259 ff., 277 ff., 286, 287–88
Phoenix Park Murders, 7, 12